THE RISE AND FALL OF THE PAPACY:

AN ORTHODOX PERSPECTIVE

The Rise and Fall of the Papacy:

An Orthodox Perspective

Patrick (Craig) Truglia

Uncut Mountain Press

THE RISE AND FALL OF THE PAPACY:
An Orthodox Perspective

uncutmountainpress.com

Interior Artwork: Public Domain or ownership from private collection
(used with permission), unless sourced otherwise.

Special thanks to John Collorafi who helped considerably with Latin
translations and interpretation.

Scriptural quotations are from the New King James Version.

Patrick (Craig) Truglia, 1985–

The Rise and Fall of the Papacy: An Orthodox Perspective — 1st ed.
Edited by Anri Sorel.

ISBN: 978-1-63941-032-3

I. Church History
II. Orthodox Christian Theology

"Believe facts rather than words."

— Saint Pope Gregory the Great

TABLE OF CONTENTS

St. Gregory the Great (540-604)

INTRODUCTION

Resetting One's Historical Presumptions

The study of history is not well understood, even though most people take a passing interest in it. Getting a good look at the past is not entirely possible. The only sources one has at his or her disposal are the "primary sources," which are documents, archaeological finds, and other pieces of evidence which actually originate from the era being studied. Historians know this well. However, most people do not interact with these, but rather with secondary sources: Wikipedia, scholarly books, polemical blogs, apologetics Youtube channels, and the like.

The crucial difference between primary and secondary sources is interpretative. Primary sources *require* interpretation, while secondary sources *provide* an interpretation. In the English language, most of the secondary sources that bear on the issue of the Papacy's rise and fall suffer from cultural biases that are inherited from the intellectual heritage of the West. The English-language reader (or any Western language) must deal with this interpretive issue whether he or she likes it or not.

Popular historical treatments of the Papacy and its role in the Great Schism are almost always written in a Western language. They presume upon Western epistemology, ecclesiology, and cultural expectations pertaining to what the Papacy is. By so doing, they (wittingly or not) presume upon the modern, Western view of the "Papacy"[1] despite many of these authors not being Roman Catholic. Protestants presume upon the modern Papacy, because they reject it. They oftentimes do not appreciate the ancient version of this institution and it is not "on their radar." Roman Catholics presume upon the Papacy in their various nuanced takes, whether "traditional" or "post-modernist," conforming it using one epistemic method or another to the Council of Vatican I (which is dogmatic). Professional historians, simply imbibing an issue which is chiefly relevant in their societies due to its import upon Protestantism or Roman Catholicism, though often skeptical of the institution's present claims, will fill the gaps found in the primary sources with anachronistic presumptions of what the Papacy is.

A good example of the preceding tendency is Henry Chadwick's relatively recent take on the Great Schism.[2] Though the following greatly simplifies his work, one may summarize its operating thesis to be that the East never conceived of the Papacy and the West, from at least the time of Pope Victor I, always had an undeveloped notion of the "Vatican I Papacy." This would include Rome laying claim to direct and universal jurisdiction, infallibility, necessity of Roman communion, etcetera. The schism, in effect, was as old as the second century and only finalized when both sides finally realized how different they were all along. Chadwick's thesis reduces the Papacy to an almost millennium-old misunderstanding.

A. Edward Siecienski's view on the topic slightly modifies this thesis in some respects and in so doing takes more care not to make anachronistic ecclesiastical assumptions.[3] However, he similarly

---

1   "Papacy" is derived from the 11th century term *Papatus*, which is a Latin term which implies the Roman Bishopric is a class above the "normal" episcopate. See Aristeides Papadakis and John Meyendorff, *The Christian East and the Rise of the Papacy: The Church 1071-1453 A.D.*. Crestwood, NY: St Vladimir's Seminary Press, 1994, 167. For the purposes of this book, the Roman Bishop will often simply be called the "Pope" and the local Roman Church "the Papacy" due to popular usage—however the 11th century implications, being anachronistic, are not intended.

2   Henry Chadwick, *East and West: The Making of a Rift in the Church*. Oxford: Oxford University Press, 2005.

3   A. Edward Siecienski, *The Papacy and the Orthodox: "Sources and History of a*

identifies the divide as originating in early times (particularly the fourth century during the semi-Arian controversy) and henceforth expanding. While this may serve the needs of present ecumenical dialogue, the idea both sides spoke past each other does not make for good history. The ancients were knowledgeable people and understood the points at issue. In fact, they arguably had a more enhanced sensitivity to differences in their own time, especially considering they were often under dire necessity to diplomatically navigate these differences.

In the popular imagination, as found in an array of Roman Catholic apologetics, the Western Church always expounded an undeveloped, but real Vatican I Papacy. Supposedly, the Eastern Church went back and forth, getting convenient amnesia about the Pope's prerogatives as an excuse to imbibe some heresy (Arianism, Monophysitism, Monothelitism, Iconoclasm, etcetera). Those opposing these heresies did not have this alleged amnesia (Saints Maximus, Theodore the Studite, etcetera) and these men are proof that the orthodox in the East had always remembered what the West had collectively held about the Pope.

This story arc does not align with the facts. Yet, because the notions surrounding it are popular, it *seems* to provide the correct interpretative lens for understanding the meaning behind some of the words that are ascribed to ecclesiastics in the first millennium Church. However, one must dispense with such a story arc. It is self-evident that the *facts* surrounding the statements from the primary sources are more useful in interpreting them than any narrative 1,000 years removed from the events.

The key to interpreting ancient sources in a neutral manner is to surmise *what the story arc should be* if all one had at his or her disposal were the primary sources alone, with no notion of the developments that occurred after the Great Schism and well into the modern era. To the pious Orthodox Christian, history is not looked upon in such a neutral sense. Instead, traditionally, history has been approached hagiographically with an eye for what the Church has historically approved of and saints teach up until the present day. However, as a

---

Debate." New York: Oxford University Press, 2017.

condescension to readers of all communions and even non-religious inclinations, the historical treatment presented here will strive for neutrality and a return to the sources in order to establish the lens for evaluating the historical development of the Papacy. This will explain the more straight-forward historical analyses of the saints in this work. Due to the press and author being Orthodox, the work still contains hagiographic glosses. Likewise, saints will be identified with their title bestowed upon them by the Church.

Having established the preceding basis, what is needed is a story arc that is actually found in the primary sources. The rest of the book will unpack in detail what is found in these sources that inform the following brief sketch of the history of the Papacy:

The early Church was an episcopal institution, where bishops presided over lower clergy and laity in a specific locale. There was always hierarchy between the bishops. These locales and hierarchies were inherited from the Apostles themselves. Those who inherited the mantles of Saints Peter or Paul (or John, or James, etcetera) were of a higher priority than those who inherited the mantle of Saints Mark, Titus, one of the blessed Seventy lesser Apostles, or whomever else. Being that Saints Peter, Paul, John, and James had evangelized specific locales, in their passing everyone they ordained had become their successors. Those who inherited their episcopate from where they died (such as Rome, Ephesus, and Jerusalem) were chief among these successors. Hence, all the successors from the evangelized territory (i.e. jurisdiction) in effect became the "local synod," with the chief successor (later known as a Metropolitan and then Patriarch) being the "CEO" of the organization.

Being that Saints Peter and Paul were the most successful evangelists in the Apostolic Era, their "territory" was by far the largest—stretching from Asia Minor, Crete, and the Balkans to Italy and Spain. Both saints were also martyred in Rome, thereby making the Roman bishop the rightful inheritor of their mantles. The spiritual authority of the Roman bishop and the synod he belonged to thereby, as a default, would be preeminent. However, as alluded to before, this did not make the Roman bishop somehow exclusive in his preeminence. Saint James was the bishop of Jerusalem and being martyred there, its jurisdiction was functionally independent. As history details, Saint John moved to Ephesus and was a bishop there. Despite the city being originally evangelized by Saint Paul, John's presence in effect "reset" the region's Apostolic Succession and rescinded Rome's initial local jurisdictional rights.

Due to no one taking offense at Saint John doing this, in effect *consenting* to this state of affairs, this is a demonstration that jurisdictions can shift and change by the consent of all. The power of consent cannot be understated, as it was the operating principle behind the Council of Jerusalem as recorded in Acts 15. When the entirety of the Church decided something, it was understood as evidence that God did so with them. The Lord taught that Church discipline worked in the same way in Matt 18:18-20. In Church history, the Holy Spirit's most ubiquitous works are not dazzling visual miracles. Rather, they are the daily workings of the Christian people in unity. When the whole Church has *consensus* on something, this is proof of the Spirit's work. Hence, the Church from Apostolic times worked with a *consensus-based epistemology* and *consensus-based ecclesiology*.

Due to scholarship up until now neglecting the issue, it is worth defining what consensus-based epistemology and ecclesiology is. As Church history unfolds, they are evidently the operating principles behind the Church's self-understanding of doctrine and ecclesiology. The drive to both identify and establish consensus is evident in all the ante-Nicene ecclesiastical controversies. Controversies are fortuitous for the historian because they draw out all sides of an issue and the presumptions intrinsic to their positions. It is most noteworthy that modern presuppositions concerning the Papacy as an institution are wholly lacking in these early controversies. Yet, the desire for consensus and the maintenance of Apostolic inheritance (both traditional/doctrinal and jurisdictional) are explicitly stated.

Conciliarity in the early Church provides evidence of consensus-based ecclesiology at work. Local councils operated according to a unanimous, as opposed to majority vote, as consensus conveyed Spiritual authority. The workings of several local synods held in concert with one another, ideally, were to all agree. In the second and

third centuries, local councils were held worldwide to determine the
day to celebrate Pascha, the jurisdictional standing of the Ephesian
church vis-à-vis the Roman church, the correct bishop of Rome
during the Novatian controversy, the correct way to receive into
the Church those baptized from other Christian groups, and the
deposition of Paul of Samosata in Antioch. Long before the Church
became "an Imperial institution," even without the logistical and
legal means to collect all the local synods into one room in an
Ecumenical Council to resolve an issue, the Church always sought
to establish universal consensus on matters of dispute. The drive to
forge consensus without any Imperial motivation was so strong that
at great expense and risk councils would be held on such questions.

The side that always "won" was the side that had the consent of
nearly all. Tellingly, Rome was the specific subject of two of these
controversies (the Ephesian ecclesiastical situation and the rebaptism
issue) and both times they "lost." Going strictly by what the primary
sources state, Rome never explicitly or implicitly asserted Vatican I
Papal prerogatives and both times they were defending their own
local views concerning disciplines and the (local) boundaries of
their jurisdiction. These positions lacked the consensus of the rest
of the Church—who in response specifically censured Rome. In
both cases, Rome afterwards reformed their views—bringing them
into line with the consensus. Papal Infallibility, direct jurisdiction,
and the like were simply not on the radar.

These controversies also demonstrate precisely *how* consensus-
based ecclesiology dealt with interjurisdictional (hereafter referred
to as interpatriarchal) matters. During the Novatian Controversy,
where Rome had a disputed election over who was Pope, Saint
Pope Cornelius wrote a "consecration letter" (or "systatic letter")
defending his own claims. His claim to be Pope required both the
consent of those within his own jurisdiction (like Saint Cyprian)
and those in other jurisdictions (like Saint Pope Dionysius of
Alexandria). This established two principles: the local synod must
consent to its Patriarch (here the Pope of Rome) and that to be
a peer with the other "Patriarchs," their consent was necessary
also. Naturally, depositions worked in the same way. When the

local Council of Antioch deposed the heretic Paul of Samosata, they sought the consent of the world's patriarchates (as they existed during that time, the term being anachronistic).

Indeed, conciliarity in the early Church was predicated by consensus-based ecclesiastical presumptions, but so were the epistemic presumptions as to what amounted to what is today called Sacred Tradition. Catholicity's meaning in its "strictest sense" according to Saint Vincent of Lerins is not merely the universal geographic dispersion of conciliar teachings, but the "faith which has been believed everywhere, always, by all."[4] Hence, consensus-based epistemology specifically identified what was the correct faith. Saint Irenaeus pointed to the apostolic pedigree (antiquity) as well as the universal geographic dispersion of the Catholic/Orthodox, as opposed to the Gnostic, approach to Scripture as well as Christianity as a whole. Eusebius of Caesarea similarly treats how one identifies canonical Scriptural books from non-canonical, discerning between what was "universally accepted" and what was not.[5] There were no local synods at that point in the early fourth century which issued a canon of the Scriptures. This demonstrates that conciliarity was not solely what demonstrated consensus, but also universal practice and acceptance.

Consensus-based ecclesiology and epistemology were necessarily intertwined. This is why Saint Augustine on the same question argues that the canonicity of *Wisdom of Solomon* (which was questioned due to its not being written by Solomon) was established:

> *since for so long a course of years that book has deserved to be read in the Church of Christ from the station of the readers of the Church of Christ, and to be heard by all Christians, from bishops downwards, even to the lowest lay believers, penitents, and catechumens, with the veneration paid to divine authority.*[6]

---

4   Vincent of Lerins, *Commonitorium*, Par 6. Open-source Patristic books/translations whenever possible will have basic citations to assist the reader in finding these sources on the internet.

5   Eusebius of Caesarea, *Church History*, Chapter 3, Par 2. See also Par 7.

6   Augustine, *On the Predestination of the Saints*, Book 1, Chapter 27.

Augustine did not solely point to bishops (or councils like the one held in Carthage in recent years). The universality of *Wisdom*'s acceptance ("heard by all Christians") from *both* clergy and laity decided the question conclusively in Augustine's mind. As stated beforehand, consensus was seen to derive from the Holy Spirit—it made apparent the origin of a given mindset behind both ecclesiastical and doctrinal questions.

When Saint Constantine ended the persecution of Christianity and began the first Imperial patronage of the Church, Christianity had already been operating for centuries upon consensus-based ecclesiastical principles. When the first Ecumenical Council occurred in Nicaea, those who attended, as well as their contemporaries, immediately recognized that the council was directed by God Himself—just as the Apostolic council in Jerusalem was centuries earlier. Unambiguously, all cited consent as the determining factor. In the subsequent semi-Arian controversy, Rome sometimes vetoed the Eastern councils due to these councils, unlike Nicaea, lacking consent—something Rome did not always provide during this era. Not surprisingly, consent was cited by Popes like Julius I. Why wouldn't he? Consensus was the exclusive criterium by which the Church had operated up to that point. No one could have even conceived otherwise.

What follows are later local and interpatriarchal controversies that repeatedly demonstrate the same dynamics at work. The Pope was explicitly rejected in the Council of Carthage (419/424, a council later received as functionally "ecumenical" in authority by Canon 2 of the Council in Trullo and Canon 1 of the Council of Nicaea II), his synod's excommunications treated as only locally binding during the Council of Ephesus, his teachings (like the *Tome of Leo*) subject to review and accusations of heresy during the Council of Chalcedon, his synod's communion treated as optional during what is popularly called the "Meletian Schism" (as Rome lacked communion with Antioch, but had communion with others who *were* in communion with Antioch), and his deposition with consent of the Patriarchs thrice repeated (and twice accepted by Rome, the one other time the Pope recanted and his deposition was reversed). If one never read a Papal honorific, one would naturally not infer even the seeds of Vatican I in the consciousness of the early Church.

Yet, the collapse of the Western Roman Empire into Germanic kingdoms had set into motion geopolitical changes. These kingdoms had only nominal allegiance to Constantinople as Roman "client states." The Roman Synod and most of its jurisdiction found itself "out in the cold." Not long afterwards, Rome was occupied by Byzantium and treated as an occupied territory, beginning the Byzantine Papacy. Popes took measures, with little success, to try to insulate their local church from Arian manipulation (at the hands of the Germanic kingdoms) and from Constantinopolitan dominance (a threat which became real when the "Byzantine Empire"[7] reoccupied Rome for the next two centuries). This is when "high Papal language," particularly in interpatriarchal contexts, began in earnest.

If one is to "believe facts rather than words,"[8] as Saint Pope Gregory the Great teaches, while the language surrounding the Papacy evolved, operating realities stayed the same. Unsurprisingly, allegedly weak Popes like Gregory explicitly asserted Rome's jurisdiction to be strictly local. Yet, even the allegedly strong Popes like Saint Martin, while stating things that *sound* very forceful, in fact reiterated the historical ecclesiology of the Church. For example, Pope Martin explicitly asserted "power was lacking" by himself "to appoint the Patriarch of Jerusalem,"[9] a statement irreconcilable

---

7   "Byzantine" is a moniker for the Roman Empire, whose capital was moved from Rome to Constantinople in the fourth century and had persisted as an empire until the 15th century. In short, there is no such thing as the "Byzantine Empire." They called themselves "Roman" and were considered solely as Roman until the Franks had adopted the term for themselves at the beginning of the ninth century. For the sake of simplicity, the term "Byzantine" will be used as it correctly implies a foreign power dominating a local power rightly called "Rome" which otherwise wished to exercise more independence or political dominance of its own.

8   Gregory the Great, *Epistles*, Book 4, Letter 40.

9   *Pope Martin to Pantaleon* in Bronwen Neil and Pauline Allen, *Conflict and Negotiation in the Early Church: Letters from Late Antiquity, Translated from the Greek, Latin, and Syriac*. Washington DC: Catholic University of America Press,

with the Vatican I doctrine of direct jurisdiction. Hence, even a Pope who is often confused by scholars as teaching direct jurisdiction because some of his words may be construed as such,[10] evidently rejects the notion. Other Popes are the same. Their actions are always inconsistent with such Vatican I ideas.

It is difficult to over-emphasize how important of a principle of weighing actions above words (in isolation) is for the historian. The scientific method, for example, tests a theory and through direct observations confirms or denies the truth of a theory. If history is a legitimate social science, surely the actions of historical actors are the tests that confirm or deny interpretations given by historians to their words.

In any event, perhaps the most important statement for the student of the pre-Great Schism Papacy is found in the minutes of the Ecumenical Council of Nicaea II. The council, in Session 6, explicitly defines what an Ecumenical Council is by contrasting itself with a pseudo-Ecumenical Council, that of Hiera:

> It [the Council of Hiera] did not enjoy the cooperation [lit. συνέργεια] of the then Pope of Rome or his priests, neither by means of his representatives or an encyclical letter, as is the rule for councils; nor did it win the assent [lit. συμφρονοῦντας] of the [P]atriarchs of the [E]ast, of Alexandria, Antioch, and the holy city, or of their priests and bishops….Nor did 'their voice', like that of the apostles, 'go out into the whole earth or their words to the ends of the world', as did those of the six holy [E]cumenical [C]ouncils.[11]

As one can see, an Ecumenical Council is not an exercise of the Pope of Rome decreeing one to be so. Rather, the Pope of Rome *cooperates* with his synod while the Patriarchs of the East "assent" (the Greek implies conviction and activity), as well as the rest of the Church worldwide. In short, consensus decided the ultimate

---

2020, 223.

10   Richard Price, Phil Booth, and Catherine Cubitt, *The Acts of the Lateran Synod of 649*. Liverpool: Liverpool University Press, 2014, 397.

11   Richard Price, *The Acts of the Second Council of Nicaea (787)*. Liverpool: Liverpool University Press, 2020, 442.

authority of a council. After all, consensus was always understood as the evidence of God's cooperation with the Church's work.

Mere years before Nicaea II, the Byzantine Papacy officially ended. Due to conflicting political players in the Italian peninsula (specifically the Franks and the Lombards), when Byzantine power collapsed, the city of Rome itself was able to play the Franks against the Lombards in order to attain a degree of political independence. In effect, the Papal States were created, with ecclesiastical reforms undertaken with the intent to further insulate Roman ecclesiastical business from foreign-political usurpation.

Over time, the Franks would dominate Papal business, but ironically this did not do much to change the independent-minded trajectory of Rome. The Franks, after all, were in a geopolitical struggle against the Byzantines and other than the briefest moments of rapprochement sought political, military, and ecclesiastical means to dominate their foe. Hence, being coerced by the Franks, Rome during the ninth century would turn decidedly against the Byzantines and expound a dramatically new ecclesiology. This sudden shift revolved around two men specifically—Anastasius the Librarian (a Frankish ghostwriter and *de facto* head diplomat for Popes Nicholas, Adrian II, and John VIII) and Saint Photius, Patriarch of Constantinople.

For the first time, Papal chanceries explicitly rejected both consensus-based ecclesiology and epistemology. Not coincidentally, at the exact same time, forged documents offering a "historical pedigree" for these changes conveniently were exploited. At minimal this included the *Pseudo-Isidorian Decretals*, but the case will be made that significant forgeries were inserted in the Latin minutes of Nicaea II and Constantinople (869-870). All of these writings either came from the pen of Anastasius or were specifically popularized internationally by himself. Anastasius also gave voice to new ideas that would become pivotal to the modern Papacy, such as Papal Infallibility. In effect, Anastasius reinvented or "rebooted" the office of the Papacy to confront the geopolitical realities of his day.

Suddenly in the 870s, the Byzantines were retaking southern Italy. Political alliances with Constantinople vis-à-vis collapsing Frankish power became preferable for the sake of the Papal States' stability. The anti-Byzantine Anastasius died or was "retired." Interestingly, his ideas were largely not set aside by Pope John VIII during the Ecumenical Council of Constantinople (879-880), but they were muted enough to make peace with Photius. This would prove to be the last gasp for the orthodox Papacy. The Roman Synod devolved into a middling, feudal faction in Italian 10th century politics and became inconsequential ecclesiastically in crucial interpatriarchal matters.

By the eve of the Crusades, however, the Papacy of Anastasius was dusted off. Eastern Frankish ecclesiastics subsumed power within the College of Cardinals. A reform program was initiated that largely depended upon precedents from Anasatasius' writings and the *Pseudo-Isidorian Decretals*. They constitutionally changed the Roman church in order to make it more independent of local Italian nobility, as well as Frankish (the Holy Roman Empire) meddling. This new Papacy had fundamentally abandoned the operating principles of its historic predecessor. Anastasius' dissemination of a slew of forgeries had allowed their innovative ideas to marinate in Rome for two centuries; these were understandably confused to be authentic Patristic witnesses. Geopolitical necessities now incentivized putting them into practice. This specific combination of historical incidents decisively changed the Papacy for good. All the Vatican I distinctives, though undeveloped, finally had some sort of concrete historical antecedent. The Papacy had finally fallen.

The preceding story arc is internally consistent, and it has a thread which can be followed from the beginning of the Church. If one looks with the eyes of a Christian where "he who is greatest among you shall be your servant,"[12] the rise and the fall of the Papacy can be easily surmised. It rose from two humble men, the Apostles Peter and Paul, who served to their deaths. Rome's primatial standing in the Church was inherited by their successors and grew when they acted as a stalwart of orthodoxy in their service to the Church (generally, there were hiccups along the way). For centuries, Rome "played by the rules" and so the Papacy rose when they were

---

12   Matt 23:11.

vindicated in controversies and repented when they fell short. Their great degree of independence from Byzantium, when compared to the other patriarchates, allowed the ecclesiastical prominence of Rome to grow as a counterweight to (often heretical) Imperial policy. When their complete independence from Byzantium effectively cut off Rome geopolitically from the rest of the canonical Church,[13] the Papacy fell when, through political necessity and the inculcation of ideas found in forgeries, the Roman Synod abandoned the consensus-based ecclesiology. This became irrevocable with their schism during the Crusades.

It is time now to unpack this story. Once unpacked, the post-schism, ethnocentric story arcs surrounding the Papacy will be exposed for what they are—the insertion of anachronistic ideas into primary sources lacking them. Consensus-based ecclesiology and epistemology are clear in the sources and do not require excessive elaboration. It is perhaps the appreciation of consensus that one will encounter most in the study of the pre-schism Papacy.

---

13 This presumes that the non-Chalcedonian sect went into schism and was no longer canonically in the Church. See W.H.M. Frend, *The Rise of the Monophysite Movement: Chapters in the History of the Church in the Fifth and Sixth Centuries*. Cambridge: Cambridge University Press, 1972.

St. Peter the Apostle

CHAPTER 1

The First Century of the Papacy

For the Papacy to have a rise, it must have a point of origin. The Scriptures provide what may be gleaned to be the earliest evidence of the institution. Before discussing the earliest historical witnesses pertaining to Saint Peter and the Roman church specifically, it is helpful to look at the first-century ecclesiology of the Church more broadly.

THE EARLIEST ECCLESIOLOGY OF THE LOCAL CHURCH

Identifying what was the earliest mode of ecclesiology is relevant to the history of the Papacy. This is especially true considering there is modern scholarship that asserts there was no original "Papacy" *per se*.[14] This scholarship posits that the Church of Rome, and the Church at-large, had a plural episcopacy that essentially operated like contemporary Presbyterians on the local level. Scriptures such as Phil 1:1 and Acts 20:28, as well as early Church documents such as 1 Clement and *The Shepherd of Hermas*, refer to there being multiple bishops in cities such as Rome and Corinth.[15] This scholarship

---

14 Eamon Duffy, "Was there a Bishop of Rome in the First Century?," *New Blackfriars*, 80:940, 1999, 301-308.

15 See 1 Clem 1, 47; *Shepherd* 2.4.8 and 3.9.7.

infers that if there are multiple "bishops," "presbyters," or "rulers" identified within singular cities in the preceding sources, this must mean they all were equals serving an identical function.

One must quibble with the insufficient evidence drawn from in making such conclusions. Where do these sources provide any textual basis for the conclusion that these multiple bishops were fundamentally equal, serving the same function? The supposed plural episcopacy is based upon inferences which ignore explicit historical evidence.

There is no example in any early Church document of there being multiple Bishops being named in one city. Even the Scriptures, such as 1 Cor 1:1, do not fail to name a single bishop despite there being schisms and potentially multiple episcopal claimants in Corinth.[16] This makes documents such as the epistles of Saint Ignatius of Antioch unexceptional in this regard. In six of his letters, the resident bishop, who is a singular bishop, is named. The chances that he would write to six cities and they all coincidentally only had one bishop, but any other church would have had a plural episcopacy is 1 in 64. It requires, without a textual basis, inferring that Ignatius was an innovator inventing the monoepiscopacy. The simplest explanation of the evidence is that cities had singular ruling bishops.

What is one to make of the aforementioned passages where the existence of several bishops are mentioned? For one, the geography of a city must be considered. Cities as large as ancient Rome or

---

16 Saint Sosthenes was likely the Bishop of Corinth (at least temporarily) as indicated by Acts 18:17 and 1 Cor 1:1. Sacred Tradition also identifies him as bishop of Colophon in modern-day Turkey. The Metropolis of Corinth lists "ΣΩΣΘΕΝΗΣ" as one of the city's first bishops, simply "Σωσθένης" (Sosthenes) in all capital letters. See "ΟΙ ΜΗΤΡΟΠΟΛΙΤΕΣ," *IEPA ΜΗΤΡΟΠΟΛΙΣ ΚΟΡΙΝΘΟΥ*, https://www.imkorinthou.org/index.php?option=com_content&view=article&id=55&Itemid=52. In any event, it is not entirely clear how literal the schisms were that are mentioned in 1 Cor 1:10, though it is likely the schismatics attached themselves to leaders, perhaps even "bishops," who claimed allegiance to Saints Peter and Apollos. See 1 Cor 1:12 and 1 Clem 47. Saint Paul may have also been obliquely referring to a Judaizing faction which had nominal allegiance to Saint James. See 1 Cor 4:6 and 2 Cor 11:5, 13, 22.

Ephesus could have easily had several bishops who exercised pastorship over particular districts and surrounding areas. For example, the earliest and more reliable tradition identifies Saint Hippolytus of Rome not as the Pope of Rome, but the Bishop of Portus (*Emporium Romanum*)—an important suburb of Rome that served as its port.[17]

It is also possible that "missionary bishops," sometimes the Apostles themselves, would be resident in a city alongside its bishop. For example, Saint Paul would have been a bishop over Crete, Ephesus, and Corinth by virtue of having begun these churches. Yet, this does not contradict the fact that these churches did have individual bishops: Titus, Timothy, and Sosthenes.

Most importantly, Tit 1:5,7 reveals there existed an episcopal hierarchy. Saint Paul wrote from Rome to Titus, acting as his bishop and, as the passage shows, Titus acted as Archbishop of Crete over local bishops he was asked to have consecrated on the island. Other Pauline epistles likewise indicate a normative episcopal succession and hierarchical arrangement. Paul, writing again from Rome, commands Timothy (as bishop, later called a "Metropolitan," of Ephesus) to "command certain men," the local bishops of the region, "not to teach a different doctrine" than his own.[18] This tradition is used to understand the Scriptures rightly.[19] The tradition is found specifically among those clergy whose job is to exhort (i.e. teach) "sound doctrine" by "holding to the faithful word [tradition] as he has been taught" by the Apostles.[20] It is explicitly passed on from Apostle to clergy,[21] clergy to clergy ("do not rebuke a presbyter,

---

17   Christian Charles Josias Bunsen, *Hippolytus and His Age: Volume 1*. London: Longman, Brown, Green, and Longmans, 1852, 205.

18   1 Tim 1:3-8. The KJV is quoted for clarity. Cf 2 Tim 2:2; Rom 16:17.

19   1 Tim 1:4-8. Cf 1 Tim 6:20-21.

20   Tit 1:9.

21   1 Tim 1:3.

but exhort him"),[22] and clergy to the people.[23] Those who teach otherwise are to be "withdraw[n]" from (i.e. excommunicated).[24]

Interestingly, the extant Scriptural evidence explicitly delineates where the tradition originates (Christ's teaching), who first taught it (the Apostles), and who is expected to faithfully preserve and teach it (the clergy, themselves ordained by those the Apostles ordained). One should infer that due to there being overlapping hierarchies of bishops within regions, that sometimes there would be several resident bishops in a given locale, just as there are today (even in areas without multiple jurisdictions). This should be considered normative for the first century, as it is the only explicit evidence from this era that is available. It leaves no room for modern speculations concerning the early Church (and thereby Papacy) operating in a crypto-Presbyterian sense.

Yet, there is still more to consider. There also appears to be a lack of attention paid to the fact that the office of *chorbishop* was common in the early Church. Technically, chorbishop means "country bishop," a reference to a priest who is given authority to appoint lesser, non-ordained clergy (such as a Reader) in the absence of a "real" bishop. Chorbishops can give judgments in synods and letters of commendation. They did not ordain bishops, priests, or deacons. Functionally, they were similar to an abbot in the modern day.

There is no contradiction in the historical inference that a city like Rome, and other local churches, would have a chief bishop and lesser chorbishops/priests assisting him. Their existence in the canons is evidence that they were widespread.[25] These canons delineate that these "bishops" are in fact simple priests. To this day, the Arabic word for the parish priest is still "chorbishop."

In summary, the monoepsicopal consensus of the early Church is easy to explain if one interprets the first-century documentation referring to multiple bishops in a city as consistent with extant

---

22   1 Tim 5:1, cf 6:2. "Presbyter" is rendered "older man" in the NKJV.

23   1 Tim 4:6, 11-13; Titus 2:15.

24   1 Tim 6:3-5.

25   Canon 13 of Ancyra, Canon 14 of Neocaesarea, and Canon 10 of Antioch.

evidence, as presented above. It is surely problematic to infer a plural episcopacy despite such evidence. Therefore, without evidence to the contrary, the traditional view that there has always been a singular bishop of Rome with succession deriving itself from Saints Peter and Paul appears to be the most justified.

Before leaving the topic of early ecclesiology and its import on the origins of the Papacy, one must consider the evidence from early Judaism. There are good grounds for presuming that early Church ecclesiology is largely a continuation of first century Jewish synagogal organization. For example, the Dead Sea Scrolls record that the local leader of the Essene community was a singular *"mevaqqer"* or *"paqid."* These Hebrew words literally mean "overseer/bishop." Below the bishop were the priests.[26] Outside of the Essenes, proto-Rabbinic synagogues (i.e. the synagogues of the first century) appeared to be part of larger organizations, themselves led by a sort of synod called the *Sanhedrin*. The *Sanhedrin* was led by a High Priest, though the High Priests did not derive themselves from an unchanging line of succession.[27] High Priests did not operate in isolation and always conferred with the *Sanhedrin*,[28] decisions being made by majority vote.[29] Subservient, local synagogues were led by regional lesser *Sanhedrins* with a singular "ruler" called a *"Nasi."*[30] One can surmise a hierarchical, synodal system not all that different from the early Church. Significant parallels can be surmised in the crypto-monoepiscopal way in which both systems were organized.

Based on the scanty early evidence on Judaism that exists, one may also infer some discontinuities between Judaism and the Early Church. In Judaism, the *Sanhedrin* appeared to be composed of a

---

26 "Qumran Community Leaders," *Hebrew University of Jerusalem, accessed 2023.*, http://virtualqumran.huji.ac.il/moreInfo/CommunityLeaders.htm.

27 As 1 and 2 Macc entail.

28 Acts 5:17-42.

29 *Babylonian Talmud: Tractate Sanhedrin*, Folios 2a and 3b, Chapter I. See "Sanhedrin," *Sefaria*, https://www.sefaria.org/Sanhedrin.2a.1?lang=bi&with=all&lang2=en. See also Acts 26:10-11.

30 Hugo Mantel, "The Nature of the Great Synagogue," *The Harvard Theological Review*, 60:1, 1967, 90.

mixture of elders and hereditary priests who had higher authority than the laymen. However, the former were mutually exclusive "offices." This may be because of the hereditary priesthood and its clan-based, Levitical character—something that the early Church dispensed with. In any event, archdeacons may serve as an early-Church analogue. It was not unknown for archdeacons to exercise considerably more authority than both priests and even some bishops. The sort of "mixed" composition of both Judaism and Christianity has some unappreciated parallels in any event.

It is likely that the hierarchy of bishop > chorbishop > priests > deacons > laity developed along the lines of local synagogue organization: synagogue ruler > lesser rulers > priests > elders > laity.[31] Lesser *Sanhedrins* were the Jewish version of a *metropolitan*, with a *Nasi* > lesser *Sanhedrin* as opposed to a Metropolitan and lesser bishops.

Taking all this into consideration, the extant historical evidence provides a basic explanation for passages such as Acts 20:28 and Phil 1:1. Paul in both passages likely was addressing some mixture of a ruling (Metropolitan) bishop and lesser bishops, if not chorbishops (or their urban equivalent). Though all of them are broadly "bishops," chorbishops do not exercise the fullness of the office. Monoepiscopacy is not a doctrinal development—in fact it appears to predate Christianity. In this regard, the monoepiscopal Papacy of Rome would have been unexceptional.

PETRINE EXCEPTIONALISM IN THE SCRIPTURES AND ITS PAPAL IMPORT

The Scriptures were written for audiences that were already Christian and would have thereby been organized among the aforementioned ecclesiastical lines. Therefore, anything of ecclesiastical import, especially when it pertained to an Apostle, would have immediately had both its importance and application recognized.

---

31   1 Clem 40 appears to similarly equate the two.

One must look at the most straightforward Scriptural texts containing a special emphasis upon the Apostle Peter (Matt 16:18, Luke 22:32, John 21:15-19, and Acts 15:6-11) with this in mind. All of these originate in the middle to late first century. Despite one's presuppositions, a surface-level reading of all these texts implies an important spiritual role belonged to Saint Peter. This would have been immediately obvious to the intended audience.

Perhaps the first true controversy that was settled in the early Church was the "Judaizing Controversy." There was a significant debate over "how Jewish" Gentile converts to Christianity were expected to be. Peter presumed initially that the "unclean" could not be made "clean."[32] This implies that the original Christian understanding (at least popularly) was that the Gentiles must first convert to Judaism, and in effect be Jews, in order to be faithful Christians. This view can be coined "Judaizing." The coming of the Holy Spirit onto the Gentiles proved with power that such a view was incorrect. This was something that initially created controversy with the rest of the Church.[33] Initially, the Church consented to Peter's view after he explained himself.[34]

Yet, the controversy was not settled decisively by Peter at this point—an interesting fact with import on the question of the Papacy. Peter himself, though not backtracking on his declared position on the matter,[35] was accused by Saint Paul of hypocrisy. Peter showed symbolic support to the Judaizers merely by eating with "men… from James" who without the latter saint's permission[36] sought to

---

32 Acts 10:14-15.

33 Acts 10:47-48 and 11:2-3.

34 Acts 11:18.

35 Paul notes that Peter "live[d] in the manner of the Gentiles and not as the Jews." (Gal 2:14.)

36 See Gal 2:12 and Acts 15:24. The latter passage states that the Church of Jerusalem, and thereby James, never gave authorization for Judaizing to be taught. Yet, crypto-Judaizing appears to be a persistent concern for James' church as evidenced by Acts 21:18-25. It is likely that James pursued a policy of rapprochement with the Jews, which had some degree of success in that he himself frequented the Second Temple. In Acts 15:21 and 21:20-25, the rules applied to Gentiles (such as not eating blood) are cited in respect to

impose the Judaizing view. Simply taking the sources at their word, the Scriptures specifically, one would never arrive at the conclusion that Peter's authority, both ecclesiastical and dogmatic, was final. On the surface, he appeared to be deferring to James on the matter.

How did the Church settle the controversy? A council was held in Jerusalem, as recorded in Acts 15:6-30. During the council, both the "Apostles and presbyters" presided. This implies the episcopate of an Apostle was functionally equal to those likewise ordained bishops.[37] During the proceedings, Peter gave a judgment citing how "a good while ago" (a reference to the events in reference to Acts 10-11), God ordained "by my mouth the Gentiles should hear the...Gospel." Certainly, Peter is laying claim to an important ministry—perhaps not coincidentally, even what would be later called a jurisdiction. Both Peter and Paul were to die in Rome and all the Gentile churches that Paul started in effect would overlap with Peter, who re-evangelized these same churches.[38]

---

them being followed so as not to offend the Jews. James' martyrdom likely spelled the effectual end of this policy. Hegesippus (*Fragments From Five Books of Commentaries on the Acts of the Church*) as well as Josephus (*Antiquities of the Jews*, Book 20, Chap 9, Par 1), both early and reliable sources, record James' martyrdom and the former indicating his closeness to Jewish leadership. Josephus interestingly records significant Jewish resistance to what was done to James, another indication that James' policy had achieved some institutional success—but not enough.

37 The Apostles themselves held the office of "bishop." See Acts 1:20 in the Greek.

38 There is a plethora of early source material asserting this. 1 Pet 1:1 is addressed to churches Paul started and 1 Cor 1:12 identifies a Petrine faction in Corinth. Additionally, 2 Pet 3:15-16 offers an admonishment to read Paul's letters rightly, implying that Peter sent his final letter to teach Pauline churches. Interestingly, Saint Dionysius of Corinth in the second century states that "both of them [Peter and Paul] went to our Corinth, and taught us in the same way as they taught you when they went to Italy; and having taught you, they suffered martyrdom at the same time." See Eusebius, *Church History*, Book 2, Chap 25. It is highly speculatory, but the episcopal quality of Paul's ministry might have been in acting as Peter's vicar. See Gal 1:18, Gal 2:6-10. Acts 13:1-3 also indicates Paul and Barnabas began in earnest their missionary work after Simeon ("who was called Niger"), Lucius, and Manaen "laid hands on them," a potential reference to a consecration to the

After Peter effectively cited historical precedent and his own authority from God in favor of the orthodox (anti-Judaizing) view, Paul and Barnabas spoke of miracles done through themselves. This is a similar claim to Peter's, but obviously less weighty as their words are not even quoted. Saint Luke's emphasis in *Acts of the Apostles* is that Peter began the ministry to the Gentiles. A sort of preeminence may be implied. Nevertheless, it is Saint James, who presided over the council, who judges: "Simon [Peter] has declared how God at the first visited the Gentiles...with this the words of the prophets agree...Therefore I judge that we should [accept the Gentiles]."

James in effect gave the first explicit judgment on the matter. He cited the Scriptures (the authority of antiquity) and recent precedent (which is also divinely authoritative) as being in agreement. For that reason, he decreed Judaizing to be heretical. Immediately afterwards, Luke records this judgment was consented to by all as "it pleased the Apostles and elders, with the whole church" to issue a synodal letter (later called a "decree") expounding the orthodox doctrine and disowning the Judaizers.

In later conciliar documents, it is not uncommon for non-Roman bishops to subscribe to a decree or issue a judgment before the Roman legate (a Roman Pope never attended an Ecumenical Council). One may go too far in definitively concluding that by James speaking authoritatively before the others this meant he had in fact the most authority. This would be an incorrect inference. However, one must surmise that all "the Apostles and elders" had to be fundamentally in agreement ("it seemed good to us, being assembled with one accord.") This was seen as proof of the Holy Spirit synergizing with, and thereby superintending, the work of the council: "For it seemed good to the Holy Spirit, and to us."

There is no indication that Peter gave the final judgment on the matter and that the consent of others was unnecessary. Rather, the opposite is the simplest interpretation of the evidence. This shows that in the council, Peter had an important role. However, more

---

episcopacy. Traditionally Antioch is a Petrine Church, so this would mean Pauline churches were in fact under Peter's oversight, the latter being the first Apostle tasked to evangelize the Gentiles.

prominent are the roles that earlier precedent, specific Scriptural warrant, and the consent of all present played. Not coincidentally, the Decree of the Ecumenical Council of Constantinople II would emphasize the preceding understanding of the Council of Jerusalem vis-à-vis the solitary decision-making of a Roman bishop:

> *they [the Apostles] met together and each of them confirmed his statements from the testimonies of the divine scriptures. Accordingly it was in common that they all pronounced judgement on the matter...The holy fathers also who convened at various times in the holy four councils followed ancient precedent and decreed in common on the heresies and problems that had arisen, since it is certain that it is through joint examination, when there is expounded what needs to be discussed on both sides, that the light of truth dispels the darkness of lies.[39]*

The ecclesiology of consent was informed by an epistemology of consent from the very beginning.

This does not mean Peter does not serve a central role in the Scriptures and Sacred Tradition. John 21:15 states that Peter "feed[s] My [the Lord's] lambs." Luke 22:32 assigns Peter a specific role—"strengthen[ing] the brethren." While other Apostles wrote epistles and preached, none had their role surmised as Peter. Such emphases cannot simply be dry, historical observations. The Lord Himself spoke these things, so such an emphasis must have significance. They had real import to the contemporary reader.

Additionally, they imply a defined ecclesiology which is not "low church," as the authors' intents must have been that Peter represented something important. Otherwise, God through the Apostles' historical documents simply left useless details. Perhaps the most significant detail about Peter in the Scriptures is that Saint

---

39   Richard Price, *The Acts of the Council of Constantinople of 553 with related texts on the Three Chapters Controversy: Volume Two.* Liverpool: Liverpool University Press, 2009, 111. Pope Vigilius at that time was not asserting infallibility, universal jurisdiction, or anything of the sort. However, his intransigence in refusing to join the council and deliberate with those present, simply because he would have been vastly outnumbered, inspired the comment. Price spells the word "judgment" according to the English spelling "judgement" in his translations.

Peter was given "keys" which can "bind and loose" sins (Matt 16:18) through the disciplinary function of the Church (Matt 18:17-18). Obviously, the giving of a literal key is not the point. The keys must mean *something*.

Due to the Orthodox (and early Church) doctrine of Sacred Tradition viewing the Patristic heritage and the Scriptures as harmonious, it is important to delineate precisely how the saints have historically understood the significance of Matt 16:18 and precisely what the ramifications of this authority was. Three perspectives may be identified: they symbolized (1) Interpretative/ preaching authority given to the Church;[40] (2) "Keys of heaven" (i.e. binding and loosing sins) given to Peter and the other Apostles/ Church at-large;[41] and (3) "Keys of heaven" given specifically to Peter and his successors in Rome.[42]

A few examples are worth drawing out. Cyprian of Carthage, a saint who in one letter briefly ascribes to the third "perspective,"[43] can be found elsewhere incorporating such a view into the larger teaching that all the Apostles and their successors have Peter's "keys." He explains:

---

40   A few examples are found in Origen (*Commentary on Revelation*, Book V, Chap 4 and *Commentary on John*, Book 2, Chap 4); Saint Jerome (*Letter 58*, Par 9; Letter 53; Homily 66's reference on Rev 3:7); Saint Augustine (*Sermon 24*, Par 1-2); and Saint Andrew of Caesarea (as quoted in William C. Weinrich, *Ancient Christian Commentary on Scripture, NT Volume 12*. Downers Grove, IL: IVP Academic, 2005, 44).

41   A few examples are found in Tertullian (*Scorpiace*, Chap 10); Saint Cyprian (*Treatise 1*, Chap 4; *Epistle 26*, Par 1); Saint Optatus (*Against the Donatists*, Book 1, Chap 12); Saint Jerome (*Letter 14*, Par 8; *Against Jovianus*, Book 1, Par 26); Saint John Chrysostom (*Homily 1 on John*; *Homily 12 on John*); Saint Augustine (*Exposition on Ps 109*, Par 1; *Tractate 50 on John*, Par 12; *Tractate 124 on John*, Par 5; *Sermon on Saints Peter and Paul*, Par 1 and 2); Saint Caesarius of Arles (*Catena on Revelation 1:18*); Saint Bede, Ibid.; Saint Isidore of Seville (*The Church*, Book 2, Par 5); Saint Pope Gregory the Great (*Epistles*, Book 7, Letter 40).

42   This will be left to other sources to prove out in the interests of space.

43   *Letter 72*, Par 11. Ironically, this letter is written in opposition to Saint Pope Stephen. Cyprian denies in the same paragraph that he was among the "betrayers of unity" as the former seems to have alleged in excommunicating him.

Our Lord, whose precepts and admonitions we ought to observe, describing the honour of a bishop and the order of His Church, speaks in the Gospel, and says to Peter: I say unto you, That you are Peter, and upon this rock will I build my Church; and the gates of hell shall not prevail against it. And I will give unto you the keys of the kingdom of heaven: and whatsoever you shall bind on earth shall be bound in heaven: and whatsoever you shall loose on earth shall be loosed in heaven. Thence, through the changes of times and successions, the ordering of bishops and the plan of the Church flow onwards; so that the Church is founded upon the bishops, and every act of the Church is controlled by these same rulers.[44]

As one can see, the second and third perspectives easily harmonize as there is no contradiction between Peter and his successors having "keys," but also the other Apostles and their successors having the same. Saint Cyprian's explicit ecclesiological views will be explained in detail in a subsequent chapter.

Cyprian's view should not be a controversial understanding. In fact, the West maintained this view far into the Middle Ages. The Fourth Lateran Council (1215) specifies:

Nobody can effect this sacrament [the Eucharist] except a priest who has been properly ordained according to the church's keys, which Jesus Christ Himself gave to the [A]postles and their successors.[45]

In summary, the saints often have multiple interpretations of verses like Matt 16:18. This is not a contradiction. Interpretative authority in the Church *complements* disciplinary authority. Peter or the Church of Rome being given "keys" *complements* other Apostles and churches being given "keys." The thread that runs through Scripture is that *Peter is the origin of the episcopate*. All bishops are in effect "Peter" and have his "keys." This is certainly a theologically

---

44 Cyprian of Carthage, *Letter 26*, Par 1.
45 *Fourth Lateran Council (1215)*, Decree 1.

slanted inference of the Scriptural passage, but it is an inference best supported by succession lists and other extant historical evidence.*

THE ORIGIN OF THE EPISCOPATE

As will be covered in more detail during the "Pascha Controversy," Saints Peter and Paul established the majority of the local churches in the Apostolic period. Presuming all the bishops who were ordained by them are their "successors" and those bishops succeeding the other bishops their "successors," one can delineate a "succession" connected to Rome, where these Apostles died. By default, this would have granted Rome the largest local jurisdiction—from Crete to Spain. This alone would make most bishops successors of Peter by default.

However, Peter's preeminence does not end there. The earliest explicit historical evidence appears to identify that Peter was considered the origin of the entire episcopate if not categorically, then at least largely so.* Eusebius of Caesarea, citing Clement of Alexandria's now lost *Hypotyposes* (a source from approximately 200 AD) reveals that Peter was involved in the consecration of Saint James the Just as the Bishop of Jerusalem.[46] The same, citing Saint Papias (a source from the early second century), asserts that Peter consecrated Saint Mark as Bishop of Alexandria.[47] In the mid-third century, Cyprian's aforementioned *Letter 26* appears to imply all bishops succeed from Peter as does his Treatise *On the Unity of the Church* which states:

> that He might set forth unity, He arranged by His authority the origin
> of that unity, as beginning from one [Peter]. Assuredly the rest of the
> [A]postles were also the same as was Peter, endowed with a like

---

46   Eusebius, *Church History*, Book 1, Chap 1.

47   Ibid., Chap 15-16, 24.

* *The points indicated in these two places are the historical conclusion of the author, but not a polemic found in recent centuries within the Orthodox Church in its dialogue with Roman Catholics. For example, the Letter of the Patriarchs (Constantinople 1848) identifies Antioch specifically as the "Apostolic Throne" of Saint Peter in Par 11.*

partnership both of honour and power; but the beginning proceeds from unity.[48]

Saint Optatus,[49] another North African writing a century later, seemingly conflates the succession from Peter with the entire episcopate receiving his keys: "[B]lessed Peter...both deserved to be placed over all the Apostles, and alone received the keys of the Kingdom of Heaven, which he was to communicate to the rest."[50] He elsewhere conflates the episcopal chairs of Cyprian (i.e. Carthage) and Peter (i.e. Rome):

> *For it was not Caecilian [of Carthage] who went forth from Majorinus [of Carthage], your father's father, but it was Majorinus who deserted Caecilian; nor was it Caecilian who separated himself from the Chair of Peter, or from the Chair of Cyprian—but Majorinus, on whose Chair you sit—a Chair which had no existence.*[51]

Fourth century sources in the East concur. Saint Gregory of Nyssa wrote that, "[Christ] through Peter gave to the bishops the keys of the heavenly honors."[52] The earliest Greek and Ethiopian Dormition homilies contain the same line, explicitly teaching that Peter was the bishop of the Apostles: "John said to him [Peter], 'You are our father and bishop; you must be before the bier until we bring it to the place [of burial].'"[53] Maximinus, an Arian bishop, asserted

---

Cyprian, *Treatise 1*, Par 4.

49 It should be noted that Optatus is only canonized by the Russian Orthodox Church.

50 Optatus, *Against the Donatists*, Book 7, Chap 3.

51 Ibid., Book 1, Chap 10.

52 PG 42, 312 cited in John Meyendorff, *The Primacy of Peter*. Crestwood, NY: St. Vladimir's Seminary Press, 1992, 71.

53 Stephen Shoemaker, *Ancient Traditions of the Virgin Mary's Dormition and Assumption*. Oxford: Oxford University Press, 2002, 326, 366. The same line was repeated in John of Thessalonica's Dormition homily in the seventh century. See Brian Daley, *On the Dormition of Mary*. Crestwood: St. Vladimir's Seminary Press, 1998, 64.

that "the see of Peter is equal and common to all the bishops"[54] taking for granted that his audience would have recognized this.

The testimony of contemporary and later Bishops of Rome is little different. In the early fifth century, Pope Innocent I wrote matter-of-factly that "all of us who are set in this place [Rome] desire to follow the [A]postle [Peter], from whom the episcopate itself and the whole authority of this name is derived."[55] Pope Boniface wrote shortly afterwards, "The universal ordering of the Church at its birth took its origin from the office of blessed Peter."[56] Saint Pope Leo the Great quoted Matt 16:18 and asserted "the universal Church has become a rock through the building up of that original Rock," likely with the preceding view of the episcopacy in mind.[57] Centuries later, Pope Gregory II plainly asserted that "the blessed [A]postle Peter was the origin of both the apostleship and the episcopate."[58]

The teaching that all bishops are successors of Peter was ubiquitous in the early Church. Succession lists from the second and third century, preserved by Eusebius, buttress the early historical authority of this consensus tradition. However, it can be argued that Saint Paul, and churches succeeding from himself, pose a historical difficulty for those who do not uncritically accept this tradition. Eusebius dryly observes that God Himself made Paul an Apostle (it is unsaid if God made him a bishop) and names several churches whose succession does not explicitly begin with Peter (Ephesus, Timothy; Crete, Titus; Antioch, Evodius).[59] None of this explicitly contradicts the later tradition (as traditionally Peter consecrated

54 PL Suppl. 1, 722 quoted in Scott Butler and John Collorafi, *Keys Over the Christian World*. United States of America: Scott Butler and John Collorafi, 2003, 78.

55 PL 20, 582-3 quoted in Ibid., 144.

56 *Letter to the Bishops of Thessaly* quoted in E. Giles, *Documents Illustrating Papal Authority AD 96-454*. London: SPCK, 1952, 230.

57 Leo the Great, *Letter 156*, Par 2.

58 MGH, Epistolae 3: 275-7 quoted in Butler and Collorafi, *Keys Over the Christian World*, 464.

59 Eusebius, *Church History*, Book 2, Chap 1; Book 3, Chap 4, 22.

Evodius and it appears Evodius' men in Acts 13:1-3 consecrated
Paul).[60]

Additionally, Eusebius preserves an oblique reference from
Clement's *Hypotyposes* which implies universal Petrine succession:
"The Lord after [H]is resurrection *imparted knowledge* to James the
Just and to John and Peter, and they imparted it to the rest of
the [A]postles, and the rest of the [A]postles to the [S]eventy, of
whom Barnabas was one."[61] On the surface this appears to be an
unexciting reference to how Apostolic Tradition was passed on
orally through the Church, perhaps a reference to Acts 1:2 ("He...
given commandments to the Apostles whom He had chosen").
However, this is not what the text, or Acts 1:2, actually states. Surely,
"the rest of the Apostles" would have had this *after* the Resurrection
as there are no recorded private meetings between Jesus Christ and
Peter/John/James the Just where significant doctrine was taught.
One may infer that this is a euphemistic reference to the origin
of the episcopacy. Similarly, Saint Clement of Rome records that
those who "received their orders" were "established in the word of
God."[62]

Early consecrations likely included the explicit passing on
of oral tradition from the Lord. Saint Hippolytus recorded that
something similar was communicated whenever communion was
shared as well as during baptism.[63] For this reason, baptism was
called "illumination" from the beginning.[64] To this day, a plethora of
doctrinal matters are passed on when consecrating bishops, because
they repeat theological confessions from the *Great Euchologion*. This

---

60 See n. 38.

61 Eusebius, *Church History*, Book 2, Chap 1.

62 1 Clem 42.

63 Hippolytus of Rome, *Apostolic Tradition*, 21:30, 40. Translation cited is by
    Kevin Edgecomb. "The Apostolic Tradition of Saint Hippolytus of Rome,"
    Saint John's Arlington, VA, https://www.stjohnsarlingtonva.org/Customer-
    Content/saintjohnsarlington/CMS/files/EFM/Apostolic_Tradition_by_
    Hippolytus.pdf

64 Heb 6:4; Saint Justin the Philosopher, *First Apology*, Chap 61; Clement of
    Alexandria, *The Pedagogue*, Book 1, Chap 6.

process in effect continues the "education" of correct doctrine during the consecration of bishops.

Thus, it appears that the widely held tradition of the Church concerning the origin of the episcopacy has dependably early attestation. Out of all historical possibilities, the idea that Peter is the origin of the entire episcopate so that all bishops can legitimately claim to be the successor of Peter is in fact the strongest. Without recorded evidence to the contrary, one would be hard-pressed to dispassionately derive a different historical conclusion.

1 CLEMENT AND ECCLESIOLOGY IN THE FIRST CENTURY

The earliest Papal letters (1 and 2 Peter) only have scanty ecclesiastical commentary. Saint Peter offers exhortations to bishops as a "fellow presbyter [i.e. priest]," identifying the Lord as "the Chief Shepherd."[65] Unpacking the third earliest Papal letter, 1 Clement, in detail helps illustrate many important aspects of early Church ecclesiology and the first century Papacy itself.

1 Clem appears to be a synodal letter written shortly after 2 Peter. It is likely written by Clement on behalf of the Church of Rome. The earliest historical evidence verifies this. Saint Dionysius of Corinth in the second century asserted Clement's authorship: "This holy Lord's day, in which we read your [the Roman Synod's] letter, from the constant reading of which we shall be able to draw admonition, even as from the reading of the former one you sent us written through Clement."[66] As for its early date, the letter identifies a maximum of two generations of presbyters succeeding from the Apostles (a number reached by the writing of Tit 1:5), it speaks of the Apostles belonging to "our generation," and it references

---

65 1 Pet 5:1-4. The NKJV renders presbyter as "elder."

66 Dionysius of Corinth, *Fragment 2*. Those who assert that the usage of terms such as "we" as evidence in favor of the plural episcopacy do so in contradiction of similar usages of such terms in Cyprian's time by the Roman Synod. They wrote under the title "the presbyters and deacons abiding at Rome" and "we." See Cyprian, *Letter 30*, Par 1. In both letters, the use of "we" is a simple synodal identification.

Jewish Temple sacrifices as something ongoing.[67]   A date past
70 AD is hard to maintain without reference to Saint Irenaeus'
dating it to the late first century. While Irenaeus may be correct, it is
hard to imagine how any of the preceding internal evidence would
correspond with a dating as late as the persecutions of Domitian.[68]

Why would Clement be writing to Corinth? Clement apologizes
that "we [the Roman Synod] have been somewhat tardy in turning
our attention to the points respecting which you consulted us."[69] In
other words, it was those at Corinth (evidently its presbyters)[70] that
wrote to the Roman Synod seeking a judgment. Likely, this was
history's earliest "appeal to Rome."

Such language sounds "loaded," because readers reflexively
equate an appeal made to Rome as an exercise in universal and
direct jurisdiction in line with Papal Supremacy. However, this
would not only be an anachronistic eisegesis, but it would contradict
the earliest evidence on the question. Dionysius of Corinth wrote to
Rome that: "Therefore you also have by such admonition joined in
close union the churches that were planted by Peter and Paul, that
of the Romans and that of the Corinthians."[71]

What was Dionysius speaking of when citing a "close union?"
"Peter and Paul" are the origin of churches they personally started.
Based upon this, there is a local "union" of select "churches" or,
in other words, the bishop is the successor of the specific Apostle
who founded it. The locale where an Apostle dies *traditionally*, not

---

67   1 Clem 41-47.

68   Some may point to persecutions being referenced in 1 Clem 1 as evidence in
favor of an approximated dating to Domitian's reign. Yet, due to there being
an obvious persecution of Christians during Nero's reign in the 60s such a
late dating is hardly necessary. Nero's death in 68 AD offers a compelling
approximation for when the letter was written, probably shortly before the
Roman campaign that destroyed Jerusalem in 70 AD.

69   1 Clem 1. John Keith's translation here is not slavishly literal with the
Greek, but accurately captures the sense of what "turning our attention"
(ἐπιστροφὴν) means, as well later comments concerning the Roman Synod's
"intercession" on Corinth's behalf. See 1 Clem 63.

70   Presbyters are identified in the plural in 1 Clem 1 and 47.

71   Eusebius, *Church History*, Book 2, Chap 25.

canonically,[72] carries with it more importance. Church hagiographies for example credit the granting of ecclesiastical autonomy/autocephaly to Cyprus to the finding of Saint Barnabas' relics due to the saint appearing in a dream to Archbishop Anthimus of Cyprus.[73] On a similar note, Columbanus wrote to Pope Boniface IV concerning "the apostles Peter and Paul, whose dear relics' have made you blessed."[74] Traditionally, Rome's authority is predicated upon relics as well.

Presuming upon this theory, Rome would be more important than Corinth. Both would be Petrine/Pauline bishoprics, but Rome would be *more so* due to having the Apostles' relics. Though not explicitly delineated by either author, it is certainly implied by Clement (in that he is replying to a Corinthian appeal made to his synod, not the other way around) and Dionysius (who above is cited stating that the Corinthians read letters from Rome for admonishment, with no mention of the opposite being the case).

Though the evidence is limited, it is the only extant evidence on the question and this exaggerates its importance. What one can gather from the evidence is that 1 Clem is an exercise in what would later be understood as "local Patriarchal jurisdiction." A local church within the jurisdiction of Peter and Paul appealed to the chief synod within this ecclesial region in accordance with Paul's admonishment that disputes be brought to the Church.[75]

When 1 Clem 1 begins with "[t]he Church of God which sojourns at Rome, to the Church of God sojourning at Corinth," it is implying not simple cities in isolation, but entire regions. While Paul wrote 1 Cor explicitly to Corinth, 2 Cor 1:1 makes clear that this was intended to be "the church of God which is at Corinth,

---

72   Canon 3 of Constantinople I and Canons 17 and 28 of Chalcedon only cite Imperial (Roman) considerations in the delineation of church jurisdictions. It appears that custom and tradition were to be honored unless "eminent domain" decided otherwise.

73   Synaxaria for June 11.

74   *Letter 5* quoted in *Letter 5* quoted in G.S.M. Walker, *Letters of Columbanus*. Cork: Corpus of Electronic Texts, University College, 2008, 49.

75   1 Cor 6:1-10.

with all the saints who are in all Achaia." Hence, "the Church of Corinth" refers to churches (plural) in an entire peninsula (and their surrounding islands) in Greece, Corinth being their metropolis. The Scriptural evidence delineates that Achaia had multiple bishops: Paul (when he was there), Sosthenes,[76] Apollos,[77] and Peter.[78] They may have had separate "cathedra" or chairs set up, technically acting as bishops in different cities within Achaia. In any event, the multiplicity of presbyters referenced in Rome and Corinth is adequately explained by the regional and synodal aspect of both local churches.

Being synodal, 1 Clem should be read as a synodal decree, as it gives a judgment concerning the appeal by the Corinthian presbyters and delegitimizes the schismatics. Second century evidence corroborates this. Irenaeus noted that "the Church in Rome dispatched a most powerful letter to the Corinthians, exhorting them to peace."[79] Why else call it powerful? Nevertheless, being synodal, the appeal is decided synodically—not by the Pope in isolation.

It is not entirely clear what the history of the Corinthian schism was. In Paul's time, there may have been local churches vouching for pre-eminence. These factions apparently attached themselves to whichever Apostle/bishop was there presently or in the past.[80] There appears to have been an invasion of Jewish Christian "eminent"/false apostles or some combination of both.[81] While this

---

76 See 1 Cor 1:1, Acts 18:17. Crispus may be the same person as Sosthenes, as the definite article in front of "ruler of the synagogue" in Acts 18:8 implies. However, tradition specifies that Sosthenes and Crispus are two separate people, as evidenced by their separate days of commemoration. Perhaps Crispus had a more prominent role in the synagogue. Tradition indicates that he was likewise a bishop within the general region of Achaia, specifically Aegina.

77 Acts 19:1.

78 1 Cor 1:12.

79 Irenaeus, *Against Heresies*, Book 3, Chap 3, Par 3.

80 A vying for regional primacy can be inferred from 1 Cor 1:10-13, 11:18-19.

81 2 Cor 11:5, 11:22. Some "Apostles" may have been impostures (i.e. Jewish Christians that were not among the original disciples of Jesus Christ), while

appears highly speculative at first glance, Clement observed that Paul "wrote to you [Corinth] concerning himself, and Cephas, and Apollos, because even then parties had been formed among you... now reflect who those are that have perverted you."[82] The original schismatics had in fact attached themselves to Apostles. The newest schismatics had no such pedigree, something that made them more illegitimate in Clement's eyes.

He describes the Corinthian schismatics in his day as "[f]oolish and inconsiderate men" who "mock and deride us [the Roman Synod], being eager to exalt themselves in their own conceits."[83] The schismatics evidently spurned Rome, likely not seeing an appeal made to them as a legitimate avenue for their ecclesiastical discipline. The terminology "exalt themselves" also implies the illegitimacy of such a tact. The tone of letter is to convince the laity in Achaia to return to validly ordained presbyters/bishops. Hence, the idea of setting oneself up as a bishop is not only scandalous (hence the next five chapters are dedicated to delineating Apostolic Succession, asserting that such an institution was set up by Christ Himself), it is completely illegitimate.[84]

Legitimate ecclesiology was consensus-based. Clement speaks of the origin of clergy via Apostolic Succession noting that "that those [present clergy] appointed by them [Apostles], or afterwards by other eminent men [those appointed by Apostles]" are so appointed "with the consent of the whole Church."[85] Clergy clearly cannot be self-appointed as the Corinthian schismatics were. In ancient times, bishops were popularly elected,[86] but succession was guaranteed by ordination with Apostolic Succession and the consent of all

---

others could have been "men from James" who knew Jesus during his ministry and had identified themselves as part of the Judaizing faction.

82   1 Clem 47.

83   1 Clem 39.

84   1 Clem 44.

85   Ibid.

86   Didache 15. Such elections persist to this day, such as in the Church of Cyprus and in a more limited fashion in the OCA, but the consent of the episcopacy to who is chosen is still necessary.

even outside the local church. Without the consent of the expelled Corinthian presbyters and the Roman Synod, that being the whole Church in this context, the new Corinthian presbyters could not be legitimate.

Clement, on behalf of his synod, writes in a fashion connoting judicial power: "Ye therefore, who laid the foundation of this sedition, submit yourselves to the presbyters [i.e. validly ordained bishops], and receive correction so as to repent."[87] The schismatics are never identified as presbyters (as that would legitimize them) and they are warned: "Those…who do anything beyond that which is agreeable to His will [i.e. abrogating the episcopacy], are punished with death."[88] He expects the repentance of the schismatics to be communicated to what were effectually Papal legates, writing: "Send back…our messengers to you: Claudius Ephebus and Valerius Bito, with Fortunatus: that they may the sooner announce to us the peace and harmony we so earnestly desire."[89] He warns the schismatics that their sedition is an issue relevant to one's salvation[90] commanding them "with all haste, put an end to this [schism]…[so] that He [God] would mercifully be reconciled to us."[91]

Clement issues such warnings so "that they may submit, not to us, but to the will of God."[92] This surely implied an *expected* obedience required to the Roman Synod, as the primatial Petrine/Pauline church. Otherwise, why specify this? Consider the next sentence: "For in this way they [who repent] shall secure a fruitful

---

87 1 Clem 57.

88 1 Clem 41. Cf 1 Clem 44: "our sin will not be small, if we eject from the episcopate those who have blamelessly and holily fulfilled its duties."

89 1 Clem 65.

90 1 Clem 46: "Let us cleave, therefore, to the innocent and righteous…Why are there strifes, and tumults, and divisions, and schisms, and wars among you?…Remember the words of our Lord Jesus Christ…'Woe to that man [by whom offences come]! It were better for him that he had never been born, than that he should cast a stumbling-block before one of my elect [i.e. the correct bishops].'"

91 1 Clem 47-48.

92 1 Clem 56.

and perfect remembrance [i.e. commemoration] from us, with sympathy for them, both in our prayers to God, and our mention of them to the saints." In other words, those who repent will be remembered liturgically *in Rome*. This shows the schismatics were at present synodically excommunicated. Hence, Church discipline even in the first century operated under Patriarchal lines, where those who refused to repent according to the standards imposed by the bishops within the synod were excommunicated—thereby handed over "to Satan."[93]

In summary, 1 Clem presumes that Corinth should be reconciled to Rome and follow proper ordination practices for clergy. Clement appears to presume upon a developed, hierarchical ecclesiology. He saw this ecclesiology as being instituted by God Himself. While some may infer from the letter some sort of exercise of universal and direct jurisdiction from the Pope, the earliest evidence such as from Dionysius of Corinth implies that the content of the Roman Synod's judgment was understood as local in nature.

SYNOPSIS OF THE PAPACY IN THE FIRST CENTURY

The earliest historical evidence, mainly the Scriptures, appears to teach that the Christian Church operated upon a consensus-based paradigm. Not only were theological matters discerned via consensus, making such a paradigm epistemically consensus-based, ecclesiastical matters were decided the same way. Bishops not only had succession from the Apostles, but they were elected locally and their elections required the consent of fellow bishops. The Church was in effect a large family, with heads of the household. However, decisions were not made in isolation.

Though the evidence is scant, the simplest interpretation of it is that the Bishop of Rome was the most prominent of these heads of the household. Whether it be in the person of Peter, or in the local churches commended to his care, or the honor he had of being the bishop of all the Apostles, there is no escaping that

---

93   1 Cor 5:5.

there was a nascent understanding that Peter and therefore Rome was the honorary head of the whole Church. This did not connote unilateral power, but as a "fellow presbyter" the Roman bishop admonished the Church at-large. At minimum, he had ultimate (but not unilateral) judicial power within the Petrine orbit of churches.

One may speculate as to what ramifications this may have on the Church at-large. This will unfold in greater detail as more sources become available in subsequent centuries. However, what never changes is the consensus-based paradigm in which the whole Church is built upon. It is perhaps the key differentiator between Christianity and Judaism, as the latter operated upon simple majority vote (as did the Roman Senate).[94] Hence, the Christian paradigm, though it has antecedents, is peculiar to itself.

---

94 Richard Talbert, *The Senate of Imperial Rome*. Princeton: Princeton University Press, 1984, 281-283.

Sts. Peter and Paul

St. Ignatius as a child

CHAPTER 2

The Second Century of the Papacy

The second century, popularly imagined as a period of "undeveloped ecclesiology," in fact evidences several relevant writings and episodes pertaining to the topic of the Papacy. The student of history who looks at the sources available in sufficient detail is compelled to conclude that there existed significant continuity between the first and second centuries; the same consensus-based, operating presumptions persisted. Interestingly, the century closes with a significant controversy that puts the consensus-based model to the test.

SAINT IGNATIUS' *LETTER TO THE ROMANS*

Before one speaks about how the second century ended for the Roman Pope, it is well worth looking carefully at how it began. This is because Saint Ignatius, who traditionally was an associate of the Apostle John, wrote to the Roman Synod.[95] His *Letter to the Romans* is a tremendously important document when read with attention to detail. This is because as bishop (later "Patriarch") of

---

95 A dating within the first decade of the century is often given, though a date approaching the 130s or 140s is not impossible.

Antioch, Ignatius in effect had written what is likely the earliest "interpatriarchal" document.

It is worth quickly unpacking the difference between intrapatriarchal and interpatriarchal documents. Those discerning the history of the Papacy rarely do this, but the failure to do so results in out-of-context analyses of the source material. For example, 1 Clem being read as an intrapatriarchal document makes it in many respects unexceptional. The Church of the first millennium had no shortage of canons, intrapatriarchal appeals, and deference being paid (or expected) due to the local primacy accorded to a Metropolitan or Patriarch. Perhaps the best example of this is Apostolic Canon 34, a document which may originate in the second century, though certainly by the third.[96] It states:

> *The bishops of every nation must acknowledge him who is first among them and account him as their head, and do nothing of consequence without his consent; but each may do those things only which concern his own parish, and the country places which belong to it. But neither let him (who is the first) do anything without the consent of all; for so there will be unanimity, and God will be glorified through the Lord in the Holy Spirit.*

The canon clearly delineates a regional hierarchy—but such hierarchy is necessarily wedded to the principle of consent. Hence, if a Papal document exhibits primacy in a local context, it is not necessarily relevant in an interpatriarchal one. One cannot simply take a deferential *intra*patriarchal document and then conclude automatically such deference automatically applies in all *inter*patriarchal contexts. In fact, explicit historical evidence across the board (Eastern and Western saints, Popes, and conciliar documents) inveighs against this.

Yet, it would be most curious that with Peter being the likely origin of the entire episcopate, there would not be some way that the Roman Pope would serve a superior function, such as the chief bishop in Apostolic Canon 34, within a consensus-based system for

---

96 John Henry Newman, *Historical Sketches, Vol. 1*. London: Longmans, Green and Co., 1920, 430.

the Church at-large. It is with this in mind one may read Ignatius' comments.

His letter begins with an honorific which is laden with meaning:

> the [Roman] Church which has obtained mercy, through the majesty of the Most High…which also presides in the place of the region of the Romans…worthy of God, worthy of honour, worthy of the highest happiness, worthy of praise, worthy of obtaining her every desire, worthy of being deemed holy, and presides over love.[97]

While "presides over [the] Love" (literally προκαθημένη [primates] τῆς [the] ἀγάπης ["agapes," Love/Goodwill as a singular genitive noun]) may be in reference to the Roman Synod presiding over Rome itself, this is an unlikely interpretation. First, it is redundant, as the same greeting already specifies the Roman Church presides in Rome. Second, the definite article before the term "Love" (meaning "Love Feast"[98]) appears to be a reference to the singular, Eucharistic body of Christ. In other words, the Church of Rome presides over the entire Christian communion. One would be hard pressed to find a more lofty ascription to the Roman Synod *in any context* until the ninth century.

The fact this was penned by Ignatius himself demonstrates that this honorific was derived from an early, plausibly Apostolic pedigree. Whether the comment is intended to be intrapatriarchal (as Antioch may have not imagined themselves, being a Petrine church, as "independent" from Rome in local contexts) or interpatriarchal is not altogether clear. However, with an absence of evidence specifying there being any time in which Antioch was once not autocephalous (locally independent), the safest interpretation is to simply presume that this is an interpatriarchal comment.

---

97   Ignatius, *Romans*, Greeting/Chap 1. The Greek can be accessed at "ΡΩΜΑΙΟΙΣ ΙΓΝΑΤΙΟΣ," *Christian Classics Ethereal Library*, https://www.ccel.org/l/lake/fathers/ignatius-romans.htm

98   A similar word is used in Jude 12. In Ignatius, *Romans*, Chap 2 Ignatius notes that Rome and Antioch are "gathered together in love," a reference to their intercommunion.

Ignatius makes several comments which illustrate the lofty
position of the Roman Church. He writes that Rome has "never
envied any one; you have taught others. Now I desire that those
things may be confirmed [by your conduct], which in your
instructions you enjoin [on others]."[99] Perhaps with the letters of
Peter, Paul, and 1 and 2 Clem in mind, Ignatius extols Rome for
the fact that they have sent teachings to the whole Church. This
appears entirely consistent with Christ's admonishment to Peter to
feed the sheep.

Yet, the motivation for this ascription appears to be tastefully
self-serving; Ignatius takes it upon himself to teach Rome! "I write
to the Churches, and impress on them all," Ignatius says in reference
to his letters.[100] Ignatius certainly issues ecclesiastical commands and
dogmatic teachings in these other letters. They were arguably sent
to jurisdictions (in Asia Minor) where Antioch was not *de jure* the
"senior" episcopate. After all, what of Ephesus (where Saint John
may have been still residing) or Rome itself (which had Peter's
relics)?

Ignatius respectfully obscures this "conflict of interests" by
immediately citing that he was writing these letters so "that I shall
willingly die for God, unless you hinder me. Allow me to become food
for the wild beasts. I do not, as Peter and Paul, issue commandments
unto you. They were [A]postles."[101] Ignatius reveals that Rome in
effect can prevent his martyrdom and, allegedly, he would never
take it upon himself to command Rome (who has the authority of
the chief Apostles) not to put a stay on his execution (via bribes,
political favors, or some other means). Yet, Ignatius then goes ahead
and does the exact opposite, pleading with Rome to let him die, and
reminding them that "[t]he prince of this world" can corrupt his
"deposition towards God" perchance Rome "help him" (the Devil!)
by preventing his martyrdom.[102] Such a passing reference seems to
lack even an inkling of the later doctrine of Papal Infallibility. In any

99 Ignatius, *Romans*, Chap 3.
100 Ibid., Chap 4.
101 Ibid.
102 Ibid., Chap 7.

event, Ignatius' words do not prove that the honorifics granted to Rome by himself were without any ecclesiastical import, but it does show that the occasion for invoking them had a specific purpose in mind.

Ignatius later makes an extremely important request to Rome: "Remember in your prayers the Church in Syria, which now has God for its shepherd, instead of me. Jesus Christ alone will oversee it, and your love."[103] The Greek breaks down to: Ἰησοῦς Χριστός [Jesus Christ] ἐπισκοπήσει [Oversee/"Bishop" as a verb] καὶ [and] ἡ [the] ὑμῶν [your] ἀγάπη ["agape," Love Feast]. In other words, in his absence, Jesus Christ and the Roman Church stand in as Antioch's bishop. "Love feast" in the Greek is not genitive and lacks a definitive article, which implies the reference to "agapes" in Chap 1 is to a body of churches, while "agape" here is the local Church of Rome.

This interpretation is buttressed by a greeting he wrote to "Polycarp, bishop of the Church of the Smyrnæans, or rather, who has, as his own bishop, God the Father, and the Lord Jesus Christ."[104] As one can see, the local bishop is in fact God, but the vicar is the man. In Smyrna, the vicar is Saint Polycarp. In Antioch, in his own absence, it is the Roman Synod (or the Pope, who is unnamed).[105] It is certainly justified to infer a Patriarchal hierarchy, with Rome placed above Antioch. One may also infer the superiority of Antioch over Smyrna, as Ignatius appears to dictate to Polycarp acting as the "senior" bishop.[106]

Thus, second century evidence of the canonical order of the local churches found in the Councils of Sardica, Constantinople I,

---

103 Ibid., Chap 9.

104 Ignatius, *Polycarp*, Chap 1.

105 This does not necessarily indicate that either Rome had no bishop due to persecution or that he was unaware of who its bishop was. Perhaps, to prevent the persecution of the Pope, he did not name him. More likely, bishops were named in letters where internal schisms were an issue. There were perhaps no local schisms in Rome and so an emphasis on the Roman Pope's name may have not been as important compared to the other letters.

106 Ibid., Chap 2-4.

Chalcedon, and especially the one held in Trullo exists.[107] Yet, Rome was not the only one to have a "say" in Ignatius' absence. Polycarp was instructed to send an assistant (*locum tenens?*) to Antioch: "O Polycarp, most blessed in God...assemble a very solemn council, and...elect one whom you greatly love...bestow on him this honour that he may go into Syria."[108]

Polycarp is then tasked with requesting other churches to do the same, perhaps to replace/assist a persecuted episcopate. Canon 2 of Constantinople I would later allow foreign bishops to partake in ordinations with permission. In his letters, Ignatius was providing permission. Perhaps, Ignatius was reacting to a harsh persecution and felt that Smyrna and Rome would be able to help reconstitute a devastated Antiochene church. Before this synod in Lebanon/Syria met, perhaps spiritual authority would reside in the resting place of Peter and Paul, Rome. Hence, Rome's preeminence surely had an honorary function with ecclesiastical import (of some sort, Ignatius does not cite anything other than Rome's teaching authority). In any event, Rome's ecclesiastical primacy did not lend itself to unilateral action, as Smyrna's involvement suggests.

Some may retort this is making too much of a couple statements that are "just honorifics." It is worth reflecting that Ignatius typically did not use empty honorifics. When he employs honorifics, he does so often in reference to something well known. His *Letter to the Ephesians* opens with a prolonged reference to predestination, an intentional echoing of Paul's letter to the same church. Similarly, Igantius' *Letter to the Philadelphians* is addressed "to the Church of God the Father, and our Lord Jesus Christ, which is at Philadelphia, in Asia, which has obtained mercy...and is filled with all mercy through [H]is resurrection,"[109] referring to Rev 3:10: "Because you have kept My command to persevere, I also will keep you from the hour of trial which shall come upon the whole world." He wrote to Smyrna that they "obtained every kind of gift, which is filled with

---

107 Trullo, Canon 36 explicitly delineates the hierarchy of the patriarchates.

108 Ignatius, *Polycarp*, Chap 7.

109 Ibid., *Philadelphians*, Chap 1.

faith and love, and is deficient in no gift,"[110] perhaps in reference to their church having an Apostolic Father as their bishop—an exceptional honor at so late a date. Not surprisingly, lesser churches without anything famous did not have such honorifics attached to them in his other letters. Therefore, any honorific about Rome must be understood as acknowledging something important.

Some final reflection on Ignatius is warranted. The Ignatian corpus not only establishes the ubiquitous nature of the monoepiscopacy, it also establishes that mere decades after the Scriptures were written, an internal hierarchical structure of the Church predicated upon the location of Apostolic relics was presumed upon in that Rome is obviously accorded superiority vis-à-vis Antioch. This not only deconstructs Protestant scholarly presuppositions (that these are developments), but also popular Orthodox ones (that Rome is "totally equal" to other churches). While the terms patriarchate and Pentarchy are not in use, their internal logic are clearly already at work, with Rome at the head.

THE SHEPHERD OF HERMAS AND THE ALLEGED "PLURAL EPISCOPACY" IN ROME

In the previous chapter, a passing reference was made to the *Shepherd* and its import on the debate over whether the early Papacy had a plural episcopacy (and thereby no single "Pope"). In one portion, the presbyters of Rome are referred to as the "rulers of the Church...that occupy the chief seats."[111] Plural episcopal scholarship infers that the rulers and their *cathedrae* (seats) were equal. It is worth pointing out that contemporary resources, written approximately a mere 20 years after the *Shepherd*, suggest that a plural episcopal inference is not compelling.

The Muratorian Fragment, which dates the Shepherd to 154 AD at the latest, itself makes mention of only a singular bishop of

---

110 Ibid., *Smyrnaeans*, Chap 1.

111 *Shepherd of Hermas* 3.9.7. (*Lightfoot*)

Rome (Pius I) when the book was composed.[112] Shortly afterward, Hegesippus records (as preserved in a fragment) Papal succession in monoepiscopal terms:

> *The Corinthian church continued in the true doctrine until Primus became bishop…On my arrival at Rome, I drew up a list of the succession of bishops down to Anicetus [approx. 168 AD], whose deacon was Eleutherus. To Anicetus succeeded Soter [approx. 174], and after him came Eleutherus [approx. 189 ad]. But in the case of every succession, and in every city, the state of affairs is in accordance with the teaching of the Law and of the Prophets and of the Lord.*

Saint Dionysius of Corinth, writing also around the same time, is no different. He identifies only a singular bishop of Rome (as preserved in a fragment):

> *ye Romans, keep up the custom of the Romans handed down by the fathers, which your blessed Bishop Soter [approx. 174] has not only preserved, but added to, sending a splendid gift to the saints, and exhorting with blessed words those brethren who go up to Rome, as an affectionate father his children.*

Dionysius' address to the Roman bishop is very specific and personal. In fact, the reference to the bishop being a "father" and those outside of Rome being his children is a solid antecedent for the title of "Pope" being accorded to the Roman bishop. The reference to Rome's "gift" shows that its primacy was certainly financial. These financial purse strings exercised their muscle in interpatriarchal contexts as well. A century later, Saint Pope Dionysius of Alexandria made mention of the Roman Synod "forwarding supplies" to take care of the material needs of "[a]ll

---

112 *The Muratorian Fragment* identifies the *Shepherd of Hermas* was written "very recently, in our times, in the city of Rome, while bishop Pius, his brother, was occupying the [episcopal] chair of the church of the city of Rome." Though this fragment makes no mention if Pope Pius I of Rome died recently, the reference to the *Shepherd* being "in our times" dates the fragment not long after 154 AD. For the entirety of the fragment see Bruce Metzger, *The Canon of the New Testament*. Oxford: Clarendon Press, 1987, 191-201.

the districts of Syria…and of Arabia."[113] This financial primacy is commented on earlier and more specifically than the spiritual criteria for Rome's primacy (the location of Saints Peter and Paul's relics). This does not mean that the importance of relics was some sort of later contrivance, but the reality is that practical considerations, as cited above and in later Church-wide canons such as Canon 3 of Constantinople I and Canon 28 of Chalcedon, bear more explicit mention. The Church's organization, though with Apostolic and traditional boundaries, has over time proved quite amenable to the practical, organizational needs of the people of God.

Back to the topic at hand, Irenaeus, himself resident in Rome in the 170s, composed a succession list which likewise presupposed singular bishops of Rome.[114] Early third century writers such as Julius Africanus, Tertullian, and Hippolytus also composed similar succession lists. The plural episcopal inference from the *Shepherd* requires mass amnesia to have occurred less than two decades after it was composed. This is simply not credible. It is easier to infer that there was always a singular Pope and several chorbishops (or their equivalents) serving in Rome. There were certainly other "ruling" bishops of Rome that had a say within the local synod, but they existed on its outskirts, such as Saint Hippolytus. There is explicit evidence of the existence of a singular Pope, but no explicit evidence of a plural episcopacy. This is enough reason to dispose with the notion.

SAINT IRENAEUS' COMMENTS IN *AGAINST HERESIES* ON THE CHURCH OF ROME

Irenaeus makes a few passing comments that are of importance. For one, he notes that "Peter and Paul were preaching at Rome,

---

113 *Letter 5 to Stephen of Rome* quoted in S.D.F. Salmond, *The Works of Gregory Thaumaturgus, Dionysius of Alexandria, and Archelaus.* Edinburgh: T&T Clark, 1882, 218.

114 Irenaeus, *Against Heresies,* Book 3, Chap 3, Par 3.

and laying the foundations of the Church."[115] He expands upon the importance of these two saints slightly later in a discussion as to why he gives only a complete succession of the Roman bishops:

> *it would be very tedious, in such a volume as this, to reckon up the successions of all the Churches, we do put to confusion all those who... assemble in unauthorized meetings; [we can avoid confusion] by indicating that tradition derived from the [A]postles, of the very great, the very ancient, and universally known Church founded and organized at Rome by the two most glorious [A]postles, Peter and Paul; as also the faith preached to men, which comes down to our time by means of the successions of the bishops. For it is a matter of necessity that every Church should agree with this Church [i.e. Rome], on account of its pre-eminent [sic] authority, that is, the faithful everywhere, inasmuch as the apostolical tradition has been preserved continuously by those who exist everywhere.[116]*

Irenaeus does not see Rome's preeminence as exclusively Petrine, as Paul is always mentioned. Additionally, he makes no reference to any sort of spiritual charism or existential necessity that Rome has this preeminence. This does not automatically discount the importance of either relics or even financial primacy, but one must consider Irenaeus' polemical purpose. It seems strange to modern interpreters, but the worldview of the Gnostics was very compelling in its day because its syncretism appeared to logically reconcile Judaism, Hellenistic philosophy, pagan mythology, and Christian teaching. An appeal to some spiritual necessity for Rome's prominence in effect lent credibility to the alleged necessity of the secret succession of private revelation from the Apostles (or directly from a divine Aeon) that the Gnostics claimed. It would make sense to avoid such an appeal.

Irenaeus rightly surmised that the Gnostics' weak spot was their lack of literal historical pedigree. Their religious movement was divorced from history. Irenaeus unsurprisingly stakes his whole

---

115 Ibid., Chap 1, Par 1.

116 Ibid., Chap 3, Par 2.

argument on the visible, historical veracity of what would become known as Orthodox Catholic Christianity vis-à-vis the Gnostics. This is the motivation behind listing Rome's Apostolic Succession list. The purpose of the list is to provide a visible demonstration that Christian doctrine in Rome, being in common with all churches with visible succession from the Apostles, is most plausibly the historical, Apostolic doctrine—unlike the secret doctrines privately passed on by the same Apostles as alleged by the Gnostics.

Roman Catholic apologists zero in on the section where Irenaeus picks Rome for this exercise because of their "pre-eminent [sic] authority." However, Irenaeus' reason for employing this language in reference to Rome is disappointingly pragmatic. He chooses Rome, because their succession was well known and that it would have been taken for granted that they preserve the same faith found "everywhere." In short, the passage is not about Rome's ecclesiastical prerogatives.

It is worth looking at the passage in some more detail. Let's unpack the passage. A more literal translation of the Latin is as follows:

> *For to this church [ecclesiam, singular], on account of its preeminent authority [potiorem], it is necessary for the Church [ecclesiam, singular] to convene [convenire], this is, those who are faithful from every side [undique], in which the tradition of the Apostles has always been preserved by those who are from every side [undique].* [117]

---

117 The passage in Latin is as follows: *Ad hanc enim ecclesiam propter potiorem principalitatem necesse est convenire ecclesiam, hoc est eos qui sunt undique fideles in quâ semper ab his qui sunt undique conservata est ea quae est ab apostolis traditio.* See George Edmundson, *The Church in Rome in the First Century.* New York: Longmans, Green and Co., 1913, 147. For the legitimacy of translating *potiorem principalitatem* as "princely authority" see Alexander Roberts and William Rambaut, "Against Heresies," in Alexander Roberts, James Donaldson, and A. Cleveland Coxe (eds.), Ante-Nicene Fathers: The Apostolic Fathers, Justin Martyr, Irenaeus; Volume 1. Peabody, MA: Hendrickson Publishers, Inc., 1995, 461. There, it is translated "potent principality" according to the same logic.

The passage appears to state that due to Rome's church having "princely authority," it is necessary for the Church of "those who are faithful from every side" to convene in Rome. "Princely authority" appears to be a reference to Rome's status as the political capital. To someone who is following Irenaeus' actual argument, and not imposing an ideology foreign to him, Rome is not preeminent merely because of its own "preserving" of the tradition of Peter and Paul, as such a charism would not impress the Gnostics. Rather, its preservation is *validated* by Christians throughout the world who bring the same tradition with them *into* Rome (as implied by *undique*) when they convene.

In short, preeminence comes from Rome's agreement with the whole, not specifically anything intrinsic to Rome. This is surprising given Saint Ignatius' comments as covered earlier, but the comments of both saints were addressing two very different situations. Irenaeus' point is epistemic: Rome is a microcosm of worldwide Christian consensus.

If a Gnostic alleged that Rome has corrupted their own tradition, Irenaeus would have to name Alexandria, Ephesus, or wherever else that agrees with Rome and likewise list their pedigrees. Irenaeus wants to avoid all the leg work. By just naming Rome and pointing to the fact that Christians from all these other places go there and agree with her teachings, Rome's tradition alone vis-à-vis the Gnostics would be sufficient in countering any claim that the historical faith was Gnostic instead of orthodox. This is because Rome's church, according to Irenaeus, exhibits a universal faith. What Irenaeus accomplishes by listing Rome's Apostolic Succession is that it proves the historicity of the faith preserved not only by Rome, but by everyone. As for Irenaeus himself, he unsurprisingly *opposed* unilateral Roman ecclesiastical authority when the situation demanded it because he, like his contemporaries, accepted a consensus-based paradigm.

THE EPHESIAN ("EASTER") CONTROVERSY

In a typical presentation of the ecclesiastical spat between the Churches of Rome and Ephesus, historians generally call it the "Easter Controversy." However, this is not the *real* controversy and doing so deemphasizes the ecclesiastical points at issue. The actual spat was over *who* had jurisdiction in Ephesus. Was the Ephesian Church functionally independent or autonomous, and thereby free to decide in isolation their peculiar dating of Pascha, or were they part of Rome's local "Patriarchal" jurisdiction and thereby compelled to reach consensus within the entire body of Petrine and Pauline churches?

The historical evidence is straightforward. In the late second century, Asia Minor (led by Polycrates, bishop of Ephesus) observed Pascha on Saturday.[118] According to Eusebius, "The rest of the world" did not.[119] Then, "[s]ynods and assemblies of bishops were held on this account" with the result that "all, with one consent, through mutual correspondence drew up an ecclesiastical decree" approving the Sunday observance of Pascha.[120] Effectually, this was a proto-Ecumenical Council via local synods sharing decrees, forging a consensus. Eusebius lists synodal documents from Palestine, Rome ("which bears the name of Bishop Victor"), Pontus, Gaul, Oshoene (eastern Turkey and Armenia), Corinth, and Alexandria all weighing in on the question.[121] Almost the whole Pentarchy besides Ephesus (which probably had jurisdiction over Byzantium, later known as the jurisdiction of Constantinople) and Antioch[122] took part in deciding the issue.

---

118 Eusebius, *Church History*, Book 5, Chap 23, Par 1.

119 Ibid.

120 Ibid., Par 2.

121 Ibid.

122 It is ultimately a mystery why the Antiochene church is not explicitly a party in deciding the question. The most probable reason is that Antioch had unrecognized claims of jurisdiction over Ephesus and Asia Minor. Therefore, they permitted diversity on the dating of Pascha and absented themselves to avoid being on the losing side. There are other plausible explanations, such

Surprisingly, in defiance of the "one consent" and "unanimous decision"[123] of the Church (Eusebius apparently was not so wooden in his idea of consensus that it did not allow for a minority opposition), Ephesus rejected the world's decrees. Interestingly, they did so in a synodal letter "addressed to Victor and the church of Rome."[124] This gets glossed over, but it must have been intentional that Ephesus responded not to the whole world who rejected them, but to the Roman Synod specifically. Unsurprisingly, this was offensive to Rome and Pope Victor (on behalf of their synod) responded to that specific letter and "*attempted* to cut off from the common unity" the Ephesian Church.[125]

The term "attempt" is intentionally used by Eusebius. It obviously implies that Rome *could not* accomplish such a task. So much for evidence of direct and universal Roman jurisdiction in the second century. Despite Eusebius' editorializing, the question is *why* this was an attempt. Was Victor claiming a novel universal and direct jurisdiction—or even an obscure, peculiar and ancient Roman claim to that prerogative? Or, was Victor exercising his rights as the senior bishop in what he believed was his local, "Patriarchal," jurisdiction? What is the best explanation of the limited evidence that exists?

It helps to sum up the entire controversy when answering this question. Eusebius records that Victor's response, despite him sharing their view on Pascha's dating, "did not please all the bishops...words of theirs are extant, sharply rebuking Victor."[126]

---

as local persecutions, an absent proto-patriarch, or their attendance at either the Palestinian or Ephesian Synod via legate. Judging from a Montanist controversy in Asia Minor that Serapion of Antioch weighed in on at around the same time (Ibid., Chap 19, Par 1-4) and the controversy over Paul of Samosata a century later (where the Antiochene Synod invited bishops from both Palestine and Asia Minor to participate in their council, as covered in the next chapter), the most likely explanation must pertain to Antioch's split between Asian and Palestinian interests.

123 Ibid., Chap 23, Par 3.

124 Ibid., Chap 24, Par 1.

125 Ibid., Par 9.

126 Ibid., Par 10.

The sharp rebuke of the Roman Pope validates Eusebius' view that the world disagreed with Rome's jurisdictional claims (whatever they were). Eusebius then records that "Irenaeus…sending letters in the name of the brethren of Gaul," referencing several synodal documents, which reiterated the date of Pascha but also "fittingly admonishes [sic] Victor that he should not cut off" the Ephesian Church.[127]

"Cut off" from whom? One may infer from the whole Church, but this is not explicitly stated. Yet, such sentiment is likewise consistent with the view that Victor should not cut off a local church. In any event, these synodal letters were sent both to "Victor" and "most of the other rulers of the churches."[128] In other words, they were a public correcting of Victor, intended to bring the weight of the world's churches against him so that the consensus of the Church would prevail over his attempted ecclesiastical actions. This in effect is history's first successful "appeal against Rome—" one of many over the centuries.[129]

Why was rejecting Rome's ecclesiastical claims over Ephesus so important that it demanded the world's synods condemn Rome on this aberrant issue as much as they condemned Ephesus over the issue of Pascha's date? Some anachronistically infer this was the first "rebellion" against the universal jurisdictional claims of the Papacy. However, not only does the weight of a universally venerated saint (Irenaeus) inveigh against imputing such an impious

---

127 Ibid., Par 11.

128 Ibid., Par 18.

129 Three simple examples of appeals against the Roman Synod are the overruling of Saint Pope Stephen on the issue of baptism, the overruling and deposition of Pope Vigilius during the seventh session of Constantinople II and Pope Nicholas' deposition by the Council of Constantinople (867). Saint Augustine in *Letter 43*, Par 19 matter-of-factly explains the decisions of the Roman Synod can be appealed to an Ecumenical Council. Appeals against Rome to the universal Church were well understood in the ancient Church. Conflicts within the local Roman jurisdiction were also solved by international appeal, such as Saint Pope Cornelius' appeal to the global churches against Novatian. All of the preceding are covered in subsequent chapters.

motive, historically Eusebius in recording the episode implies not
a hint of this. The fact is there is no explicit evidence that Victor
actually excommunicated the Ephesians (i.e. "attempted"), nor
that it was even perceived at the time as an exercise of universal
jurisdiction or an attempt to claim it. There is simply no textual
basis for such claims.

The textual evidence best supports that the world's churches took
interest in this specific ecclesiastical dispute, because they rejected
Rome's claims of local jurisdiction over Ephesus and recognized the
latter synod's ecclesiastical autonomy/autocephaly. A close look at
the evidence reveals this. The Ephesian Synod wrote their letter to
Rome specifically *after* all the synods made judgments on the dating
of Pascha, but *before* Victor "attempted" excommunicating them.[130]
Rome's excommunication therefore was specifically motivated by
the contents of their response, not the date of Pascha specifically.

What was found in this response that was not specific to Pascha?
In Polycrates' letter, the Church of Ephesus asserts that the relics of
(1) the Apostles Philip and John are in Asia Minor (Hieropolis and
Ephesus respectively), (2) three of Philip's daughters are in Ephesus,
(3) martyrs Polycarp and Thraseas are in Smyrna, (4) Sagaris is
in Laodicea, (5) Papirius and Melito are in Sardis, and (6) all of
Polycrates' relatives who were bishops of Ephesus likewise were
there.[131] In short, the letter contains a prolonged emphasis on relics.

For some reason, the location of the relics is glossed over in
analyses of the controversy, but evidently it was central to the
reasoning of Polycrates, and offensive enough to instigate a breach
in Roman communion. As discussed previously, the traditional
importance of relics is that they delineate under whose jurisdiction
a church belongs. By listing Philip, Polycarp, and other saints who
had succession presumably from the *Apostle John*, Polycrates was
most likely asserting that Ephesus and its synod was *Johnnine and
Philippine, not* Petrine and Pauline—despite the latter Apostles' initial
evangelism of the region. This is relevant, because Paul started the
church in Ephesus and sent Timothy, presumably from Rome (Heb

---

130 Ibid., Par 1.

131 Ibid., Par 2-5.

13:23) to Ephesus to be their bishop (1 Tim 1:3,2 Tim 4:12). This theoretically *should* have put Ephesus under Rome's *local jurisdiction*, just like Corinth evidently was at the time 1 Clem was written.

The appeal to these relics was effectively a claim made by Ephesus of having *its own* Apostolic See and thereby ecclesiastical independence. One can infer that Polycrates was simply listing a litany of relics to add "Patristic authority" behind his claim favoring his dating of Pascha. Yet, this is called into question by a most interesting omission of yet another Ephesian saint—Timothy, Paul's right-hand man. His relics were likewise in Ephesus. The *Acts of Timothy* locates his death in Ephesus and the Latin manuscript tradition of these acts identifies *Polycrates* was its author.[132] Hence, there is reliable (and a historically convenient) attestation that Polycrates was fully aware that he omitted Timothy. Even if such authorship is apocryphal, which is likely, the point that Timothy's relics were in Ephesus was evidently common knowledge in the entire Christian world. Timothy's relics were transferred to Constantinople from Ephesus in the mid-fourth century. The day this occurred is commemorated by Orthodox (January 22nd), Roman Catholics (January 26th) and Oriental Orthodox (Tobi 27th) alike.

Memories of the jurisdictional importance (and motivation) behind the transfer of relics were long lasting. Anania of Shirak, a seventh century Armenian ecclesiastic not in communion with the Church of Ephesus, recalled:

> they [Jerusalem] kept it [the feast of the Nativity] freely and openly, except in the metropolises of the four Patriarchs, who had the thrones of the holy Evangelists. For at that time [in 335 AD] they had not forcibly transferred the throne of Saint John from Ephesus to Constantinople.[133]

---

132 "Acts of Timothy Acta Apostoli Timothei," *NASSCAL: North American Society for the Study of Christian Apocryphal Literature*, https://www.nasscal.com/e-clavis-christian-apocrypha/acts-of-timothy/

133 Appendix I quoted in Abraham Terian, *Macarius of Jerusalem: Letter to the Armenians, A.D. 335*. Crestwood, NY: St Vladimir's Seminary Press, 2008, 144. Terian notes that, "The four metropolitan archbishops of the ancient Apostolic centers of Christianity, of Rome, Alexandria, Ephesus (later transferred to Constantinople), and Antioch, were all given status

In other words, Ephesus was understood to have had a patriarchate *until* John's relics were transferred. This gave Constantinople the "traditional" right to now claim Ephesus' early charism. It is most probable that it was explicitly this charism that Polycrates was asserting in the second century. The location of Timothy's relics were likely *deliberately* left out of the Ephesian letter for that specific reason. Naming Timothy's relics would substantiate that Paul had sent Timothy there before his death, enhancing claims that Ephesus was under Rome's local jurisdiction.

This history explains the connection between Ephesus' letter starting with the discussion of relics and then ending ominously by quoting Acts 5:29—"We ought to obey God rather than man." The Ephesians, in asserting their independence from Roman practice, were allegedly being obedient to their Apostolic origin which is from God. Hence, the authority to observe their practice is theirs alone derived from God, and not from man's (the Roman Synod's) permission.

It was this situation that was the real "deal breaker" for Pope Victor—not the dating of Pascha itself. In his defense, Rome's local jurisdictional claim was traditionally valid. However, the Christian world saw Polycrates' claim as stronger. In effect, the residence of John in Ephesus created an "Apostolic Succession reset" as surely the living bishop and Apostle would have carried more authority than the individuals who succeeded from Timothy.

Aside from the pious, traditional reasons for the jurisdictional arrangement situating itself around John's relics, there is also a significant geopolitical reason. Ephesus was probably the third or

---

of Patriarchs by the Council of Nicaea (325)." This is implied by Canon 6 ("other provinces...retain their privileges,") though it would seem that Ephesus technically had autonomy under Antioch (similar to the Ukrainian Orthodox Church and Orthodox Church of America in relation to the Moscow Patriarchate today). Canon 7 appears to exclude Jerusalem from having truly equal status at this juncture, which explains them not being numbered as among the four Patriarchs in 335 in Anania's account. Concerning Ephesus' status as a patriarchate see also Leroy Froom, *The Prophetic Faith of our Fathers: The Historical Development of Prophetic Interpretation: Volume I.* Washington D.C., Review and Herald, 1950, 502.

fourth biggest city in the Roman Empire, with significant political independence from Rome. John's relics justified a purposeful jurisdictional shift along Imperial Roman provincial lines, something that would later by implicitly canonized by Nicaea I (Canons 4-6) and Chalcedon (Canon 17). As stated previously, practical arrangements were the most decisive factor in determining jurisdictional questions—even at this early a stage.

Irenaeus' rebuke of Victor contains an episode which has implications upon what has been discussed. It states that "when the blessed Polycarp was at Rome in the time of [Pope] Anicetus, and they disagreed a little" over the dating of Pascha, but "they immediately made peace with one another."[134] It is stated that Polycarp attributed the peculiar observance to Saint John as justification.[135] In the end, "Anicetus *conceded* the administration of the Eucharist *in the church to Polycarp*, manifestly as a mark of respect."[136]

The whole context behind the exchange is lost to those who do not understand Greek liturgical practice. What the episode demonstrates is that *Smyrna* had earlier cited their Johannine authority. By "conceding the administration of the [E]ucharist" Polycarp presided over the liturgy, *not* Anicetus. In liturgics, only superiors or equals preside over a liturgy. Irenaeus appears to be communicating that Anicetus in this episode acknowledged Asia Minor's, or more narrowly Smyrna's, independence—a sort of granting of proto-autocephaly. This is relevant to Polycrates' claim because Saint Polycarp of *Smyrna*'s authority is derived from his succession from John—whose relics were in Ephesus.

The fact that Irenaeus takes the time to write the above and include the details that he does is not a superfluous attention to detail, something moderns too easily impute to ancient sources whose significance they do not understand. Rather, the reported incident and its importance was common knowledge. Jurisdiction was the actual point at issue.

134 Eusebius, *Church History*, Book 5, Chap 24, Par 16.

135 Ibid.

136 Ibid., Par 17.

In the third century, an Asian bishop (Saint Anatolius of Laodicea in Syria) in reporting the episode, observes the same:

> *even today all the bishops of Asia…were celebrating Easter when it was the fourteenth day of the month [Nisan], not acquiescing to the authority of some, that is, the successors of Peter and Paul…Therefore a certain contention arose between some of their successors, namely Victor, bishop of Rome, and Polycrates, who at that time appeared to have the primacy among the bishops of Asia.*[137]

The term "appeared" implies that there was notable dispute particularly over episcopal primacy in Asia Minor. One may also infer Anatolius' favoring of the Roman practice, considering his Paschal calculations did not accord with the Ephesian practice, but rather that of Antioch. Nevertheless, he accurately records the true nature of the controversy—disputed ecclesiastical primacy in Asia Minor specifically.

In summary, the simplest interpretation of the Pascha controversy's relevance upon the Papacy is *not* that the Pope was asserting universal jurisdiction over the church or even that Eusebius and others were critiquing such an idea. Rather, Victor was responding to a letter purposely addressed to his synod (and no one else's) which insultingly omitted mention of Paul and Timothy's (and thereby Rome's) importance in establishing the Ephesian church and its customs.

One may infer that perhaps Ephesus' whole impetus behind having an aberrant date for Pascha was explicitly to express their individuality and thereby independence. It appears that the whole fiasco amounted to jostling over who had local jurisdiction in Asia Minor. There are too many details supporting this explanation versus no details whatsoever supporting the universal jurisdiction inference. In the end, the Church sided with Ephesus and the latter Church enjoyed autonomy (though they apparently competed with Caesarea, which will be covered later) until their prerogatives were subsumed by Constantinople. Despite three councils in Ephesus

---

137 *The Paschal Canon* in PG 10, 217 quoted in Butler and Collorafi, *Keys Over the Christian World*, 19.

during the fifth century, with the Third Council of Ephesus successfully declaring a restoration of Ephesus' "former constitution" (i.e. their autonomy and local jurisdiction),[138] ultimately Ephesus' claims were dropped. At this point, they are mostly forgotten.

SYNOPSIS OF THE PAPACY IN THE SECOND CENTURY

The history of the Papacy in this century is controlled by what inferences the historian draws. Too often, novel plural episcopal or anachronistic Papal Supremacist views are imposed upon the source material. However, if one draws inferences based upon the geopolitical context of the churches, contemporary source materials, and with an attention to detail that treats the writers as serious and deliberate in their work, a much different picture results. The second-century Church shows an expected continuity with the first century. Additionally, the Papacy shows itself as a prominent, but local, Roman synodal institution that is the honorary head of other local, prominent, institutional churches.

In Ignatius' letters, nothing explicitly asserts universal jurisdiction. Rather, what is said pertains to Rome having some sort of real spiritual authority over Antioch, but this authority for all ecclesiastical intents and purposes is shared with Smyrna in Asia Minor. This suggests that the Roman Synod did not have a universal and direct jurisdiction over other local churches. Another second-century source more explicitly delineates precisely what Rome's jurisdiction was, the letter from Dionysius of Corinth quoted in the preceding chapter. Rome and Corinth were "joined in close union" because their "churches...were planted by Peter and Paul."[139] 1 Clem 1 delineates that judicial appeals existed within this "union."

In light of these sources, the idea that Rome did not have Vatican I distinctives, but rather was an almost unexceptional proto-patriarchate among other proto-patriarchates is not even an inference. Rather, it is the only *explicit* explanation of the evidence

---

138 Zachariah of Mitylene, *Syriac Chronicle*, Book 5, Chap 5.

139 Dionysius of Corinth, *Fragment 3*.

that actually exists. That any historian would impose later categories of thought in search of explaining the occurrences at this time instead of operating with the explicit ecclesiastical statements that are extant exposes severe chronological and sometimes ideological bias. It is not justifiable. The simplest explanation is to interpret evidence consistently with what is found most explicitly in the primary sources.

When this is done, some of the inferences drawn here revolving around issues such as the importance of relics during the Ephesus Controversy are not innovative "stretches of the imagination." They are entirely justified, and in fact, the best explanation of the evidence at hand. If one maintains this consistent approach to history, the third century will unsurprisingly reveal that identical operating principles were held by both the Roman Synod and the Church at-large.

St. Ignatius the God Bearer

St. Hippolytus of Rome

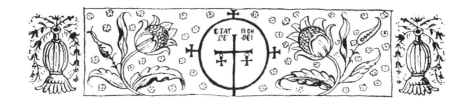

CHAPTER 3

The Third Century of the Papacy

By the third century, many undeveloped analogues to the modern Roman Papacy can be found, perhaps not in concrete antecedents, but at least addressed in some context. This does not mean that one can necessarily find the "seeds" of the modern Papacy in this century. In fact, the third-century Papacy is in effect no different than that found in the second century. Nevertheless, one can find certain epistemic and ecclesiastical principles expressed in sources from this era which inform the student of history how alien later popular conceptions of the Roman Synod at this time really are.

THE RIGORISTS AND THE ABSENCE OF ANY NOTION OF PAPAL INFALLIBILITY

Moral rigorists, those who expounded very high ethical standards as to what the Church can and cannot tolerate from Christians, had a significant following in Christianity until the eve of its official toleration. For example, since the late fourth century a soldier who sheds no blood may not have a penance, but if he does there is a minimal penance of three years in which a soldier cannot commune.[140] However, earlier authorities

---

140 Basil the Great, *Letter 188*, Canon 13.

recommended that commanders and those shedding blood would be excommunicated for life.[141] Similarly, the rigorists would impose a lifetime excommunication upon the divorced.[142] Later authorities and canonical interpretations are more lenient.

The rigorist tendency in the early Church appears excessive in light of 1 Cor 5 and Saint Paul's treatment of the penitent. Perhaps it arose when Christianity got big enough to incite Roman persecutions. For most of the second century, morals within the Church were so purified by persecutions (because lackluster people would never pretend to be Christians) and by general asceticism (Saint Athenagoras spoke of Christian couples partaking in relations "only for the purpose of having children")[143] that sins like divorce and adultery among Christians were rare and scandalous.

By Tertullian's time (the turn of the second to third century), exceptions began being made if a martyr or a confessor vouched for an individual. These were called "indulgences," because a bishop would "indulge" the request of a confessor to "go easy" on the penitent. These are different from the Roman Catholic indulgences of the Middle Ages and modern day.[144] Apparently, the perceived change in the Church's policy was due to the esteem given to martyrs.

This is the context of Tertullian's critique of the "Pontifex Maximus," which is pertinent due to it being a potential moniker for the Bishop of Rome. He denigrates the bishop and then quotes a synodal statement he evidently ascribes to him:

> *The Pontifex Maximus — that is, the bishop of bishops — issues an edict: I remit, to such as have discharged (the requirements of) repentance, the sins both of adultery and of fornication.*[145]

---

141 Hippolytus, *Apostolic Tradition*, 16:9-11. Cf "Hippolytus' Canons," 14.

142 Council of Elvira, Canon 8. Cf *Shepherd of Hermas*, Book 2, Commandment 4, Chap 1 on a related noted seems to impose lifetime excommunication for adulterers.

143 Athenagoras, *A Plea For Christians*, Chap 33.

144 Tertullian, *On Modesty*, Chap 22.

145 Ibid., Chap 1.

It is possible "bishop of bishops" may be a reference to the Metropolitan of Carthage as head of the North African synod that Tertullian was part of. However, a later reference to Matt 16:18 adds to the probability that the text was cited by a Roman Synod which decided against the rigorist view. While it is not impossible for another Petrine bishop (like Carthage's) to cite the passage, the reference to a synod against rigorism appears to correspond with a contemporary critique by Saint Hippolytus concerning Pope Callistus, as covered later. Back to the critique at hand, Tertullian writes:[146]

> *I will descend even to this point of contest now, making a separation between the doctrine of [A]postles and their power.*

Why even say this unless *someone* was claiming they held both the Apostles' doctrine and power? The point at issue was the apostolic power of binding and loosing sins: "Who, moreover, was able to forgive sins? This is His alone prerogative: for who remits sins but God alone?" Tertullian categorically denies the entire concept of Church discipline carrying any definitive bearing on an individual's spiritual standing (in contrast with Matt 18:19). A Montanist (a sort of ancient Pentecostal) at this juncture of his life, Tertullian certainly would have been excommunicated and thereby disciplined by the Church body he was criticizing. This reveals that ecclesiology at this juncture, as it did in Saint Clement of Rome's time when he warned the Corinthian schismatics of damnation, operated upon the principle that Church excommunication effectively removed someone from God's good grace. Tertullian disagrees and in so doing reveals much about ecclesiology in his day. The passage is long, and is best understood when quoted in full with added emphasis:

> *If it were agreed that even the blessed [A]postles had granted any such indulgence (to any crime) the pardon of which (comes) from God, not from man, it would be competent (for them) to have done so, not in the exercise of discipline, but of power. For they both raised the dead, which God alone (can do)...If, however, you [i.e. the Catholics/Orthodox]*

---

146 Ibid., Chap 21.

have had the functions of discipline alone allotted you, and (the duty) of presiding not imperially, but ministerially; who or how great are you, that you should grant indulgence, who, by exhibiting neither the prophetic nor the apostolic character, lack that virtue whose property it is to indulge? But, you [the Catholics/Orthodox] say, the Church has the power of forgiving sins. **This I acknowledge and adjudge more (than you; I) who have the Paraclete Himself in the persons of the new prophets**, *saying,* **The Church has the power to forgive sins; but I will not do it**, *lest they commit others withal…If, because the Lord has said to Peter, Upon this rock will I build My Church, to you have I given the keys of the heavenly kingdom; or, Whatsoever you shall have bound or loosed in earth, shall be bound or loosed in the heavens, you therefore presume* **that the power of binding and loosing has derived to you, that is, to every Church akin to Peter**, *what sort of man are you, subverting and wholly changing the manifest intention of the Lord,* **conferring (as that intention did) this (gift) personally upon Peter**?*…in accordance with the person of Peter, it is to spiritual men that this power will correspondently appertain, either to an [A]postle or else to a prophet… And accordingly the Church, it is true, will forgive sins: but (it will be) the Church of the Spirit, by means of a spiritual man;* **not the Church which consists of a number of bishops**.[147]

In this text, Tertullian teaches that the Montanists only had the power to forgive sins *because* they worked miracles. He makes the audacious claim that "I," as in Tertullian, can forgive sins by the grace of the Holy Spirit, but he simply refuses to do it. This he denies belongs to "every Church akin to Peter," which evidently sourced their authority in Matt 16:18. These churches consisted of "a number of bishops" in the Roman Synod or in the Catholic/Orthodox Church at-large.

In what may be the earliest exegesis to Matt 16:18, Tertullian in disagreeing with the Church reveals the passage's popular

---

147 Emphasis is added due to the difficulty of following the logic of such a long passage.

interpretation. The Church cited the passage as pertaining to disciplinary power exercised by the entire episcopate—not the Pope of Rome in isolation. Apparently, "every church" was "akin to Peter," which makes sense if it was a well understood tradition that Saint Peter was the origin of the entire episcopacy. Additionally, Tertullian refers to there being a "bishop of bishops"—a title which appears to be a common, non-exclusive insult in the third century.[148] The term appears to be a pejorative for a bishop who does not submit to conciliarity or consensus in that he asserts illegitimately expansive episcopal prerogatives. Due to this usage, it is not necessarily the case that one may infer a hierarchical episcopal arrangement typical of a patriarchate or metropolis in every circumstance that it is used.

Saint Hippolytus, a contemporary, was also a rigorist like Tertullian. However, he was within the Church. Some assert that Hippolytus became an antipope over rigorism issues and concerns over Modalism (a Trinitarian heresy). However, he never identifies himself in *Refutation of All Heresies* as *the* bishop of Rome. As covered previously, the best evidence points to Hippolytus being a bishop in a Roman suburb. In any event, he identifies himself as part of the "high priesthood."[149] He uses the term "we," implying he was the head of a faction of rigorists within the Roman Synod.[150]

There is no evidence contemporary to Hippolytus' time that he was a schismatic. Further, no known parallel line of episcopal succession stems from him, such as can be found among other rigorist schismatics like the Novatianists. This may even imply he was a chorbishop or a rough equivalent (i.e. auxiliary bishop) without the capacity to ordain other bishops. In any event, he certainly makes negative comments about Popes of Rome. Details in these comments help reveal what the nature of the Papacy was during that time.

---

148 Saint Cyprian of Carthage likewise uses the term not only in reference to the Pope of Rome (Council of Carthage 256, Par 1), but also other bishops such as Florentius. See Cyprian, *Letter 68*, Par 3.

149 Hippolytus, *Refutation of All Heresies*, Book 1, Preface.

150 Ibid., Book 9, Par 6.

For example, Pope "Zephyrinus imagines that he administers the affairs of the Church—an uninformed and shamefully corrupt man."[151] Contextually, "Church" here is in reference to the *whole* Church,[152] interestingly implying that Zephyrinus asserted some sort of *worldwide* Papal prerogatives. Similar to Saint Ignatius' passing reference to Rome teaching others, it appears Hippolytus likewise has some sort of teaching function in mind. He accuses Popes Zephyrinus of Modalism and "heresy."[153] Likewise, Pope Callistus allegedly disseminated Modalism "throughout the entire world."[154]

These accusations appear to be exaggerations. In making his case that they are heretics, Hippolytus' actual quotations from them unintentionally appear to prove that neither Zephyrinus nor Callistus were true Modalists. They were certainly poor communicators of Orthodox/Catholic doctrine and were *too tolerant* of Sabellius (the chief expounder of Modalism). For example, Hippolytus quotes Zephyrinus' public statements, such as the denial of the Father suffering on the cross, that are Orthodox and anti-Modalist.[155] Hippolytus begrudgingly admits this and says Zephyrinus was being insincere and at that point, Sabellius was pretending not to be a heretic. This reveals that Zephyrinus was actually *not* teaching Modalism (and perhaps at that juncture, even Sabellius may have been "keeping a lid on it"). However, it does demonstrate that Zephyrinus was tolerant of Sabellius, which is probably what elicited Hippolytus' ire.

Despite the similar accusations made against Callistus, Sabellius was eventually excommunicated for "not entertaining orthodox opinions" by the same Pope. This was allegedly to curry favor with

---

151 Ibid., Par 2.

152 Ibid., Par 1-2.

153 Ibid., Par 2.

154 Ibid., Par 8. It should be noted that these accusations unintentionally met the precise standards necessary for Papal Infallibility as delineated centuries later during Vatican I, surely not a concept appreciated at that time.

155 Ibid., Par 6.

Hippolytus![156] These statements demonstrate that Sabellius *was* in communion with Zephyrinus, so Hippolytus had real causes for concern. It also implies that Hippolytus was perhaps not an antipope, as getting his approval in that event would have been meaningless. Despite excommunicating Sabellius, Callistus allegedly maintained semi-Modalist Christology, accusing Hippolytus of being a "Ditheist."[157]

Before unpacking the perceived doctrinal differences between Hippolytus and his opposition, it is worth pointing out that Hippolytus exhibits no understanding whatsoever of "Papal Infallibility." His accusations of Popes being heretics are made with no thought paid to the idea that this would scandalize anyone within the Roman Synod, let alone the Christian world. Additionally, the Popes do not counter Hippolytus citing their alleged doctrinal infallibility. Both of these facts imply the doctrine's non-existence in any form. One may also infer that the Popes were stuck dealing with Hippolytus, as there is no direct evidence that he was excommunicated. Apparently, Hippolytus had enough support within the synod to prevent this (as being an alleged "Ditheist" surely they would have wanted to if given the opportunity).

The disagreement between Hippolytus and the Popes on Modalism to the modern observer appears to be over nominal, instead of truly doctrinal, differences. For example, Hippolytus quotes Callistus:

> *For, says (Callistus), 'I will not profess belief in two Gods, Father and Son, but in one. For the Father, who subsisted in the Son Himself, after He had taken unto Himself our flesh, raised it to the nature of Deity, by bringing it into union with Himself, and made it one; so that Father and Son must be styled one God, and that this Person being one, cannot be two.' And in this way Callistus contends that the Father suffered along with the Son; for he does not wish to assert that the Father suffered, and is one Person, being careful to avoid blasphemy against the Father.*[158]

---

156 Ibid., Chap 7.

157 Ibid.

158 Ibid. Cf Ibid., Chap 6 where Hippolytus reports: "Callistus brought forward

Taken at face value, Callistus avoided specifically confessing Modalism. However, he taught what would logically amount to a theologically equivalent doctrine: "the Father...subsisted in the Son Himself." If one carries the logic through, despite him not asserting the Father was crucified, he did not explicitly divide the hypostases/personalities of the Holy Trinity. Yet, Hippolytus betrays that Callistus may have simply been confused over terms: "therefore this one person [i.e. hypostasis], (according to Callistus,) is divided nominally [i.e. in name], but substantially not so [i.e. not in essence]."[159]

Hippolytus appears ahead of his time in positing the doctrine of the particular hypostasis (a fourth-century Cappadocian doctrine). Callistus appears to equate hypostasis with essence/substance (as the Nicene Creed does, incidentally), therefore allowing for only a division in names but not in hypostasis. Conceptually, Callistus is teaching there being three Persons of the Holy Trinity, but one essence/substance. He is simply using "hypostasis"/"subsistence" in a non-particular sense. It is unclear if Callistus (despite his Greek name) was schooled in Greek and why he would reject Hippolytus' orthodox parsing of the issue, but likely it was due to the customary usage of the term "hypostasis" at that time.

The Modalist controversy was later settled in Rome. Pope Dionysius, the author of the synodal decree *Against the Sabellians*, appeals to the fact his fellow bishops "are men filled with the Spirit" and would discern "absurd results" of false doctrine. Hence, it is expected that bishops can issue their own judgment, in agreement or against, the Pope. This discernment process is apparently Spirit-led, likely a reference to consensus in judgment evidencing God's work within the synod. Yet, Dionysius makes no appeal to a profound

---

Zephyrinus himself, and induced him publicly to avow the following sentiments: 'I know that there is one God, Jesus Christ; nor except Him do I know any other that is begotten and amenable to suffering.' And on another occasion, when he would make the following statement: 'The Father did not die, but the Son.' Zephyrinus would in this way continue to keep up ceaseless disturbance among the people."

159 Ibid., Book 10, Chap 23.

Papal charism—one that may be expected if Papal Infallibility was a known doctrine in that day.

While Callistus may have never been a Modalist, Hippolytus was correct in his accusations that the Pope allowed for scandalous moral laxity in the Church. He allowed priests to remarry and those with multiple marriages to be ordained.[160] Callistus apparently also allowed for concubinage, which Hippolytus considered "adultery."[161] This laxity created synodal instability:

> anyone…called a Christian, should he commit any transgression; the sin, they say, is not reckoned unto him, provided only he hurries off and attaches himself to the school [i.e. faction] of Callistus.[162]

In other words, Callistus would give easier absolution, and admit people to communion other bishops within the same synod would not. In effect, this was a means of invalidating the discipline of another bishop within the synod. This likely evidenced a split within the Roman Synod along two schools of thought—although an outright schism between the two is not impossible (despite it not being explicit in the written evidence).[163] Interestingly, Hippolytus notes that "after such audacious acts, they, lost to all shame, attempt to call themselves 'a Catholic Church!'"[164] This implies that the Roman Church identifies itself among the churches of the Catholic

---

160 Ibid., Book 9, Par 7.

161 Ibid. The Council of Toledo (400) likewise tolerated concubinage, so historically *economia* allowed for some extreme allowances such as this.

162 Ibid.

163 If there were rival communions, they likely were in communion tangentially (i.e. the North Africans or foreign patriarchates would be in communion with both factions, despite the factions not being in communion with one another). This was fairly common in the ancient Church. Canon 101 of Carthage (419) is written predicated upon Rome and Alexandria not being in communion with one another over controversy surrounding the Synod of the Oak. This breach in communion was resolved by Saints Isidore of Pelusium's and Atticus of Constantinople's mediation, leading to Alexandria liturgically commemorating Saint John Chrysostom. See Theodoret, *Church History*, Book 5, Chap 34-35.

164 Ibid.

Church. There is a notable lack of exclusivity in this claim. After all, this was an in-house debate between multiple direct successors of Saints Peter and Paul. Interestingly, Hippolytus implies that the Papal faction forfeited the right of being Catholic through their heterodoxy, this being an underappreciated definition for the term "Catholic" that maintained usage in the early Church.[165]

Between Tertullian and Hippolytus, one can glean what Roman prerogatives were claimed to be at this time. Due to these writers being opposed to the Popes, one would expect they would exaggerate the things they disagree with. Yet, even their exaggerated critiques lack reactions to Vatican I like claims. Rome was simply understood as "a Catholic Church," which could make doctrinal errors. Nonetheless, the Pope was *perhaps* perceived as a "bishop of bishops" for the whole Christian world. However, this slanderous term was not exclusively used for Popes or even Metropolitans. Therefore, one must be careful not to infer that the euphemism was in reference to some sort of interpatriarchal (or even intrapatriarchal) ecclesiastical overreach. In any event, Hippolytus' accusation that the Pope imagined himself administering "the affairs of the whole Church" does lend plausibility that there was some sort of global teaching function that Rome was acknowledged to have since Clement's time. Being an "honorary" head, it does appear that Rome was expected to follow after Peter and "strengthen the brethren."

THE NOVATIANIST SCHISM

The rigorist undercurrent in Rome did not end with the martyrdom of Hippolytus. His martyrdom was one of many, as the Christians in Rome were regularly persecuted in the mid–third century. Novatian, a priest in Rome popular among the rigorists, amidst the violence and chaos secured himself a questionable ordination to the episcopacy over against the valid ordination of Saint Pope Cornelius to the same bishopric.

---

165 "Catholic" is used in the sense of "orthodox"/correct doctrine by Vincent of
     Lerins, *Commonitorium*, Par 6.

Cornelius recounted the episode in his "consecration letter." A "consecration letter" is a letter a Patriarch sends to their suffragan bishops and fellow bishops worldwide, usually delineating the legitimacy of their consecration and a creedal affirmation of orthodox doctrine. The idea behind such a letter is to gain the consent of their fellow bishops to their election and ordination.[166] The Pope of Rome, like the Pope of Alexandria, or any other Patriarch was no exception to this rule and only "abandoned the practice" in the 11th century because it "would have been construed as a sign that the Roman pontiff was willing to defer to the judgement (and possible censure) of his brother bishops in the East."[167] In any event, Cornelius' consecration letter detailed that Novatian:

> compelled them [the ordaining bishops] by force to confer on him the episcopate through a counterfeit and vain imposition of hands…One of these bishops shortly after came back to the church, lamenting and confessing his transgression. And we communed with him as with a layman…And we ordained successors of the other [schismatic] bishops.[168]

The quote demonstrates that the consecration was invalid due to the lack of consent of the bishops involved. Later in the letter, Novatian's up-until-then recognized priesthood is declared invalid due to his irregular reception into the Church, his baptism being by

---

166 This is acknowledged by the 2016 "Chieti document" expounded by Orthodox and Roman Catholics in the "Joint International Commission for Theological Dialogue." See Par 17 in "Synodality and Primacy During the First Millennium: Towards a Common Understanding in Service to the Unity of The Church," *Diacastery for Promoting Christian Unity*, http://www.christianunity.va/content/unitacristiani/en/dialoghi/sezione-orientale/chiese-ortodosse-di-tradizione-bizantina/commissione-mista-internazionale-per-il-dialogo-teologico-tra-la/documenti-di-dialogo/testo-in-inglese1.html

167 Papadakis and Meyendorff, *The Christian East and the Rise of the Papacy*, 77. The spelling of judgment here is according to the English, as opposed to American, norm.

168 Eusebius, *Church History*, Book 6, Chap 43, Par 9-10.

"affusion" and lacking chrismation.[169] The situation is justification for replacing the bishops who willingly participated in the schism, as they are apparently in communion with a non-bishop who was ordained non-canonically.[170] By concelebrating Eucharistically with a layman, they effectually deposed themselves.[171] Otherwise, Cornelius' actions could not be understood as the replacing of deposed bishops, but rather the creation of a schismatic parallel bishopric in its own right.

Cornelius obviously needed the consent of the Christian world for such an action in order to avoid being deemed a schismatic himself—hence the letter. At the very beginning, "a very large synod" was held in Rome that included sixty bishops with "a great many more presbyters and deacons" who excommunicated all the Novatianists.[172] Receiving word of Rome's Synod, intrapatriarchal councils in Rome's jurisdiction in Africa and elsewhere were held: "the pastors of the remaining [Western] provinces deliberated in their places privately concerning what ought to be done."[173]

Not only was intrapatriarchal consent required for Cornelius' election, but so was interpatriarchal consent. Eusebius recounts:

> *There have reached us epistles of Cornelius, bishop of Rome, to Fabius, of the church at Antioch, which show what was done at the synod at Rome, and what seemed best to all those in Italy and Africa and the*

---

169 Ibid. Par 14-15. After all, one cannot make a non-Christian a bishop, as allegedly the baptism by affusion should have prevented him being a priest. See Ibid., Par 17. This is an ironic criticism given the later stance Saint Pope Stephen would take on the issue of baptism vis-à-vis Saint Cyprian of Carthage.

170 Ibid., Par 20 speaks of "five presbyters" originally joining the schism. Being that only one repented, it is safe to presume the compulsion was not as evident in the participation of the other schismatics in Novatian's ordination.

171 Apostolic Canon 31 deposes such clergymen.

172 Eusebius, *Church History*, Book 6, Chap 43, Par 2. Cf Cyprian, *Letter 51*, Par 6.

173 Ibid.

regions thereabout. Also other epistles, written in the Latin language, of
Cyprian and those with him in Africa, which show that they agreed.[174]

This shows the Novatian matter, when the schism spread past the
Roman local jurisdiction, called into question Cornelius' legitimacy.
Cornelius did not simply dictate terms, nor could he. He required
Patriarchal recognition to join their ranks.

Cornelius' care to delineate himself as the right party in the
matter and Novatian a schismatic was motivated by the fact that
at that time schism was understood as a serious moral crime. Saint
Dionysius, the Pope of Alexandria, in Alexandria's synodal response
to Novatian and Cornelius' consecration lamented,

> *For it were better to suffer everything, rather than divide the Church of*
> *God. Even martyrdom for the sake of preventing division would not be*
> *less glorious than for refusing to worship idols.*[175]

The African Synod through Saint Cyprian of Carthage
condemned Novatian with similar reasoning:

> *Novatian had been made bishop; disturbed by the wickedness of an*
> *unlawful ordination made in opposition to the Catholic Church, we*
> *considered at once that they must be restrained from communion with*
> *us...I and several of my colleagues, who had come together to me,*
> *were awaiting the arrival of our colleagues Caldonius and Fortunatus,*
> *whom we had lately sent to you as ambassadors, and to our fellow*
> *bishops, who were present at your ordination, in order that, when they*
> *came and reported the truth of the matter...[T]hey are striving here*
> *also to distract the members of Christ into schismatical parties, and*
> *to cut and tear the one body of the Catholic Church...if they confess*
> *themselves to be maintainers of the Gospel of Christ, they must return*
> *to the Church.*[176]

Cyprian obviously reaffirms Cornelius' reasoning, but likewise
reveals that Cornelius was in effect (partially) Africa's chosen

174 Ibid., Par 3.

175 Ibid., Chap 45, Par 2.

176 Cyprian, *Letter 40*, Par 1-2.

Pope of Rome. The African legates Caldonius and Fortunatus, by participating in Cornelius' consecration, in effect revealed who they had sided with from the beginning. Novatian and his faction could under no circumstance be acceptable. Further, their schism rendered them as categorically outside the veil of the Church and Christendom. Cyprian warned that, "he who is not in the Church of Christ" due to the Novatian schism "is not a Christian."[177] This logic applied to all schismatics. Cyprian complained that a different set of schismatics who were anti-rigorist/lenient:

> *are promising to bring back and recall the lapsed into the Church, who themselves have departed from the Church. There is one God, and Christ is one, and there is one Church, and one chair founded upon the rock by the word of the Lord. Another altar cannot be constituted nor a new priesthood be made, except the one altar and the one priesthood. Whosoever gathers elsewhere, scatters.*[178]

As covered previously,[179] it was understood that the chair of Peter and Matt 16:18 applied to all Bishops. This is why establishing a parallel church and setting a bishop against any Orthodox/Catholic bishop was and still is schismatic. There is one chair founded upon the Rock, Peter, by God's stipulation. This central, foundational ecclesiastical premise was evidently shared by the entire Church at this juncture and it is precisely why the Novatianist schism was responded to in the manner that it was.

THE REBAPTISM CONTROVERSY AND THE ESTABLISHMENT OF CONSENSUS

The controversy over whether the Church can receive Christians from schismatic (and heretical) groups without "rebaptism" is to this day not something completely settled within Orthodoxy. It

---

177 Ibid., *Letter 51*, Par 24.

178 Ibid., *Letter 39*, Par 5.

179 See Cyprian's comments in the first chapter, *Letter 26*, Par 1 specifically. Saint Optatus' comments in the same chapter follow identical logic.

suffices to say that the Church's canons have preserved diversity on the question, some being categorically restrictive[180] and others that accept the baptism of some and not others generally following the criterium of a baptism having proper form (i.e. the sacrament is performed correctly).[181] Saint Basil the Great, who drew up his own list of canons, explicitly accepting Cyprian's teaching on the matter, allowed more diversity on the question according to the level of discretion/*economia* a given region traditionally exercised.[182] The degree of *economia* favored by different sides historically has led to misunderstandings.

This was no different during the first intra- and interpatriarchal debate on the question of rebaptism. Saint Cyprian defended the restrictive, rigorist view and Saint Pope Stephen of Rome, a miracle worker and martyr, *seems* to have defended the exact opposite—that every sort of baptism is acceptable. Upon reviewing all the extant primary sources on the question, two things are clear. First, Cyprian's explicit view was within the pale of the canons as delineated above, while Stephen's was understood to have permitted all baptisms despite their schismatic source or wrong form. This is non-canonical. Second, the relevance of this to the question of the Papacy is that Stephen's view was put under review before the whole Church, who refused to consent to it. As it will be shown, Rome later relented and without fanfare abandoned Stephen's view. This reveals what ecclesiastical presumptions the Church held during this time.

Due to his controversy with the Pope of Rome, people popularly confuse Cyprian as some sort of anti-Roman ideologue. But this is

---

180 Apostolic Canons 47 and 68; Cyprian's Canon 1 ("Cyprian's Canon" in the Photian Nomocanon). Cf Apostolic Canon 50 which also delineates the necessity of baptism having proper form, a criterium endorsed by the Ecumenical Councils (see n. 181).

181 Canon 7 of Constantinople II; Canon 95 of Trullo. Cf Decree 15 of Council of Jerusalem (1672) states: "heretics who renounce their heresy and join the Catholic Church are received by the Church; although they received their valid Baptism with weakness of faith." The question of validity obviously presumes upon proper form. Similarly, Decree 16 speaks of those "rightly baptized," assuming the necessity of proper form.

182 Basil's Canons 1 and 47.

not true, as he consciously followed the model of Apostolic Canon 34 and recognized the Pope of Rome as spiritual head of the Western jurisdiction. Cyprian in fact followed the judgment of the Roman Synod in an appeal made to Rome[183] and appealed to the same Roman Synod (there was no Pope at the time) looking for a judgment in his favor.[184] It is likely that despite Rome not having a Pope, the synod was led by Cornelius who was then an important deacon. At this time, Rome limited itself to seven deacons in accordance with ancient practice.[185] Usually, the most influential deacon would run things (sometimes even when a Pope was around) and being that Cornelius was soon elected, he must have already had notoriety within his synod. This increases the chances that he wrote everything on behalf of the Roman Synod before his consecration to the episcopacy. When Cornelius finally became Pope, Cyprian wrote to his synod asking for an appeal not to be ruled against him.[186] Only after Rome's schism did Cyprian appeal *from* Rome, to Saint Firmilian of Caesarea.[187] Appeals against Rome were therefore possible, just as Irenaeus had done during the Ephesian Controversy and Rome's appeal against a part of itself during the Novatian Controversy demonstrates.

Cyprian's appeal to Cornelius gives one a good window into how the former understood the Papacy. Cyprian describes an adversarial African bishop's appeal against him to the Roman Synod:

> *a false [schismatic] bishop…set sail…to bear letters from schismatic and profane persons to the throne of Peter, and to the chief church whence priestly unity takes its source; and not to consider that these were*

---

183 Cyprian, *Letter 14*, Par 3.

184 Ibid., *Letter 22*.

185 The practice of having seven deacons was derived from Acts 6, but was violated for the first time in Rome during the Laurentian Schism in the sixth century as a means for (anti?) Pope Symmachus to replace legitimate clergy who had rejected his episcopacy. See John Moorhead, "The Laurentian Schism: East and West in the Roman Church," *Church History*, 47:2, 1978, 133.

186 Cyprian, *Letter 54*.

187 Ibid., *Letter 74*, Par 4.

*the Romans whose faith was praised in the preaching of the [A]postle,
to whom faithlessness could have no access [for appeals].*[188]

Rome's great faith as recognized by Saint Paul in his *Letter to the Romans* is seen as an honorifically insulating influence against foolish "faithless" appeals. Cyprian makes no explicit reference to relics, but he certainly treats Rome's capacity to hear appeals as a matter of settled precedent. On that note, he identifies Rome as the "source" of unity and the "chief church," something he sincerely means as he repeats the same idea in a letter he wrote *in opposition* to Pope Stephen.[189] It is most likely that he is acknowledging an interpatriarchal primacy of some sort, similar to Ignatius of Antioch—why else would he identify Rome as the "source" of the priesthood? This is a reference to the idea that the entire episcopate originated in Peter (as covered previously).

Cyprian certainly had a high view of the Roman Church and saw Rome as a "root" of unity—but only to an extent. One must always take care to read not just words, but evaluate how they apply to the facts surrounding them. Consider how the same letter ends:

I know, dearest brother, from the mutual love which we owe and manifest one towards another, that you always read my letters to the very distinguished clergy who preside with you there…yet now I both warn and ask you to do by my request what at other times you do of your own accord and courtesy.[190]

As one can see, Cyprian believes that the Pope cannot act unilaterally—the Pope "owes" love and a sort of obedience. In fact, Cyprian actually makes a sort of threat to Pope Cornelius ("I warn you") and elsewhere he does the same,[191] which shows there was an

---

188 Ibid., *Letter 54*, Par 14.

189 For example, "the Church founded by Christ the Lord upon Peter, by a source and principle of unity, is one also." See Ibid., *Letter 69*, Par 3.

190 Ibid., *Letter 54*, Par 20.

191 Cyprian admonishes/commands Pope Cornelius in other instances: "you ought to send these letters also to the other churches." *Letter 45*, Par 3; cf *Letter 44*. Acknowledging that saints act "politically" may appear impious.

understood limit to the aforementioned honorifics. Rome obviously consented to Cyprian's repeated dictating to them what they ought to do and until Pope Stephen, never corrected him.

Cyprian was being forceful in that his consent to Cornelius' actions was necessary. Unsurprisingly, Cyprian had an explicit ecclesiology of conciliar consent.[192] Other than the preceding footnote, the following passages from Cyprian are illustrative:

> our proceedings…ought to be united and to agree in all things.[193]

> communicate to as many of our colleagues as you can, that among all these, may be observed one mode of action and one agreement.[194]

> the place of Fabian, that is, when the place of Peter and the degree of the sacerdotal throne was vacant; which being occupied by the will of God, and established by the consent of all of us, whosoever now wishes to become a bishop, must needs be made from without; and he cannot have the ordination of the Church who does not hold the unity of the Church.[195]

In short, the "place of Peter" is held by the entire Roman Synod ("consent of all of us") which includes Africa, within Rome's jurisdiction. A true successor of Peter must have the consent of that local synod, obviously following the logic of Apostolic Canon 34.

The ecclesiology of consent permeated the Church and the Roman Synod in the third century was no exception. The Roman Synod heartily concurred before the Papacy of Stephen, writing (likely from Cornelius' hand):

The necessity for honest historicity aside, one should be understanding that saints like people today live in a fallen world and often fight hard for their partisans or flock, sometimes creating friction and evidencing strategizing.

192 See Ibid., *Letter 13*, Par 2; *Letter 17*; *Letter 18*; *Letter 22*, Par 4; *Letter 32*, Par 1; *Letter 52*; *Letter 64*, Par 1; *Letter 66*, Par 1.

193 Ibid, *Letter 14*, Par 13.

194 Ibid., *Letter 19*.

195 Ibid., *Letter 51*, Par 8.

> *that cannot be a firm decree which shall not appear to have had the consent of very many.*[196]

> *it becomes us all [Africa and Rome] to watch for the body of the whole Church.*[197]

Perhaps the most profound expounding of the ecclesiology of consent can be found in the Roman Synod's (again, likely Cornelius') letter to Cyprian where it is written:

> *they [bishops] owe their conscience to God alone as the judge yet desire that their doings should be approved also by their brethren themselves. It is no wonder, brother Cyprian,…we should be found not so much judges of, as sharers in, your counsel.*[198]

These words became a sort of rallying cry that Cyprian repeated soon afterwards. When Cornelius was Pope, Cyprian paraphrased these words back to him: "he [the bishop] shall give an account to the Lord in the day of judgment"[199] and "every bishop disposes and directs his own acts, and will have to give an account of his purposes to the Lord."[200] It appears that Cyprian expected Cornelius' to immediately recognize what authority he was citing.

This ecclesiology was shared between Rome and Africa immediately prior to the spat between Cyprian and Pope Stephen over the issue of rebaptism. Before that controversy erupted, Cyprian was sent an appeal from Gaul which was *also* sent to Rome. In a letter to Rome, Cyprian "behooves" Stephen to share in Africa's excommunication of their Gaulish opposition and affirm bishops recognized by Africa.[201] The appeal was likely sent to Cyprian first because Cornelius was martyred and Stephen only recently

---

196 Ibid., *Letter 30*, Par 5.

197 Ibid., *Letter 29*, Par 4.

198 Ibid., *Letter 30*, Par 1.

199 Ibid., *Letter 53*, Par 5.

200 Ibid., *Letter 51*, Par 21.

201 Ibid., *Letter 66*, Par 2.

elected.[202] Cyprian's thinly-veiled commands were something he had gotten away with in the past, but now they were likely perceived as stepping on the Roman Synod's (Stephen's) toes.

The African Synod also took an appeal from the Spanish Synod.[203] Spain excommunicated two bishops and Africa affirmed their judgment. The Roman Synod under Stephen did not accept their excommunications. Suddenly, and likely not coincidentally, an argument over rebaptism erupted.

Stephen's letters during this controversy have been lost to history, so everything one can gather from them is quoted from his opponents. Several quotations from Stephen, or paraphrases of a letter of his, are relevant to the study of the Papacy. For example, Cyprian recalls:

> *For neither did Peter, whom first the Lord chose, and upon whom He built His Church, when Paul disputed with him afterwards about circumcision, claim anything to himself insolently, nor arrogantly assume anything; so as to say that he held the primacy, and that he ought rather to be obeyed by novices and those lately come.*[204]

From Cyprian's quote, one can infer that Stephen must have demanded "to be obeyed" due to holding "primacy."[205] Cyprian rejects this sort of unquestioning obedience, not rejecting Petrine authority; but presuming both that Peter can be corrected (as Saint Paul had done)[206] and obedience be negotiated. After all, consent to the primatial bishop is always necessary.

Rejecting Stephen in a regional council, Cyprian slyly refers Stephen to the Roman Synod's (likely Cornelius') words, telling him:

> *For neither does any of us set himself up as a bishop of bishops, nor by tyrannical terror does any compel his colleague to the necessity of*

---

202 Ibid., Par 3.

203 Ibid., *Letter 67*.

204 Ibid., *Letter 70*, Par 1.

205 Cf *Letter 75*, Par 8.

206 Gal 2:14-16.

obedience; since every bishop, according to the allowance of his liberty and power, has his own proper right of judgment, and can no more be judged by another than he himself can judge another. But let us all wait for the judgment of our Lord Jesus Christ.[207]

The statement was not a duplicitous excuse for disobeying a Pope of Rome. It cited Rome's (likely Cornelius') former teaching as reason to reject Stephen's call for unquestioning obedience.

During this controversy, Stephen "excommunicated" Cyprian and Firmilian for opposing him. Apparently, Stephen, in the words of Saint Dionysius (Pope of Alexandria), "depart[ed] from their communion."[208] Dionysius understood that Stephen had the capacity to break himself off from others, but not excommunicate outside of his jurisdiction. The concept of universal and direct jurisdiction is notably absent in the primary sources.

Firmilian's opposition to Stephen was well known. In his synod's letter responding to Cyprian's appeal, Firmilian wrote: "they who are at Rome…vainly pretend the authority of the [A]postles… defaming Peter and Paul."[209] This conveys not only Firmilian's resistance, but demonstrates that Stephen cited his authority derived from Peter and Paul when excommunicating. The citing of Peter and Paul likely was a reference to their historical churches, or in other words, Stephen breaking the communion of others from Rome's local jurisdiction.

---

207 Decree of the Carthaginian Council in 256 ("On the Baptism of Heretics"). Cyprian says almost the same exact thing in Cyprian, *Letter 72*, Par 26.

208 *Letter 6* in Alexander Roberts and James Donaldson, *Ante-Nicene Christian Library: Translations of the Writings of the Fathers Down to A.D. 326 Vol. XXI.* Edinburgh: T. & T . Clark, 1882, 218. Other translations of the same passage concur. See Charles Feltoe, *St. Dionysius of Alexandria: Letters and Treatises.* New York: The Macmillan Company, 1918, 55 and Arthur Cushman McGiffert, "Church History (Eusebius)" in Philip Schaff and Henry Wace (eds.), *Nicene and Post-Nicene Fathers, Second Series, Vol. 1.* Buffalo: Christian Literature Publishing Co., 1890, 176.

209 Cyprian, *Letter 74*, Par 16.

This explains why Firmilian interpreted Stephen's actions as schismatic, writing to Cyprian that "Stephen has now dared to" ruin the unity of the Church by "breaking the peace."[210] He explains:

> he [Stephen] is really the schismatic who has made himself an apostate from the communion of ecclesiastical unity. For while you [Stephen] think that all may be excommunicated by you, you have excommunicated yourself alone from all.[211]

This may imply that Stephen did assume the authority of excommunicating "all," but it also may be a reference to those within his own jurisdiction. The former reading is preferable because internal details in the letter indicate that Stephen broke communion with Firmilian at that juncture.[212] Firmilian in castigating Stephen reveals more details relevant to the question at hand:

> [Stephen] boasts of the place of his episcopate, and contends that he holds the succession from Peter, on whom the foundations of the Church were laid…the Christian Rock is overshadowed, and in some measure abolished, by him when he thus betrays and deserts unity.[213]

Firmilian's point is that schism and rejecting the unity of the Church (implicitly in his unilateral actions instead of seeking consensus) "abolishes" any claim to Petrine authority. This is probably intended to be a larger critique of Rome forfeiting its position as honorary head through faithlessness. Firmilian does not fail to point out elsewhere that "the [A]postles alone" and "the bishops who succeeded to them by vicarious ordination" constitute the disciplinary authority of the Church at-large.[214] Such an

---

210 Ibid.

211 Ibid., Par 24.

212 Ibid., Par 25. The fact that Firmilian identifies with the "[E]astern churches" may indicate that he was speaking for the "Ephesian Patriarchate" in some sense, as he uses the term "we" to speak for his synod. Caesarea at this juncture vied for primacy within the jurisdiction and would later attain to it. See n. 317.

213 Ibid., Par 17.

214 Ibid., Par 16.

emphasis indicates that interpatriarchal prerogatives played some role in the debate.

Cyprian shared Firmilian's view of the episcopacy. By rejecting consensus, the former likewise argues, Stephen implicitly separated himself from the Church: "we [the Catholic rebaptizers] who hold the head and root of the one Church know, and trust for certain, that nothing is lawful there outside the Church."[215] In other words, those who stay in communion with the rest of the Church (here, the rebaptizers) are not the schismatics; but those who break unity (like the Novatians and Stephen if he is obliquely being referenced) are. Even if these words were not a measured response to Stephen specifically, which is highly unlikely given the occasion for the letter's writing, it reveals an ecclesiology which places the onus of schism on the party which deserts the unity of the Church.

This ecclesiology matches the one Cyprian expounded before Stephen's schism from Carthage—an ecclesiology which at the time was accepted by Rome. In Cyprian's *On the Unity of the Catholic Church*, written against the Novatianists, Cyprian defends the view that the whole Church originated in Peter, whose ordination of the Apostles to the episcopate created the unity the Church was built upon. "[T]he beginning proceeds from unity."[216] Elsewhere Cyprian explains the origin in the Church in more detail:

> And in the Apocalypse the Lord directs His divine and heavenly precepts to the seven churches and their angels, which number is now found in this case, in the seven brethren, that a lawful consummation may be completed. With the seven children is manifestly associated also the mother, their origin and root, who subsequently begot seven churches, she herself having been first, and alone founded upon a rock by the voice of the Lord.[217]

Schism is, very simply, leaving the unity which was established from the Church's beginning. Cyprian's view of schism can

---

215 Ibid., *Letter 72*, Par 2.

216 Ibid., *Treatise 1*, Par 4. For more details on this passage, see the first chapter.

217 Ibid., *Treatise 11*, Par 11.

be summed up as "the one who started it is at fault." In *On the Unity of the Catholic Church*, he discussed the issue of schism as it pertained to the Novatianists thusly: "For we have not withdrawn from them, but they from us...they have forsaken the Head and Source of the truth."[218] "Head," "Source," "root," and "mother" are the actual Christian unity of Petrine bishops which existed from the beginning—not the Pope of Rome in isolation. For example, Cyprian wrote to Cornelius concerning the Novatianists:

> *the adverse party has not only rejected the bosom and the embrace of its root and Mother, but even, with a discord spreading and reviving itself worse and worse, has appointed a bishop for itself.*[219]

In criticizing Florentius, a Novatianist that Cyprian who like Stephen was called by the pejorative "bishop of a bishop:"

> *the bishop is in the Church, and the Church in the bishop; and if any one be not with the bishop, that he is not in the Church...the Church, which is Catholic and one, is not cut nor divided, but is indeed connected and bound together by the cement of priests who cohere with one another.*[220]

In other words, breaking from a legitimate bishop, as the Novatians did, is definitionally schismatic. This applies not only to Rome, but to any bishop who rejects the consent of the Church ("cement of priests") as the Novatianists did (being that the Church rejected Novatian's ordination). According to Cyprian's ecclesiology, which appears to be the universal ecclesiology of the day, it is clear that Stephen had fomented a schism in his own right and Saints Firmilian and Dionysius of Alexandria recognized this.

Much of this will appear new or even bizarre to readers, because presentations of this era rarely portray Stephen as "the odd man out." The origin of this confusion may be the popular idea that Cyprian had picked the wrong view on baptism during

---

218 Ibid., *Treatise 1*, Par 12.

219 Ibid., *Letter 41*, Par 1.

220 Ibid., *Letter 68*, Par 8.

the controversy, and had made subsequent ecclesiastical errors as a result. This is wrong for two reasons. First, as just shown, Cyprian's ecclesiology was consistent before and after the controversy. In fact, before and after Stephen, as the previously-discussed letters of Cornelius and Dionysius of Rome demonstrate, consensus-based ecclesiology was the explicit ecclesiology that the Roman Church both expounded and received. Second, all the primary sources detail that Cyprian's contemporaries sided with him against Stephen—not the other way around.

Later saints such as Jerome, Augustine, and Vincent of Lerins had concluded otherwise and as a result, moderns presume upon their reading of history. However, these men were interpreting the same primary sources that presently exist. The fact none of them quote anything new from Stephen indicates that even by the fourth century his correspondence was already (intentionally? tragically?) lost.

Cyprian (representing the African Synod) and Firmilian (representing the Asian/Ephesian Synod, possibly including Antioch given his later interference there during the controversy surrounding Paul of Samosata) as detailed previously rejected Stephen emphatically. Only one other figure's writings who participated in the controversy are preserved: Pope Dionysius of Alexandria. Writing on behalf of the Egyptian Synod to Stephen, he clearly supported Cyprian:

> *For these reasons, that we may be in accord, church with church and bishop with bishop and elder with elder,* **let us be careful in our utterances**. *Moreover in judging of and dealing with particular cases [of baptism]… we give instructions to the local primates who under divine imposition of hands were appointed to discharge these duties; for they shall give a summary account to the Lord of whatsoever they do.*[221]

---

221 Dionysius of Alexandria, *Armenian Letter 1*. The letter is accurate as proved by the same quote being found in a Syriac fragment and a Greek Catena on Deuteronomy. See Feltoe, *St. Dionysius of Alexandria*, 53-54.

As one can see, Dionysius commands Stephen to "be careful" with his "utterances," a rejection of the latter's policy of excommunication. Weighing in on baptism, he does not actually detail in this letter what his instructions are, but he not so coincidentally refers to the Roman Synod's teaching that each bishop is individually judged by God for what he does. His specific reference to giving "a summary account" appears to be a direct quotation to one of Cyprian's letters,[222] clearly identifying whose side he is taking.

In a letter after Stephen's martyrdom, Dionysius writes to Pope Sixtus II of Rome that the Alexandrine practice on baptism is that:

> *those over whom there has not been invoked the name either of Father or of Son or of the Holy Spirit, these we must baptise, but not rebaptise. This is the sure and immovable teaching and tradition.*[223]

Dionysius is clearly asserting that proper form is required for baptism. This view is more lenient than Cyprian's, though both Cyprian's and his own are both explicitly found in the canons (unlike Stephen's who was accused of accepting all baptisms).[224]

---

222 Cyprian, *Letter 71*, Par 3 or *Letter 53*, Par 5.

223 Dionysius of Alexandria, *Armenian Letter 2*.

224 Cyprian, *Letter 72*, Par 4 allegedly quotes Stephen as saying that "even those that came from" the Marcionites (a Gnostic sect) "did not need to be baptized, because they *seemed* to have been already baptized in the name of Jesus Christ." This implies the Holy Trinity was not invoked. Elsewhere his opposition (likely Stephen, cf *Letter 74*, Par 21) is quoted as saying, "What, then, shall become of those who in past times, coming from heresy to the Church, were received without baptism?" in Ibid., *Letter 72*, Par 23. This implies there was no discernment whatsoever how the baptism was performed. Such allegations may or may not be exaggerated. Stephen is quoted in Ibid., *Letter 73*, Par 1 stating, "If any one, therefore, come to you from any heresy whatever, let nothing be innovated (or done) which has not been handed down, to wit, that hands be imposed on him for repentance; since the heretics themselves, *in their own proper character*, do not baptize such as come to them from one another, but only admit them to communion." The italicized may imply they had proper form according to the Catholic measure, or it may imply the opposite, that the heretics' form was correct according to their own standards. The fact that Stephen allegedly accepted

Interestingly, Dionysius of Alexandria did not feel that his view was at odds with Cyprian's, because when he asserted that "these [with improper form] we must baptize, but not rebaptise," he evidently was quoting Cyprian: "we say that those who come thence are not re-baptized among us, but are baptized."[225] Contrary to later assumptions about the controversy, no one was approvingly quoting Stephen on the issue. Cyprian was the one who was quoted authoritatively.

How does one explain the historical confusion of later saints, whose evaluations of the controversy are so contrary to the primary sources?[226] The confusion appears to originate in the only other ecclesiastical writer who weighed in on the issue that was at least alive in the third century: Eusebius of Caesarea. Eusebius was likely not born when the controversy occurred, but reflecting on it decades later he favored what he understood to be[227] the Roman custom:

> *the ancient custom prevailed in regard to such, that they should receive only the laying on of hands with prayers… Cyprian, pastor of the parish of Carthage, maintained that they should not be received except they*

the baptisms of "Valentinus and Apelles, and of others who blaspheme against God the Father; and to say that remission of sins is granted in the name of Jesus Christ where blasphemy is uttered against the Father" (Ibid., *Letter 73*, Par 7) implies certain Gnostics did not include the Father's name in baptism over scruples that the God of the Old Testament was in fact an inferior *aeon* (generally called the *demiurge*). These letters, if an accurate synopsis of Stephen's views, demonstrates he accepted baptisms with improper form. Saint Firmilian does not explicitly impute to Stephen the practice of accepting baptisms with improper form, but he broadly condemns the schismatic and heretical character of those baptisms which Stephen admitted to accepting. See Ibid., *Letter* 74, Par 5, 7, 12, 22.

225 Ibid., *Letter 70*, Par 2.

226 These later saints do not take the wrong canonical view of baptism, as even Augustine maintained that proper form was necessary (*On Baptism, Against the Donatists*, Book 3, Par 20), in agreement with the canons.

227 It is likely the Roman view by this point was modified to incorporate the teaching of Dionysius of Alexandria that proper form was necessary for a baptism. This revision may explain how all of Stephen's writings were evidently lost even by Eusebius' day, as he quotes none of them. This preserved Stephen's memory at the expense of Cyprian's.

had been purified from their error by baptism. But Stephen considering it unnecessary to add any innovation contrary to the tradition which had been held from the beginning, was very indignant at this.[228]

Interestingly, Eusebius quotes a (different) letter from Dionysius of Alexandria's letter to Sixtus II that seems to contradict his very point. Dionysius of Alexandria wrote:

He [Pope Stephen] therefore had written previously concerning Helenus and Firmilianus, and all those in Cilicia and Cappadocia and Galatia and the neighboring nations, saying that he would not commune with them for this same cause; namely, that they re-baptized heretics. But consider the importance of the matter. For truly in the largest synods of the bishops...decrees have been passed on this subject, that those coming over from heresies should be...washed and cleansed from the filth of the old and impure leaven. And I wrote entreating him [Stephen] concerning all these things.[229]

Dionysius of Alexandria boasts that "the largest synods of the bishops" decreed contrary to Stephen and that he entreated the latter concerning this. Does this sound like Dionysius agrees with Stephen? Eusebius does not explain, but continues with an interesting statement he records which ends the same letter:

I [Dionysius of Alexandria] wrote also, at first in few words, recently in many, to our beloved fellow presbyters, Dionysius [future Pope of Rome] and Philemon, who **formerly had held the same opinion as Stephen**, *and had written to me on the same matters.*[230]

The fact that Dionysius of Alexandria references Dionysius of Rome (the future Pope who would succeed Sixtus II) and Philemon (another Roman clergyman) "formerly had held the same opinion as Stephen" serves as proof that Rome had already begun changing

---

228 Eusebius, *Church History*, Book 7, Chap 2-3.

229 Ibid., Chap 4-5.

230 Ibid., Chap 5.

their teaching in the face of popular opposition.[231] The fact their position was evidently modified proves that Stephen's teaching was probably portrayed by Cyprian and Firmilian accurately. Rome, by accepting the premise that proper form is necessary for baptism in obedience to Dionysius of Alexandria's teaching, had in effect made a necessary concession needed to maintain unity in the Church. Further, it may have been a return to their initial practice considering Pope Cornelius' concern for proper baptismal form, as revealed by his consecration letter. Hence, the traditions preserved by Dionysius of Alexandria and Cyprian are to this day found in the canons. Stephen's are not. They were evidently disowned and then lost to history—likely in respect to his sanctity in other respects. In summary, Stephen was perceived as wrong on rebaptism during his day based upon the sources that are actually contemporary to the events. The presentation given here should not be viewed as a revisionist portrayal, but the default given it is the only interpretation allowed by the sources which survive. Nevertheless, this is not in and of itself important for the study of the Papacy. Rather, the fact that the whole Christian world refused to submit to Stephen's view or recognize his excommunication is entirely relevant. In fact, Stephen was viewed as schismatic by three different saints and their synods. On top of this, Rome evidently re-entered communion and even modified their baptismal practices *in response* to being scolded by Alexandria. The ecclesiology of conciliarity and consent won out over Stephen's intransigence on this matter.

Despite the appearance of conciliarity, one may still pose the question, is it possible that Stephen may have been asserting some

---

231 In a letter to Philemon of Rome, Dionysius not only defends the African and Asian customs, he expresses that those who left the Church having already received baptism after adopting some sort of heresy did not require another baptism after re-entering the Church. The significance of this is that it demonstrates Stephen's position was (likely) deliberately contrasted. One then can surmise Dionysius' of Alexandria's position as follows: the baptism in the Church is valid among those who become heretics, but the baptism received among heretics was not necessarily valid. See *Letter 7 to Philemon Presbyter of Sixtus* in Salmond, *The Works of Gregory Thaumaturgus, Dionysius of Alexandria, and Archelaus*, 219-220.

sort of Papal Supremacy in seed form? He surely excommunicated Cyprian and he refused to commune with Firmilian. However, no documented source implies, let alone states, that Stephen understood his actions as removing Firmilian from the Church at-large. In fact, Dionysius of Alexandria implies only a local separation of communion. The simplest interpretation is that Stephen was acting in a local context, determining who his synod specifically held in communion. When this created the threat of schism with Alexandria, Rome evidently backed down.

Interestingly, Sixtus II's and Dionysius of Rome's capitulation proved to be more effective in cowing the North Africans than Stephen's hard stance. Over time, the Latin-centric, as opposed to indigenously aligned, North Africans gained prominence in the African Synod. They followed the modified Roman (Alexandrian) practice, likely due to their closer ethnic affinity with those in Rome. The "indigenous" Punic-speaking North Africans, who would become the Donatist schismatics, followed Cyprian on the question of baptism (though their ecclesiology was ironically Novatianist and not Cyprianic).[232] Historical circumstance effectively culled the sacramentology of Cyprian from the canonical African Church, even if it did not from other churches within the Orthodox Catholic communion.

As a result, history was (unintentionally) revised to the detriment of the Donatists. It was forgotten that Rome had modified their baptismal tradition in response to being censured and that the Latin North Africans had subsequently adopted the modified Roman practice—not Stephen's specifically. As referenced above, the ecclesiastical and sacramental details of the points at issue are found in a corpora of manuscripts, many of which were entirely lost (Stephen) or exist only in fragments (Dionysius of Alexandria). So, the history was simplified to cast Stephen as upholding the moderate position and Cyprian a hyper-rigorist one. This negative recasting of Cyprian was a means of denouncing the Donatists,

---

232 The ethnic divide which undergirded the Donatist schism is discussed by W.H.M. Frend, *The Donatist Church: A Movement of Protest in Roman North Africa*. Oxford: Oxford University Press, 1952, 246.

who were faithful to Cyprian on that specific issue (though not others). The historical truth of the matter, as has been shown, is more complicated; but not elusive.

THE FIRST PATRIARCHAL DEPOSITION: PAUL OF SAMOSATA

Paul of Samosata was the bishop of Antioch, later known by the honorary title of "Patriarch." In Orthodoxy, a Patriarch can only be deposed by Patriarchs, as "recent" synods such as Moscow 1666 (deposed Moscow's Patriarch) and Istanbul 2005 (deposed Jerusalem's Patriarch) demonstrate. This theology of Patriarchal deposition existed throughout early Church history, as this study entails. The first instance was that of Paul of Samosata.

His heresy is not important for this book's purposes, but it was identified in the 260s. Due to Paul of Samosata being propped up by the Palmyrene Empire (a Roman break-away state that had control over Egypt, Roman Syria/Palestine, and most of Asia Minor), it took years to depose him both ecclesiastically and pragmatically (because he refused to leave). Initially, Eusebius indicates the local Antiochene Synod and those nearby deposed him:

> *Firmilianus, bishop of Cæsarea in Cappadocia; the brothers Gregory and Athenodorus, pastors of the churches in Pontus; Helenus of the parish of Tarsus, and Nicomas of Iconium; moreover, Hymenæus, of the church of Jerusalem, and Theotecnus of the neighboring church of Cæsarea; and besides these Maximus, who presided in a distinguished manner over the brethren in Bostra.*[233]

Iconium and Caesarea represented notable Ephesian sees (Ephesus it should be remembered is the primate of Asia at this time, effectively holding the place Constantinople would in the future).[234] Jerusalem also had representation. In effect, three patriarchates were directly weighing in during the Council of Antioch (269). Eusebius

233 Eusebius, *Church History*, Book 7, Chap 28, Par 1.

234 Arguably, Caesarea vied for primacy in Asia Minor with Ephesus, as covered n. 317.

explains that "his false doctrine [was] clearly shown before all, and he was excommunicated from the Catholic Church under heaven."[235] As one can see, the excommunications of Polycrates, Firmilian, and Cyprian were never described by Eusebius as "excommunications from the" entirety of "the Catholic Church under heaven." This is likely because they did not involve the input of multiple Patriarchs. The Council of Antioch (269), in deposing Paul of Samosata, did.

One may infer that it was "irregular" for Patriarchs from "lesser" sees to depose a superior Patriarch. Certainly, the Apostles of Ephesus (John) and Jerusalem (James the Just) were less important than Antioch's, who claimed for itself Peter, the Prince of the Apostles. According to Eusebius:

> *The pastors who had assembled about this matter [the Antiochene Synod with Jerusalem and Asia Minor], prepared by common consent an epistle addressed to Dionysius, bishop of Rome, and Maximus of Alexandria, and sent it to all the provinces.*[236]

They required the acceptance of all the Patriarchs—Ephesus (Asia), Jerusalem, Alexandria, and Rome—and their synods ("all the provinces"). The former two already approved, the latter were pending. It is likely the latter two were recognized as being more important, but not for any real spiritual reason. Antioch arguably is more Petrine than Alexandria (traditionally begun by Saint Mark). Yet, Rome and Alexandria were definitely the wealthiest, most geopolitically important cities in the Roman Empire. The priority granted to their respective patriarchates is not uncoincidentally correlated with this.

The Antiochene Synod, in conjunction with the Asian and Jerusalem Patriarchates wrote "[t]o Dionysius [of Rome] and Maximus [of Alexandria] and to all our fellow-ministers throughout the world…to the whole Catholic Church under heaven"[237] explaining that they "called many of the bishops from a distance

---

235 Ibid., Chap 29, Par 1.

236 Ibid., Chap 30, Par 1.

237 Ibid., Par 2.

to relieve us from this deadly doctrine; as Dionysius of Alexandria [now deceased] and Firmilianus of Cappadocia."[238] They justified their actions:

> we have been compelled to excommunicate him [Paul of Samosata], since he sets himself against God, and refuses to obey; and to appoint in his place another bishop for the Catholic Church. By divine direction, as we believe, we have appointed Domnus, who is adorned with all the qualities becoming in a bishop... We have informed you of this that you may... receive letters of communion from him.[239]

In short, the council asserted that it was directed by the Holy Spirit and sought the acceptance of their new Patriarch on the grounds that the former one was rightly deposed as a heretic. Claiming "divine direction" was a purposeful citation of Acts 15:28. Accepting Domnus of Antioch's communion would consummate that consensus had been achieved, laying claim that God had resolved a hitherto unknown issue—deposing a Patriarch against his wishes. In some respects, the Council of Antioch (269) was functionally little different than an Ecumenical Council in points of doctrine, ecclesiastical prerogatives, and the genuine consensus that it achieved with the acceptance of the Alexandrian and Roman Synods. However, its deposition was unprecedented in its day, even if the settling of jurisdictions (Ephesian Controversy), choosing between a disputed Patriarch (Novatian Controversy), and the discerning of practical and doctrinal matters (Rebaptism Controversy) was not.

The Palmyrene Empire and their Patriarch of choice, Paul of Samosata, did not really care for Church consensus nor history in the making. Eusebius records that: "Paul [of Samosata] refused to surrender the church building"[240] in Antioch. The Church lacks an army to enforce its will so Paul simply defied it. However, the Palmyrene Empire after reaching its zenith in 271 AD was quickly

---

238 Ibid., Par 3.

239 Ibid., Par 17.

240 Ibid., Par 19.

defeated by Rome. The Church, knowing "the enemy of my enemy is my friend" looked to the pagan victors for help. Eusebius records:

> *the Emperor Aurelian was petitioned; and he decided... the building to be given to those to whom the bishops of Italy and of the city of Rome should adjudge it. Thus this man was driven out of the church, with extreme disgrace, by the worldly power.*[241]

This was the first instance of a secular power being exploited to solve a Church dispute. Interestingly, a pagan Emperor obliged. Why? Certainly, it was seen as a means of subverting the remnants of Palmyrene power, which would have hung on after Rome's re-conquest of their former provinces. Eusebius appears to take for granted that while the Antiochene Synod spiritually settled matters, "the worldly power" enforced the Church's court order—viewed as a disgrace for Paul of Samosata, who should have obliged from the beginning.

What is one to make of "the bishops of Italy and of the city of Rome" judging matters? One may infer from this evidence in favor of Papal Supremacy in the third century, but this does not appear justified given the facts at hand. For one, the passage indicates the Pope of Rome did not decide matters individually, but as part of a synod. Additionally, it would be unlikely that a pagan Emperor, in sensitivity to the Church's alleged Papalist ecclesiastical sensibilities, for that reason deemed it necessary for Rome to have the definitive say on the issue. Rather, it was evidently a practical move. The Roman Synod was the only synod among all the patriarchates (this would later be called "the Pentarchy") that had not recently been under total or partial Palmyrene control. It made sense that bishops where Aurelian had unquestioned control would determine matters in the Roman Empire's favor.

It is clear the Antiochene Synod imagined itself as having settled the matter, as evidenced by its invocation of "divine direction." The Synod merely sought the acceptance/acquiescence of Alexandria and Rome because no one in their synods, even legates, attended the council. Yet, Paul of Samosata's refusal to submit created a new

---

241 Ibid.

precedent—the first ever interpatriarchal appeal to the Roman Synod. While Eusebius downplays this appeal to apply only to who must vacate a church building, surely the real significance was that Rome was given the role of actually approving the work of the Antiochene, Jerusalem, and Asian Synods—thereby giving Rome the final say.

Future appeals frequently would be made to Alexandria and Rome—even to other cities like Jerusalem and Thessalonica. Yet, Rome's primacy now not only had a spiritual legacy due to Saint Peter and Paul's relics; it finally had a specific, juridical precedent. It would be all but forgotten that earlier interpatriarchal appeals had actually went against Rome during the Ephesian and Rebaptism Controversies.

Due to this precedent, it is historically fitting that Roman primacy was later canonically defined as political in nature,[242] considering that the inauspicious origin to interpatriarchal appeals to Rome was likewise political in orientation. This precedent would be cemented by the semi-Arian controversies during the fourth century, which gave mutual occasion for Rome to both receive interpatriarchal appeals and, more importantly, be on the side defending Orthodoxy.

One cannot conclude that appeals to Rome are historically illegitimate due to their political origin. Similarly, appeals made elsewhere, particularly to the Church at-large as seen during the Ephesian, Novatian, and Rebaptism Controversies, are not invalidated by their solely ecclesiastical origins. However, one can conclude that appeals followed a specific model, that being ecclesiastical consensus, was the final (and decisive) arbiter in all disputes.

Synopsis of the Papacy in the Third Century

The third century brings to bear many more sources pertaining to the Church of Rome. In what they detail, not a faint indication of Papal Supremacy is to be found. Without controversy, saints

---

242 Canon 3 of Constantinople I and Canon 28 of Chalcedon.

and other prominent ecclesiastics alike assumed that Rome can make doctrinal errors (as the Rigorist and Modalist Controversies demonstrate), go into schism, be appealed from, and make disciplinary errors (Rebaptism Controversy). As opposed to any ideas pertaining to direct and universal jurisdiction, all of the explicit historical evidence points to Roman excommunications being local in nature. Rome was seen as one of many Petrine, Catholic Churches. Additionally, the Roman Synod in letters (likely written by later-Pope Cornelius) and Pope Dionysius of Rome clearly presumed upon the ecclesiology of consent. This shows marked continuity with the ecclesiology of the Church of previous centuries.

It is not coincidental that Rome's adherence to such an ecclesiology was quoted against them when Saint Pope Stephen proved exceedingly inflexible on the issue of rebaptism. Such inflexibility appears to have been trumped up as a cover for disputes with Africa pertaining to appellate jurisdiction over Spain and Gaul. It pushed Rome into schism. A weak foundation for pursuing a controversy could not endure. After Stephen's martyrdom, Rome quickly relented and submitted to Alexandria's view of rebaptism. If history ended then, it would seem that the Roman Synod had fallen from its honorary prominence without having attained any notable notches on their belt. This is especially true considering their additional international humbling during the Ephesian Controversy and their weakness during Novatian's disputed election to the Papacy.

Yet, like the mythological phoenix cited by Saint Pope Clement of Rome, greatness was about to rise from the ashes. The Palmyrene Empire's quick rise and collapse foisted a hugely important matter, the decision over the status of an already-deposed Patriarch of Antioch, into the Roman Synod's hands. Having been appealed against, overruled, and humbled repeatedly in the span of a few decades, it was finally the Roman Synod's time in the sun—a time graciously granted to them by a pagan Emperor for strictly political reasons. Imperial meddling proved to be providential in Rome's case and would lead to their synod taking an increasingly prominent role which would historically otherwise seemed to have disappeared shortly after the penning of Saint Ignatius of Antioch's lofty epistle. The Papacy's precipitous rise will be something for the world to behold for the next two centuries, though it does not reach the heights that many expect.

St. Constantine the Great

CHAPTER 4

The Fourth Century of the Papacy

The beginning of the fourth century is the last time the Church would plausibly be a counter-cultural institution in the Roman Imperial context. The Church had experienced its worst persecution up until that point under Diocletian. This persecution was so fierce it even led to the apostasy, episcopal abdication, and repentance of Saint Pope Marcellinus of Rome.[243] Yet, the moment Christianity was officially tolerated by the Edict of Milan thanks to Saint Constantine the Great, the Church quickly made use of Imperial patronage and power. While this led to many conversions to Christianity and the salvation of countless souls, it also created a new set of circumstances that would prove to endure for centuries.

In short, the Roman state (centered in Rome, Nicomedia, then Constantinople) became the most powerful arbiter of ecclesiastical matters. When the state reacted correctly to Church appeals, this put schismatics and heretics at a decisive disadvantage. However, when the state sided with the heretics, this would create wholesale persecutions of Orthodox Catholic Christians, leading even to the apostasy of saints such as Pope Liberius of Rome. In effect, Church history after this point becomes a repetitious cycle of some doctrinal and/or ecclesiastical dispute in which the Roman state generally

---

243 By virtue of his repentance the Serbian Orthodox venerate Pope Marcellinus.

makes the wrong decision initially, leading to untold conflict; only
to correct its previous error, but in using brute force when doing so
flames further conflagration.

To the uninitiated, it would appear that the early Church
was lost and totally absorbed by a secular institution. However,
as controversies unfold over Donatism, Arianism, and disputed
jurisdictions (again in Antioch), the Church proves itself quite
resilient to institutional, ecclesiastical change. The Church, as well
as the Roman Papacy, continued operating under the same consent-
based ecclesiastical and epistemic presumptions which existed in
previous centuries. This continuity, despite the massive changes in
the Church's overall circumstances, demonstrates the endurance of
God's people in the face of the world's changing currents. To some,
the Papacy proves to be a most important institution—a Stone of
Gibraltar. It helped maintain the Church's anchoring in the Gospel
promise given to Saint Peter centuries beforehand: that the gates of
Hell would never prevail. Yet, such a view is simplistic, if not wholly
an encomium, considering details which do not accord with this as
the following will demonstrate.

THE DONATIST SCHISM AND ITS ECCLESIASTICAL RAMIFICATIONS

Donatism was a schism similar to Novatianism in that it was
rigorist and it theoretically disallowed for lapsed clergy. As mentioned
beforehand, it was in fact an ethnic schism in response to changing
demography in North Africa, especially between urban versus rural
Christianity. Its relevance to the question of the Papacy pertains
to how the Church of Rome's role was understood. Additionally,
epistemic and ecclesiastical presumptions are brought out that are
relevant to the consensus-based understanding the early Church
operated under.

Donatism erupted after a disputed election for the Bishop of
Carthage occurred, split among ethnic lines (Latin versus Punic
Africans). Punic Africans were the backbone of Donatism. The
Donatists appealed to the Roman Synod under Pope Melchiades
(Synod of Rome, 313), where 19 bishops favored Caecilian of

Carthage (representing the Latin faction).[244] Interestingly, the Donatists then appealed to Saint Constantine despite the fact Christianity had only been a legal religion for a few months at this point. Christians immediately seemed to identify a Christian Emperor as fulfilling some sort of function as an arbitrator. Perhaps a Christian Emperor effectively baptized the civil magistrate so that it would not be a violation of the Apostle's command to *not* press lawsuits there,[245] though surely such tactics were pursued simply for practical reasons. Ironically, Constantine was probably not baptized for another two decades.[246]

Fittingly, Constantine refused to decide the issue and sent it to a wider council in Arles (314). Clergy (about 30 bishops and a few more priests) from Africa, Italy, Sicily, Sardinia, Britain and Gaul attended. The Pope's legates subscribed after Marinus of Arles, likely in respect to his episcopate and local jurisdiction.[247] Saint Augustine, writing decades later, called this a "a plenary Council of the whole world."[248] This was surely a pious exaggeration and likely a reference to Western Europe in isolation.[249] As will be shown, Augustine would later specify that Arles was not on the level of an Ecumenical Council. In any event, after Arles, the Donatists appealed again to Constantine. This was the second time the Pope

244 Augustine, *Letter 43*, Par 4.

245 1 Cor 6:4.

246 Sources in the fourth century including Eusebius of Caesarea, Saint Jerome, and Saint Ambrose note Constantine's baptism near the end of his life. Hagiographic sources, like the *Acts of Sylvester*, credit his baptism to the Pope of Rome in the 310s.

247 *Letter to [Pope] Sylvester from the Council of Arles (AD 314)*.

248 Augustine, *On Baptism, Against the Donatists*, Book 4, Par 9; cf Ibid., Book 2, Par 14.

249 The ancients would regularly exaggerate what the "world" or "universe" was in an honorific sense. Saint Paul claimed the Gospel had reached "the ends of the world" (Rom 10:18) *before* Christian missionary work occurred in Spain. Saint Columban centuries later called "Rome...the head of the churches of the world" only to specify this meant he was the "head of all the churches of all Europe." See Butler and Collorafi, *Keys Over the Christian World*, 443.

was appealed from. Constantine then decided the issue in Milan, surely not in isolation from the local church there.

The Donatists understood the process of appeals in the Church. They evidently did not ascribe final authority to the Pope of Rome. However, one may rightly point out that being schismatics, their ecclesiastical presumptions would be highly suspect. Nevertheless, the Catholic party likewise did not view the Pope of Rome as above dispute. This is evidenced by Augustine's reflection on these course of events:

> They [the Donatists] chose, therefore, as it is reported, to bring their dispute with Cæcilianus [of Carthage] before the foreign churches [in Rome]...the common outcry of all worthless litigants, though they have been defeated by the clearest light of truth—as if it might not have been said, and most justly said, to them: "Well, let us suppose that those bishops who decided the case at Rome were not good judges; **there still remained a plenary Council of the universal Church**, in which these judges themselves might be put on their defence; so that, if they were convicted of mistake, **their decisions might be reversed.**" Whether they have done this or not, let them prove: for we easily prove that it was not done, by the fact that the whole world does not communicate with them; or if it was done, they were defeated there [Arles] also, of which their state of separation from the Church is a proof.[250]

Augustine matter-of-factly observes that the Church of Rome's decisions can be appealed to a "plenary council of the universal Church." What he means specifically is an Ecumenical Council. This was not an innovative idea, as in previous centuries Rome was appealed against during the Ephesian and Rebaptism Controversies.

It is worth saying that Augustine's observation was not intended to be anti-Papal in any way. Arles itself, though a "plenary council," was viewed by Augustine as superfluous as it was given to the Donatists "as a concession to their stubbornness."[251] The original

---

250 Augustine, *Letter 43*, Par 19.
251 Ibid., Par 20.

appeal should have settled matters and the follow-up appeals, ultimately to the same source (Rome), were exercises in futility in Augustine's mind. Nevertheless, despite feeling this way, Augustine acknowledged that a legitimate appeal above the Roman Synod was possible.

In light of this, Arles was understood by Augustine as a Roman-Patriarchal council—not a literal "plenary Council of the universal Church" which can overturn such a council. Augustine did not believe that every "plenary council" was one of the universal Church. Augustine speaks of multiple plenary councils that are "often corrected by those which follow them."[252] Augustine's letters[253] as well as the canons of Carthage, use the term "plenary" for regional councils.[254]

Augustine evidently believed local councils can err, but not ecumenical ones. He classifies two kinds of plenary councils, those "embraced by the whole Church, or at least [those who] represented our brethren beyond the sea."[255] It appears councils of the "whole Church" require participation of the Eastern churches. "Brethren beyond the sea" means the rest of the Roman Patriarchate outside of Africa. While the Donatists alleged that their own "plenary councils" had an "unerring voice,"[256] Augustine countered that only councils "of the whole Church" had "the full illumination and authoritative" quality.[257]

Augustine's understanding of ecclesiastical infallibility is as follows:

> the safe course for us is, not to advance with any rashness of judgment in setting forth a view which has neither been started in any regionary Council of the Catholic Church nor established in a plenary one; but to

---

252 Augustine, *On Baptism, Against the Donatists*, Book 2, Par 4.

253 Ibid. *Letter 64*, Par 4; *Letter 215*, Par 2.

254 Council of Carthage (419) Canons 48, 77, 85, 90, 97, 98, and 127.

255 Augustine, *On Baptism, Against the Donatists*, Book 2, Par 14.

256 Augustine, *Letter 51*, Par 2; cf *On Baptism, Against the Donatists*, Book 2, Par 4; *Answer to Petilian the Donatist*, Book 1, Par 11.

257 Augustine, *On Baptism, Against the Donatists*, Book 2, Par 5.

assert, with all the confidence of a voice that cannot be gainsaid, what has been confirmed by the consent of the universal Church, under the direction of our Lord God and Saviour Jesus Christ.[258]

This was the contemporary conception of what is usually called today "ecumenicity." One can immediately gather that the definition hearkened back to Acts 15:28—consensus verified the work of the Spirit was involved.

Thus one may conclude the following: First, the early Church had a view of infallibility which was consensus-based, and this had earlier explicit precedents, such as the synodal decree of the Council of Antioch that was held to depose Paul of Samosata. Second, the decision of the Roman Church in isolation did not meet this criterion (as Augustine allowed for local plenary councils to err and be appealed from); but a Church-wide consensus did. Even if in *On Baptism, Against the Donatists* Augustine oversells the potentially ecumenical nature of the Council of Arles (314) for polemical reasons, this was not the position he was wed to. It was Churchwide consensus that was the ultimate authority.

The Council of Nicaea: The First True Ecumenical Council

The Council of Nicaea was understood in its time as an exercise in infallible, consensus-based ecclesiology. Revolving around an Egyptian Christological controversy (Arianism), it is telling that the controversy in Egypt was not settled in Rome by the Roman Emperor. It was deliberately clarified in Nicaea by the whole Church, due to the understanding that only Church-wide consensus could definitively settle a matter.

This was well-understood in its own time. The council was described by Eusebius, who was an attendee that modified his views to align with the council,[259] as follows:

---

258 Ibid., Book 7, Par 102.

259 Eusebius, *Letter to the Church of Caesarea.*

when they were all assembled, it appeared evident that the proceeding was the work of God inasmuch as men who had been most widely separated, not merely in sentiment but also personally, and by difference of country, place, and nation, were here brought together, and comprised within the walls of a single city.[260]

Consensus of the whole Church in every land is what made clear God's work. Constantine described the council in the same way:

We have received a complete blessing from Divine Providence, namely, we have been relieved from all error and been united in a common confession of one and the same faith…At the command of God, the splendor of truth has dissolved all the poisons so deadly to unity…This ruling, made by the collective judgment of three hundred bishops, cannot be other than the doctrine of God, especially where the Holy Spirit has illuminated the divine will by placing it upon the minds of so many dignified persons.[261]

Another attendee to the council, Saint Athanasius, described the council's work as similar to that of God's in the Scriptures:

Vainly then do they run about with the pretext that they have demanded Councils for the faith's sake; for divine Scripture is sufficient above all things; but if a Council be needed on the point, there are the proceedings of the Fathers, for the Nicene Bishops did not neglect this matter, but stated the doctrine so exactly, that persons reading their words honestly, cannot but be reminded by them of the religion towards Christ announced in divine Scripture.[262]

Athanasius' contemporary, Saint Basil the Great, described Nicaea identically: "the three hundred and eighteen who met together without strife [at Nicaea] did not speak without the

260 Eusebius, *Life of Constantine*, Book 3, Chap 6.

261 *Constantine to the Church of Alexandria*, Verse 1-2, 8.

262 Athanasius, *De Synodis*, Par 6.

operation of the Holy Ghost."[263] More than a century later, Saint Pope Leo the Great speaks of Nicaea as "framed by the Spirit of God and hallowed by the whole world's reverence."[264] There would be no parallel statements from anyone for centuries expressing anything remotely similar about a Pope of Rome.

Not surprisingly, no one invoked the idea that the Bishop of Rome, or even the Roman Emperor, in isolation could settle Arianism. This was despite the fact that honorary "infallibility"/"supremacy" statements were made about the Roman Emperor during this era.[265] Nevertheless, the Roman Synod was part of the Church-wide consensus. Eusebius explains that, "The prelate of the [I]mperial city [i.e. the Pope] was prevented from attending by extreme old age; but his presbyters were present, and supplied his place."[266] In conclusion, universal consent is the only explicit criterion for discerning whether a council is ecumenical and therefore the

---

263 Basil the Great, *Letter 114*.

264 Leo the Great, *Letter 14*, Chap 3.

265 Saint Constantine described himself to the Palestinian Synod as "the instrument whose services He chose, and esteemed[,] suited for the accomplishment of his will." See Eusebius, *Life of Constantine*, Book 2, Chap 28. A century later Pope Leo wrote in even more extreme terms concerning the Byzantine Emperor, also named Leo: "your clemency's most excellent faith to be in all things enlarged by the gifts of heavenly grace, and I experience by increased diligence the devotion of a priestly mind in you. For in your Majesty's communications it is beyond doubt revealed what the Holy Spirit is working through you for the good of the whole Church...I know you, venerable Prince, imbued as you are with the purest light of truth, waver in no part of the Faith, but with just and perfect judgment distinguish right from wrong, and separate what is to be embraced from what is to be rejected...I am very confident of the piety of your heart in all things, and perceive that through the Spirit of God dwelling in you, you are sufficiently instructed, nor can any error delude your faith." See Leo the Great, *Letter 162*, Parts 1-3. It should be noted this was intended as mere lofty language. Leo in the same letter instructs the Emperor what he ought to do in order to avoid error. Another contemporary, Theodoret, said of Constantine that he was "a prince deserving of all praise, whose calling, like that of the divine Apostle, was not of men, nor by man, but from heaven." See Theodoret, *Ecclesiastical History*, Book 1, Chap 1.

266 Eusebius, *Life of Constantine*, Book 3, Chap 7.

work of God Himself. Epistemic and ecclesiastical claims in later centuries merely reiterate the same idea when addressing the issue of ecumenicity.

THE SEMI-ARIAN CONTROVERSY AND THE COUNCIL OF SARDICA

Following Nicaea, Arianism was reinvented along less extreme lines. Following the death of Constantine, who appeared to politically favor certain prominent semi-Arians, his heir in the East (Constantius II) imposed a pro-Semi-Arian policy. His heir in the West (initially Constans I) favored the Nicaeans. In effect, a religious divide began with the permanent split between the Eastern (Byzantine) and Western Roman Empires that followed Constantine's death. During the sole reign of Constantius II, the Eastern Roman Emperor acquired both halves of the Empire, and unsurprisingly the Western Church went officially semi-Arian. This included even high-profile figures that would become saints. Pope Liberius under torture and others such as Saint Hosius of Cordova in Spain (himself the president at Nicaea) capitulated.

So, despite all the lofty words about Nicaea, much of the Church turned their backs on the council. They either had "buyer's remorse" or through incremental compromises and Imperial strong arming endorsed a sub-Nicene Christology. However, semi-Arianism was magnified far beyond its actual serious adherents. When Imperial persecution stopped against Nicaeans, the yes-men changed sides, and Arianism mostly disappeared within the Roman Empire. It would endure centuries longer among the Germanic tribes as it was politically expedient to be out-of-communion with the Church, which was largely "Imperial" and centered in the new Roman capital, Constantinople.

During this controversy, for the first time detailed statements are made that may legitimately be construed as teaching some sort of Papal Primacy. For example, Athanasius quotes Pope Julius[267]

---

267 Julius is wrongly identified as a saint by some, but he is commemorated in no
   Orthodox synaxarion.

and the Roman Synod (on whose behalf he explicitly wrote for)[268] responding to the semi-Arian Council of Antioch (341) as follows: "Are you ignorant that the custom has been for word to be written first to us, and then for a just decision to be passed from this place?"[269]

While one may infer that Julius is claiming the right to make a final decision, over and above a council, a detailed reading of this letter does not permit such an ecclesiastically unilateral interpretation. Rather, Julius unsurprisingly expounds a consensus-based ecclesiology, as former Roman Popes have done.

The context behind the statement is that it was common for synods to send their decisions worldwide so that their work could be assented to. This is something that was seen during earlier controversies, discussed beforehand. Irenaeus and his synod did this several times in opposition to Pope Victor and Pope Cornelius and his synod did the same during the Novatian controversy. Antioch themselves did this when deposing their Patriarch, Paul of Samosata. Imagine the shock of Julius when he had to write *first* to those assembled in Antioch (including Emperor Constantius II) about the work of their council, instead of Antioch sending him correspondence looking for his synod's consent.[270] Julius' ire over not being consulted, considering this is precisely how consensus-based ecclesiology is supposed to work, is understandable.

In response, Julius summoned Antioch to a council,[271] which those at Antioch scoffed at. They wanted their work to be final without Rome's (and the Western Empire's) consent, settling things "in house." Yet, no Church-wide council has ever been final without everyone's consent. So, while Julius' words seem innovative as they imply to some that Rome has some sort of "final say," one must take care to note that Julius never claims this. Rather, he is claiming that Rome has a right to *a* say. Julius cites Nicaea's reception as precedent:

---

268 Athanasius, *Apologia Contra Arianos*, Part 1, Par 36.

269 Ibid., Par 35.

270 Ibid., Par 21.

271 Ibid., Par 22.

The Bishops who assembled in the great Council of Nicæa agreed, not without the will of God, that the decisions of one council should be examined in another [i.e. Rome's]…if you are unwilling that such a practice should be adopted in your own case [Antioch's council], though it is of ancient standing, and has been noticed and recommended by the great Council, your refusal is not becoming.[272]

What Julius is expounding is a legitimate clarification of Rome's claims consistent with the necessity for Church-wide consensus. His citation of God's will, similar both to Acts 15:28 and earlier synodal claims such as Antioch's in the previous century, is intended to delineate that a true consensus is needed for a council's work to be superintended by God. It is perhaps for this reason that Antioch exaggerated that their own council expressed consensus, claiming "that unanimity prevailed in the Churches" due to their council.[273] If such a thing had indeed occurred (which clearly did not), then their council would have had the Spirit's implicit endorsement and would have been above question.

It is clear that the Church in both the East and West understood consensus as the deciding factor. Ironically, due to the canons of this council gaining Church-wide consent,[274] there is a certain respect in which the Council of Antioch was correct in its claims. During the Ecumenical Councils of Ephesus and Chalcedon a century later, its canons (particularly on depositions) were treated as binding.[275]

---

272 Ibid.

273 Ibid., Par 34.

274 Canon 1 of Chalcedon; Canon 2 of Trullo.

275 Specifically, Canon 5 of Antioch (341), though Apostolic Canon 74 more clearly applies in both situations. However, the Western Church did not include the Apostolic Canons above 50 in their canon law since the work of Dionysius Exiguus. Yet, the same Dionysius accepted the canons of Antioch. Later canonists such as Saint Nicodemus the Hagiorite treat both canons as little different. This is not a stretch of interpretation as the Roman Synod likely understood the procedure of deposition in Ephesus and Chalcedon as following the canonical demands of Antioch. As for Antioch's canons, they are explicitly quoted as authorities during Chalcedon. See Richard Price and Michael Gaddis, *The Acts of the Council of Chalcedon: Volume Two.* Liverpool: Liverpool University Press, 2005, 167-168; Ibid. *The Acts of the Council of*

Antioch (341) essentially pretended to be an Ecumenical Council with the authority to depose Athanasius without Alexandria's or Rome's consent. Earlier, Athanasius was deposed by a council in Tyre (335) based upon trumped up charges, the chief one being that he would impede the shipment of grain to the capital in Constantinople. Athanasius appealed directly to Saint Constantine, who refused to overturn the synod (in a replay of what occurred to the Donatists). An antipope of Alexandria was consecrated to replace him. The deposition and replacement of Athanasius apparently lacked the consent of a substantial contingent (approximately 100 bishops) of the Alexandrian Synod, which refused to recognize it in 339.[276]

Just like with Paul of Samosata, the consent of *all* the Patriarchs and their synods is necessary for the deposition of a Patriarch. What Julius and similar Papal letters were asserting was thereby completely in line with tradition—Rome's consent is necessary alongside the other patriarchates.

Appeals to Rome and Roman intransigence with semi-Arian conciliar claims during this time must be understood in this light. Appeals are part of a system where the Church worked out its problems with the goal of establishing consensus. It was understood that an appeal below an Ecumenical Council, even to Rome, does not restore someone to worldwide communion—it simply established local communion. Pope Julius of Rome wrote: "I [Julius] have written the foregoing, that you may understand that we [the Roman Synod] acted not unjustly in admitting them [Athanasius and his allies] to *our* communion."[277]

In response to Antioch (341), a true Ecumenical Council was attempted in Sardica a few years later. It failed to be one due to the semi-Arian faction leaving (and thereby not consenting to it). Canons 3-5 of this council pertain to details regarding appeals to the Pope of Rome for judgment. Requiring centuries to be accepted

Chalcedon: Volume Three, 10-11.

276 Charles Hefele, *History of the Councils of the Church: Vol.* 2. Albany, OR: Books For the Ages, 1997, 45.

277 Athanasius, *Apologia Contra Arianos*, Part 1, Par 34.

in the East,[278] these canons were understood as local in character
by every Eastern canonist on the question.[279] In the words of one
scholar discussing Rome's machinations during the ninth century,
inferring an interpatriarchal appeal (as opposed to intrapatriarchal
ones as the Orthodox canonists understand Sardica):

> *was a remarkable stretch of what Sardica did, or could have, set out
> in the mid-fourth century, long before (that is) the system of Pentarchy
> reached its mature form. Whether the canons in question could, five
> centuries later, provide any justification for Rome's interference in the
> affairs of another patriarchate was wholly a matter of interpretation.
> There was certainly no clear precedent.*[280]

Yet, the Sardican canons seem to *at least* imply interpatriarchal
appeals to Rome. The occasion behind their composition, an appeal
of Saint Athanasius and the Alexandrian Synod against Antioch
(341), would seem to inveigh against a strictly intrapatriarchal
application. On top of this, its canons were added to Rome's
collections in Nicaea's name and were understood as applying to
interpatriarchal appeals.

For example, Saint Pope Leo the Great in hearing an appeal
from Saint Flavian of Constantinople cited Sardica's "canon"
requiring an "appeal to command a special Synod in Italy…to
it should also come the bishops of all the [E]astern provinces…
[from] the whole world."[281] In other words, he cited the canon as
interpatriarchal in import, but specifying that a Pope as part of
an Ecumenical Council that is fully representative of the Church
acts as the final place of appeal. In other words, consensus-based
ecclesiology rules the day. Leo's interpretation not only excludes the

---

278 Canon 2 of Trullo.

279 See Saint Nicodemus the Hagiorite's comments on Canon 9 of Chalcedon
where he cites Zonaras as well as Byzantine law on this point.

280 The words belong to Federico Montinaro. See Richard Price and Federico
Montinaro, *The Acts of the Council of Constantinople of 869-70*. Liverpool:
Liverpool University Press, 2022, 8.

281 Leo the Great, *Letter 43*, Par 3.

understanding that the Pope of Rome can overrule consensus, but also a strictly intrapatriarchal reading.

While Sardica may be rightly understood as Rome having a final say *locally*, the canonists are correct in surmising that this would not apply to interpatriarchal appeals. If an interpatrarichal gloss was intended, it must be kept in view that Sardica occurred while Julius was Pope. It makes sense that it was canonizing Rome's consent in conciliar matters and their capacity to extend local communion.

After all, that was all he was arguing for in opposition to Antioch (341). Canon 4 of Antioch (341) disallows (binding) appeals over regional synods. The Latin West at this time likely did not disagree with this canon. As Augustine stated concerning the disputes with the Donatists, only an Ecumenical Council can actually overturn a local synod, in that case Rome's. However, the same logic surely applied to a synod anywhere such as Antioch's (as Julius was writing against) or Ephesus' a century later (the occasion Pope Leo was writing in response to above).

Understanding the semi-Arian controversy is useful because it illustrates a consistent pattern for the next few centuries of Church history. The Imperial politicization of ecclesiastical matters often coincides with a more prominent Papacy. This is because politically-motivated depositions and imposed doctrines constantly proved to be fertile grounds for interpatriarchal appeals. While these appeals did not always go to Rome (they sometimes went against the Roman Synod in fact), they often did as the Eastern patriarchates jockeyed for prominence in the Eastern Roman Empire. Rome (in the West) was by default insulated from Eastern Roman/Byzantine policy which made the success of an appeal against such a policy more likely to succeed.

The preceding reality gave Rome, whether *de facto* or *de jure*,[282] the "highest spot" in appeals below an Ecumenical Council. In any

---

282 It is not entirely clear, depending on how one interprets Canon 3 of Constantinople I and Canons 9, 17, 28 of Chalcedon whether Rome implicitly had truly the "highest" level of appeals below an Ecumenical Council. No canon explicitly says so and neither does anyone explicitly delineate this before the ninth century. Hence, the *de jure* element of Roman preeminence (or Constantinople or Alexandria being second in receiving

event, as Pope Julius' letter reveals, Rome can only extend their own communion in an appeal. It was not understood that the Roman Synod had a final, decisive say. This was reserved for an Ecumenical Council and the letters of future Popes of Rome correspond with this idea.

The Papacy certainly "rose" due to such political undercurrents. But, this rise is quite a bit "iconified" because such a rise in defense of Orthodoxy was not without its "dips." During the semi-Arian controversy, Rome's Patriarchate (meaning, the entire Western Synod) capitulated twice (in Arles and Milan between 353-355) to semi-Arianism and Athanasius' deposition. This was due to torture and intimidation exacted upon the Western bishops at the behest of the state. There were few exceptions. As referred to previously, Pope Liberius of Rome likewise capitulated for the same reason: "Liberius after he had been in banishment two years gave way, and from fear of threatened death subscribed."[283]

It would be dishonoring to the memory of several saints including Liberius to assert that any of these saints or their synods outright "taught error." They certainly did not always exercise the unyielding bravery that the situation called for. Nevertheless, the Orthodox teaching is that unless someone freely consents to a sin, its force is removed. While future Roman claims to synodal indefectibility (usually inferred in an anachronistic manner to be teaching the personal infallibility of a Pope) would need to be highly qualified due to the existence of apostate Popes (including Saints Liberius and Marcellinus) and Western capitulations, they would have made some sort of sense despite the preceding facts.

THE SECOND ECUMENICAL COUNCIL: CONSTANTINOPLE I

appeals, and so on among the patriarchates) is questionable. In any event, history clearly shows that *de facto* the Church often operated with Rome being treated below the Ecumenical Council and Constantinople's Synod in the third place. There were temporary aberrations, such as Alexandrian primacy being asserted particularly in the late fourth to the sixth centuries.

283 Athanasius, *History of the Arianism*, Book 5, Par 41.

It would be fair to say that semi-Arianism's death knell was the Council of Constantinople I, as without Imperial patronage the force behind its adherence was almost entirely diminished. While the reverberations of the controversy continued during the Roman Schism with Antioch (covered in the next section), it no longer proved to be a Church dividing issue, despite the increasing encroachments of Arian Germanic tribes.

Before putting an official end to semi-Arianism, Saint Theodosius the Great, the Eastern Roman Emperor, created a government edict that made Christianity the official Roman religion (as compared to Constantine, which only made Christianity an officially tolerated religion). Called the "Edict of Thessalonica," it stated:

> *Edict to the People Of Constantinople. It is our desire that all the various nations which are subject to our Clemency and Moderation, should continue to profess that religion which was delivered to the Romans by the divine Apostle Peter, as it has been preserved by faithful tradition, and which is now professed by the Pontiff Damasus and by Peter, Bishop of Alexandria, a man of apostolic holiness...*

The edict is useful, because it gives a window as to how the Roman Synod was understood in its day. Not looking to rock any boats or "pick sides," the edict simply equated the Popes of Rome and Alexandria as notable for preserving the faith "delivered...by the divine Apostle Peter."

While Constantinople at this point was the most important city in the Roman world, its apostolic pedigree was questionable. The transfer of Saint Timothy's relics to Constantinople, occurring a few decades beforehand, had apparently failed to bestow the Petrine authority to that city which Alexandria traditionally enjoyed through the relics of Saint Mark.[284] The translation of Saint Andrew's relics from Patras to Constantinople at around the same time would prove to be more important, as Andrew's traditional evangelism in the

---

284 These relics were translated centuries later to Italy (allegedly) by Venetian sailors at some point in the ninth century according to the earliest written tradition, the *Translatio*. See Edward Muir, *Civic Ritual in Renaissance Venice*. Princeton, NJ: Princeton University Press, 1981, 80-84.

region bestowed a more legitimate Apostolic pedigree upon the specific city.[285]

Nevertheless, the traditional priority ascribed to Rome and Alexandria exclusively was questionable as Alexandria was not directly connected to Peter. Other patriarchates had more concrete Petrine claims than Alexandria. Peter likely sent delegations to Antioch in Acts 11:22-27 and actually visited Antioch according to Gal 2:11. Further, Jerusalem once housed not only the Bishop of the Apostles (Peter) himself, but was where the Lord Himself resurrected! Traditional claims to authority and jurisdiction aside, the reality one can infer from Theodosius' edict is that honorifics were bestowed upon cities which had political prominence and importance. Obviously, Rome and Alexandria were more important that Antioch, Ephesus, or Jerusalem.

For this reason, the Council of Constantinople I is refreshing. Canon 3 of the council essentially "cut to the chase" and simply delineated "honorary" jurisdiction according to the civil model:

> Let the Bishop of Constantinople, however, have the priorities of honor after the Bishop of Rome, because of its being New Rome.

What exactly this "honorary" jurisdiction entailed is considerably more muted than modern imagination allows. In short, it bestowed two important things. First, the bishop of Constantinople would be chaired before the other Patriarchs in council and would give a judgment before them (with the exception of the Roman Patriarch). This had occurred in the Council of Constantinople (394),[286] and Chalcedon where a Roman legate cited Canon 3 of

---

285 *Acts of Andrew*, v. 8-9. Cf Eusebius, *Church History*, Book 3, Par 1.

286 During the Council of Constantinople (394) Saint Nectarius of Constantinople spoke before Theophilus of Alexandria and Saint Flavian of Antioch, though the minutes interestingly contain the detail that Theophilus "decreed" in accordance with his *own* judgment. This is perhaps a face-saving move for Alexandria which may have been inconsistent with their acceptance of Canon 3 of Constantinople I.

Constantinople I during its first session in criticism of improper seating arrangements.[287]

Second, it was implied that the canon gave Constantinople jurisdiction over what was once Ephesian territory, officially subjugating Ephesus, Caesarea, and all of Asia Minor to Constantinopolitan jurisdiction. This can be gleaned from the explicit assertion the Council of Chalcedon makes in its 28th Canon:

> *Following in all things the decrees of the holy fathers and acknowledging the canon just read of the 150 most God-beloved bishops who assembled under the then emperor Theodosius the Great of pious memory in [I]mperial Constantinople New Rome, we too define and decree the same regarding the privileges of the most holy church of the same Constantinople New Rome. The Fathers appropriately accorded privileges to the see of Senior Rome because it was the [I]mperial city and, moved by the same intent, the 150 most God-beloved bishops assigned equal privileges to the most holy see of New Rome, rightly judging that the city which is honoured with the [I]mperial government and the [S]enate and enjoys equal privileges with [I]mperial Senior Rome should be exalted like her in ecclesiastical affairs as well, being second after her,* **with the consequence** *that the [M]etropolitans alone of the Pontic, Asian and Thracian dioceses, and also the bishops from the aforesaid dioceses in barbarian lands, are to be consecrated by the aforesaid most holy see of the most holy church at Constantinople.*[288]

In Chalcedon's letter to Pope Leo, they referred to the ordaining of Metropolitans in the Pontic, Asian and Thracian dioceses by the church of Constantinople as "[t]he long prevailing custom." This implied that Canon 28 was nothing new, but merely making more explicit what Canon 3 of Constantinople I had already delineated.[289] It made sense if the Roman capital had a jurisdiction following the civil model, that the New Rome would likewise (implicitly undoing the "traditional" local primacy of Ephesus/Caesarea). It is not a

---

287 Price and Gaddis, *The Acts of the Council of Chalcedon: Volume One*, 144.

288 Ibid., *Volume Three*, 75-76.

289 Leo the Great, *Letter 98*, Par 4.

coincidence that Chalcedon's canon was on the heels of the Council of Ephesus II where both Ephesus and Alexandria had picked the losing geopolitical side. Details of this will be covered in the next chapter.

Back to Constantinople I specifically, Constantinople's jurisdiction at this time was modified by the historical prerogatives of Ephesus and Caesarea, preserved intact along with other Eastern jurisdictions in Canon 2. The same canon prevented "bishops" from "go[ing] beyond their dioceses to churches lying outside of their bounds" conducting "ordination[s] or any other ecclesiastical ministrations, unless they be invited." Even though Constantinople would not have much trouble in manipulating ecclesiastical matters occurring in their backyard, on paper the council preserved everyone's prerogatives inviolate. All things told, its canons were not particularly controversial in its day.

Alexandria appeared to implicitly accept the canons,[290] and a preponderance of evidence suggests the Roman Synod did as well. For one, as stated previously, a Roman legate (Paschasinus) cited Canon 3 during Chalcedon, implying his synod accepted it. Second, another Roman legate (Lucentius) in criticizing Canon 28 of Chalcedon for "not [being] contained in the conciliar canons" noted in passing that it was wrongly added after "the definitions [canons] of the 318 [Nicaea I] and to those of the 150 [Constantinople I]."[291] Third, Eusebius of Dorlyeum, a pro-Roman partisan during

---

290 N. 286.

291 This is found in the Greek minutes. See Price and Gaddis, *The Acts of the Council of Chalcedon: Volume Three*, 84. The Latin rendering disputes this, stating that the canons of "the 150…are not among the conciliar canons." In determining what is the more likely rendering, internal consistency favors the Greek. Later in the same session, the canons of Constantinople I are "read from the same book" of canons. (Ibid., 86) Constantinople I's canons were in the book of canon law used by the council. Hence, the statement from the Roman legate (as rendered in the Greek) would have been common knowledge to all present. It is possible that one may infer that due to the Roman legates only reading Canon 6 from Nicaea I and not continuing to read from their book of canon law, that this implies the canons of Constantinople I's absence from the said book. However, such an inference is unnecessary. Following the minutes of the council itself, it is more likely

Chalcedon, asserted that he had personal acquaintance with Pope Leo and that the latter "accepted" Canon 3.[292] Additionally, Latin canon law, including even the earliest fifth-century Prisca collection, always included Canons 1-4 of the aforementioned council.[293]

There are additional evidences that are less explicit, but relevant to the question at hand. For example, the Constantinopolitan Creed was paraphrased in the July 22nd minutes of the Council of Ephesus.[294] The Roman Synod regularly received correspondence from Constantinople with the Creed cited, so they surely were aware that its Creed was deemed an authority.[295] This is a bizarre detail unless Constantinople expected Rome to recognize what they were citing was authoritative. Additionally, the *Tome of Leo* quotes

---

those favoring Canon 28 scoffed at the falsified canon of Nicaea I read by the Roman legates and so not only was the correct rendering of this canon read, Lucentius was confuted by continuing to read the canons of Constantinople I thereby disproving his claim Canon 28 had no canonical precedent.

292 Ibid., 89.

293 Hefele, *History of the Councils of the Church: Vol.* 2, 281. Hefele notes that "in the Prisca the canons of Constantinople are only placed after those of the fourth General Council" implying "that they were not contained at all in the oldest Greek collections of canons, and were inserted after the Council of Chalcedon." A later canonical revision due to Canon 1 of Chalcedon is unlikely, as one would expect that all seven canons of Constantinople I would have been included as a result. Because only the first four canons were accepted in the West, this implies an early acceptance dated approximately to 382 before additional Constantinopolitan canons were added to Constantinople I's traditional list. Additionally, the amount of other evidence pointing to their early acceptance inveighs against Hefele's theory. More likely, the placement of Constantinople I's canons may simply be because of post-Chalcedonian controversy. Due to this controversy, they were treated as an authoritative local council like other eastern councils, and so were numbered after the Ecumenical Councils. See *The Acts of the Council of Chalcedon: Volume Three*, 94. The fact they were accepted in any event shows their authority was not in doubt in the Latin West, despite Roman interpatriarchal posturing to the contrary.

294 Richard Price and Thomas Graumann, *The Council of Ephesus of 431.* Liverpool, Liverpool University Press, 2020, 460.

295 See the *Protest Concerning Nestorius* and *Nestorius' Second Letter to Celestine* in Ibid., 96, 101.

a Creed held by "common and not discordant confession which is professed by the whole multitude of the faithful"[296] which matches either the Constantinopolitan Creed or a variant of the Apostles' Creed.

In any event, what cannot be doubted is that Saint Ascholius of Thessalonica, designated as the Papal Legate to Constantinople I,[297] had accepted the council. While Saint Ambrose of Milan claimed that the West lacked sufficient participation through just "A[s]cholius, a single Bishop,"[298] traditional authorities as far away as Egypt claimed that Pope Damasus approved of the council through "legates."[299]

The whole debate over Constantinople I was not over Canon 3. Rather, tensions were high over disputed Patriarchal elections. The acceptance of the Antiochene Synod's consecration of Saint Flavian and the Constantinopolitan Synod's election of Saint Nectarius had occurred without the West's consent. The reason why this was so controversial will be covered in the next section, but in short the West at this juncture had sided with two non-canonical bishops, Paulinus of Antioch and Maximus the Cynic (in Constantinople).

Ambrose, on behalf of the West, demanded the right "according to the customs of our predecessors" for those at Constantinople I "to have sought the decision [on Flavian] of the Churches of Rome, of Italy, and of all the West."[300] He continued, "We do not claim any special privilege of examining such matters, but we ought to have had a share in a united decision." The Ecumenical Council itself, in its synodal letter, felt that the imposition of non-canonical bishops upon them was tyrannical and responded:

> *you have shown your brotherly love for us by convoking a synod in Rome, in accordance with God's will, and inviting us to it, by means of*

---

296 Price and Gaddis, *The Acts of the Council of Chalcedon: Volume Two*, 15.

297 Butler and Collorafi, *Keys Over the Christian World*, 73.

298 Ambrose, *Letter 13*, Par 7.

299 This is claimed in the Coptic Synaxarion, quoted in Butler and Collorafi, *Keys Over the Christian World*, 74.

300 Ambrose, *Letter 13*, Par 4.

a letter from your most God-beloved [Western] emperor, as if we were
limbs of your very own…you should not now reign in isolation from
us, given the complete agreement of the emperors in matters of religion.
Rather, according to the word of the [A]postle, we should reign along
with you.[301]

In short, Constantinople I was received by the whole Church, making it ecumenical. Letters of contemporaries, like Ambrose, show that the criterium for ecumenicity is not a "special privilege" of a Western synod like Rome's to decree a council as ecumenical, but rather that all the Church must consent to it. In fact, the debate over the council was over consensus. According to the so-called "letter of the law," the West technically was in the right for demanding that their consent to Patriarchal elections occur. After all, the replacement of two Patriarchs being presented as a *fait accompli* was no trivial matter.

However, the East according to the "spirit of the law" was under no constraint to be in perpetual limbo over its Patriarchs due to the West favoring what were in fact illegitimate and unsavory candidates. The fact that the Church had forgotten about this debate after the Roman Schism with Antioch and fully received the council's Creed and canons demonstrates that consensus was eventually reached. The "spirit of the law" won out.

THE ROMAN SCHISM WITH ANTIOCH (OTHERWISE KNOWN AS THE "MELETIAN SCHISM")

Popularly, the schism between the churches of Rome and Antioch stretching from the 360s to approximately 400 AD is called the "Meletian Schism." The moniker is not a good one for several reasons. First, there were multiple bishops of Rome (Liberius, Damasus, Siricius, and Athanasius I) and Antioch (Meletius and Flavian) that were not in communion. Second, the schism was initiated by Liberius and after it was healed temporarily, it was re-initiated by Damasus. Third, the term "Meletian Schism" implies

---

301 The synodal letter is usually dated to 382.

that Antioch was the guilty party when in fact it was the Roman Synod who ultimately repented. For the sake of historical accuracy, this schism will be rightly called "the Roman Schism."

For the purposes of this history, not many details concerning the fomenting of the schism are necessary. Meletius was a pro-Nicene bishop who was cast as a semi-Arian. In opposition, a rival semi-Arian bishop and an uncanonically ordained Nicene Bishop (Paulinus) competed with him. The Roman Synod recognized Paulinus of Antioch. The synods surrounding Constantinople, all of Asia Minor, and Antioch favored Meletius.

Lucifer of Cagliari in Sardinia had effectively started the schism by single-handedly ordaining Paulinus (a canonical violation) when he was in exile in 361-362.[302] The Roman Synod, in support of their own, recognized this improper ordination, initiating the schism. Paulinus' foreign support netted him no patriarchal legitimacy. The historian Socrates records that, "Paulinus only retained a small church within the city, from which Euzoïus [the Arian bishop] had not ejected him, on account of his personal respect for him."[303] Paulinus' claim was a joke—his "jurisdiction" consisted of one small church. He did not have a synod.

This explains the disbelief of Saint Jerome when in 377 he visited the city. He was beside himself that his bishop (Pope Damasus) could possibly recognize Paulinus:

> *As I follow no leader save Christ, so I communicate with none but your blessedness, that is with the chair of Peter. [Honorifics follow]...I cannot, owing to the great distance between us, always ask of your sanctity the holy thing of the Lord. Consequently I here follow the Egyptian confessors who share your faith, and anchor my frail craft under the shadow of their great argosies. I know nothing of Vitalis; I reject Meletius; I have nothing to do with Paulinus. He that gathers not with you scatters; he that is not of Christ is of Antichrist.*[304]

---

302 Socrates, *Ecclesiastical History*, Book 3, Chap 6.

303 Ibid, Chap 9.

304 Jerome, *Letter 15*, Par 2.

Contextually, Jerome pays homage to the Pope, as he came from Rome and belonged to their jurisdiction. He acknowledges the breach in communion with the Egyptians and Rome with Antioch. However, he questions whether this is right by not holding communion with Paulinus. Paulinus was in communion with Rome for *15 years* at this point. Jerome seems to have acquired his rejection of Paulinus from the Egyptians, who apparently at this juncture did not recognize him.

While the preceding passage is often misinterpreted as an expression of fealty to Damasus, its intended purpose is transparently the exact opposite. Jerome and the Egyptians are obviously opposing Rome's Patriarch of Antioch. Jerome, no stranger to Papal politics as he himself desired Papal consecration, is opposing Damasus in the nicest possible way. Jerome did not relent in this, writing a year later (378) to the same effect:

> *Meletius, Vitalis, and Paulinus all profess to cleave to you, and I could believe the assertion if it were made by one of them only...Only tell me by letter with whom I am to communicate in Syria.*[305]

This reveals a couple of things. First, Rome's schism was unilateral. Meletius apparently commemorated Damasus. Second, Jerome appears to be "political." He is akin to a local commander asking for "clarification" from headquarters for a field decision as a way of delaying putting into action something he does not agree with. This is not surprising given what Jerome believed concerning the episcopate, writing elsewhere, "If you ask for authority, the world outweighs its capital [Rome]."[306] The Roman Synod did not have the final say in his mind.

Perhaps due to this pressure, Damasus' unconditional support for Paulinus began to waver. One year later (379), Damasus uncoincidentally struck a deal with Meletius. The contents of the deal reveal that the former still supported Paulinus but had lost the "political capital" to do so forcefully. A *Tome of Damasus* was sent

---

305 Ibid., *Letter 16*, Par 2.
306 Ibid., *Letter 146*, Par 1.

to Antioch and it was sent back without acceptance of its ninth ban/canon which asserted that Meletius' consecration in exile was non-canonical. This indicates that Papal documents were subject to revision for diplomatic reasons and conditional acceptance was allowed. In any event, this deal resulted in re-established communion between not only Rome and Antioch, but even Paulinus and Meletius.[307]

Signs of unilateral Roman decision-making are wholly absent. Interestingly, the deal exclusively endorses a temporarily parallel bishopric in Antioch, designed to come to an end when either Paulinus or Meletius died—the survivor becoming the sole Patriarch. This did not please "the Luciferians," Paulinus' strongest partisans, who went into schism.[308] During the Council of Constantinople I, Meletius died. The Antiochene Synod broke the deal and consecrated Saint Flavian to replace Meletius—despite him previously taking an oath to abide by it.[309] In the estimation of Theodoret, due to these events "a lasting hostility arose among the Romans and the Egyptians against the East, and the ill feeling was not even destroyed on the death of Paulinus."[310] The schism recommenced.

The schism was incomplete, however. The Alexandrian Synod maintained union with Constantinople (and initially Antioch)[311] and

307 Lester Field Jr., *On the Communion of Damasus and Meletius: Fourth-century Synodal Formulae in the Codex Veronensis LX*. Toronto: Pontifical Institute of Mediaeval Studies, 2004, 171-172.

308 Socrates, *Ecclesiastical History*, Book 5, Chap 5. It should be noted the actual "Luciferians" were not partisans of Paulinus of Antioch, but Socrates used the term as a moniker for their faction. See Colin Whiting, *Christian Communities in Late Antiquity: Luciferians and the Construction of Heresy*. Riverside, CA: University of California, Riverside (PhD dissertation), 2015, 101-103.

309 Ibid.

310 Theodoret, *Church History*, Book 5, Chap 23.

311 One month after the Council of Constantinople I, a Roman law records that communion was established between Constantinople, Alexandria, and Antioch. See Theodosius Code (16.1.3): "It will be established that the bishops of the Church of Constantinople, as well as Timothy, bishop of Alexandria in Egypt, are united in communion with them. They are also to be united in

Rome was in union with Alexandria. Similar to modern Orthodox schisms, the tangential communion established through such a scheme made circumstances very different than today's Roman Catholic and Oriental Orthodox schisms. Even if Alexandria had subsequently broken communion with Antioch after Constantinople I as Theodoret's words imply, by 394 Egypt had re-entered communion with Antioch as evidenced by the conciliar decree of Constantinople (394) where Flavian takes part alongside Theophilus of Alexandria and Nectarius of Constantinople.

Yet, even up until Pope Anastasius I (consecrated in 399), Rome refused to hold communion with Flavian. They even lobbied the Emperor to summon Flavian to trial in Rome (presumably for his non-canonical consecration).[312] Flavian viewed such a trial as beneath him, responding that he would agree to trial if he was accused of heresy, "[b]ut if they are contending about see and primacy...I will give way and resign my bishopric."[313] According to Theodoret, "The Emperor admired his manliness and wisdom, and bade him go home again, and tend the church committed to his care."[314]

Flavian essentially said that *if* the trial is merely about Rome picking king maker, he considers it below his dignity to go. The

the eastern parts with Pelagius, bishop of Laodicea, and Diodorus, bishop of Tarsus; in Asia, with Amphilochius, bishop of Iconium, and the excellent bishop of Antioch; in the Pontic diocese, with Helladius, bishop of Caesarea, and Otreius, bishop of Melitene, and Gregory, bishop of Nyssa, Terentius, bishop of Scythia, and Marmarius, bishop of Marcianopolis." In Latin: *quos constabit communioni nectari episcopi Constantinopolitanae ecclesiae nec non Timothei intra Aegyptum Alexandrinae urbis episcopi esse sociatos; quos etiam in Orientis partibus Pelagio episcopo Laodicensi et Diodoro episcopo Tarsensi: in Asia nec non proconsulari adque Asiana dioecesi Amphilochio episcopo Iconiensi et optimo episcopo Antiocheno: in pontica dioecesi Helladio episcopo Caesariensi et Otreio Meliteno et Gregorio episcopo Nysseno, Terennio episcopo Scythiae, Marmario episcopo Marcianopolitano communicare constiterit.* See "TITULI EX CORPORE CODICI THEODOSIANI," *Ancient Rome,* https://web.archive.org/web/20120127105031/http://ancientrome.ru/ius/library/ codex/theod/liber16.htm#1

312 Theodoret, *Church History*, Book 5, Chap 23.

313 Ibid.

314 Ibid.

invocation of "primacy" is an interesting detail. It appears that Flavian's rejection of Roman primacy was the basis for the Emperor to drop charges against him. This may imply that Rome asserted "primacy" and this was rejected. It may also be an exaggeration on Flavian's part designed to make Rome's request sound tyrannical and they had, in fact, not explicitly cited "primacy." The mere mention of primacy could have been seen as an embarrassing slander.

Most likely, Rome had laid claim to some kind of honorary "primacy." Honorifics such as "primacy" and equivalent rhetoric were applied commonly at this time. Saint Basil the Great earlier in the schism spoke of Meletius as "in authority over the Churches of the Lord" and asserts that the latter "stands at the head, so to say, of the whole body of the Church, and all else are mere disjointed members."[315] He asked rhetorically "what part is more vital to the Churches throughout the world than Antioch?"[316] Saint Gregory Nazianzus, another contemporary, wrote of Basil's city (Caesarea)[317] as "the Mother of almost all the Churches" and "worthy of the Primacy," both likely references to the region of Asia Minor.[318] In short, Flavian might have felt that Rome's summoning of himself was an affront to him as a Patriarch. After all, he could not be judged by an equal, but only an Ecumenical Council (which had already approved of him).

---

315 Basil the Great, *Letter 67*. The letter was addressed to Athanasius of Alexandria.

316 Basil the Great, *Letter 66*. The letter was likewise addressed to Athanasius of Alexandria.

317 Caesarea apparently vied with Ephesus for primacy in Asia Minor. Saint Firmilian of Caesarea, who likewise represented the synod in Asia Minor as Basil the Great did, during several third-century controversies spoke on behalf of the synod—implying Caesarea's regional primacy. Likely, Asia Minor was *de facto* split between east and west, Caesarea exercising primacy only over the eastern half. *De jure*, the *Notitiae Episcopatuum* (a document specifying the hierarchy of Metropolitans within Constantinople's jurisdiction) lists Caesarea as the first see and Ephesus as the second one.

318 Gregory Nazianzus, *Letters*, Section II, Epistle 41.

Taking Flavian's side, the Emperor then had a meeting with the Roman Synod. Theodoret records it went as follows:

> *The emperor…[said] he himself was Flavianus and had become his protector. The bishops rejoined that it was impossible for them to dispute with the emperor. He then exhorted them in future to join the churches in concord…the [E]astern churches accepted Flavianus as their bishop… all Illyricum recognised his authority.[319]*

It should be noted that Illyricum was under Roman Patriarchal jurisdiction. Hence, Rome's excommunications were so localized, they were not even deemed definitive within their own patriarchate. This is not surprising if one presumes upon Apostolic Canon 34 being in full force, as inferior bishops have the right to not consent to what the Metropolitan (or here, Patriarch) is doing (presuming it is wrong). Rome subsequently cowed to the Emperor's "counsels" and so "the Western bishops promised to bring their hostility to a close."[320] In other words, the Pope and the local Roman Synod relented and entered into communion with Flavian. Therein ended the Roman Schism.

SYNOPSIS OF THE PAPACY IN THE FOURTH CENTURY

The Papacy in the fourth century was approaching its historical zenith in defense of Orthodoxy against semi-Arian heresy. The Nestorian and Monophysite controversies in the next century would firmly establish Rome's reputation as a Christian stalwart, something which only added to its honorary authority as the traditional church of Saints Peter and Paul. Yet, details reveal that such an iconic gloss can only be taken so far. In the past, it was acknowledged that the Roman Synod can err and be appealed from. In fact, two Popes apostatized within a few decades during this century. Rome fomented a schism with Antioch which after decades resulted in the former eating humble pie. Rome, when pushing its prerogatives,

---

319 Theodoret, *Church History*, Book 5, Chap 23.
320 Ibid.

was hardly lording itself over the Church—they were struggling to simply have a place at the table.

However, this "place at the table" was something that earlier precedent guaranteed. Despite the locus of authority shifting to Constantinople, the canons preserved Rome's rights inviolate. Consensus-based ecclesiology would prove to be a mitigating factor against the Eastern Roman/Byzantine Empire, centered in Constantinople, becoming the sole mediator of all things Christian. In the next century, this *modus operandi* merely continued. This indicates that the ecclesiology of the first-century Church continued to be preserved intact.

St. Cyril of Alexandria

CHAPTER 5

The Fifth Century of the Papacy

The fifth century proves to be the zenith of Rome's prominence in the early Church. The Church was cohered as the Roman Empire, East and West, remained intact. Further, Rome would not be under foreign domination for most of this century, which made currying their favor relevant in the midst of doctrinal disputes that often had political intrigue mixed in. In other words, East versus West politics were always at work. During this century, honorary language in interpatriarchal disputes is applied to Rome, a true rhetorical advance. If read divorced from events and historical context, this can be confused with a much more muscular Papacy than had in fact existed. Rather, what comes out most clearly and consistently is the expounding of an explicit ecclesiology, and epistemology, of consensus. Nevertheless, when the Roman Empire fragments and the West is lost, the first seeds of ecclesiastical change start appearing in the West—even if no one, including the Popes, appreciated it at the time.

THE COUNCILS OF CARTHAGE (419, 424) AND INTRAPATRIARCHAL APPEALS

In the previous chapter, not only was Donatism discussed, but also the Council of Sardica. It is mysterious why Sardica was not universally understood as deciding the issue of precisely how intrapatriarchal appeals were to be understood. As the Donatist Controversy unfolded, it became apparent that not only had the churches in North Africa failed to receive Sardica (or at least conveniently forgot), the way they viewed intrapatriarchal relations more strictly followed the lines delineated in Apostolic Canon 34. That is, inferiors can refuse to consent to superiors, nullifying their decisions and policies.

The West's intrapatriarchal ecclesiology can be discerned by studying the era's intrapatriarchal appeals. Donatism and then Pelagianism created many appeals to Rome, Milan, and the Roman Emperor—none of which were perceived as the sole deciding authority on disputed questions in the West.[321] Usually, the appeal was made to Rome in order to specifically get access to the Emperor in a foreign city, as the canons delineated that the appeals be forwarded to him. This is disconcerting considering the reality that the traditional authority of Rome should have required that ecclesiastical appeals be decided by their own synod. As usual, practical and overtly political considerations won out. The Emperor was more likely to "get things done."

The way intrapatriarchal appeals were regulated can be surmised from the canons produced during this era. The African Synod sought tough regulations giving them local control over appeals. Carthage (393) in Canon 27 forbade "bishops...to travel beyond the sea, unless they have consulted the bishop of the first see of their respective province" and received his permission.[322]

---

321 See Carthage (419) Canons 94 and 106 which speak of letters that are sent to Rome that then go to "court," meaning the Emperor. Canon 104 dictates the Emperor would forward cases to episcopal judges.

322 Geoffrey Dunn, "The Appeal of Apiarius to the Transmarine Church of Rome," *Journal of the Australian Early Medieval Association*, 8, 2012, 11-12. See

Carthage (419) in Canon 125 (Latin numbering) disallowed foreign appeals for local clergy:

> *let them not carry the appeal except to African councils or to the primates of their provinces. But whoever shall think of carrying an appeal across seas he shall be admitted to communion by no one in Africa.*[323]

During the Pelagian Controversy, Celestius (a Pelagan) was condemned in Carthage. He appealed to Rome before escaping to the East. Pelagius likewise escaped to the East, where in Jerusalem it was decided that this was a matter pertaining to another patriarchate. The case was referred back to Rome.[324] In 416, a Carthaginian council condemned Pelagianism and likewise referred to Rome for intrapatriarchal consensus. They wrote to Pope Innocent "that the authority of the Apostolic See should also be added to the statutes of our lowliness."[325]

Pope Innocent responded approvingly that he ought to be referred to for his "judgment," because "whatever be done, even in distant provinces, not be concluded until it be brought to the knowledge of this see."[326] The "distant provinces" here are contextually those in the West's own patriarchate. This is the language of consensus, similar to previous Papal letters, such as Julius I's letter to the Council of Antioch (341). By 417, in response to having received appeals from Africa, Rome had held two synods condemning Pelagianism. This created a precedent for decisively rejecting this heresy in the West.[327]

Shockingly, Pope Zosimus reneged on this in 418. Slyly, the African bishops assembled in Carthage rejected Zosimus on the grounds that "the sentence against Pelagius and Coelestius by the

---

n. 10 therein for the Latin being quoted.

323 Cf Canon 19 of Council of Carthage (419), which dictates that annual synods would be held to deal with local issues.

324 Butler and Collorafi, *Keys Over the Christian World*, 142.

325 Ibid.

326 Ibid., 144.

327 See Ibid., 151 and Augustine's *Sermon 131*.

venerable Pope Innocent… remain."[328] Zosimus responded that "our authority is such that nobody may review our sentence."[329] Intrapatriarchal appeals cannot be above the Patriarch, so the Africans appealed to Rome's previous judgment as a way of nullifying Zosimus' current judgment, thereby avoiding the appellate process. Zosimus considered this avoidance a "review," and rejected the permissibility of it. One should note that neither of these positions disallows for interpatriarchal appeals, which Augustine explicitly notes in *Letter 43* are in fact able to overturn Rome.

In any event, African pressure evidently led both the "[E]astern and [W]estern" Roman Emperors to force Zosimus to re-visit the issue. He condemned Pelagius in letters written to the whole Church.[330] One may infer that this demonstrates that Zosimus was censured globally and a global recantation was necessary. Others may infer that this shows the primacy of the Pope, but both such readings of the evidence presume upon polemical concerns foreign to the time. Pelagianism had made waves in the Jerusalem Patriarchate. The Pelagians had for a short while one prominent "defender" *somewhere*. The intent was to make it clear that this was not the case, thereby settling the issue. The Pelagians later appealed from Rome to Constantinople when the latter was under Patriarch Nestorius, only to be condemned by the Council of Ephesus along with him.

During this time of friction over Pelagianism, Zosimus had accepted an appeal from an otherwise unknown priest: Apiarius. This African priest was canonically deposed, but was *de facto* entered into Roman communion. In reality, Zosimus gave his decision to overturn Apiarius' deposition to legates with the command to hold a council in Africa on the issue which would canonically restore Apiarius. Zosimus threatened local Roman excommunication if those in Africa did not comply with his intentions to reinstate Apiarius and excommunicate Boniface, Apiarius' former bishop. This convoluted way of restoring Apiarius instead of just decreeing

328 Ibid., 148.

329 Ibid., 151.

330 Ibid. See also Edward Denny, *Papalism*. Christian Resources, 2013, 247.

it from the onset betrays the canonical irregularity of what Zosimus was trying to accomplish. Deposing a local priest is something a local, regional synod can do. Overturning the decision of the bishops in such a synod was not something Zosimus thought was possible—even though he was *the* Pope of Rome. In effect, he hoped to have the local, regional synod held again so they would decide in his favor.

While this idea seems strange today, as the Pope or a Patriarch seem like "more" of a bishop than another bishop, canonically and traditionally this is not the case. In the words of Saint Jerome, who was alive at the time of the dispute over Apiarius:

> *Wherever there is a bishop, whether it be at Rome or at Engubium, whether it be at Constantinople or at Rhegium, whether it be at Alexandria or at Zoan, his dignity is one and his priesthood is one. Neither the command of wealth nor the lowliness of poverty makes him more a bishop or less a bishop. All alike are successors of the [A]postles.*[331]

The motivation for Rome to take such an interest in some far away local priest is hard to explain. One scholar speculates that it was Zosimus' revenge for being overturned on Pelagius,[332] but perhaps he simply had family connections in Rome or something of the sort. One must also consider that it was intentional Roman pushback against earlier Carthaginian canons that were abrogating the Pope's right to hear appeals within the patriarchate. Whatever the motivation, the Roman Synod needed the African Synod to comply with their wishes for their machinations to have any force. This is why Roman excommunication, essentially the "nuclear option," was threatened. Rome had no other means to try to get their way.

Interestingly, as canonical precedent for their actions, the Roman legates cited "Nicene" canons concerning regulations pertaining to appeals made to Rome. The African Synod, assembled

---

331 Jerome, *Letter 146*, Par 1.

332 Bernard Green, *The Soteriology of Leo the Great*. Oxford: Oxford University Press, 2008, 20.

at the Council of Carthage (419), appealed to Alexandria, Antioch, and Constantinople on this question. They had no record of such "Nicene" canons. It is now known in retrospect that Rome added Sardican canons to their Nicene collection. The Africans, not knowing this, asked Rome to present proof of the Nicene canons from their records. Faustinus, the Roman legate, tried assuaging the concerns of the Africans in a condescending manner:

> *Let not your holiness do dishonour to the Roman Church…by saying the canons are doubtful…it suffices that the most blessed bishop of the city of Rome should make enquiry just as your holiness proposes doing on your part, that there may not seem to have arisen any contention between the Churches.*[333]

Despite the air of superiority, what is actually stated demonstrates that the African appeal was legitimate. Additionally, the reference to avoiding "contention" demonstrates that Rome paid homage to the ecclesiology of consensus.

"Aurelius, Valentine of the primatial See of Numidia,[334] and others present with…the number of 217 [bishops] from the whole council in Africa," as well as the Roman legates, wrote Carthage's (419) synodal decree.[335] It was addressed to Pope Boniface (Zosimus had died). They cited their synod's "mutual consent" and asserted that Carthage's censuring of Apiarius should have been final ("this case should be thus closed"). However, Apiarius' appeal to Rome (as well as other appeals) would be considered open *temporarily* until the matter of the "Nicene" canon was settled.[336] However, this was

---

333 Faustinus is quoted in the preface to the canons of the Council of Carthage (419).

334 The term "primatial" as an adjective was used as an honorific for other cities such as Rome, but this term lacked exclusive connotations.

335 Council of Carthage (419), Canon 134.

336 As quoted in Council of Carthage's (419) Canon 134: "it is allowed to bishops to appeal to Rome and that the causes of clerics should be settled by the bishops of their own provinces…we were willing to observe these provisions for a little while without any injury to him, until the search for the statutes of the Council of Nicaea had been finished…we have read very

itself presented as a condescension on Africa's part as apart from the Sardican canon being found in:

> *the most accurate copies of the Nicene Council…in no way could we be compelled either to endure such treatment as we are unwilling to mention or could suffer what is unbearable.*[337]

In other words, Africa gave Rome the benefit of the doubt pending hearing back from the Eastern patriarchates. They would not stand for such intrapatriarchal prerogatives for a second longer than they had to.

This statement is jarring given the tradition of both intrapatriarchal *and* interpatriarchal appeals to Rome up to this point. However, the fact that Africa demanded canonical precedent perhaps implied that such appeals, though traditional, were ultimately non-binding. Apart from an *ecumenical* canon, Africa (even within the same patriarchate) was not obligated to recognize Roman decisions on their clergy. Rome, for their part, could only enter someone into their own local communion at the risk of provoking their own excommunication. At this juncture, Africa had not received Sardica (allegedly) and certainly did not treat Papal decretals as equal to synodal decisions.

"Canon 138" of the council, actually written by a follow-up council in 424 to Pope Saint Celestine, is even more harshly worded. The case surrounding Apiarius was re-opened and Celestine personally entered into communion with him. Unlike Zosimus, who

---

many copies, yet never have we read in the Latin copies that there were any such decrees as are contained in the commonitory before mentioned. So too, because we can find them in no Greek text here, we have desired that there should be brought to us from the Eastern [c]hurches copies of the decrees, for it is said that there correct copies of the decrees are to be found. For which end we beg your reverence, that you would deign yourself also to write to the pontiffs of these parts, that is of the churches of Antioch, Alexandria, and Constantinople, and to any others also if it shall please your holiness, that thence there may come to us the same canons decreed by the Fathers in the city of Nice, and thus you would confer by the help of the Lord this most great benefit upon all the churches of the West."

337 Ibid.

had referred the matter back to a Carthaginian council, Celestine acted unilaterally. This sent the African bishops into a frenzy:

> *we earnestly conjure you [Pope Celestine], that for the future you do not readily admit to a hearing persons coming hence, nor choose to receive to your communion those who have been excommunicated by us…whosoever thinks himself wronged by any judgment may appeal to the council of his [p]rovince, or even to a General Council unless it be imagined that God can inspire a single individual [i.e. the Pope] with justice, and refuse it to an innumerable multitude of bishops (sacerdotum) assembled in council. And how shall we be able to rely on a sentence passed beyond the sea, since it will not be possible to send there the necessary witnesses…?*[338]

This stern rebuke contains several interesting points. First, the use of the term "readily" implies that Rome ought not to take appeals from African clerics, but that they *can*. At this point, the Africans have acknowledged the evidence that the canons earlier disputed were not Nicene. Either due to acknowledging they were canons from somewhere (such as Sardica) or simply traditional precedent, appeals to Rome were interestingly dissuaded yet allowed. Second, the synod rebukes the Pope of Rome, here Celestine, for acting *unilaterally*. They asserted that a council should have decided the matter. The epistemic presumption behind the critique is that God's Spirit inspires only a consensus of bishops—not individuals acting in a solitary manner. With no comprehension of future doctrines such as Papal Infallibility (or direct jurisdiction for that matter), the council simply presumed that the Pope of Rome lacked the capacity to act because the binding and loosing of the Church is through the act of the Spirit. He is only evident in the work of a whole assembly of bishops where consensus is reached. Third, the Africans make a practical critique, disqualifying Celestine's judgment. They reasoned that distance prevented them from providing their *necessary* input in Rome (or vice versa) so that a consensus (and thereby binding) judgment can be made.

The Africans' critique continued on the same note:

---

338 Canon 138 ascribed to the Council of Carthage (419).

For that your Holiness should send any on your part [to dictate to us] we can find ordained by no council of Fathers…whoever desires you to delegate any of your clergy to execute your orders [i.e. the observing of Apiarius' successful appeal to Rome], do not comply, lest it seem that we are introducing the pride of secular dominion into the Church of Christ.[339]

Here, they ordered Celestine to desist. The council rejected that a "single individual" (i.e. the Pope) can overturn a local conciliar judgment. They accused this of being akin to "secular dominion" (i.e. the autocratic rule of an Emperor), as there would have been no ecclesiastical precedent or Scriptural basis where the Pope of Rome was able to act thus. The Council of Carthage in effect clarified precisely how appeals were understood in the Church of the day. Rome can take appeals in extreme situations, but consensus was necessary to make any judgment binding. The idea that the Pope of Rome can decide matters in isolation, an innovative ecclesiastical ploy that Celestine *allegedly* was doing, is soundly rejected.

As for the truth of the matter (whether Apiarius was railroaded, there were serious canonical issues with the deposition in Africa, etcetera) much of this is lost to history, so it is difficult to ascertain whether Celestine was *actually* overstepping his authority or remotely acting tyrannical. Matters are surely different if there were major abnormalities with Apiarius' deposition. As Pope Julius had done with Athanasius and Celestine would soon do with Nestorius, Rome had and would continue to issue non-binding judgments in response to appeals made to it. They had the right to re-enter whomever they pleased into their local communion and excommunicate whomever else from the same. In all likelihood, Zosimus and Celestine were operating under such ecclesiastical presumptions.

THE COUNCIL OF EPHESUS AND INTERPATRIARCHAL ECCLESIOLOGY

The context behind the Council of Ephesus was that Constantinople's Patriarch, Nestorius, was teaching Adoptionism.

---

339 Ibid.

Perhaps more disconcertingly, as it carried the weight of possible persecution, it was understood that Nestorius threatened to use his influence with the Roman Emperor (Saint Theodosius the Younger) to impose his view over the entire Church. Saint Cyril, Pope of Alexandria, warned Celestine of Rome that "by using the authority of his see to scheme against all, he [Nestorius] will induce us and everyone else to adopt his beliefs."[340] Evidently, Constantinople's authority was truly not understood to be in its (translated) relics, but necessarily attached to the secular authority of the Roman Emperor. There was no pretended charism of Constantinopolitan supremacy. Interestingly, it is taken for granted that the Roman Emperor can impose beliefs. During this era, the Pope of Rome is never described in this same way—an indication that the Vatican I concept of the Papacy did not exist at this juncture.

Perhaps due to legitimate fear of the power Nestorius wielded, Cyril exhibited considerable caution in trying to get Nestorius to recant. When patient letter writing did not convince Nestorius, Cyril got ready for an ecclesiastical "war." "War" meant finding allies and building a consensus against Nestorius, as the consent of the Patriarchs was necessary to depose a Patriarch (as previously covered with the cases of Paul of Samosata and Saint Athanasius). It is with this in mind that Cyril cajoled Celestine to support him by citing that "all the bishops of the East…especially…Macedonia [i.e. Thessalonica]" already agree with him.[341] "We shall prompt them [the rest of the Church], as they desire," Cyril continued to Celestine, noting that they would be working together to establish Church-wide consensus in order "to make a joint stand with one soul and one mind…to contend for the orthodox faith."[342]

There is nary an indication that Cyril is the junior partner. It is interesting to note the fact Thessalonica's/Illyricum's support was not a given even though they were under Roman jurisdiction. The Councils of Carthage (419 and 424) were evidently not exceptions

---

340 *First Letter to Celestine* quoted in Price and Graumann, *The Council of Ephesus of 431*, 130.

341 Ibid.

342 Ibid.

to how intrapatriarchal ecclesiastics operated. Agreement, let alone submission, to the Pope of Rome was not a default. In fact, it was presumed *not* to be the case. The Roman Synod did not have supremacy even within its own local jurisdiction. Instead, the Pope of Rome experienced pushback as one would expect from a local church operating under the presumptions of Apostolic Canon 34.

Celestine decided to cooperate with Cyril's plan. Similar to some of the strongly-worded correspondence sent to Africa the previous two decades, Celestine subsequently makes interpatriarchal statements uncharacteristic of Roman correspondence in the past. For example, Celestine's *Letter to Nestorius* warned the latter that "you have been totally expelled from the universal fellowship."[343] His *Letter to the Clergy of Constantinople* asserted the same: "you are expelled from the communion of the universal [C]atholic [C]hurch."[344] The same letter cited that "the authority of our see has decreed that no one… is to be considered either deprived or excommunicated," thereby theoretically restoring the holy orders of those deposed locally by Nestorius and restoring them into Christian communion.[345]

Due to the common, anachronistic presuppositions imposed upon "Papal-sounding language," one can prematurely conclude that a nascent Vatican I Papacy is being expressed here. However, the correct way to interpret such words is to compare them to their immediate context. For example, the same *Letter to the Clergy of Constantinople* states that its "sentence" is that one must agree with what "is held by the Roman and the Alexandrian and the universal [C]atholic [C]hurch."[346] *The Letter of Celestine to John of Antioch, Juvenal of Jerusalem, Rufus of Thessalonica, and Flavian of Philippi,* states the exact same thing.[347] This implies that Celestine was taking it upon himself to speak on *behalf* of the Church, not *for* the whole Church.

---

343 Ibid., 141.

344 Ibid., 154.

345 Ibid., 153.

346 Ibid.

347 Ibid., 155.

This is verified by how Cyril described Celestine's actions. Cyril's *Letter to Constantinopolitan Clergy* speaks of Nestorius being "excommunicate by all"[348] and wrote to John of Antioch that:

> the holy council of Rome issued a decree [excommunicating Nestorius] and indeed wrote to your piety [John Patriarch of Antioch] the instructions that must be followed by those who wish to remain in communion with all the West…for we ourselves [Alexandria's Synod] shall follow his judgement, fearing to lose the communion of so many.[349]

The excommunication was understood to be a joint effort, with each locality excommunicating Nestorius. These local actions combined reflected the joint action of a whole entity: the Church. Papal prerogatives were not advanced in any real way. Rather, the rhetoric used by the Church of Rome was evolving.

This interpretation is further verified by the Council of Ephesus specifying that Roman excommunications were purely local affairs. A good example is the *Letter to Theodosius II After June 22ⁿᵈ Session*, written before the Roman legates arrived because Cyril wisely began the council early on June 22, 431 to avoid being outmaneuvered by Nestorius. The letter states that "our [the council's] verdict [against Nestorius] was ratified by all the West."[350] This obviously refers not to the Roman legates' participation in the council, as they were not there yet. Rather, it demonstrates that they understood the Pope's earlier excommunication of Nestorius ("you are expelled") as a reference to expulsion from the Roman Synod specifically—not the whole Church.

As for the council itself, several statements are relevant concerning the consensus-based ecclesiology of the Church during this time. Theodosius the Younger in his capacity as Emperor in his *Letter of Convocation* wrote that: "Before the most holy council and the decree that it is going to issue by common vote, no fresh step, obviously, is

---

348 Ibid., 172.

349 Ibid., p. 159. In Price's translations "judgment" is spelled according to the English norm, "judgement."

350 Ibid., 355. See also *Report to Theodosius II Sent Via the Envoys of the Council* which is similar in the same regard in Ibid., 553.

to be taken individually by anyone."[351] This demonstrates a lack of awareness that the Pope, *or anyone*, can function independently of an Ecumenical Council. He presumes this is obvious. The concern evidently is not about Roman domination, but Alexandrian overstepping. Theodosius similarly warned Cyril, demanding that consensus must freely be formed:

> *For from old these ["doctrines of piety"] have been defined for us not by threats of someone domineering...but by the deliberation of the holy fathers and the sacred council...not through imperiousness but consent.*[352]

During the council itself, explicit statements were made concerning the necessity of "common decision and assent" (as stated by Theodotus of Ancyra).[353] Capreolus of Carthage, in his letter to the council, noted the necessity of both "the authority of the [A]postolic [S]ee *and* a unanimous priestly vote."[354] Though the letter speaks highly of the council, asserting that "the Holy Spirit" is "present in your hearts during the proceedings,"[355] the intent was not to delineate a doctrine of conciliar infallibility. That was taken for granted by the bishops undertaking a conciliar action. Nor was the intent to contrast the magisterial work of the council with the Roman or Alexandrian Papacies, which were never described in such terms in either the fourth or fifth centuries. Simply, Capreolus' motivation was to ensure on the record that the West had a seat at the table, as their input was necessary for a true Spirit-led consensus.

Capreolus' concerns were justified. When the Roman legates arrived, they were not happy that they were not included in the council's decisions. They had been sent by Celestine with the following instructions: "you are to pass judgement on their

---

351 Ibid., 198.

352 Ibid., 199.

353 Ibid., 277.

354 Ibid., 279.

355 Ibid.

statements but not descend to the controversy."[356] Essentially, the legates were not expected to actually take an active part in the council, but merely to cooperate with its work by assenting to it (presuming it went the way they wanted). This was part and parcel of previous and future councils where the debate was generally between Eastern clergy. It would be these ecclesiastics that devised the conciliar decrees and canons. The Roman Patriarchate simply would receive them, establishing consensus and thereby completing the work of the council. As it will be covered later, this criterion was effectively canonized during the Council of Nicaea II.

The legates had a vested interest in insuring that their input mattered—it mattered during Nicaea I, after all. Pope Julius I vigorously defended such a prerogative a century previously. During the July 10th session of the council, the legates demanded that Celestine's letter to the council be read, reminding the audience to "observe the care he takes of all the churches."[357] The language was intentionally paternalistic, intended to defend Rome's right to take an interest in Eastern affairs—not a given considering how Constantinople I treated Maximus the Cynic and Paulinus of Antioch. They did not want a precedent where Rome was excluded from such a council, as Constantinople I implied this can be the case (though the attendance of Ascholius of Thessalonica, an authentic Papal legate, disproves this).

Celestine's letter was modest in tone, using somewhat more circumspect language than the legates would during the session. This was likely because Celestine did not expect that Cyril would have acted without him. His letter expressed consensus-based ecclesiology in the interest of including his far away jurisdiction in the decision-making process: "let us, as is beneficial, be 'of one mind and one conviction...' Let the whole assembly in common join us."[358] On the same note he wrote that "we," as in the synod, "are

---

356 Ibid., 205.

357 Ibid., 369.

358 Ibid., 372.

confident that this [Rome's deposition of Nestorius] will receive the assent of your holinesses."[359]

The council, smarting from the implication that their work would have been illegitimate without Celestine's input, responded, "To Celestine the new Paul! To Cyril the new Paul!"[360] The purposeful avoidance of citing Saint Peter, and the bestowing of the same Apostolic title to both Celestine and Cyril, was intended to convey the council's legitimacy despite them acting apart from the Roman legates. Firmus of Caesarea, defending the work of the council, stated, "There was a previous [Roman] verdict...we [the council] put the decree into effect."[361] This response framed the council's work as legitimate, effectively presuming upon Rome's preemptive consent to the council's deposition of Nestorius. Hence, the bishops at Ephesus, Celestine, and Cyril all understood the deposition of Nestorius by the Roman Synod to be local in nature. This would mean the council effected the excommunication of Nestorius, not Celestine, as a local excommunication would not be binding upon the whole Church.

Further evidence that Celestine's excommunication was not treated as final can be gleaned from the fact that Nestorius was tried as a bishop, retaining his ecclesiastical title. Only after the council had gone through the literal canonical motions of deposition was Nestorius declared excommunicate and stripped of such titles.[362] Celestine had in effect consented to this in advance, writing to Cyril before the council:

For you [Cyril] ask whether the holy council ought to receive a man who condemns what he himself has preached, or whether, because the period of respite has now passed,[363] the sentence [of excommunication]

359 Ibid., 373.

360 Ibid., 374.

361 Ibid.

362 Ibid., 231, 232, 250-254, 281.

363 Celestine is referring to a ten-day deadline for Nestorius' excommunication to take effect, a deadline that had already passed thereby demanding the excommunication to be in force.

*already passed must hold…I am zealous for universal peace, and I am
zealous for the salvation of one who is perishing, if indeed he is ready
to acknowledge his sickness. Our reason for saying this is lest we appear
to fail one who wishes to reform. If however, while he look for grapes
he has grown thorns, let the earlier decree stand.[364]*

As the letter details, only if Nestorius did not repent in the
council would the excommunication (implicitly then by the council)
be put into force. This may even imply that locally, Rome had
rescinded (conditionally) their own excommunication.[365]

The Roman legates, displeased from the council's purposefully
dismissive response to the reading of Celestine's letter, made a point
of extolling the Pope. This led to a petty, put polite, exchange:

*Philip [Roman legate]: "[the Pope is]…the holy head; for your
beatitude is aware that the blessed Peter the Apostle is the head of the
whole church as also the [A]postles."*

*Theodotus bishop of Ancyra said [in reply]: "The God of the
universe has shown the decree of the holy council to be just by means
of the visitation, by letter, of the most religious Bishop Celestine…
your religiousness has requested most reasonably to be informed of
the proceedings, the minutes of the proceedings concerning Nestorius'
deposition will fully satisfy…"[366]*

Philip's citation of the Pope of Rome's primacy was treated as
an honorific by Theodotus, who understood the actual import of the
statement as pertaining to the council's deposition of Nestorius. In
effect, Theodotus merely repeated the rationale of Firmus: that the
council had put into effect what Rome had already consented to. This
is how the July 10th Session closed. Philip, apparently acknowledging
that this was a correct response to his words, admitted during the

---

364 Ibid., 203.

365 Implications of potential episcopal restoration by Rome's local synod in
   anticipation of an ecumenical deposition is more explicit in Saint Pope Leo's
   treatment of Dioscorus, as covered in the next section.

366 Ibid., 375.

session held on the next day, "By a reading of the proceedings…
the whole trial was conducted canonically."[367] Here, Philip is
acknowledging that the council's defense of its actions, though not
necessarily respectful to the legates, was acceptable. The deposition
was canonical, even without the Roman Synod's presence.

During the July 11th Session, the whole "Holy Council" (likely
its chairman with a few assenting voices) soon defended itself again
on the same grounds. The reason for this defense is not clear in the
written words of the minutes. It may have been elicited in response
to the tone or demeanor (perhaps sarcastic) of the Roman legates
in admitting to the council's canonicity. The "council" responded:

> *we are of necessity obliged by the canons and by the letter of our most
> holy father and fellow minister Celestine bishop of Rome to proceed this
> melancholy sentence against him…the same Nestorius is excluded from
> episcopal dignity.*[368]

Philip, apparently wanting the council to speak more repentantly
for acting apart from himself and the other legates, responded:

> *It is doubtful to no one, rather it has been known in all ages, that the
> holy and most blessed Peter, the leader and head of the [A]postles, the
> pillar of the faith, and the foundation of the [C]atholic [C]hurch,
> received the keys of heaven from our Lord Jesus Christ the saviour and
> redeemer of the human race…he lives and performs judgment, until
> now and always, through his successors.*[369]

Modern observers may confuse the Papal honorific as some sort
of proof of Papal Supremacy. However, as stated previously, the
point at issue was the Roman Synod's explicit assent to the council's
work. Thus the statement must be read as intending to address that
specific concern. Cyril, responding to the exchange (and surely
orchestrating the council's posturing in this exchange with the
legates), exhibited precisely this sort of understanding:

---

367 Ibid., 376.

368 Ibid., 377.

369 Ibid.

They [the Roman legates] have pronounced as representatives of the
[A]postolic [S]ee and of the entire holy college of the most God-beloved
and most holy bishops of the West…they have given their assent to the
verdict against the heretic Nestorius.[370]

Cyril, being mindful that the exchange was entered into the
minutes, framed the point at issue. Rome was to officially give assent
to the council's work. The "entire" council pressed the legates:

Since the…legate[s] of the [A]postolic [S]ee have spoken most
fittingly, it is appropriate that they fulfill their promise and confirm the
proceedings by subscription.[371]

The legates were given an opportunity to grieve the early
initiation of the council. They, particularly Philip, have made their
point. Now, they had to submit. And submit they did. Projectus,
one of the other legates, signed the June 22nd minutes, stated
subserviently:

I hereby sign the just judgement of this holy [E]cumenical [C]ouncil,
of which we learned from the proceedings, putting into effect in every
way the deposition of the impious Nestorius.[372]

"Putting into effect in every way" is a reference to the June
22nd session being canonical, but making this conditional upon the
Roman delegation's present assent. Interestingly, a few days later,
the council read the entirety of the June 22nd minutes simply so
everyone, including the Roman legates, can all accept at the same
time. The obvious motivation was to prevent any critiques of
canonical irregularity.

In summary, Celestine acted as Patriarch of the West and
exhibited no jurisdiction over the entire Church during Ephesus.
Consistent with Pope Julius a century previous, Rome had the right
to consent to the council, which is why their subscription "in every
way" effected the deposition of Nestorius. The ecclesiology of

---

370 Ibid., 380.

371 Ibid.

372 Ibid., 381.

consent is explicitly found in the sources surrounding this council. Later notions of Papal Supremacy are conspicuously absent.

SAINT VINCENT OF LERINS AND THE EXPLICIT EPISTEMOLOGY OF CONSENSUS

Saint Vincent of Lerins in the *Commonitorium* was the first to put pen onto paper and explicitly delineate the epistemology of consensus. He described how it can decide doctrinal matters. The occasion that demanded his attention appears to be questions surrounding the Council of Ephesus, though the Donatist controversy was also a concern of his. The Council of Ephesus initially failed to attain to consensus specifically because the Antiochene Patriarchate did not assent, creating a schism. In 433, the schism was healed after Cyril of Alexandria penned a confession explaining the Christology of Ephesus in an acceptable, non-Apollinarian, manner.

Nevertheless, the situation required some reflection as the competing synodal claims between Antioch and those assembled in Ephesus laid bare the difficulty in simply appealing to the grace of the Spirit as ensuring the correctness of a council. A convocation containing bishops, something the Council of Carthage in 424 asserted as proof of their authority, was something the Antiochenes were also able to lay claim to during the Council of Ephesus. Now, both sides were reconciled and neither side recanted as being in error. This made looking back at who was precisely in error difficult at first glance.

Traditionally, doctrinal differences such as the Arian and Apollinarian controversies in the fourth century were settled through argumentation over the Scriptures. The Scriptures were understood as the primary doctrinal authority of the early Church. However, the early Church believed, as evidenced by the writings of Saints Irenaeus and Hippolytus as well as others such as Eusebius of Caesarea, that the those with Apostolic Succession had preserved Apostolic Tradition. Further, they had authority to expound the meaning of the Scriptures.

As theological controversies drifted from broad and obvious (i.e. the divinity of Christ or the Holy Spirit) to more minute questions of more precise theological import (Apollinarianism, Nestorian adoptionism, etcetera), a tendency prevailed that for all practical intents and purposes, the writings of the fathers were equally as useful as the Scriptures in addressing such questions.[373] This tendency has been observed by scholars to be so exacting, that the writings of the fathers were regularly treated in a matter that imbued upon them a "sacred, indeed inspired, character, not unlike the words of Scripture."[374] This tendency was applied by contemporaries even to the minutes of Ecumenical Councils (coined "conciliar fundamentalism.")[375] One scholar put it succinctly:

---

373 David Gwynn, "The Council of Chalcedon and the Definition of Christian Tradition" in Richard Price and Mary Whitby (eds.), *Chalcedon in Context: Church Councils 400-700*. Liverpool: Liverpool University Press, 2009, 7-26. Gwynn notes Irenaeus and Eusebius held to a view of Patristic authority. Another early expounder of such a view was Saint Hippolytus, a thinker who on musing on the preservation of "the Apostolic Tradition" noted that if anything was not recorded, "God will reveal it to those who are worthy, steering [the] Holy Church to her mooring in the quest haven." See *Apostolic Tradition* 43:4. The presumption is that the "worthy" (i.e. saints) would preserve and expound the Apostolic deposit of faith, even if it is not written down, through the inspiration of the Spirit.

374 Nicholas Constas, *On the Difficulties of the Church Fathers: Volume I*. Harvard University Press: Cambridge, MA, 2014, xiii.

375 Price, *The Acts of the Council of Constantinople of 553: Volume One*, 98. The term "conciliar fundamentalism" is a pejorative and should actually be coined "conciliar contextualism," as the saints were not extremists. They posited the reasonable idea that the minutes of a council informed the intent and meaning of its decree. A contradiction between what is stated in the minutes and decree renders the latter impossible to interpret. Additionally, if the council's primary theological teaching as found in the decree is correct, it is due to the trustworthiness of the conciliar fathers involved in teaching Orthodox doctrine. Spiritual illumination, it was understood, guaranteed this. Oftentimes, the same fathers issued secondary teachings in passing during the minutes. If they made errors concerning such secondary theological matters, then on what basis was their teaching on the primary topic at issue trustworthy? Hence, the saints were not so much "fundamentalists" in viewing the minutes of councils as authorities, but reasonable and informed by context. For the authoritative Orthodox

[P]atristic authority shared a footing with biblical authority. Just as the biblical authors, understood to have been guided by the Holy Spirit, could never be said to have "gone astray," so too were the fathers now thought to be divinely inspired and therefore correct and unswerving in everything they wrote.[376]

This should not be understood to mean that the early Church saw themselves as abrogating the authority of the Scriptures with that of the fathers, or even making them equal partners. Rather, it was understood that it was indispensable to the study of theology to understand Christian doctrine as found in the Scriptures in a way consistent with the fathers. In effect, the consensus of the fathers was the magisterium of the early Church. They offered the context in which the Scriptures, and even individual statements of the fathers and councils, were to be evaluated.

Vincent merely put pen to paper and made this idea explicit. He mused:

I have often then inquired earnestly and attentively of very many men eminent for sanctity and learning, how and by what sure and so to speak universal rule I may be able to distinguish the truth of Catholic faith from the falsehood…we must, the Lord helping, fortify our own belief in two ways; first, by the authority of the Divine Law, and then, by the Tradition of the Catholic Church.[377]

As one can see, the primary authority is "the Divine Law" (i.e. the Scriptures) and *then* "the Tradition" which was understood as a mixture of Patristic writings, conciliar authorities, and widely adhered to customs. A century later, the Council of Constantinople II surmised the work of all councils was to "confirm statements

teaching on conciliar contextualism, see the *Synodical Tome of the Synod of Constantinople (1351)*, Par 12. Therein, it anathematizes "those who did not embrace the Acts of the ecumenical councils…" This can be accessed at "The Synod of Constantinople (1351)," *Μαξιμολογία*, https://maximologia.org/2020/05/17/the-synod-of-constantinople-1351/

376 Yonatan Moss, *Incorruptible Bodies: Christology, Society, and Authority in Late Antiquity*. Oakland: University of California Press, 2016, 107-108.

377 Vincent of Lerins, *Commonitorium*, Par 4.

from the testimonies of the divine scriptures."[378] Yet, this council, like Vincent, treated Tradition functionally equivalent. Vincent gives the exact reason why:

> some one perhaps will ask, "Since the canon of Scripture is complete, and sufficient of itself for everything, and more than sufficient, what need is there to join with it the authority of the Church's interpretation?" For this reason — because, owing to the depth of Holy Scripture, all do not accept it in one and the same sense.[379]

Vincent presumes that the Scriptures are fully capable of addressing all doctrinal matters. However, there is a "need" to "join" the Scriptures to "the authority of the Church's interpretation" simply because a magisterium is needed to prevent wrong interpretations inconsistent with the original prophetic and Apostolic intent of the Scriptures' authors. Vincent understood this magisterium to be a historical consensus of Christian authorities on a given question. He describes it as follows:

> We shall follow universality if we confess that one faith to be true, which the whole Church throughout the world confesses; antiquity, if we in no wise depart from those interpretations which it is manifest were notoriously held by our holy ancestors and fathers; consent, in like manner, if in antiquity itself we adhere to the consentient definitions and determinations of all, or at the least of almost all priests and doctors.[380]

The (near) consensus of the saints was not merely some sort of historical verification of how the Church always understood this or that parsing of Scripture. Rather, such a consensus was an indication of nothing other than the illumination of the Holy Spirit:

> Great then is the example of these same blessed men, an example plainly divine, and worthy to be called to mind, and meditated upon continually by every true Catholic, who, like the seven-branched candlestick, shining

---

378 Price, *The Acts of the Council of Constantinople of 553*, 111.

379 Vincent of Lerins, *Commonitorium*, Par 5.

380 Ibid., Par 6.

with the sevenfold light of the Holy Spirit, showed to posterity how…
[heresy] might be crushed by the authority of hallowed antiquity.[381]

The epistemology is later explicitly applied to the workings of
"the whole priesthood of the Catholic Church, with the authority of
a General Council,"[382] which he then poses the Council of Ephesus
as his chief example:

> *the whole body of priests there assembled, nearly two hundred in*
> *number, approved of this as the most Catholic, the most trustworthy,*
> *and the best course, viz., to bring forth into the midst the sentiments of*
> *the holy Fathers, some of whom it was well known had been martyrs,*
> *some Confessors, but all had been, and continued to the end to be,*
> *Catholic priests, in order that by their consentient determination the*
> *reverence due to ancient truth might be duly and solemnly confirmed,*
> *and the blasphemy of profane novelty condemned…we recorded the*
> *names and the number (though we had forgotten the order) of the*
> *Fathers, according to whose consentient and unanimous judgment, both*
> *the sacred preliminaries of judicial procedure were expounded, and the*
> *rule of divine truth established.*[383]

On the preceding basis, Vincent concluded that Nestorius was
outside the consensus, and in so doing "confidently asserted that
the whole Church was even now in error, and always had been in
error."[384] This could not but imply that Nestorius was devoid of the
Spirit that guided the Church and was therefore incorrect.

In summary, Saint Vincent provided a written explanation of
the operating principles the Church had been using for centuries.
It would be incumbent upon contrarians to establish any other
epistemic principle whatsoever that had such currency in the early
Church. The epistemology clearly preceded Vincent and it persisted
afterwards.

---

381 Ibid., Par 15.

382 Ibid., Par 77.

383 Ibid., Par 77-78.

384 Ibid., Par 83.

THE COUNCIL OF CHALCEDON AND THE SEARCH FOR CONSENSUS

Traditionally, Rome was always more important than Alexandria. In the modern day, one presupposes Roman primacy. However, Rome's official status on paper was not always without equal. As the Edict of Thessalonica delineates, both Rome and Alexandria faithfully represented the divine witness of the Apostle Peter. In fact, Canon 3 of Constantinople I may have been the only actual documentation the Roman Synod was able to point to in order to buttress their traditional claims. It is uncoincidental, as discussed previously, that Latin canon law without exclusion contained this canon. Yet, this canon predicated Rome's authority upon geopolitics—something problematic as the fifth century drew on and the city of Rome increasingly became less important.

As the city of Rome decreased in importance alongside historical Eastern cities such as Ephesus and Antioch, other Eastern cities clearly eclipsed all of them. Constantinople, as the capital of the more prosperous Eastern Roman Empire, by the close of the fourth century had taken geopolitical preeminence. However, the city, as discussed previously, did not have a traditional ecclesiastical basis for primacy.

The same could not be said about Alexandria. The city was an "Apostolic See" of Peter through Saint Mark *and* it was a geopolitical powerhouse. It also had a solid track record up to this point of having the most important say on varying ecclesiastical matters. Alexandria settled the Rebaptism Controversy, moderating both the rigorist and excessively lax (Roman) view of the day. Later, Alexandria exercised a decisive role in the Councils of Nicaea, Constantinople I, and then Ephesus. Rome played second fiddle. To someone living in the mid-fifth century, it may even appear that there was a Roman primacy according to honor and an Alexandrian primacy according to geopolitical and ecclesiastical reality.

This may surprise modern readers as they are used to only reading about the triumphant ecclesiastical history of Rome and honorifics applied by its own bishops to themselves and by others. However, similar honorifics were not lacking for Alexandria during this time. Pope Dioscorus of Alexandria was called "ecumenical [i.e. universal] archbishop,"[385] the "Archbishop" and "great guardian of the faith,"[386] and "a personage unique in the world."[387] Similar appellations were retained in the subsequent century, as antipope Theodosius of Alexandria was called "the head of the bishops" by Jacob Bar Addai.[388] This is despite the latter being one of the most important macro-historical individuals in the history of Christianity. Jacob nearly single-handedly formed the entire episcopacy of the non-Chalcedonian Church, known today as the Oriental Orthodox Church.

Pope Dioscorus of Alexandria was the successor of Cyril. It is outside of this study's scope, but it suffices to say that he was politically lest tactful than Cyril and had at the cost of Church's unity pursued a policy of Alexandrian primacy. During the Council of Ephesus II (449), the synod deposed Saint Flavian of Constantinople and several other bishops, such as Antioch's, non-canonically. In short, the council was an exercise in tyranny, resorting to not merely threats but overt physical violence so that Dioscorus could get his way. When he was posed with the reality of these canonical irregularities, he was dismissive and laid the responsibility at the emperor's feet.[389] Dioscorus openly defied both

---

385 S.G.F. Perry, *The Second Synod of Ephesus: Together with Certain Extracts Relating to It.* Dartford: Orient Press, 1881, 287.

386 Ibid., 155.

387 Ibid., 127.

388 *Letter of the Anti-Chalcedonian Bishops to the Faithful* in Neil and Allen, *Conflict and Negotiation in the Early Church*, 158.

389 See Dioscorus' reply to *Canon the 70ᵗʰ of the Holy Apostles* in Perry, *The Second Synod of Ephesus*, 438-441. In response to the deposition of Domnus II (the Patriarch of Antioch) he simply says that everyone should "decide for himself" equating his deposition with that of Ibas of Edessa. This response is not compelling as the latter was deposed by a local synod, unlike the former (which he calls "Mar Paul," likely an insulting reference to Paul of Samosata). Dioscorus likewise justifies Theodoret of Cyrus' deposition *in absentia* on shaky canonical grounds, asserting that he was a heretic and undeserving. Flavian of Constantinople, who died shortly after the council, is not mentioned. Leo in *Letter 56* notes having received an "appeal" from

canonical procedure and the wishes of Constantinople's Patriarch (Saint Flavian) and the Roman Synod, represented through the legates. When the Roman Synod received interpatriarchal appeals from Flavian, Theodoret of Cyrus and others, Dioscorus went as far as to excommunicate Leo. Leo reciprocated.

The whole context behind the Ecumenical Council of Chalcedon (451) was that one way or the other, the Church was going to take "revenge" against Alexandria due to their tyrannical machinations at Ephesus II. Rome and Constantinople were the main parties in this council, as they were particularly humbled by the earlier one. It did not hurt Rome's cause that Saint Marcian, the Byzantine Emperor, had less means to secure the allegiance of the Roman Synod in the fragmenting Western Roman Empire than he had to accomplish the same with the Alexandrian Synod, which was securely under his thumb (especially when they were held captive in Constantinople itself). This political backdrop is necessary in order to understand how the Pope of Rome is described and his role understood during Chalcedon.

Considering the honorifics surrounding Alexandria at the time, the ones applied to Rome during the council are not surprising. The legates use honorifics such as "Rome, the head of all the churches"[390] and "the [A]postolic [S]ee."[391] The Council of Chalcedon itself, in its letter to Leo, does not shy away from calling

---

Flavian (which is extant) and presumes he could be restored—which means that it was thought the latter was still alive at the time the letter was written, sometime before October 15, 449—the dating of Leo the Great, *Letter 59*. The traditional date for Flavian's death is August 11th, 449, but some push the date out as far as February 450. See Rafal Kosinski, "The Exiled Bishops of Constantinople from the Fourth to the Late Sixth Century," *Studia Ceranea*, 5, 2015, 237-238.

390 Price and Gaddis, *The Acts of the Council of Chalcedon: Volume 1*, 129.

391 Ibid. This was not an exclusive title. During the Council of Ephesus (431) in its July 16th Session Saint Juvenal of Jerusalem calls his own patriarchate an "[A]postolic [S]ee." See Price and Graumann, *The Council of Ephesus of 431*, 390. Eastern patriarchates were also in passing called "[A]postolic [S]ees" during Nicaea II. See John Mendham, *The Seventh General Council, the Second of Nicaea, Held A.D. 787, in which the Worship of Images was Established*. London: William Edward Painter, 1850, 101-102.

him "the head" and themselves "the children."[392] One may even infer that there was a "battle of honorifics" of some sort between Ephesus II and Chalcedon. In opposition to Alexandrian primacy, Chalcedon effectively settled upon traditional Roman primacy as historically expressed in Saint Ignatius' *Letter to the Romans*, Canon 3 of Constantinople I, and its own Canon 28 (the latter canon surely providing the pretext for ascribing the title to Leo). As discussed in the previous chapter, the aforementioned canons applied to the Synods of Rome and Constantinople respectively the two highest statuses in the Church. This was strictly honorary. Jurisdiction was believed to be applied in a strict, local context, while the honorary status only decided how people were seated and in what order they would be allowed to subscribe or speak during a council.

The list of interpatriarchal honorifics for Rome up to this point in history is by modern standards (which presumes upon Roman preeminence) surprisingly short. If it were not for Saint Ignatius' early citing of the idea in passing, one would be tempted to think the idea was purely a creation of Constantinopolitan Synod in 381-382 to justify their own status. In other words, Constantinople placed all its weight behind a sort of Roman honorary preeminence, as it gave greater weight behind their own claims of being second in such preeminence. This is something that the Church would have not automatically granted in that day and only after controversy assented to. Perhaps this was even the direct impetus behind the expansion of honorifics. In any event, this does not mean, due to the location of the relics of saints Peter and Paul, it would have been without all traditional merit. It was not wholly an invention and Sacred Tradition does not treat it as such.

Nevertheless, it does seem that the Roman Synod took to the title "head of all the churches" more to heart than the rest of the Church. Chalcedon applied this title in a self-serving way in order to convince Leo to overrule his legates, who did not accept Canon 28 during Session 16 of the same council. An alternate rendering of the minutes during Session 3 of Chalcedon demonstrates the enhanced emphasis this title had to some within the Papal chancery.

---

392 Leo the Great, *Letter 98*, Par 4.

During that session, according to one early witness (Leo's *Letter 103* written to the bishops of Gaul, which quotes Session 3), the legates allegedly refer to "the holy and most blessed [P]ope, the head of the universal church...endowed as he is with the dignity of Peter the Apostle, who is called the foundation...the rock...," etcetera.[393] Contrary to this rendering, *all* of the Latin and Greek manuscripts of Chalcedon speak of "the most holy and blessed Leo, archbishop of Great and Senior Rome,[394] through us [the legates] and the present most holy council, together with the thrice-blessed and wholly renowned Peter the Apostle, who is the rock," etcetera.[395]

There are clear signs that one rendering or the other has been deliberately manipulated. The former alleged rendering portrays the Pope as head of the Church by virtue of a charism from Christ. Surely, this specifically, and not being called "head of the universal church" in particular, is a significant advance beyond what the ecumenical canons endorsed during this era. The latter, official rendering in the minutes, lacks the title "Pope" or reference to the headship of the Church. Instead, it speaks of Leo through the council pronouncing sentence with Peter, the significance of this being an invocation of a common, Church-wide Petrine function.

What is the story behind the alternate rendering? The actual Latin translation of Chalcedon is thought to have originated about

---

393 Price and Gaddis, *The Acts of the Council of Chalcedon: Volume 2*, 70.

394 The title "Senior Rome" was used throughout the Council of Chalcedon by its participants. Its first usage is in the attendance list for a Roman legate during Session 1. See Ibid., *The Acts of the Council of Chalcedon: Volume 1*, 124. The use of this title by a Roman legate may imply the Roman Synod's tacit acceptance of Canon 3 of Constantinople I, as this canon identifies Constantinople as "New Rome." This by default makes the original Rome "Senior." Nevertheless, "New Rome" was an official political designation for Constantinople since its founding.

395 Ibid., *The Acts of the Council of Chalcedon: Volume 2*, 69-70. See Mansi 6, 1047 for the rendering in the Latin minutes: *Unde sanctissimus & beatissimus archiepiscopus magnæ & senioris Romæ Leo, per nos & per præsentem sanctam synodum, una cum ter beatissimo & omni laude digno beato Petro apostolo, qui est petra & crepido catholicæ ecclesiæ, et rectæ fidei fundamentum...*

100 years after it occurred, probably for usage by Pope Vigilius.[396] The variant rendering from *Letter 103* predates the three Latin versions of Chalcedon originating from the mid-sixth century. Because no version of Chalcedon (Latin or Greek) contains this rendering, at no point was its sentiment officially received by the Church's synods. In fact, this rendering appears to be written before an aborted attempt to translate Chalcedon.[397] In 453, Leo admitted that:

> *We have no very clear information about the acts of the Synod, which were drawn up at the time of the council at Chalcedon, on account of the difference of language. And therefore I specially enjoin upon you [Julian], brother, that you have the whole collected into one volume, accurately translated of course into Latin, that we may not be in doubt on any portion of the proceedings.*[398]

Hence, the Papal statement as preserved in *Letter 103* could not be what was rendered in Chalcedon by any known witness to the earliest acts. This is because Leo admits ignorance of what was explicitly recorded in the same minutes. *Letter 103*'s rendering would have had to be derived from some independent source.

Contrary to what the primary sources state, some scholars surmise that *Letter 103* allegedly preserves what must have been read at Chalcedon.[399] Such a view cannot but presume that *Letter 103*'s rendering was covered up by those writing the minutes and that the motive for this was that there had to be some degree of animosity over interpatriarchal ecclesiastical prerogatives *in the East*. This textual theory is built upon multiple unproven assumptions. Further, it is uncharacteristic of the council. Chalcedon's minutes

---

396 Ibid., *The Acts of the Council of Chalcedon: Volume 1*, 83-84.

397 Ibid., *The Acts of the Council of Chalcedon: Volume 2*, 69-70. The "pro-Papal" Latin rendering is from Leo the Great, *Letter 103* as found in PL 54, 991-992. Leo commissioned Julian of Cos to make a translation of Chalcedon in 453, but this evidently never materialized. See Ibid., *The Acts of the Council of Chalcedon: Volume 1*, 83.

398 Leo the Great, *Letter 113*, Par 4.

399 Price and Gaddis, *The Acts of the Council of Chalcedon: Volume 2*, 69-70.

are so painfully faithful to every verbal statement of those present
that even the "series of utterances" recording the physical "checking
of the minutes" when a session was closed were preserved.[400] A
simpler textual theory suffices.

The best theory, as it preserves the integrity of all the primary
sources' renderings, is that the rendering as preserved in *Letter
103* was what was written *in advance* for the Papal legates to state
at the council. This is the only explanation that allows for the
statement to be extant in writing before any attempt to translate
the council *and* to be authentic. During the council, the statement
was likely diplomatically revised for Greek consumption when
the judgement was actually given and recorded into the minutes
themselves. Intrapatriarchal texts in the West tend to have more
exalted statements about the Pope of Rome written by the Papal
chancery. Such idiomatic language is fitting when deference to
the local Patriarch was expected and there were no ecclesiastical
or political equals to him in that context. In an interpatriarchal
context, such language (unless one was angling for a fight) would
have been perceived as disrespectful, even strange coming from
what was fast becoming a political and economic backwater. This
increases the probability that the statement was written more for
local rather than interpatriarchal consumption.

However, one must consider an additional possibility. It is possible
that *Letter 103* was manipulated to exaggerate Papal prerogatives
relevant to current events during the mid-fifth century. This was
perhaps necessary due to earlier ecclesiastical conflict in Gaul that
required Roman law to preserve (local) Papal ecclesiastical rights
there.[401] Another, stronger possibility, was that it was a response to
the debate surrounding Canon 28 during the council's final session.
Scholarship recognizes, "The Roman delegates had certainly been
slow to wake up to the importance of the issue."[402] This is because,
as covered in the previous chapter, all the extant primary source

---

400 This includes mundane statements such as "I have read" and "[i]t is
    complete." See Ibid., *The Acts of the Council of Chalcedon: Volume 1*, 365.

401 Denny, *Papalism*, 90-91.

402 Price and Gaddis, *The Acts of the Council of Chalcedon: Volume 3*, 70.

evidence suggests that the Roman Synod had accepted Canon 3 of Constantinople I before Chalcedon ever occurred. This canon expressed a pragmatic understanding of ecclesiastical prerogatives, linking Patriarchal rank to a synod's connection to an Imperial capital. Canon 28 of Chalcedon was similar in this regard. With Old Imperial Rome's fortunes waning, this was a dangerous canonical precedent which could ultimately unseat the Roman Synod from its primacy.

This demanded revisionism among those in the Papal chancery over the question of Canon 3 of Constantinople I, as simply rejecting Canon 28 of Chalcedon would not have sufficed. Now, Canon 3 was allegedly *never* accepted by the Roman Synod and for a specific reason: Rome's preeminence was *not* of an Imperial nature at all, but entirely dependent upon inviolable canons and their Apostolic Succession from Peter. Leo wrote indignantly to Saint Anatolius of Constantinople after the council:

> *you…try to break down the most sacred constitutions of the Nicene canons as if this opportunity had expressly offered itself to you for the See of Alexandria to lose its privilege of second place, and the church of Antioch to forego its right to being third in dignity…that state of things which was truly ordained by the Holy Spirit in the canon of Nicæa could in any part be overruled by any one. [sic]…For your purpose is in no way whatever supported by the written assent of certain bishops given, as you allege, 60 years ago [during Constantinople I], and never brought to the knowledge of the Apostolic See by your predecessors. [i.e. Rome never consented to Canon 3] The See of Alexandria may not lose any of that dignity which it merited through S. Mark, the evangelist and disciple of the blessed Peter…The church of Antioch too, in which first at the preaching of the blessed Apostle Peter the Christian name arose, must continue in the position assigned it by the Fathers, and being set in the third place must never be lowered therefrom…* [403]

Here, Leo makes two arguments. First, the Nicene canons guarantee that synodical ranks cannot change. This is a more than liberal gloss of Canons 6-7 of Nicaea I and one that was not held

---

403 Leo the Great, *Letter 106*, Par 2.

by the Roman Synod by the ninth century. At that point, they supported Canon 21 of Constantinople 869-870 (which recognized Constantinople being in the second place of preeminence). Second, more crucially, Leo specifies that a direct connection to the Apostle Peter is *the* basis for a patriarchate's rank. Hence, *Letter 103* may have deliberately revised the statement of the Roman legates in Chalcedon to match Roman ecclesiastical posturing as a response to Canon 28 of Chalcedon during Session 16.

In fact, the Papal legates presented an interpolated version Canon 6 of Nicaea I during the same session specifying, "The church of Rome has always had primacy."[404] Presuming this canon was not doctored on the spot in response to Canon 28 of Chalcedon, this means that a Papal chancery had previously modified documents for domestic use in order to emphasize Rome's prerogatives. If this corruption was old, it could have been forgotten that it was inauthentic.

Unlike the textual theories lacking motive that simply assume that somehow *all* the Latin and Greek minutes of Chalcedon render the disputed passage in Session 3 incorrectly, postulating that *Letter 103* was deliberately manipulated can actually work. The motive existed. Controversy over Canon 28 demanded a response from Rome. Further, another contemporary forgery (Canon 6 of Nicaea I) demonstrates that contemporary Papal chanceries would knowingly produce or use such modified documents to defend their prerogatives in an intrapatriarchal context at the very least. Lastly, Leo's chancery has a track record of enlisting to their support a forgery to deal with an ecclesiastical controversy at the time of the penning of *Letter 103*. If *Letter 103* contained another forgery, or at best a rough draft of the legate's judgement that was never actually read at Chalcedon (but deceptively presented as if it were), this would not be out of step with what Leo's chancery was already doing.

Due to probability dictating that in any event *Letter 103*'s rendering was not actually read out at Chalcedon, the authentic passage provides evidence that everyone (including the Papal legates

---

404 Price and Gaddis, *The Acts of the Council of Chalcedon: Volume 3*, 85.

themselves) understood that there was a common, as opposed to exclusive, Petrine work of the council. There were concurrences with this idea during the council. The Oriental Bishops for example praised Peter of Corinth for leaving Dioscorus' side by saying "Peter thinks like [Saint] Peter. Orthodox one, you are welcome."[405] Antioch is also identified as a "See...of Saint Peter."[406] These examples are limited in utility as both Corinth and Antioch are traditionally Petrine, but they are suggestive nonetheless.

Honorifics aside, the real "muscle" behind Roman Papacy was in their receiving of interpatriarchal appeals surrounding Ephesus II. As discussed previously, Flavian appealed to Rome specifically during Ephesus II. He did this not only in a written appeal, but also directly to the Roman legate Hilary when Ephesus II was in session. The legate famously replied *"contradictur,"* which does not mean he instantly undid Ephesus II by virtue of Papal authority, but in Hilary's own translation "means, 'An objection is lodged.'"[407]

Evidently, this was understood to mean another, more fair council would take up the case. Flavian's written appeal explicitly demanded that "an united synod of the fathers both of West and East may be held."[408] Theodoret appealed to Leo likewise, but without reference to another Ecumenical Council:

> *I await the sentence of your [A]postolic [S]ee. I beseech and implore your holiness to succour me in my appeal to your fair and righteous tribunal...you to tell me whether I ought to put up with this unrighteous deposition or not; for I await your decision. If you bid me abide by the sentence of condemnation, I abide; and henceforth I will trouble no man, and will wait for the righteous tribunal of our God and Saviour.*[409]

Though Theodoret was received locally by Leo in advance of Chalcedon, the "glorious officials" asserted that "[i]t...remains for a

405 Ibid., *The Acts of the Council of Chalcedon: Volume 1*, 188.

406 Ibid., *The Acts of the Council of Chalcedon: Volume 2*, 247.

407 Price and Gaddis, *The Acts of the Council of Chalcedon: Volume 1*, 344.

408 *Appeal of Flavian*, Par 8.

409 Theodoret, *Letter 113*.

decree to be issued" by the council "just as the most sacred Archbishop Leo has also pronounced."[410] The Papal legates concurred with this sentiment, demonstrating that similar to the Council of Ephesus, it was understood that a definitive interpatriarchal appellate judgment is made via consensus. The council officially puts in effect what the Pope earlier tentatively decided.

The same applied to Leo's excommunications. Leo conceded this immediately before Chalcedon, writing, "I modified[411] [lit. 'lessened'] my practice…they [whom I excommunicated] still retain their sees and their rank as bishops."[412] What was the "lessening"? It would be incorrect to read this as if Leo was condescending himself in rescinding an alleged interpatriarchal prerogative to excommunicate other Patriarchs on behalf of the whole Church. The most likely interpretation is borne out by Leo's "sentence" against Dioscorus and Eutyches to the Council of Chalcedon.

Therein, Leo refers to Disocorus as "bishop of the city of Alexandria" but does not identify Eutyches' by his clergyman title because he "had been lawfully condemned by his own bishop."[413] This demonstrates that Leo's decisions were evidently not binding in an interpatriarchal context (only an Ecumenical Council's was). Further, Leo had actually *reversed* his local excommunication. Hence, the "lessening" of his practice was that he now recognized Dioscorus as a bishop, as reflected in an official document. Eutyches' condemnation was intrapatriarchal and decided by Constantinople's own synod.[414] Constantinople's decision over their

---

410 Price and Gaddis, *The Acts of the Council of Chalcedon: Volume 3*, 255.

411 In the Latin the term *minuisse* is used. See PL 54, 944.

412 Leo the Great, *Letter 95*, Par 4.

413 Price and Gaddis, *The Acts of the Council of Chalcedon: Volume 2*, 69.

414 Leo the Great, *Letter 34*, Par 1 states that his excommunication of Eutyches was contingent upon "if he perseveres in his perversity." Perhaps this indicated he was willing to receive Eutyches' appeal to himself and give a positive, local judgment provided he repented. Eutyches appealed to "Rome, Alexandria, Jerusalem, and Thessalonica" after his deposition by the Council of Constantinople (448). See Price and Gaddis, *The Acts of the Council of Chalcedon: Volume 1*, 264. This is yet more evidence that interpatriarchal appeals were not a solely Roman phenomenon.

own clergyman was binding and canonical, hence recognized by Leo. Otherwise, a simple priest can never be defrocked without holding an Ecumenical Council.

After the reading of Leo's sentence, the Roman legates requested the council "to pronounce, as justice bids, a canonical verdict against the aforesaid Dioscorus."[415] Contextually, this shows that Leo through the legates sought a final and binding sentence against Dioscorus, something that only the council can canonically provide. Being that Leo had interpreted the Sardican canons to apply to the work of an Ecumenical Council, not simply an appeal to Rome in isolation,[416] it makes sense that he would have nullified his own local judgment and deferred to the Ecumenical Council.

There are certain procedural elements during Chalcedon that are relevant to this study. For example, during Session I of Chalcedon, debate broke out over Ephesus II not reading Leo's letter.[417] Dioscorus and Saint Juvenal of Jerusalem were called to task for this, as it was obviously perceived as a serious affront—especially for a council such as Ephesus II that was theoretically supposed to be a demonstration of consensus-based ecclesiology. Both men, defending themselves, did not say, "it was unnecessary." Disocorus claimed that he tried to and Juvenal alleged that a letter from the Emperors distracted him. If Rome's cooperation with an Ecumenical Council was not viewed as absolutely necessary at this time, one would expect this incident would not bear mention.

Further, there were indications that at this time Rome viewed their prerogatives as canonical in origin—i.e. according to agreed-upon custom, which has the force of ecclesiastical law. Earlier in Session I, the Papal legates made clear they cannot "go against the instructions" of the Pope of Rome "nor against the ecclesiastical

---

415 Price and Gaddis, *The Acts of the Council of Chalcedon: Volume 2*, 270. It should be noted that Dioscorus lacked his title as bishop at this juncture due to his Imperial deposition in Session 1 of the same council. The quotation here is in reference to a canonical, ecclesiastical deposition.

416 Leo the Great, *Letter 43*, Par 3.

417 Price and Gaddis, *The Acts of the Council of Chalcedon: Volume 1*, 148-150.

canons or traditions of the fathers."[418] Hence, an interesting equivalence is made between Papal instructions and ecclesiastical canons, something that is discussed in detail in an excursus that follows this section.

Another interesting event is that, despite the council being held to vindicate both Rome and Constantinople, Chalcedon did not kowtow to either synod. This was especially visible in the debate surrounding Leo's *Tome*. Bishops had to give their assent and even debated the *Tome*—including Illyrian bishops within Rome's local jurisdiction. When Rome objected to Chalcedon's first draft definition, the Illyrians called the Roman legates along with the Orientals (Syrians) "Nestorians."[419] In Leo's reply to Theodoret (two year later after the Council of Chalcedon), Leo makes a candid reference to the event:

> *For lest the assent of other Sees to that which the Lord of all has appointed to take precedence of the rest might seem mere complaisance, or lest any other evil suspicion might creep in, some were found to dispute our decisions before they were finally accepted.*[420]

It is telling that Leo interpreted such pushback as reflecting the authenticity of the consensus that formed around the *Tome*. He evidently viewed not "mere complaisance," but authentic "assent" as necessary.[421]

The last event of note is immediately after the council where Leo affirmed his "assent" to "what the synod had passed concerning the faith," but rejected Canon 28 "on the absolute authority of the Nicene canons."[422] This reflects a tiered understanding of authority, that being the superiority of ecumenical canons over all

---

418 Ibid., 130.

419 Price and Gaddis, *The Acts of the Council of Chalcedon: Volume 2*, 200.

420 Leo the Great, *Letter 120*, Par 1. This letter is dated to 453.

421 Leo's thought is without comparison with later Roman Catholic ideas. Consider Decree 9 of the Council of Vatican I, which states that "definitions of the Roman pontiff are of themselves, and not by the consent of the church, irreformable."

422 Leo the Great, *Letter 117*, Par 1.

other ecclesiastical authorities. This is relevant because Leo does not cite his own authority or mere pleasure for his decisions, but an acknowledgment of the superiority of the canons.

In closing, Chalcedon evidences the existence of consensus-based ecclesiology. There were certainly some references to the Roman Synod's spiritual headship. This emphasis makes sense given Alexandria's attempt to usurp the same. At no point does the historical evidence bear out any anachronistic ecclesiastical prerogatives pertaining to Papal Supremacy. This also manifests itself in the writings of Leo himself. In Chalcedon, there was a marked continuity with the Council of Ephesus and ecclesiastical business in previous centuries.

AN EXCURSUS ON THE DEVELOPMENT OF WESTERN CANON LAW AND THE CANONICAL IMPORTANCE OF PAPAL DECREES

As mentioned in the previous section, there appeared to be a special emphasis applied to Papal "instructions" in that they were spoken about in the same sentence with canons and Patristic tradition. This idea was expounded somewhat more clearly in the Council of Rome (465) in their first canon, which ordered "that the canons of Nicaea and the decrees of the [A]postolic [S]ee be observed."[423] Eventually, though this did not occur in the fifth century, Papal decrees would find themselves published next to ecumenical canons in all Latin copies of canon law. It is necessary to discuss *why* Western canonists accepted this and what significance they attached to it. To do so, one must look at the slightly different nature of canon law between the East and West.

Canon law was established with the Apostolic Canons in the second or third century. Saint Dionysius of Alexandria issued his own local canons in the same century as did Saint Cyprian of Carthage. All of these canons were received by the whole Church. Even in

---

423 Edward Landon, *A Manual of Councils of the Holy Catholic Church, Volume 2.* Edinburgh: John Grant, 1909, 87.

local councils, the Holy Spirit was thought to be at work.[424] Perhaps uncoincidentally, *all* of the existing canons of the East, provided they were considered authentic synodal products, were ultimately received as ecumenical in authority.[425] In fact, Eastern canon law in the first millennium is simple, because there were *no* "local canons" not already in force Church-wide. All the *Eastern* local councils (and a few Western ones) within the Roman Empire had their canons received as ecumenical officially by the Council in Trullo, though they were treated as binding long before then in Ecumenical Councils such as Ephesus and Chalcedon. Chalcedon's first canon presumes upon it: "We have judged it right that the canons of the Holy Fathers made in *every synod* even until now, should remain in force." Synods subsequent to Trullo, such as Nicaea II and several councils in Constantinople (all but one being local synods), likewise had their canons received as part of the Photian Nomocanon.

The Council of Constantinople (920) (including all the Patriarchs with the exception of Rome's) agreed to make the Photian Nomocanon the basis of Orthodox canon law. In total, 22 different local councils have "ecumenical authority" due to this; no purely local council was held in the East between the fifth and most of the eighth centuries. It appears that once the Byzantine state began to incorporate ecclesiastic canons into civil laws, local synods other than Constantinople's avoided issuing canons. Perhaps the other synods would wait for an Ecumenical Council to decree such matters, despite the fact that these synods soon existed outside of the Byzantine Empire. In short, out of 22 local councils, only four were held after the early fifth century, and all were Constantinopolitan.

---

424 Even local councils made the explicit claim of acting concertedly with the Holy Spirit. The Council of Antioch (approximately 269) and Carthage (424) as discussed previously both made this claim. In addition, Antioch (341) similarly claims that those there assembled were "together with unity of mind and concord and the Spirit" with "the Holy Spirit, uniting in our definitions."

425 The Apostolic Canons were treated as authentic. Other questionable canonical sources, like those ascribed to Saint Hippolytus, being inauthentic were excluded from ecumenical reception.

Now, one must compare the "streamlined" list of canon law from local synods in the East to what the West had to deal with. During the first millennium, the West accepted all of the local Eastern councils before Chalcedon, probably due the latter council's first canon. On top of this, they had a slew of local councils that, though issuing canons, never received pan-Eastern nor Western acceptance:[426] Elvira (300),[427] Arles (314), Rome (378),[428] Rome (386), Carthage (393, 398),[429] Toledo (400), Milevis (402), Rome (402), Rietz (439), Orange (441), Vaison (442), Ireland (456),[430] Rome (465), Vannes (465), Rome (499), Agatha (506), Orleans (538), Orleans (549), Tours (567), Braga (572), Macon (585), Toledo (589), Toledo (633), Toledo (638), Lateran (649), Toledo (655), Nantes (660), Rouen (650), Merida (666), Toledo (681), Toledo (684), Toledo (694), Compiegne (756), Rome (769), Cealchythe (785), Ratisbon (796), Aix-La-Chapelle (802), Mayence (813), Cealchythe (816), Paris (829), Mayence (847), Worms (868), Pavia (876), Ravenna (877), Metz (888), Ravenna (898), and Reims (991).[431] This is a total of 48 local councils at minimal, 12 times more local councils purely of a Western import in contrast to the paltry four Eastern local councils

---

426 The Roman councils contrarily had some degree of pan-Western acceptance, as discussed in this excursus.

427 The canons traditionally ascribed to Elvira (300) may have actually belonged to a series of councils in Elvira over the course of years.

428 This Council had the "Tome of Damasus" whose canons the Antiochene council in 379 received all but one of. Yet, these canons hold no subsequent importance in the East after the end of the Roman Schism from Antioch during the early fifth century.

429 Several councils were held in Carthage and it appears that canons from earlier Carthaginian councils were conflated with the work of later Carthaginian councils.

430 Allegedly two councils were held in Ireland in the same year that issued canons.

431 The list and dates are gleaned from all the volumes of Landon, *A Manual of Councils of the Holy Catholic Church* with the exception of the Council of Agatha, whose date is given by Evangelos Chrysos, "Minors as Patriarchs and Popes," in Alexander Beihammer, Bettina Krönung, and Claudia Ludwig (eds.), *Prosopon Rhomaikon: Ergänzende Studien zur Prosopographie der mittelbyzantinischen Zeit.* Berlin, Boston: De Gruyter, 2017, 222.

that lacked Western acceptance. In the creation of so many canons, the West continued operating as the Church always had. This was unlike the East, who for centuries allowed the prerogatives of local synods to issue canons, only for them to fall into virtual disuse in response to Imperial interests.

Yet, in the West, not all of the canons in force for one local synod were canonical in another local synod. This was a situation unknown in the East, which for the first 1,000 years of Church history appeared to hold the work of local synods in the highest regard, seemingly Spirit-led and non-negotiable. Local synods regularly received the canons of other local synods. Imperial centralization certainly hastened this consensus. The West, unable to establish consensus due to political chaos and the more contradictory nature of their canons, evidently did not accord to local canons the sort of authority the East did to their own councils.[432] Also, as covered previously, Augustine speculated aloud that councils can contradict one another, even though the same saint in Carthage (424) appears to take a more "fundamentalist" view of a council's work. Perhaps, the former private speculations won out in the popular imagination of Western Christians over the canonical judgment of the same saint. The geopolitical situation made the former easier to stomach.

While the non-fundamentalist Augustinian view seems "sensible" according to Western presumptions of what is allegedly an authoritative tradition, Scripturally and traditionally it makes no actual sense. On what authority can ecclesiastics issue canons if the Holy Spirit is not granting them disciplinary authority (Matt 18) as He had in Jerusalem in Acts 15? If the Holy Spirit is not present, then how do these canons have any authority whatsoever, even in a strictly local context? And, if He is indeed present, then would that not demand that even the canons of a local council are just as important as those issued by even the largest of Ecumenical

---

432 It appears the refusal (likely for practical and political reasons) to have local Western canons translated into Greek and submitted to other local synods for reception in effect invalidates any later claim these canons carried disciplinary authority in the sense that their teachings would be applicable to all Christians.

Councils? These rhetorical questions illustrate precisely why the East historically had treated Patristics and councils as authorities akin to Scripture, while the West seems to rank their magisterial authorities so that some are more authoritative than others.

This chaotic understanding of what makes a synod authoritative in the West, without any literal unifying force, created a canonical wasteland. Indeed, Rome (465) required that the decrees of the Pope (i.e. local synodal decrees) and the Nicene canons (the only canons up to that point Rome *admitted* to receiving due to squabbles over Canon 28 of Chalcedon)[433] both be in force. However, this did not mean they accorded Papal decrees equal authoritative rank. For example, the Council of Rome (496) lacked any mention of Papal decrees despite delineating what they precisely understood to be the only authoritative documents of the Church. This included the Canon of Scripture, four ecumenical councils, and the canonical "works of Saints Cyprian, Athanasius, Gregory of Nazianzen, Basil, Cyril of Alexandria, John Chrysostom, Hilary, Ambrose, Augustine, Jerome, and [sic] Prosper, and Theophilus of Alexandria, and the letter of St Leo to Flavianus [i.e. the *Tome*]."[434]

This indicates that Rome, during this period, had a lower view of their own councils than the East did and reveals a subtly different epistemology existed. It also reflects that Papal decretals were not seen as authoritative documents, but perhaps pastoral applications of authoritative canonical writings.

What motivated this different epistemology? The West encountered the basic reality that their canons were so widely disparate, it was impossible to reconcile and accord them with the authority of being non-negotiable.[435] For example, Toledo (681)

---

433 The canons of Sardica during this period were still treated by the Roman Synod as if they were from Nicaea I. Canon 28 of Chalcedon was rejected by Rome due to it assigning Rome's primacy to its geopolitical position in the Empire, something that subtly made their position tentative. This was traditionally unacceptable.

434 Landon, *A Manual of Councils of the Holy Catholic Church, Volume 2*, 90.

435 From a religious standpoint, if Western ecclesiastics did not even expect their work to be Spirit-led, even nominally so, it would be unfair to demand that their work meet such an exacting epistemic standard.

allowed for divorce only in cases of adultery. However, Compiegne
(756) allowed for a man to divorce a woman for being a former
slave and to remarry. The latter also allowed the dissolution of
a marriage if someone had leprosy. Placing varying weights to
canonical authorities and holding disciplinary canons to be fallible
was a sensible, epistemic response.

As for first millennium Western collections of canon law that
are not fraught with forgeries, there is a small list for the historian
to glean from (in chronological order): Hispana, Prisca, those of
Dionysius Exiguus (compiled sometime after the year 500 in Rome),
Quesnelliana (also compiled in Rome at almost the same time),[436]
Capitula Martini, the Spanish Epitome, Isidoriana, the Concordia
of Creconius Africanus, and the Collectio Canonum Hibernensis.
Not surprisingly, only the lists of canons from Rome or those
directly dependent upon these (such as the Concordia of Creconius
Africanus, Spanish Epitome, Isidoriana, and Hibernesis) included
Papal decretals.

Dionysius wrote in Rome. His work was commissioned for
Roman use and according to the canonical demands of Rome
(465). The pre-Dionysian texts lack Papal decretals. The oldest
Latin canonical lists include the Eastern (consensus) collection of
canon law, including the local Eastern councils. There are only
minor variations in these local canons.

Collections of canon law in the West were tailored for each
specific locality, as they would include the consensus canon law and
their own, peculiar, local canons. For example, Spain would have
Spanish canons. Rome, understandably, had Roman canons. Papal
decretals would have only been relevant in the locality of Rome
if it were not for the popularity particularly of Dionysius' canons.
Roman collections of canon law were exported to England,[437] the
Carolingian Empire,[438] and as already covered, Africa and Spain.

436 Michael Elliot, *Canon Law Collections in England ca 600–1066: The Manuscript
      Evidence*. Toronto: Centre for Medieval Studies University of Toronto (PhD
      dissertation), 2013, 221.

437 Ibid., 204.

438 Lowe Elias Avery, *Codices Latini Antiquiores. A Palaeographical Guide to Latin*

Not surprisingly, the oldest collections of Latin canon law such as Hispana and Prisca lack Papal decretals. Before Rome (465), even Roman collections would have lacked such decretals, as Prisca demonstrates.

Interestingly, even though most of the Western Church by happenstance had absorbed local Roman canon law, that does not mean they received the Roman canons as being in force. One late historical account illustrates this. Arnulphus of Orleans during the Council of Reims (991) taught: [439]

> *[if] the Church of Rome was ever to be held in honour on account of St Peter, and that the decrees of the pope should always be received when they are not contrary to the canons; 'if,' said he, 'any one pretends with Gelasius, that the Church of Rome is judge of all, whilst she is judged of none, let him place at Rome a pope whose judgment cannot err.' He then proceeded to show that even Rome herself had approved that bishops, when accused, should be judged on the spot, without reference to the holy see; that the primitive rule and custom had been broken in upon by false [Pseudo-Isidorian] decretals;[440] that he advocated deference to the pope by consulting him; 'but,' said he, 'if his judgment be not just, let us obey the [A]postle, and not listen even to an angel speaking contrary to the gospel.'*

In short, Papal decrees are not in force when they contradict the canons or when they are in error. Not controversial for its time, the rationale given for this is the automatic presumption that the Pope is fallible. Reims (991) invalidates any honorary

---

Manuscripts Prior to the Ninth Century. Part VII: Switzerland. Oxford: Clanderon Press, 1954, 12.

439 Landon, *A Manual of Councils of the Holy Catholic Church, Volume 2*, 70.

440 "False Decretals" appears to be a gloss from Landon. Arnulphus of Rheims, who was being prosecuted by Arnulphus of Orleans, employed the *Pseudo-Isidorian Decretals* in his defense. These were rejected on the basis that Papal decretals were not the final say. Eventually, the former Arnulphus was restored when the next Pope applied more diplomatic pressure in his support. "Thus the claims of the *Decretals of Pseudo-Isidore* triumphed." See Froom, *The Prophetic Faith of our Fathers*, 540, 543.

precedence or equivalence that the Pope's decrees may have in contrast to canons.

Such a convoluted approach to Papal (non) authority was not original to Reims. A century previous, Charles the Bald (a Carolingian monarch) wrote to Pope Adrian II that, "the privilege of Peter does not persist when judgment is not passed with equity" in nullifying Rome's judgment over a deposition.[441] Simply, Roman canons and Popes could be ignored when they were wrong. It should go without saying that when Popes were correct that they (or their decretals) would be concurred with.

From this, one must conclude that though Western canon law included Papal decretals, this must not be inferred to be evidence that there were Vatican I ecclesiastical doctrines, even in seed form, circulating in the West. Papal decretals were secondary texts existent in canon law simply due to local churches using the best Latin version of the canons then available: the work of Dionysius Exiguus. The paradigm under which Western canon law worked allowed for Papal decretals to be ignored or followed whenever it suited the situation. By not absorbing the entirety of Western canons, all the meanwhile fully accepting all the Eastern canons with only few exceptions,[442] the West essentially operated under a peculiar working order: all Western-specific canon law was negotiable other than what their own local synod demanded. Eastern canon law, providing it was synodically received, carried unyielding authority.

Similar to how the Western view of canon law drifted and evolved after the fall of the Western Roman Empire, the Orthodox East centuries later had its own, different kind of drift. In the second millennium, local councils (in Russia[443] and

---

441 This concerns the deposition of Hincmar of Laon, as covered in a later chapter. See George Tavard, "Episcopacy and Apostolic Succession according to Hincmar of Reims," *Theological* Studies, 34:4, 1973, 616.

442 Western canon law never accepted Canons 5-7 of Constantinople I.

443 The Russian Synod issued canons in the Pan-Orthodox Council of Moscow in 1666-1667 as well as during the local Moscow Synod of 1551, the former abrogating the latter. The former council contained elements of intimidation

Georgia[444]) issued their own canons. Strangely enough, these canons ultimately fell into disuse and were never accepted by the Church at-large. However, local synods to this day regularly issue "decrees," "statutes," "regulations," and "orders" (as they are coined by the Moscow Patriarchate),[445] which effectively act as canons on procedural and disciplinary matters.

Since Moscow (1666), no such *de facto* canons have been submitted for Pan-Orthodox review, so they are effectively purely local in character. While this may be considered a "return to form" as the issuing of local canons had a long period of disuse, the fact that these *de facto* canons are often considered "secondary" and not in force in a Church-wide context is a peculiar historical development. The lack of will to issue *de jure* canons since the first millennium is also difficult to explain.

Part of the explanation may be that the second-millennium Orthodox Church had treated legal and canonical interpretations

and alleged bribery of the Patriarchs which call into question the authentic reception of their canonical decisions. In Moscow (1666-1667), Patriarch Macarius of Antioch (an alleged apostate to Roman Catholicism) played a leading role in asserting the theology that was the foundation of many of the canons. See Steven Runciman, *The Great Church in Captivity: A Study of the Patriarchate of Constantinople from the Eve of the Turkish Conquest to the Greek War of Independence*. Cambridge: Cambridge University Press, 1986, 234. In the case of the Stoglav Synod (Moscow 1551), Greek monks in attendance (presumably acting as legates for Constantinople, Russia not having autocephaly until approximately 1590) expressed their disputes with its decisions. Historians do not believe that its episcopal consensus was otherwise forced by the Tsar, as the council appears to have operated quite freely. See Sergei Bogatyrev, "Reinventing the Russian Monarchy in the 1550s: Ivan the Terrible, the Dynasty, and the Church," *The Slavonic and East European Review*, 85:2, 2007, 276.

444 The Georgian Synod issued local canons in the early 12th century at the Council of Ruisi-Urbnisi. See Manana Javakhishvili, "Canon Law in Georgia in the Middle Ages," in Pavel Kraft (ed.), *Sacri Canones Servandi Sunt, Ius canonicum et status ecclesiae XII-XIV*. Prague: Historický ústav AV ČR, 2008, 308.

445 "Statute of the Russian Orthodox Church: Adopted by the Council of Bishops in 2000, Amended by the Council of Bishops in 2008 and 2011 and Adopted As Amended by the Council of Bishops in 2013," *Moscow Patriarchate USA*, https://mospatusa.com/files/STATUTE-OF-THE-RUSSIAN-ORTHODOX-CHURCH.pdf

as evolving, substituting for the need for new canons. These interpretations underwent a process of reception. In Serbia, Romania, Bulgaria, and Russia the *Syntagma* (essentially an edited version of the Photian Nomocanon with Byzantine civil law) and the Serbian *Kormchaia* (a similar document with Serbian civil law) were translated. They formed the basis of local canon law in the aforementioned localities. In Russia, the *Ulozhenie* was yet another similar collection of juridical and legal understandings that for a short period also served the same function.

In reality, the first millennium's canon law was the only agreed-upon gold standard of canons. Juridical precedents and interpretations effectively allowed for the evolution of *de facto* canons which made no claim of being explicitly graced by the Spirit in their penning. This, in light of the Spiritual (Acts 15:28) authority local councils accorded to themselves earlier in history, was without earlier precedent. In 2016, Patriarch Daniel of Romania spoke of the "immutable canonical tradition of the Orthodox Church."[446] No one appears to apply this to the local, *de facto* canons that exist today—despite their wide dissemination. Perhaps, they are to be understood strictly as pastoral condescension falling short of actual canon law. Such a concept is lacking from the first millennium Church, at least on the synodal level.

Both the first millennium Eastern and early-medieval Western paradigms of canon law, as neither are the popular understanding of modern Orthodox[447] or Roman Catholics, seem bizarre. The original Eastern approach to all things legitimately conciliar being graced by the Spirit is clear conceptually, but the Western multi-tiered view of authority appears to be a more pragmatic solution (especially in light of their canonical heritage). Though the West was divergent with the East, the fact that the East's canons were

---

446 In Romanian: *canonice imuabile a Bisericii Ortodoxe*. See "MISIUNE ORTODOXĂ ÎN SINODALITATE ASTĂZI," *Biserica Ortodoxa Romana*, https://patriarhia.ro/misiune-ortodoxA-n-sinodalitate-astAzi-8703.html

447 Nevertheless, local councils are still cited on questions of authority. For example, discussions concerning the Orthodox view of organ donation and vaccinations often invoke the positions of local councils.

accepted in both the East and West until the ninth century made the difference uncontentious. However, having identified this subtle epistemic difference between East and West originating mainly in the fifth and sixth centuries, one can realize how this contributed to a theological drift (and epistemic confusion), which would ultimately lead the West to adopt radically different ecclesiastical assumptions.

THE FALL OF THE WESTERN ROMAN EMPIRE AND THE ACACIAN SCHISM

When the Western Roman Empire fragmented, Constantinople's pro-Roman policy went away. It was seen as more prudent to end religious conflicts in the remaining Roman Empire than waste Imperial resources seeking doctrinal and ecclesiastical rapprochement with the West. This required capitulation to the non-Chalcedonians (an ecclesiastical minority, but no small contingent of the population in Egypt and the Near East). The *Henotikon* was concocted as a doctrinal confession to bring non-Chalcedonians back into Church communion. This was done with the allowance that Chalcedon was still on the books in Constantinople, as they jealously guarded the privileges made explicit by Canon 28 of the same council.

This occurred during Acacius of Constantinople's bishopric. At the same time, Rome was under Ostrogothic domination, and their synod adopted an anti-Byzantine policy. For the first time, the bulk of the Christian world was fundamentally split. While the Christian religion existed as far as Persia and India (where there existed no small number of believers), these peripheral regions represented ecclesiastically unimportant portions of Antioch's Patriarchate. While their geopolitical separation at the behest of the Sasanian Empire was an event (though traumatic) of some importance, it ecclesiastically was not cataclysmic.

As discussed previously, while the Church had ecclesiastical customs derived from precedents, relics, and Patristics, oftentimes these gave way to practical realities. The Church proved quite amenable to becoming an institution largely subjugated, or at least guided, by the Roman state. They even drew their local jurisdictions along Imperial diocesan (provincial) lines[448] and radically re-oriented regional primacies. This occurred in Asia Minor and as well as in Palestine (where Jerusalem became a small patriarchate).[449]

Due to the Church being historically so reflexive to practical necessity, it should not be a surprise that the collapse of the Western Roman Empire created a distancing in ecclesiastical matters. For example, in Pope Gelasius' *Epistle to Faustus* (a dignitary of King Theodoric), he is dismissive of how "the canons" are cited by Eastern bishops, citing "the canons" of Sardica in support of Rome's chief appellate role:

> *Against us they oppose the canons, while they do not know what they are talking about. They make known that they themselves are against the canons [of Sardica] by the very fact that they avoid obeying the first see when it recommends what is sound and upright. These are the very canons that intended the referral of appeals from the entire church to this see for examination, but that* **these people have ordained henceforth on no occasion should be appealed by this see.** *And by this means the canons have instructed that this see is to sit in judgement on the entire church, to pass to nobody's judgement [juidicium], nor ever to be judged by its judgement, and they have determined that its verdict should never be undone, and ordered instead that its decisions are to be followed.*[450]

Such a tone is hard to imagine in a united Roman Empire. As for its intended meaning, the emboldened implies that Eastern bishops completely deny the canons of Sardica or an interpatriarchal

---

448 Canon 17 of Chalcedon.

449 Canon 3 of Constantinople I and Canon 28 of Chalcedon. For Jerusalem's official patriarchal elevation and its geographic jurisdiction see Price and Gaddis, *The Acts of the Council of Chalcedon: Volume 2*, 247.

450 *Letter* 10 in Bronwen Neil and Pauline Allen, *The Letters of Gelasius I (492-496): Pastor and Micro-Manager of the Church of Rome.* Turnhout: Belgium: Brepols Publishers, 2014, 111. "Judgment" in Neil and Allen's writings is spelled according to the English norm, "judgement."

interpretation of its appellate canons.[451] Other translations render the emboldened as "they [the canons] have decreed that no appeal anywhere should be in any case made from it [Rome]"[452] and "from it they [the canons] decreed also that no appeal whatsoever ought to be made."[453] The latter translations appear to be more accurate. The difference in translations affects how one is to interpret the passage in question. If it is the canons that are being spoken of, Gelasius is stating that no one can appeal above Rome according to the canons.

In interpreting the passage, one may infer that the Roman Synod is above the judgment of the whole Church. However, this inference is not explicit in the text. One must consider that Gelasius was using his words in an intentionally lawyerly fashion. Gelasius indeed was correct in observing that Sardica never explicitly stated that a *single* patriarchate, such as Constantinople, can review or overturn Rome's appellate judgement. The canons never order that Rome's judgment should be subject to such a judgment. However, the Latin does not demand that one infer the judgment of the whole Church is excluded. In fact, *judicium* (translated "nobody's judgement") is in the singular, not the plural (such as *judicia*), which one may expect if the concurrent judgment of several patriarchates was implied.

Indeed, this is exacting and technical; but Gelasius would have been correct in presenting the Sardican canons as such. Obviously, his intent was to extol his own patriarchate's honor (especially in light of the City of Rome's diminishment under Ostrogothic domination). He was not interested in other technicalities such as local judgments (whether they be Rome's or anyone else's) being

---

451 Later Orthodox canon law interprets the Sardican canons as purely local in import as covered in the final chapter.

452 Denny, *Papalism*, 399-400.

453 Butler and Collorafi, *Keys Over the Christian World*, 266-267. In the Latin: *nusquam prorsus appellari debere sanxerunt.* See PL 59, 28. The whole passage is as follows: *Ipsi sunt canones, qui appellationes totius Ecclesiæ ad hujus sedis examen voluere deferri. Ab ipsa vero nusquam prorsus appellari debere sanxerunt; ac per hoc illam de tota Ecclesia judicare, ipsam ad nullius commeare judicium* [singular], *nec de ejus unquam præceperunt judicio judicari...*

non-binding. Therefore, nothing in Gelasius' words disallows the potential Church-wide censuring of Rome, which in this study is the real point at issue. Such censuring did indeed occur in previous and subsequent centuries. The fact that this accords with the details surrounding Roman ecclesiology in the first millennium Church makes this interpretation, in light of the literal rendering of the Latin, the most likely one. It is unlikely Gelasius was asserting an explicit exception from Church-wide judgment.

Further, despite Gelasius' magnified Papal posturing, consensus-based ecclesiology was evidently incorporated into his thinking. For example, in defense of the accusation that Rome was acting unilaterally against consensus in refusing communion to those adhering to the *Henotikon*, Gelasius replies:

> But as for Euphemius [of Constantinople], who says that Acacius could not have been condemned by one person, I am surprised if he does not realise his own ignorance himself. Yes, does he not realise that Acacius was condemned according to the formula of the synod of Chalcedon?... the instigators of Acacius' error were condemned by a majority vote of bishops (sacerdotum)...[454]

As one can see, Gelasius denies that Rome operates apart from consensus. Rather, he lays claim to it by expressing solidarity with the bishops of Chalcedon, who themselves represent a consensus. Another example of consensus-based ecclesiology can be inferred when Gelasius claims:

> No true Christian should be ignorant of the rule of each synod, one approved by the assent of the whole church, to the effect that no see ought to have a greater executive role [than Rome].[455]

Elsewhere Gelasius writes similarly:

> the authority of the [A]postolic [S]ee has been put at the head of the universal church in all Christian centuries, it is strengthened both by a succession of canons of the Fathers and by a complex tradition. But

---

454 *Letter 10* in Neil and Allen, *The Letters of Gelasius I*, 110. Cf *Letter 1* in Ibid., 83.

455 Price, *The Acts of the Second Council of Nicaea (787)*, 171.

from this, whether somebody can appropriate something contrary to the ordinances of the synod of Nicaea...[456]

Rome's prerogatives were envisioned by Gelasius as canonical in their origin, requiring the Church's consensus to be authoritative. Rome's "executive role" is nowhere described to include the sort of prerogatives that moderns automatically infer. Surely, he had in mind Rome's honorary prerogatives and the Sardican canons.

Why is it that those both in favor and against the Roman Catholic concept of the Papacy tend to interpret Gelasius' statement on the Sardican canons as some sort of fifth century statement on Papal Supremacy? As warned against in the introduction, the danger in interpreting history is that one often imports modern concepts and presuppositions. Consider the medieval Russian saying, "no one is to judge the bishop's cases; the bishop himself judges them."[457] In isolation, one can conclude the Russian bishop is under "nobody's judgement." But, due to there being no ingrained Vatican I presuppositions about Russian bishops, the reader automatically knows not to interpret the words in this sense. Following the same principle of analysis, if one removes modern Roman Catholic presuppositions from Gelasius' words, then an interpretation more in line with contemporary ecclesiology is most compelling.

In any event, Gelasius' strong rhetoric is clearly an intentional advance fitting the geopolitical and theological situation. During the Acacian Schism, there was intercommunion between non-Chalcedonian and Chalcedonian partisans in the East. Despite Gelasius' efforts, Rome would prove not immune to succumbing to this peculiar sort of communion. Tangential communion between Rome and the non-Chalcedonians occurred immediately after Gelasius' Papacy, when Pope Anastasius II between 497-498 entered into communion with Andrew of Thessalonica. This was due to the embassy of Photinus of Thessalonica. Thessalonica was in communion with several non-Chalcedonian churches in

---

456 *Letter* 12 in Neil and Allen, *The Letters of Gelasius I*, 78.

457 George G. Weickhardt, "The Canon Law of Rus', 1100-1551," *Russian History*, 28:1, 2001, 416.

the East. Thessalonica, still part of the intact Byzantine Empire but also nominally within Rome's local jurisdiction, was a fitting "middleman."

Other Western bishops rejected Photinus. Yet, Pope Anastasius II wanted rapprochement and even explicitly recognized Acacius' holy orders as valid.[458] Anastasius II wrote flowery words to the Byzantine Emperor (Anastasius I), flattering him as God's "vicar" (lit. "*vicarium*") on Earth.[459] Photinus was sent to Alexandria to try to broker a peace over Leo's *Tome*, alleging the *Tome* in Latin was consistent with Miaphysitism (the non-Chalcedonian's Christology). The Alexandrian Synod wrote a letter to the Roman Synod trying to effect a direct, as opposed to a tangential, union on the basis of receiving a Miaphysite explanation of the *Tome*.[460]

It is beyond the purview of the history presented here to speak of this in the detail it deserves, but it is plausible that before Severus of Antioch, Miaphysite Christology was *not Severian* and less developed. This, if true, made it more reconcilable with the *Tome*. However, the Alexandrian position would prove to be unacceptable because it held that Chalcedon, in the Greek, was heretical. At this juncture, they still wanted to reject Chalcedon simply to save face and did not admit to its reconcilability with the theology of Cyril of Alexandria.

The desire of some in Rome's Synod to maintain some sort of communion with the East led to a dispute in the subsequent century between rival claimants to the Roman Papacy: Laurentius and Symmachus. The former, though commonly called an antipope, exercised his bishopric within the confines of the actual city. He,

---

458 *Anastasius II of Rome to Emperor* Anastasius in Neil and Allen, *Conflict and Negotiation in the Early Church*, 47.

459 The context pertained to God's authority over secular domains. The full passage is as follows: *Pectus clementiae vestrae sacrarium est publicae ut per instantiam vestram quam velut vicarium Deus praesidere jussit in terris evangelicis apostolicisque praeceptis non dura superbia resistatur sed per obedientiam quae sunt salutifera compleantur.* See Andreas Thiel, *Epistolae Romanorum Pontificum Genuinae: et quae ad eos scriptae sunt A.S. Hilaro usque ad Pelagium II.* Braunsberg: In aedibus Eduardi Peter, 1868, 620. The term "vicar" was also an honorific bestowed upon Pope Gelasius by the Council of Rome (495). See Denny, *Papalism*, 401.

460 Neil and Allen, *Conflict and Negotiation in the Early Church*, 51-52.

like Anastasius II, maintained the policy of rapprochement until approximately 507.[461] Contrary to the popular imagination, during the entire Acacian Schism, a potentially legitimate Pope of Rome was in communion with the East for about 30 percent of its duration.

SYNOPSIS OF THE PAPACY IN THE FIFTH CENTURY

The fifth century proves itself to be the most crucial in the study of the Papacy. This is not because there were any critical ecclesiastical developments in Rome or elsewhere. Events prove out that the Church, including those in Rome, presumed upon consensus-based ecclesiology in both intra and interpatriarchal contexts. The African Synod exhibited a desire for regional independence that was tempered by the necessity of patriarchal oversight in (canonically regulated) appellate matters. The history surrounding the appeals over Apiarius therefore followed the ecclesiastical model of Apostolic Canon 34. In interpatriarchal contexts surrounding the Councils of Ephesus and Chalcedon, the Roman Synod likewise took appeals, but by the explicit admission of its Popes did not view these as binding upon the entirety of the Church. Additionally, Pope Leo observed that the testing of his *Tome* was a matter which vindicated that his view of Christology was authentically consented to.

Writing between Ephesus and Chalcedon, Vincent of Lerins expounded an explicit epistemology of consensus. This "Vincentian Canon," as it is commonly called, gave a specific explanation for what the significance was behind centuries of doctrinal controversies. They revealed how the Church's epistemology worked. This epistemology was intrinsic to the ecclesiology of the Church and, in effect, the ecclesiology of the Church was threaded into Vincent's epistemology. The acknowledged source of authority and knowledge, that being the work of the Holy Spirit in God's people, was central to its conception.

---

461 Moorhead, "The Laurentian Schism," 125.

During Chalcedon, one cannot help but observe that the Papacy attains to its absolute zenith. The council deposes Leo's enemy, Dioscorus, putting to death serious claims of Alexandrian primacy. It accepts his doctrinal definition as well as vindicates those ecclesiastics who have appealed to him. The council, needing Rome's assent, implores Leo to accept Canon 28—which he exercises his right not to accept. The Papacy is strong, needed, independent, teaching the whole Church, solving interpatriarchal disciplinary matters, and facilitating binding decisions in an Ecumenical Council. Leo played by all "the rules" and effectively "won the game."

Yet, after the rise comes the fall. During Chalcedon, the Byzantine/Eastern Roman Emperor (Marcian) wanted to facilitate unity with the Western Roman Empire simply because he was more able to exact "persuasive methods" in the East than in the politically independent West. Rome was essential to the East for this reason. After his death, when the Western Roman Empire began its precipitous collapse, this was no longer true. The East effectively snubbed Chalcedon and Leo's *Tome*.

The city of Rome itself was now politically controlled by Arian Ostrogoths. Romans had two choices. On one hand, they could facilitate closer connections with their disinterested kinsmen still independent in the East at the expense of forfeiting their doctrinal principles. On the other, they could strike out an independent path that maintained these principles, but effectively insulated themselves both from their Arian overlords and their Eastern brethren who abandoned the earlier, orthodox consensus.

This independent path was not only understandable, it seems to be the only principled option. However, in so doing, this appears to have led to developments which planted seeds for future problems which would have surely raised their heads sooner if it were not for Rome's geopolitical reincorporation into Byzantium. For one, the West, being isolated from the centralizing influences in the East, appears to have pursued a cavalier approach towards canon law. This introduced a tiered understanding of canonical authority, and authority in general, which did not have earlier precedents in Church history. Additionally, the verbiage of Gelasius, which was intended to give the impression that the Roman Synod's review was final and irrevocable, was advanced upon soon afterwards. As a review of the Papacy of Symmachus in the sixth century will prove, Gelasius' purposefully intransigent tone was advanced to the point that God Himself was the Pope's judge of last resort!

Such subtle developments in epistemology and ecclesiology had no practical effects, because of Rome's changing geopolitical situation. It would not be until Rome's geopolitical fortunes changed again during the eighth and ninth centuries for the "dust" to be blown off some of these fifth and sixth century statements, peculiar as they were for their era. With minor embellishment and reimagination, these "ancient" texts became the basis for a new concept of ecclesiology, bringing with it the final fall of the Papacy.

S . CELIVS SIMMACVS . PAPA . I . SARDV

Pope Symmachus

CHAPTER 6

The Sixth Century of the Papacy

The sixth century Papacy started "off with a bang," headed by a clique (called by one scholar the "Symmachan old guard"[462]) of fiercely pro-independent ecclesiastics. This included Pope Symmachus and three deacons he ordained that later became Popes themselves: Hormisdas, Felix IV, and Agapetus. Pope John I was likewise a deacon under Symmachus (one who left Laurentius' side). Others not directly connected to Symmachus himself were part of the same clique. At the end of what can be coined a dynasty, Hormisdas' own son, Silverius, became Pope. The "Symmachean Dynasty" was unceremoniously uprooted when Silverius was unfairly deposed and replaced by Vigilius—the latter perhaps exercising the most disastrous, capitulatory Papacy of the first millennium. With Vigilius began the era of the "Byzantine Papacy." This in effect put a pause on any ecclesiastical developments, even if purely rhetorical, that were being floated by the "Symmachean Dynasty."

---

462 This is a moniker used throughout Jeffrey Richards, *The Popes and the Papacy in the Early Middle Ages.* London: Routledge and Kegan Paul, 1979.

THE SYMMACHEAN FORGERIES

At the very beginning of the sixth century, a series of forgeries were made during a period of dispute called the Laurentian Schism. This moniker is not entirely justified as while there was a disputed election between Popes Symmachus and Laurentius, it was the latter that had the support of native Roman clergy and the rest of the Church. This was despite Laurentius accepting Symmachus' election on paper a year into the dispute.[463] The latter, wisely towing a middle line between the Ostrogoths and complete independence, commanded the allegiance of the episcopacy in the rest of Italy. His claim to the Papacy would win out only after many years and "persuasion" from the Ostrogothic King, Theodoric.

Laurentius was clearly the spiritual successor of Pope Anastasius II. He favored the Miaphysite *Henotikon* and had Byzantine support, favoring the continuation of Anastasius II's conciliatory attitude towards the East. However, Theodoric (an Arian and Ostrogoth) *initially* supported Symmachus as a bulwark of Roman independence from the Byzantine Church (i.e. against the *Henotikon*). The Roman Senate (in opposition to the Ostrogoths) supported Laurentius' cause and sought the deposition of Symmachus for violations of law.

As a result, Symmachus lost much of his support and Laurentius assumed control of the churches in Rome, as he had more support from local priests.[464] It appears Symmachus always had more support from Italy's bishops, likely due to his non-capitulatory stand against the Ostrogoths and Byzantines. Theodoric's support for Symmachus had apparently wavered in the middle of the controversy. In fact, Theodoric was unable (or unwilling) to even keep Symmachus safe in Rome itself, as he was nearly murdered re-entering the city in 501, despite Imperial protection.[465] It is ironic that in modern

---

463 Laurentius signed onto Rome (499) as an "archpresbyter," not accepting the bishopric of Nuceria at this time. See W.T. Townsend, "Councils Held Under Pope Symmachus," *Church History,* 5:3, 1937, 236.

464 Moorhead, "The Laurentian Schism," 133-134.

465 Townsend, "Councils Held Under Pope Symmachus," 248.

times the Basilica of Saint Paul contained the Papal portrait not of Symmachus, but Laurentius among the Popes, so serious was his claim.[466] Symmachus eventually regained Theodoric's support to the point that Laurentius' retirement was forced.

In order to protect Symmachus from deposition, several forgeries were concocted to prevent the Pope of Rome from being judged. This was important, because the concern that Theodoric's allegiance or sensibilities can shift was justified. The potential of Church-wide censuring, which was not impossible under the *Henotikon*, does not appear to be an explicit motivation.

In some respects, these forgeries did not say anything new. For example, in the Pseudo-Council of Sinuessa, it was claimed that "the first seat is not judged by anyone."[467] The false proceedings of a Pseudo-Council of Rome during the pontificate of Saint Silvester asserted that "the supreme leader will not be judged by anyone."[468] Indeed, this was similar to Pope Zosimus' assertion to the Africans 85 years previously that "our authority is such that nobody may review our sentence." However, the latter statement was specifically about the review of an intrapatriarchal appellate judgment. The former statements pertain to an intrapatriarchal deposition.

Yet, these fraudulent statements were not a remarkable advance beyond what Pope Gelasius had written less than a decade previously. In effect, the forgeries were the continuation of Gelasius' thought, but adding an allegedly more ancient pedigree so as to bestow upon them greater authority. The fact that a more ancient pedigree was deemed necessary reveals that the interpretations of Sardica from Gelasius were not considered authoritative in their own right. This

---

466 Moorhead, "The Laurentian Schism," 134. It has not been confirmed if this is still the case today, but presently Symmachus now has a portrait (perhaps replacing Laurentius).

467 The Latin is: *prima sedes non judicatur a quoquam*. See "Pope Saint Marcellinus," *Catholic Encyclopedia*, https://www.newadvent.org/cathen/09637d.htm

468 The Latin is: *neque praesul summus a quemquam iudicabitur*. See Eckhard Wirbelauer, *Zwei Papste in Rom: Der Konflikt Zwischen Laurentius und Symmachus (498-514)*. Munchen: Tuduv-Verlagsgesellscaft, mbH, 1993, 236.

was because Sardica's pedigree was in question and/or Gelasius' assertions were not understood as binding.

Details in the forgeries also broadened Gelasius' thought. The Pseudo-Council of Rome allegedly had the participation of 57 Eastern bishops via letter,[469] implying that Rome's exception from judgment was a Church-wide prerogative. This sealed the deal that Gelasius' had correctly interpreted Sardica and that its canons were a reiteration of a previous consensus.

Yet, such an implication can be emphasized too much. Consider the decree of the Synod of Palmaris (502) which concluded God was the Pope of Rome's judge of last resort:

> *Pope Symmachus, bishop of the [A]postolic [S]ee, has been charged with certain misdemeanors. Because for reasons set forth above, the whole affair has been reserved for divine judgement…Whence, according to the fundamental precepts which concede this to our power, we place back in his hands whatever of ecclesiastical jurisdiction is within or without the sacred city of Rome; and reserving the whole cause to the judgement of God we exhort, that, as occasion demands, people receive the sacred communion from him [Symmachus]…[470]*

One can infer that the Pope being under the judgment of God means that there was no other ecclesiastical body or bodies able to judge the Pope of Rome. However, this is not the likely intent of the authors of Palmaris' decree. As the statement shows, the matter is treated by the local council as outside of their own jurisdiction. The appeal to God is a figurative throwing of one's hands in the air and absolving oneself of responsibility—something that needed to be done in light of Theodoric's repeated requests that Symmachus be tried at this juncture. It does not directly address the function of a Church-wide judgment, something that by implication would be

---

469 Ibid., 73. Ironically, the same forgery ruled that Rome may only have seven deacons, a rule Symmachus himself would be the first to break. See Ibid., 74.

470 Townsend, "Councils Held Under Pope Symmachus," 251. Townsend renders "judgment" according to the English spelling "judgement."

God's judgment as it was understood that consensus carried with it the grace of the Spirit.[471]

In the end sum, the forgeries served the narrow purpose of addressing a local situation. They provided a local solution. Not surprisingly, the same synod removed the legal necessity that a king of Italy (then, Theodoric) consent to a Pope's election. Palmaris' goal was to insulate Rome from Ostrogothic interference. Interpatriarchal interference, though definitely a concern in these days, was likely not considered categorically impossible.

The topic of Papal depositions addressed by Palmaris is an interesting one. Up to that point, there was no "official" Papal deposition. Saint Pope Marcellinus might have legitimately resigned, or simply died before any action was taken against him. Saint Liberius signed the Arianized Creed. These men were the Papacy's only two lapsed Bishops at that time. Despite lapsing, no recorded depositions occurred.

Now, compare Rome to the other patriarchates. Both local and interpatriarchal synods have deposed Patriarchs of Alexandria (Saint Athanasius, Dioscorus), Constantinople (Maximus the Cynic, Nestorius), Antioch (Paul of Samosata, Domnus II), and Jerusalem (Saint Maximus III). Yet, Roman Patriarchs never were judged during the same time. The forgeries surrounding Symmachus were not without some historical pedigree.

Rome can legitimately be viewed as a special "exception to the rule" in the early sixth century. Such novel thinking, though with some historical justification, ultimately did not figure prominently in Rome's thinking on intrapatriarchal depositions. Pope Silverius three decades later was deposed by Imperial decree and this was accepted by the Roman Synod, as they (with Imperial "persuasion") elected and consecrated Vigilius. A century later, the Imperial deposition of Saint Pope Martin was accepted and Pope Eugene was consecrated against the will of the former while he was still

---

471 This may also indicate that Rome at this juncture did not view their local councils as graced in the Spirit as Carthage 80 years previously did. See the discussion of the Council of Carthage and the excursus in the previous chapter.

alive. The Symmachean forgeries failed in their attempt to create in Rome a novel understanding of ecclesiology in which the rules of intrapatriarchal deposition did not apply to the Pope. As for interpatriarchal depositions, Vigilius was deposed by the Ecumenical Council of Constantinople II.

In light of this, the Symmachean forgeries may seem inconsequential. However, their real import was two-fold. First, in time as memory faded concerning their questionable origin, they added ancient precedent to the ideas of Gelasius. Second, Palmaris created a juridical precedent wherein the Pope could not be judged in intrapatriarchal disputes other than by God. By the eighth and ninth centuries, by which point the forgeries and Palmaris were seen as authentic parts of the Christian tradition in the West, this justified an odd understanding of Papal depostions. The Roman Synod would continue deposing Popes, but because of the theoretical impossibility of anyone other than God doing so, the depositions all surrounded the alleged non-canonical character of a Pope's consecration. In effect, instead of depositions surrounding trumped-up charges of infidelity, they surrounded trumped-up charges of invalidity.

It would take until Anastasius the Librarian, when confronted by a valid Church-wide deposition exacted against Pope Nicholas in 867, to apply the logic of exception to intrapatriarchal depositions (by then accepted fully in Rome) to interpatriarchal ones. He also potentially wrote the "third address" of Pope Adrian II to the Council of Constantinople (869-870), which summed up the issue surrounding Palmaris and its import upon interpatriarchal depositions:

> *Who of you, I pray, ever heard of such a thing or encountered such immense presumption, at least in reading [i.e. Constantinople (867)'s deposition of Nicholas]? Although we have read of the Roman of the Roman pontiff passing judgement on the prelates of all the churches, we have not read of anyone having passed judgement on him...We remember, however, that, when Theodoric king of Italy wanted at one time to get Pope Symmachus condemned and therefore ordered as many bishops as possible to come to Rome...the venerable bishops replied that*

it was the one who was said to be under accusation who ought to have convoked the synod. For they knew that first the merit and pre-eminence of the [A]postle Peter and then the authority of the venerable councils, following the Lord's injunction, had conferred on him unique power in the churches…[472]

The stiff legalism of Gelasius, the imagination of Symacchus' clique, and the off-hand comment of Palmaris had created a Papal Supremacist seed—even though it had nothing specifically to do with interpatriarchal depositions. The later inventiveness of Anastasius the Librarian would play the decisive role in reapplying these in a novel way.

THE END OF THE ACACIAN SCHISM AND THE *FORMULA OF HORMISDAS*: AN OVER-EMPHASIZED "MILESTONE"

The *Formula of Hormisdas* is understood by some to be a document which explicitly laid out a muscular doctrine of the Papacy that was accepted by the whole Chalcedonian Church.[473] The truth of the matter is considerably more subdued in what the document claimed, what it was supposed to accomplish, and how it was received.

Hormisdas, being part of the Symmachean clique and involved in the dissemination of the Symmachean forgeries,[474] was not a stranger to the careful use of language to attain to his goals. At this juncture of history, Rome lacked a *Henotikon*-leaning faction.

472 Price and Montinaro, *The Acts of the Council of Constantinople of 869-70*, 314-315. Price, as in his other works, renders "judgment" according to its English spelling, "judgement."

473 Adrian Fortescue, *The Reunion Formula of Hormisdas*. Garrison, NY: Chair of Unity Apostolate, 1955. This tract is highly polemical, but still cited by modern scholarship due to containing multiple Latin versions of the *Formula*. See Volker-Lorenz Menze, *Justinian and the Making of the Syrian Orthodox Church*. Oxford: Oxford University Press, 2008, 67-69.

474 Future Pope Hormisdas "read material on behalf of Symmachus" during the Synod of Palmaris (502). See Moorhead, "The Laurentian Schism," 131. This suggests a role in the dissemination and, potentially, creation of the forgeries.

Rapprochement with Rome required the Byzantines to meet them on their terms, not the other way around. When the Byzantine Emperor Anastasius I died childless, the commander of the palace guard, Justin, outmaneuvered his competition and seized the throne. Justin sought to solidify his relations with the West by re-establishing a Church union with the Roman Synod.

In short, Constantinople needed to capitulate, unambiguously accept the Council of Chalcedon and disown the *Henotikon*. This would come at the expense of offending subjects who were opposed to these actions, not to mention the disgrace of reversing decades of ecclesiastical policy. Yet, only Alexandria at this juncture was strongly non-Chalcedonian. Antioch, Jerusalem, and Constantinople had several Patriarchs during the Acacian Schism that were Chalcedonian. In effect, Justin was giving up on Anastasius I's policy of trying to make everyone happy, because clearly it was not working. He picked what was the majority—the Chalcedonians. This, politically, was a reasonable choice at the time.

Hormisdas had already penned the *Formula* in 515, before Justin attained the throne. It was perhaps a reunion formula whose acceptance would be necessary for Roman participation at a council called by Emperor Anastasius I in Heraclea.[475] Upon Justin's ascension to the throne, Hormisdas requested that this same formula, at this point already subscribed to by those within his own patriarchate in Spain and the Balkans, as well as those from beyond such as by some Syrian monks, to be accepted officially in *all* the East.

The document was deliberately penned to leave no doubt that its signers disowned Acacius' policy of rapprochement with the non-Chalcedonians and an admission that Rome was right all along. There would be no ambiguous re-interpretations of the *Tome of Leo* such as what was being floated during the Papacy of Anastasius II. No face-saving or compromising of Saint Leo's doctrine would be allowed. The *Formula* ran as follows. The demands for the unambiguous acceptance of Chalcedon and the *Tome* are

---

475 Menze, *Justinian and the Making of the Syrian Orthodox Church*, 71.

underlined and the sections relevant to the Papacy emboldened in order to assist the reader in discerning the true purpose of the text:

The first condition of salvation is to keep the norm of the true faith and in no way to deviate from the established doctrine of the Fathers. **For it is impossible that the words of our Lord Jesus Christ, who said, "Thou art Peter, and upon this rock I will build my Church," [Matthew 16:18], should not be verified. And their truth has been proved by the course of history, for in the Apostolic See the Catholic religion has always been kept unsullied.** *From this hope and faith we by no means desire to be separated and, following the doctrine of the Fathers, we declare anathema all heresies, and, especially, the heretic Nestorius, former bishop of Constantinople, who was condemned by the Council of Ephesus, by Blessed Celestine, bishop of Rome, and by the venerable Cyril, bishop of Alexandria. We likewise condemn and declare to be anathema Eutyches and Dioscoros of Alexandria, who were condemned in the holy Council of Chalcedon, which we follow and endorse. This Council followed the holy Council of Nicaea and preached the apostolic faith. And we condemn the assassin Timothy, surnamed Aelurus ["the Cat"] and also Peter [Mongos] of Alexandria, his disciple and follower in everything. We also declare anathema their helper and follower, Acacius of Constantinople, a bishop once condemned by the Apostolic See, and all those who remain in contact and company with them. Because this Acacius joined himself to their communion, he deserved to receive a judgment of condemnation similar to theirs. Furthermore, we condemn Peter ["the Fuller"] of Antioch with all his followers together with the followers of all those mentioned above.* **Following, as we have said before, the Apostolic See in all things** *and proclaiming all its decisions, we endorse and approve all the letters which Pope St Leo wrote concerning the Christian religion.* **And so I hope I may deserve to be associated with you in the one communion which the Apostolic See proclaims, in which the whole, true, and perfect security of the Christian religion resides.** *I promise that from now on those who are separated from the communion of the*

> *Catholic Church, that is, who are not in agreement with the Apostolic*
> *See, will not have their names read during the sacred mysteries.*

The obvious emphasis in the *Formula*, as the amount of underlined text proves, was the unambiguous acceptance of the Council of Chalcedon/the *Tome* and the rejection of those Rome has anathematized both past and present. The significance of the latter was to disallow for the sort of intercommunion between Chalcedonians and non-Chalcedonians the *Henotikon* allowed. The *Formula's* purpose is clear: a complete repudiation of the *Henotikon* and its spirit, something that was not possible during the reign of Anastasius I.

In light of this, the Roman honorifics (in bold) appear to serve the function of admitting Rome was right all along during the Acacian Schism, thereby delegitimizing the *Henotikon*. An interpretation that emphasizes that some sort of ecclesiastical primacy or infallibility/ indefectability concessions were being sought does not appear to fit the context.[476] Evidence for this is seen in that the *Formula* extols Rome's orthodox stands in explicitly the Nestorian and Eutychian controversies, but not any others. If the intent was to argue in every possible respect that Rome was eternally orthodox and this was the basis under which Hormisdas should be heeded,[477] one would

---

476 Menze emphasizes that the language left "no doubt that *only* Rome remained
    permanently faithful," (emphasis added) citing anathematization of the
    heretics in the other patriarchates as proof for this contention. See Ibid.,
    69. This gloss puts too heavy of an ecclesiastical emphasis beyond what
    Hormisdas likely intended. First, the Jerusalem Patriarchate is not implicated
    in the anathemas, which inveighs against the inference Menze is drawing.
    Roman exceptionalism is not strictly intended in the anathemas. Second,
    the names of those that are condemned are invoked so as to make clear who
    cannot be liturgically commemorated, one of the central demands coupled
    with the acceptance of the *Formula*. The obvious point of this demand was
    to undo the sort of inter-sectarian commemoration the *Henotikon* permitted.

477 Some wrongly infer that the *Formula* is attempting to convey the absolute
    necessity of Roman communion in the words "one communion which the
    Apostolic See proclaims." This is anachronistic and would have called into
    question Pope Anastasius II's conciliatory policy, not to mention the Roman
    Synod's errant stand during the Meletian Schism. Nevertheless, there are
    fifth century statements which more convincingly appear to argue for the

expect that it would have included Rome's role during the Arian Controversy. However, this is not explicitly laid out in the *Formula*, because the only point at issue was Chalcedon/the *Tome*—not a broader claim. This is why only Chalcedon and Ephesus are noted, the citation of Ephesus serving the function of proving that Chalcedon and the *Tome* were not crypto-Nestorian as the non-Chalcedonians alleged.

It would be inferring too much that Hormisdas was deliberately leaving unsaid the capitulations to semi-Arianism that occurred in the Roman Patriarchate, or other examples of questionable acts from Roman Popes such as Zephyrinus' friendliness with Sabellus, Marcellinus' apostasy, and Liberius' creedal affirmation of semi-Arianism. Unlike what the modern imagination races to, ascribing infallibility to the Pope of Rome would have been completely alien to anyone's thinking at this time.[478] Inferring a deliberate omission of the preceding demands that infallibility was central to the

---

absolute necessity of the aforesaid communion. Pope Boniface I asserted to the Bishops of Thessaly: "Certain, therefore, is it that this [Roman] Church is to the Churches spread throughout the world, as it were, the head of its own members, from which whoever cuts himself off is expelled from the Christian religion, inasmuch as he has ceased to be within the one structure." "Churches spread throughout the world" appears to be a euphemism for those within Rome's own patriarchate, as what follows this warning is a criticism of "certain bishops, despising the apostolic right…striving to separate themselves from the Apostolic See's communion" in abandoning Rufus of Thessalonica. In short, the statement is intrapatriarchal in import. Such a statement does not appear to be a serious assertion that in recent memory, Saints Flavian and Meletius of Antioch were not in Christian communion. However, Boniface would have been in his right in asserting Rome's synodical assent was necessary to grant *full legitimacy* to a fellow Patriarch. See Butler and Collorafi, *Keys Over the Christian World*, 115.

478 Siecienski wrongly ascribes to Dorotheus of Thessalonica the belief in Hormisdas' personal infallibility in *The Papacy and the Orthodox*, 183. The actual passage merely asserts that "champions [lit.: *propugnatores*] of the faith never err" concerning the churches making up the Church at-large. See the plurals for the words "sacred churches" (*ecclesiarum sanctarum*) in PL 63, 371. Ironically, Dorotheus broke with Hormisdas and temporarily sided with the non-Chalcedonians.

document's penning, which radically decontextualizes it from the polemical demands of the time.

Further evidence can be gleaned by the response of some Syrian monks to the *Formula*. There is no doubt that the Syrian monks believed their response, though not *ad verbatim* following the *Formula*, to be a subscription to it. In fact, it references providing an answer to a Roman legate (lit. *angeli* or "messenger") and describes itself as "having the power of *Formulas*" (i.e. a reference to the *Formula of Hormisdas*; lit. *"virtutem habente libelli"*).[479] In subscribing to it, the majority of their letter complains about their persecution, before in the end making vague references to the document in question.[480] Their confession issues different, equally lofty Papal honorifics. Hormisdas is called in the Latin the "blessed [P]atriarch of the whole world." This was a deliberate slap against Constantinople's bishop, a Patriarch they were not in communion with who *also* laid claim to the title "Ecumenical Patriarch" (the Latin surely being a translation of this). Additionally, Syria is called "your province," as these Syrian monks had broken off local communion due to the local bishops' rejection of Chalcedon and Byzantine oppression of their partisans. They would have needed a bishop to be in communion with, why not Hormisdas?

As for the ecclesiastical honorifics concerning Rome, the letter shows no awareness that they are serious doctrinal assertions that must be confessed. Instead of citing Matt 16:18 as the *Formula* does, it cites Matt 16:19. Additionally, their letter asserts that Rome's authority to bind and loosen comes from both "Peter… and Paul," not specifically Peter as the *Formula* specifies. Lastly, it makes no reference to the "unsullied" faith of Rome, likely not out of disagreement but in proper recognition that the actual point

---

479 PL 63, 411. Latin: *Ad perfectam autem notitiam vestri sancti angeli anathematizamus in eadem nostra deprecatione virtutem habente libelli omnes projectos et excommunicatos a vestra apostolica sede.*

480 Collectio Avellana, Letter 139 is the same letter as Ibid.. Subsequent English translation is provided by Cornelia Horn in "The Correspondence Between the Monks of Syria Secunda and Pope Hormisdas in 517/518 A.D.," *Maronite Institute*, http://www.maronite-institute.org/MARI/JMS/october97/The_Correspondence_Between.htm

of the passage was the delegitimization of the *Henotikon*. Fittingly, the Syrians then without reservations anathematize everyone that Rome sought to have anathematized.

Hormisdas' recorded response indicates his pleasure with what was stated. He wrote, "For we hold as a guaranty [sic] the firmness of your faith in its profession up to the individual letters."[481] He even embraces the altered honorifics ascribed to him. In approving of the Syrians' acceptance of the *Tome*, he comments that the document has:

> *been set up from the hearts of the [A]postles [Peter and Paul] themselves. In these [Apostles] the banner of faith, in these the ramparts of truth, in these Christ is recognized, in these the hope and cause of our redemption is preserved. This is the foundation...* [482]

Such a reply surely indicates that all Hormisdas was looking for was unqualified communion with his synod, and acceptance of Chalcedon/the *Tome*. Roman ecclesiastical prerogatives are apparently not on anyone's radar.

When the same *Formula* was posed to Constantinople's Synod as a requirement for Roman communion in Justin's time, Hormisdas was in a more negotiating mood than he was previously. Initially, he wanted several dead Patriarchs and their followers to be removed from liturgical commemoration—otherwise the *Henotikon* would still be in force for the dead. Due to this, Hormisdas actually instructed his legates via letter to lie that the *Formula* could not be altered whatsoever. However, not wanting to miss the opportunity to have Constantinople reenter communion (mostly) on his terms, the same letter of instructions indicates that the *Formula* could be altered *if* opposition to his demands was too strong.[483] The alteration agreed to in the *Formula* was minor and can be reduced to recognizing the holy orders of Acacius' successors. This was an obvious concession as not doing so would have called into question the capacity of

---

481 Collectio Avellana, *Letter 140* in Ibid.

482 Ibid.

483 Denny, *Papalism*, 472-473.

those he was negotiating with to even enter his communion. In fact, Hormisdas was merely admitting what Pope Anastasius II had already made clear 20 years previously.

Typical of Byzantine politics, Constantinople's Patriarch, Saint John II, sought something in return for admitting to his patriarchate being in the wrong for about 40 years. In accepting the *Formula*, which as established beforehand had the sole purpose of unambiguously affirming the Council of Chalcedon and the *Tome*, John took the opportunity to emphasize his ecclesiastical prerogatives enshrined in Canon 28 of the aforementioned council. In his signature he added:

> *I hold the most holy churches of your elder and our new Rome to be one church; I define that the see of the Apostle Peter [Rome] and this of the [I]mperial city [Constantinople] to be one see.*[484]

It is possible that the significance of Rome and Constantinople being "one" is simply a reference to union. However, it has been rightfully interpreted as an invocation of the "equal privileges" accorded to Constantinople in virtue of it being "the same" as "Senior Rome" as Canon 28 of Chalcedon delineates.[485] The *Formula* lacked such a parsing of elder/senior and new. The insertion of this could mean nothing other than the smug implication that by accepting Chalcedon, Canon 28 comes with the package. The usage of the terminology "I define" implies that John II is acting as an equal, imposing his own views.

The Papal legate Dioscorus, himself a deacon from Symmachus' time and later a short-tenured Pope of Rome, realized the indignity intended by the signature. He wrote apologetically to Hormisdas that John II "tried to make out it [the *Formula*/*libellus*] was a letter rather than a *libellus*" and "appropriate for a *libellus*" allowed for

---

484 Collectio Avellana, *Letter 159* quoted in Frederick Puller, *The Primitive Saints and the See of Rome*. London: Longmans, Green, and Co., 1900, 400.

485 Frend, *The Rise of the Monophysite Movement*, 239. Frend infers that accepting the "presbeia" of Old Rome was a sort of ecclesiastical concession, but much the opposite is the case.

the aforementioned signature.[486] In other words, John had initially intended on receiving the letter in a sense that treated the *Formula* like correspondence, not an explicit repudiation of Constantinopolitan policy. Dioscorus seems to be saying that he did not oppose the signature as stated, because this made clear that the *Formula* was an official document which required Constantinopolitan agreement to its stipulations. Hormisdas, not bound by someone else's signature (despite it being a "decree"), simply did not make an issue out of John's obvious intransigence. John II and his synod officially dumping the *Henotikon*, the goal all along, was good enough.

In light of these events, what happened next is not terribly surprising. Hormisdas continued a policy of subtle compromises provided that those re-entering Roman communion unambiguously accepted Chalcedon and the *Tome*. Initially, he sought to have the *Formula* accepted with the minimal changes that he had accepted from Constantinople. However, despite supporting the use of "fire and sword" and "threats and persuasions" to impose an unmitigated acceptance of the document,[487] Hormisdas soon gave up on this. Justin cautioned Hormisdas that coercion was not working and that it was necessary to:

> unite everywhere the venerable churches, and especially the Church of Jerusalem, on which all bestow their good will, as being the mother of the Christian name, so that no one dares to separate himself from that church.[488]

Hormisdas decided that he would drop requirements pertaining to not liturgically commemorating deceased individuals, as this was proving divisive. Additionally, the *Formula* did not have to be confessed *ad verbatim*. Hormisdas demanded only that Chalcedon

---

486 Collectio Avellana, *Letter 167* quoted in Neil and Allen, *Conflict and Negotiation in the Early Church*, 81.

487 Collectio Avellana, *Letter 196* and *232* quoted respectively in Puller, *The Primitive Saints and the See of Rome*, 401. Hormisdas' reply in *Letter 238* amounted to an admonishment to "compel uniformity" on the question of the *Formula*. See Ibid.

488 Collectio Avellana, *Letter 232* quoted in Ibid.

and its doctrines be affirmed and "keep to these things as defined by the Fathers."[489] This would be done via a "written profession of faith" sent to both Constantinople and then forwarded to Rome for review, in which it would be accepted as long as it was "written however in the same tenor" as either the formula itself, or more likely, the Chalcedonian teachings found in the same letter.[490] While this has been asserted to have been a deliberate tempering of the allegedly "extreme" ecclesiastical claims in the *Formula*,[491] this is not credible, considering no such claims were actually made nor intended. In asking for a confession in a "similar tenor," Hormisdas was simply requesting what he was always insisting upon since the inception of the *Formula* itself. In other words, a statement similar to what the Syrians sent a few years previous sufficed to meet his requirements.

The true indignity for Hormisdas was in dropping the requirement for ceasing the liturgical commemoration of deceased non-Chalcedonians. By dropping any necessary anathemas concerning who was not to be liturgically commemorated,[492] he had in effect removed the requirement of repudiating the spirit of the *Henotikon*. In effect, Hormisdas had adopted the rapprochement policy of Pope Anastasius II not on behalf of the living, but the dead. This was a definite retraction of Symmachus' posturing on the same question. However, it was a necessary move as there was no other way to make peace. Even notable contemporary

---

489 Hormisdas, *Letter 80*. See translation by John Collorafi in "Pope Hormisdas Letters 77 and 80: A Translation," *Orthodox Christian Theology*, https:// orthodoxchristiantheology.com/2021/08/26/pope-hormisdas-letters-77-and-80-a-translation/. The "Fathers" intended must have been the same that were approved by Rome (496) and who, uncoincidentally, were later largely approved by Constantinople II in Session 3. See Price, *The Acts of the Council of Constantinople of 553: Volume One*, 224.

490 Ibid.

491 See Denny, *Papalism*, 307 and Puller, *The Primitive Saints and the See of Rome*, 398.

492 Puller, *The Primitive Saints and the See of Rome*, 424.

non-Chalcedonians, such as Severus of Antioch, adopted an identical policy.[493]

It is ironic that the *Formula* has been reimagined in later centuries as some sort of Papal ecclesiastical zenith. The actual history on the question reveals the document had no ecclesiastical import and that its modified acceptance was in some respects humiliating for the Roman Synod. However, unity was attained throughout most of Christendom. In light of the actual purpose of the *Formula*, one can rightly evaluate that Hormisdas was successful in redeeming Chalcedon and the *Tome*. Hormisdas made the right compromises to accomplish his task. The sands of time have since ground away the significance of his liturgical concessions.

THE COUNCILS OF CONSTANTINOPLE IN 536: AN EXERCISE IN CANONICAL PATRIARCHAL DEPOSITION

In terms of actual history of the Papacy, the consecration of Saint Menas of Constantinople by Pope Agapetus carries little importance on the question. However, due to there being undue emphasis attached by polemicists to the nature of this consecration, it will be discussed in brief.

Anthimus of Constantinople had Miaphysite leanings and was pressured by Saint Justinian, the Byzantine Emperor who replaced his uncle Justin, to resign in March 536 (or he was deposed). Menas was ordained on March 13th, 536 by Pope Agapetus. This happened during the first Council of Constantinople of 536, a small synod with mostly local clergy. Menas' letter to Jerusalem's Synod boasted of his ordination by a Pope, as this surely was more impressive than whatever minor bishops also took part.

It is falsely believed, due to the hagiographic witness not naming any other bishops, that Agapetus singularly deposed Anthimus and ordained Menas. This is not credible. Menas obviously did not have a non-canonical ordination with only one bishop presiding. Multiple bishops signed onto Menas' consecration letter indicating they took

---

493 Moss, *Incorruptible Bodies*, 91.

part in the ordination.[494] Due to Anthimus only resigning (or being deposed by Imperial decree and rubber-stamped by the Home Synod in Constantinople and the Pope of Rome), a council was necessary to win the assent of the Patriarchs for his replacement. This was a replay of ecclesiastical procedure for Patriarchal depositions from previous centuries.

Due to Alexandria and Antioch arguably having Miaphysite patriarchs, the follow-up synod in Constantinople went through specific motions. It anathematized Severus of Antioch (who had been deposed years earlier). At that time, the episcopacy in Alexandria was disputed between two non-Chalcedonians (Theodosios of Alexandria and a Julianst, Gainas, who died shortly thereafter). Theodosios, due to his exile, and Gainas' soul (due to being dead) were not in the city itself. The Patriarchal deposition of Anthimus therefore did not need Alexandria's consent until they had a new Patriarch. The next year, Paul of Alexandria (Chalcedonian) served this role.

As for the more intact patriarchates, Jerusalem held a synod in the same year accepting the work of Constantinople's council.[495] There is no record of a council in Antioch, but there are indications that Saint Ephraim of Antioch was cooperative[496]—implying his synod's concurrent acceptance. Anthimus was canonically deposed by the Patriarchs of Rome, Antioch, and Jerusalem—with the explicit acceptance of Jerusalem's and Constantinople's Synods and implied synodal acceptance of Rome and Antioch. Alexandria would rubber-stamp matters after the fact. In short, the standard procedure of Patriarchal deposition, requiring synodal consensus, was followed.

---

494 Maria Constantinou, "Synodal Decision-Making Based on Archived Material," in Wolfram Brandes, Alexandra Hasse-Ungeheuer, and Hartmut Leppin (eds.), *Konzilien und kanonisches Recht in Spätantike und frühem Mittelalter: Aspekte konziliarer Entscheidungsfindung.* Berlin: De Gruyter, 2020, 87-88.

495 Landon, *A Manual of Councils of the Holy Catholic Church, Volume 1,* 306.

496 Zachariah of Mitylene, *Syriac Chronicle,* Book 10, Chap 1.

THE BEGINNING OF THE BYZANTINE PAPACY

In 536, Pope Silverius, Hormisdas' son, was made Pope with Ostrogothic support in the time immediately preceding their geopolitical collapse in Italy. This was probably with the hope he would not be a Byzantine puppet as he represented the more independent Symmachean Dynasty. Shortly afterwards, Byzantium retook Rome from the Ostrogoths. Suspecting Silverius of sedition, he was deposed at the Byzantine General Belisarius' command. Vigilius, the Roman legate to Constantinople, was tapped to replace Silverius with the support of a sizable faction within Rome's clergy. Despite this, Silverius appealed to Justinian that his deposition was arbitrary and capricious. Justinian overruled Silverius' enemies and sent Silverius to Rome for a retrial. Vigilius had Silverius arrested again and the latter died in exile.[497]

This account is a good example of the harshness and subjugation that the Byzantine Papacy often manifested. Pope Vigilius would later be deposed as a heretic, though he was reinstated after recanting. Saint Pope Martin would be arrested and replaced against his wishes while still being alive. Byzantine policy was to force the Pope to act as a tax collector for the local garrison and to toe a line sympathetic to Eastern ecclesiastical demands. Rome, being far away from Constantinople, was often able to buck the trend when Byzantine geopolitical fortunes waned. Politics decided whether Rome "got away with it" or meekly went along with the Byzantine program. The preceding dynamic governed what shape Papal controversies would take over the next two centuries.

VIGILIUS AND THE FIFTH ECUMENICAL COUNCIL: A MICROCOSM FOR FIRST MILLENNIUM ECCLESIOLOGY

It is fitting that the continued dastardly political machinations of Vigilius would result in the greatest humiliation in Papal history

---

497 Eamon Duffy, *Saints and Sinners: A History of the Popes*. London: Yale University Press, 2014, 66.

immediately after the Ecumenical Council of Constantinople II. Unfortunately for the Roman Synod, Vigilius' tenure would prove to be the nadir of Papacy. The council excommunicated him and the same Pope repented and blamed his doctrinal errors on Satan. The council issued in its decree an explicit endorsement of consensus-based ecclesiology and with its acceptance by all the patriarchates, including Rome, the matter of ecclesiology was dogmatically settled.

As a result of the rhetorical developments since the Papacy of Gelasius, Vigilius often expressed himself with high-Papal language. Relevant to this study is the fact that he did so due to indications that he was going to be forced (again) by Justinian to anathematize certain crypto-Nestorian statements recorded in the "Three Chapters." At this time, synods in the West saw such anathemas as tampering with Chalcedon and therefore a repudiation of orthodox Christology. Vigilius knew better than this, but not wanting to be deposed or assassinated, he took a firm stance in "defense" of Chalcedon and excommunicated all those who did not adopt the majority stance of the West.

For example, in a letter excommunicating those who subscribed to Justinian's *Edict* (whose contents essentially became the meat of Constantinople II), Vigilius identifies himself as from "the primatial see."[498] He boasted of "the role and authority of the blessed Peter the [A]postle" and "decreed" that those who disagreed with him were "stripped both of priestly dignity and catholic communion" and that they "may recover" their "rank...through the mercifulness of either myself or, after my death, my successor."[499] Such strong wording is innovative in an interpatriarchal context. Taken at face value, Vigilius seems to say that Rome has the highest rank and can unilaterally decide who is catholic and who is not.

This is when one must separate rhetoric from substance, words from facts. For one, it is unlikely that after centuries of Popes of Rome never asserting any such ecclesiastical prerogatives that suddenly they exist so as to merit reference. Second, Vigilius expounded

---

498 Price, *The Acts of the Council of Constantinople of 553: Volume One*, 163.
499 Ibid., 164.

consensus-based ecclesiology and viewed his excommunications as purely local in character. For example, his resistance to Justinian's *Edict* was predicated upon it being "transact[ed]" without "resolution by the [i.e. Ecumenical] council."[500] In a Papal encyclical written to "the holy catholic church of the city of Rome to the whole people of God,"[501] Vigilius asserts that Justinian and everyone else are "obliged to wait for a common resolution" and that they were "suspended as transgressors," being excluded "from communion with the see of the blessed [A]postle Peter."[502] He specifies this as "our communion."[503] This indicates that Vigilius understood his excommunications were not binding Church-wide—mitigating against the literal wording of his original excommunication. Vigilius based his authority upon his see and "the ecclesiastical canons,"[504] an expected detail but one that would eventually drop out of Papal discourse in later centuries.

The interpretation that Vigilius identified his own excommunication as only locally binding is strengthened by a contemporary document weighing in on the same question. The *Letter of the Church of Milan to the Frankish Envoys*, written contemporarily with the preceding documents, delineates which local communions those opposed to Vigilius were excluded from:

> the most blessed pope [Vigilius] admonished all the bishops in the following words: 'Whoever agrees to give the edict [of Justinian] his assent is to know that he is suspended from the communion of the [A]postolic [S]ee.' The holy Datius of Milan also gave his testimony before all when he exclaimed loudly, 'Mark that both myself and all the priests of the region which my church belongs, that is, Gaul, Burgundy, Spain, Liguria, Aemilia, and Venetia [i.e. from Spain to Italy], attest

---

500 Ibid., 162.

501 The encyclical's name is *Dum in Sanctae Euphemiae*. See Ibid., 170.

502 Ibid., 171.

503 Ibid., 172.

504 Ibid., 171. Cf Ibid., 164.

that whoever assents to the edict will be excluded from communion with the bishops of the above-mentioned provinces. [505]

Vigilius' in his *First Constitutim* likewise expounded consensus-based ecclesiology. Concerning what contains dogmatic authority he specified that "whatever was affirmed orthodox in those places by common consent with the legates…we revere and accept as orthodox…without revision or alteration."[506] This same document defended the *Letter to Maris* (among the "Three Chapters") as orthodox in its content, an ironic position given that he'd soon condemn the same document as heretical after Constantinople II. As Saint Columbanus recalled a few decades later to Pope Boniface IV, "you are alleged to favour heretics…Vigilius himself died under such a taint."[507]

Before he backtracked on the alleged orthodoxy of the *Letter to Maris*, Vigilius reversed his own demands for an Ecumenical Council. When it was convened, Vigilius refused to attend. The council responded by excommunicating Vigilius and teaching consensus-based ecclesiology in a firm repudiation of his intransigence.

Concerning Vigilius' excommunication, it was intentionally predicated upon his heresy in not imputing heterodoxy to the "Three Chapters." Earlier Patriarchal excommunications were more strictly procedural. The Council of Chalcedon deposed Dioscorus of Alexandria for failing to answer three summonses. During the Council of Ephesus, Nestorius was effectively excommunicated twice: once for failing to answer three summonses to attend the council and again for being a heretic. Vigilius would receive an Imperial deposition for heresy. Only Paul of Samosata was strictly deposed for heresy beforehand (though it is possible he was summoned three times, but this was lost to history). Similar to Paul of Samosata, what made Vigilius' deposition binding (not that anyone was going to question an Imperial decree in Constantinople) was the consent of the world's synods, as represented in the Ecumenical

---

505 Ibid., 168.

506 Ibid., *The Acts of the Council of Constantinople of 553: Volume 2*, 146.

507 *Letter 5* quoted in Walker, *Letters of Columbanus*, 45.

Council, to it. While Vigilius was summoned twice to the council, a third summons was likely deliberately avoided.

The excommunication is condensed as follows:

> *The Holy Council Said: 'May the sacred decree be duly received and read.' [Decree of Justinian]: '...we have pronounced that his name [Vigilius] is alien to Christians and is not read out in the sacred diptychs...' The holy council said: 'What has now seemed good...Let us therefore preserve unity with the [A]postolic [S]ee of the sancrosanct church of Elder Rome, transacting everything according to the tenor of the texts [i.e. the decree] that have been read.*[508]

It is common knowledge that when a "[c]hurch named a person in the diptychs, she professed her communion with that individual."[509] After this action, Vigilius is never mentioned with his ecclesiastical title by the council, the deposition knowingly being in effect. Hence, Pope Vigilius himself was excommunicated; but not the Roman Synod itself, whose consent (with the other synods) to the council was necessary for it to establish "consensus." Immediately prior to the deposition, Vigilius' own condemnations of the "Three Chapters" were posed as evidence that he had already accepted the work of the council in advance. Such a move is not unknown in Ecumenical Councils, as Nicaea II essentially did this during its third session (in reference to the Oriental Patriarchs accepting iconodulia 18 years *previously*).

Why was an Imperial deposition for heresy, as opposed to a failure to answer three summonses, opted for? In short, it allowed for the recantation of the heresy. A third summons could not be undone. It was hoped that Vigilius could be "persuaded" to recant, thereby nullifying the excommunication. Indeed, if Vigilius would not recant, he, like his *deposed* predecessor Pope Silverius, would simply be replaced with someone more manipulable. But, Vigilius had flip-flopped before. A third summons would make matters

---

508 Price, *The Acts of the Council of Constantinople of 553: Volume 2*, 99, 101.

509 Butler and Collorafi, *Keys Over the Christian World*, 130.

more laborious than necessary. Vigilius would be kept under house arrest until he changed his tune again.

There can be no doubt that the excommunication had taken place. It is preserved in whole in the only extant manuscript of Constantinople II.[510] This manuscript so happens to be a Latin translation, the Greek being lost to history. It is believed that a second, doctored version of Constantinople II was made in response to Vigilius' excommunication in the hope of preserving his reputation. It survives presently in fragments, but is allegedly preserved entirely in a 1567 published edition. Interestingly, in this version Vigilius' titles are restored and any mentions of his intransigence and deposition are removed from the final two sessions of the council. In the conciliar decree, Vigilius is called "*Vigilium religiosissimum*"[511] ("Most Religious Vigilius") instead of simply "Vigilius."

Presuming the authenticity of this tradition, it appears to have been created soon after the council by the same translators as the full Latin tradition. Due to their identical rendering of the Latin in sections not putting Vigilius into disrepute, this indicates that a second round of Latin translation is extremely unlikely. Rather, the version lacking Vigilius' excommunication is essentially an *ad verbatim* copy of the original Latin tradition containing the excommunication (represented by the sole extant manuscript that presently survives). Scholarship identifies the translator of all the Latin traditions of Constantinople II as "the same source" which translated Chalcedon, due to its identical translational style.[512]

This most plausibly identifies Vigilius' own chancery. He would have needed Chalcedon translated when he was penning the *First Constitution* and an extant Latin tradition for Chalcedon does not pre-exist this era. Similarly, Vigilius would have required the entirety

---

510 Price, *The Acts of the Council of Constantinople of 553: Volume 1*, 104.

511 Laurentius Surius, *Concilia omnia, tum generalia, tum provincialia atque particularia*. Calenius & Quentel, 1567, 590.

512 Price, *The Acts of the Council of Constantinople of 553: Volume 1*, Preface, x. The surviving Greek portions of Constantinople II preserved in fragments point to a "literal and faithful" translation just like Chalcedon's, where the same is surmised by comparing the entire set of the Greek minutes with the Latin.

of Constantinople II translated for his review and as indicated previously, the near-identical nature of the two Latin variants identifies a time of composition immediately after the council (or several centuries in the future when the council's original contents would have been scandalous). Certainly, the modified version was made after Vigilius' recantation, as this is the only motive that makes sense. For a modified version to be made, the pre-existing Latin translation with the excommunication had to already exist.

After Vigilius' recantation and acceptance of Constantinople II, the second, edited, version outlived its purpose. Vigilius died (or was murdered) on his way back to Rome and there was no compelling reason to protect his reputation, especially considering the next Pope handpicked by Justinian (Pelagius I) was rumored to have been involved in his death.[513] Vigilius' chancery evidently preserved, and the Roman Synod later received, both manuscripts of the council. This explains their textual survival. Nobody thought it problematic to receive a document which recorded the Pope's interpatriarchal excommunication. There was nothing doctrinally problematic about the concept at the time. Probably the only reason the edited version survived despite no one caring about Vigilius' memory (presuming its authenticity) is because paper was expensive and textual criticism non-existent. The copy was maintained and re-copied before being totally lost to history sometime after it was lucky enough to be published in print.

So much for Vigilius' deposition. As noted previously, Constantinople II's decree is relevant to this study, because it expounded upon consensus-based epistemology and ecclesiology:

> *Vigilius was staying in this [I]mperial city and ought to have taken part...our most pious emperor...urged both Vigilius and ourselves to meet together, since it is appropriate for priests to impose a common solution...we recalled to his [Vigilius'] memory the great example of the [A]postles and the traditions of the fathers. For even though individual [A]postles abounded with the grace of the Holy Spirit so that they*

---

513 "Papa Pelagio I," *Liber Pontificalis*, https://fontistoriche.org/papa-pelagio-i/. The *Liber Pontificalis* briefly notes that Pelagius I cleared himself from blame for Vigilius' death, indicating this was a response to accusations.

*did not need the advice of others...they met together and each of them confirmed his statements from the testimonies of the divine scriptures... The holy fathers also who convened at various times in the holy four councils followed the ancient precedent...since **it is certain that is through joint examination,** when there is expounded what needs to be discussed on both sides, **that the light of truth dispels the darkness of lies. For neither is it permissible in the case of faith for anyone to anticipate the judgement of the church in her totality...**[514]*

As noted previously, Vigilius is not identified as a bishop. This is a standard conciliar way of identifying people who are not clergy. More striking is the emphasis put upon "joint examination." It is identified as morally "certain" that it is the only way "the light of truth" is discerned. The establishment of consensus is considered non-negotiable and the idea any individual can make a singular judgment for the Church, with the Pope of Rome specifically in view, is disallowed. By any consistent theological standard, this conciliar decree must be understood as expressing the dogmatic ecclesiastical and epistemological view of the entire early Church. This obviously includes Rome, which accepted this conciliar decree.

As indicated previously, Vigilius capitulated to Justinian under pressure. He wrote to Constantinople's Patriarch, Eutychius, blaming "the enemy of the human race" for deceiving him into writing against the "Three Chapters" and then "annul[ed the *First Constitution*] by the authority of our present letter."[515] The ignominy of Vigilius, though not preventing local reception of the council in Rome itself, led to parts of the West not consenting to the council's work. This was despite Papal ratification. For example, decades later Saint Pope Gregory the Great wrote several letters imploring foreign synods to accept Constantinople II. The Councils of Toledo in 643 and 684, though their synods were in communion with

---

514 Ibid., *The Acts of the Council of Constantinople of 553: Volume 2*, 110-111. The modified Latin rendering maintains this passage. See Surius, *Concilia omnia, tum generalia, tum provincialia atque particularia*, 591.

515 Ibid., 215, 218.

Rome, likewise failed to recognize Constantinople II. This is despite the latter synod's acceptance of the sixth Ecumenical Council (Constantinople III).

If there is any episode in history that thoroughly demonstrates how anachronistic modern conceptions of the Papacy are, it is Vigilius and the events surrounding Constantinople II. Consensus-based ecclesiology (and epistemology) is accepted by all parties involved and dogmatized. The Pope teaches heresy and blames Satan for it. The Pope's deposition and excommunication is accepted as fact by all parties involved. Apostolic Canon 34 remains in full force as Rome's acceptance and promotion of Constantinople II fails to win the assent of those within their own patriarchate, despite them being in full Roman communion. By any measure, the earliest ecclesiology of the Church as delineated in previous centuries is on full display. This is despite all of the medieval rhetorical conventions and Imperial meddling that had become mainstream by this point in time. Old habits died hard.

SYNOPSIS OF THE PAPACY IN THE SIXTH CENTURY

The Papacy experienced a significant development during the end of the fifth through the beginning of the sixth century. Rome clarified a view of appeals where their synod could not be appealed from to another jurisdiction. This is something that was technically true in a narrow context. However, on top of this rhetorical advance, Papal partisans concocted forgeries which made such a view more ancient than the Sardican canons. In a flourish of creativity, they invented an ecclesiology which theoretically prevented the deposition of a Pope in a local council. Being an innovation, such a view had no traction—not even in Rome itself, which consented to a deposition of a Pope three decades later. This proved to be the advent of the Byzantine Papacy.

The consensus-based ecclesiology of the Church is so ingrained during this era that when the strong Papal rhetoric is put to the test on an international stage by Vigilius, it is portrayed as consistent with the same ecclesiastical model. When he became intransigent, an excommunication and deposition kept him "honest." In short, the events of the sixth century would seem to convey very little promise for the growth of Papal pretensions. Roman bishops would find themselves considerably sidelined during much of the Byzantine Papacy. Nevertheless, intellectual seeds were sown which, with the right ingenuity, could later be reinterpreted into a radically new vision of ecclesiology. It was this that gave birth to the Papacy of the modern day.

Pope Hormisdas

St. Gregory the Dialogist

CHAPTER 7

The Seventh Century of the Papacy

The study of the Papacy in this century is useful because it clarifies ecclesiastical realities that became especially clear in the previous century. During this time, the Byzantine Papacy was in full force for a little more than 100 years until, under pressure from the Caliphate, Byzantine power experienced an international collapse. This power vacuum was similar to the absence of Eastern Roman power when Rome was under the Ostrogoths. A more muscular, independent Papacy arose. This is seen particularly during the pontificate of Saint Pope Martin I. Yet even then, a new Papal ecclesiology is entirely absent, despite some of the desperate measures taken.

Nevertheless, the Byzantines licked their wounds, reasserted themselves, and Roman policy reverted to its less independent self. But this short Byzantine revival was the beginning of the end. The Byzantine Papacy experienced a slow death as decade by decade control over the Italian peninsula slipped away. Rome would not accept the canons of Trullo in this century and Emperor Justinian II was repudiated by the local Roman garrison when he tried to impose their acceptance. This cannot be confused with Rome adopting a new ecclesiology, as local synods maintained the right to not receive canons. Soon, in the next century, Justinian II would reassert Byzantine power in Italy and succeeded in "persuading" Pope Constantine (after arresting him) to accept Trullo's canons. Nevertheless, the canons' initial hiccup was a harbinger of things to come. By the iconoclast controversy in the next century, Byzantine collapse continued incrementally and the Papacy started gaining attributes which would have been unrecognizable in earlier centuries.

Before this occurs, one can perceive instances of pushback against Byzantine domination. The seventh century has the seeds of future Papal ecclesiastical expansion. They are not doctrinal, however. They are geopolitical.

SAINT POPE GREGORY THE GREAT: THE PAPACY AT A STASIS

Unlike the sixth century, which started with a bang under the Symmachean Dynasty, the seventh century begins with a Papacy that is rather par for the course during its Byzantine captivity. In polemical debates some people cite Gregory as "proof" of Roman resistance to the notion of Papal Supremacy. However, this is anachronistic, because such an ideology did not even exist. Gregory approaches the Papacy for what it was and so his correspondence is most useful for the historical task at hand.

Gregory appears to anticipate that upon becoming Pope of Rome, many compromises and worldly dealings would be required of him. Reflecting on this he laments that, "I am stricken with so great sorrow that I can scarcely speak...through earthly cares I have lost works of righteousness."[516] The honeymoon period at the beginning of his Papacy lacks excessive controversy. His consecration letter addresses all the Patriarchs, uncontroversially including the bishop of Constantinople.[517] Constantinople is addressed first in accordance with Canon 3 of Constantinople I. In the letter he accepts without qualification all five Ecumenical Councils. These

---

516 Gregory the Great, *Epistles*, Book 1, Letter 6.

517 Ibid., Letter 25.

details are notable such as when controversy demanded it. Gregory would prove to be quite flexible with these details.

The ecclesiology that Gregory presumes upon is unsurprisingly consensus-based. He comments on this extensively. Concerning the discipline of a monk-turned Byzantine Patrician he writes, "I will call the whole Church together into counsel on this question...I will in no wise contradict, but gladly fulfil and subscribe to what is decided in common."[518] Commenting on the election of the legally autonomous bishop of Prima Justiana (a jurisdiction within the Roman Patriarchate but under Byzantine civil law independent), he writes that "the consent of all should concur in the election," which he defines as "the unanimous consent of the whole council and the will of the...prince."[519] He explains that only after this bishop (John) attained to this consent did he "appoint" him "vicar of the Apostolic See."

This demonstrates that Papal vicariates were understood as exercises in consensus—not unilateral exercises in direct Papal jurisdiction. Nevertheless, Gregory's motivation is to deny the legal independence of Prima Justiana. He recognizes the role of the "prince" in approving the bishop's election, but the election must still be fair and received by the whole local synod. By sending "the pallium according to custom" to John,[520] Gregory is rubber-stamping his election (because he really had no choice in the matter) and asserting that his consent, within his own contested jurisdiction, was still necessary. In other words, such tactful writing is indicative of Rome's political weakness at this juncture.

Gregory also recognizes that ecclesiastical "primacy" was something delineated in precise, jurisdictional ways. For example, he cites the episcopate of Carthage's "dignity of primacy" over the African church.[521] The Roman Patriarchate is very much on the

---

518 Ibid., Letter 34.

519 Ibid., Book 2, Letter 23.

520 Ibid. This custom bestowed honor from the Pope of Rome, but by receiving this honor it is a recognition of some sort of honorary subjugation within the jurisdiction.

521 Ibid., Book 1, Letter 77.

backfoot during his Papacy and so Gregory emphasized traditional privileges as doing so helped maintain a status quo which seemed tenuous due to geopolitical circumstances.

Without circumstances forcing him to do otherwise, Pope Gregory initially "played by the rules" and was cautious in his claims. However, the "honeymoon period" of Gregory's Papacy ends and, historically speaking, one starts seeing some tactful stratagems employed in defense of his local synod and the Roman population. This should not be a scandal to the pious as Saint Cyril used bribes, Saint Justinian employed brute force, and other saints made compromises in order to do the right thing. Gregory's reticence in becoming Pope is justified because such actions were not taken lightly by the saints.

For example, when Vicar John of Prima Justiana overrules an appeal made to Rome based on his see's authority as an independent ecclesiastical jurisdiction, Gregory has little choice but to excommunicate him and "decree that, the decrees of your judgement being first annulled."[522] Gregory was exercising his rights under Apostolic Canon 34 as head of this jurisdiction. In so doing, he calls into question the ecclesiastical legitimacy of Prima Justiana's legal autonomy. As Pope Zosimus asserted two centuries previously, in the Roman Patriarchate (which by accepting the pallium John admitted being part of), the Pope's judgement was not subject to review.

Soon afterwards, through Byzantine string-pulling, the city of Salona ordains a bishop "without our consent and permission," according to Gregory.[523] To justify his position that the election was invalid he specifies that an election must have "the voluntary consent of all…and there should be no one to dissent from his being ordained."[524] The importance of universal consensus theoretically was that it showed the cooperation of the Holy Spirit as seen in

---

522 Ibid., Book 3, Letter 6. The translation renders "judgment" according to the English instead of the American spelling.

523 Ibid., Book 4, Letter 10. Cf Ibid., Book 5, Letter 21.

524 Ibid.

Acts 15. The sacramental grace of episcopal consecration requires the participation of God Himself.

Theological high-mindedness aside, Gregory's defense of the consensus-based ecclesiology of the Church proves to be self-serving. He is asserting his role as the head of the patriarchate and denying the role of civil power being a final arbiter. Clearly, the idea the Pope of Rome had direct jurisdiction to decide such questions did not exist at this time, or Gregory would have never appealed to universal consensus as being the deciding matter.

Gregory had problems. Not only were Byzantine machinations chipping away at the Pope's intrapatriarchal authority, the city of Rome had financial issues that were Byzantium's fault. The Byzantines notoriously "usurped" the finances of churches they occupied—in other words, they raided the churches and taxed the populace that belonged to their patrimonies.[525] This likely had a direct effect on the Roman Synod's finances. To add insult to injury, Gregory was often forced to reimburse the Byzantines for garrisoning Rome against the Lombards *and* pay the latter tribute. He reflected, "How much is expended on them daily by this Church, that we may be able to live among them, is not to be told."[526]

Not coincidentally, while this is occurring Gregory excommunicated Saint John the Faster, the Patriarch of Constantinople, over the latter's usage of the title "Ecumenical Patriarch." Gregory apparently takes things so seriously he breaks communion with John and even effectually calls him the "Antichrist."[527] He cites his grievances about money and Salona in the same letter. While this excommunication appears to be political and economic in its motivation, Gregory's theological rationale is that ascribing oneself with such a title is an arrogation of the entire episcopate into one person. This he rejects as abhorrent.

For example, he complains that the honorific of "Ecumenical Patriarch" displays "an eminence of singularity."[528] He complains

---

525 Ibid., Book 5, Letter 26.

526 Ibid., Letter 21.

527 Ibid.

528 Ibid., Letter 18.

that "if one…is [a] universal bishop, it remains that you are not bishops."[529] In response to the Pope of Alexandria who ascribes to Gregory the title "Universal Pope," obviously with the intent of dismissing the seriousness of an honorific title, Gregory responds that such a title is just as reprehensible as "Universal Bishop… For if your Holiness calls me Universal Pope, you deny that you are yourself what you call me universally."[530] Ironically, in future centuries, such scrupulosity will be dropped by the Papal chancery with Pope Gregory VII boasting four centuries later, "Only the Pope can with right be called 'Universal.'"[531] When explaining previous instances of the Pope of Rome being called by similar titles, Gregory claimed they were empty honorifics bestowed by others and that the Pope did not arrogate the title for himself.[532]

Clearly, the whole issue was a tempest in a teapot. All of the Patriarchs in receipt of such reproofs responded with either nothing or with a dismissive attitude. Nevertheless, an exaggerated controversy helps bring to light some statements of ecclesiastical import. For example, Gregory declares to John the Faster that his recourse is not to himself, but "if I am despised in my reproof, it remains I must have recourse to the Church."[533] A Church-wide appeal is obviously seen as the highest possible "court" for such matters. He also asserts that bishops are all fundamentally equal (referencing Is 14:13 as proof), noting that the local jurisdiction of churches was delineated by Peter and the other Apostles being identified as "heads of *particular communities*…under one Head [Christ]."[534] The significance of "particular communities" in identifying a bishop as merely having local jurisdiction serves the purpose of contradicting the "universal jurisdiction" implied by there being an alleged "universal bishop." Gregory, not conceiving

---

529 Ibid., Book 9, Letter 68.

530 Ibid., Book 8, Letter 30.

531 *Dictatus Papae*, 2.

532 Gregory the Great, *Epistles*, Book 5, Letter 43.

533 Ibid., Letter 18.

534 Ibid.

of universal and direct jurisdiction, had no clue that he forfeited Papal claims to universal jurisdiction centuries in the future.

Gregory made other assertions which delineate what the conception of the Roman Papacy was at this time. For one, he asserts that there was no "universal [A]postle," including Peter. Therefore, no one can be a "universal bishop."[535] Petrine prerogatives are not exclusive to Rome, as they belong to both Antioch[536] and Alexandria.[537] To both Alexandria and Antioch he wrote that:

> *Peter, Prince of the [A]postles…sits on it in the persons of his successors…with regard to the principality itself the See of the Prince of the [A]postles alone has grown strong in authority, which **in three places is the See of one**…by Divine authority three bishops now preside, whatever good I hear of you, this I impute to myself. If you believe anything good of me, impute this to your merits.[538]*

Unintentionally contradicting the future impetus behind Papal Infallibility, Gregory declares that a "universal church" stands or falls with a universal bishop.[539] "[I]f one bishop is called Universal," he warns, "the Universal Church comes to ruin."[540] The implication is that consensus is the safeguard against a singular bishop with Church-wide prerogatives falling into error. Gregory made other comments concerning interpatriarchal prerogatives for Rome and other jurisdictions. Churches can abrogate portions of councils they do not agree with. For example, he claims that Rome abrogated the usage of "Ecumenical Patriarch" as set forth in the Council of Constantinople (588).[541] He additionally asserts that Rome fails to "possess" canons and the "acts" of Constantinople I, and so has

---

535 Ibid, Letter 20.

536 Ibid., Letter 39.

537 Ibid., Book 6, Letter 60.

538 Ibid., Book 7, Letter 40.

539 Ibid., Book 5, Letter 20.

540 Ibid., Book 6, Letter 27.

541 Ibid., Book 5, Letter 21; Book 9, Letter 68.

not "accepted them."[542] The latter is not strictly true, historically speaking; because every Latin collection of canon law both before and after Gregory had the canons, as discussed in a previous chapter. It also appears to contradict at least the spirit of his confession in his consecration letter.

Nevertheless, it reveals the theoretical right for a local church to pick and choose what they accept from a council. For example, Gregory notes in the same letter that "the Church of Ravenna" (despite accepting the Ecumenical Council of Constantinople II) "reject[s] the twelve chapters of Cyril."[543] This demonstrates that only what is received locally is binding to the given church and such a privilege is not understood to be exclusive to Rome.

It is with this in mind that Gregory asserts Rome can overturn Constantinopolitan depositions "by our definite sentence."[544] Rome, like Ravenna, can apply the logic of picking and choosing what from another patriarchate they accept, thereby locally nullifying the other patriarchate's decision. As seen in previous centuries, such a view of appeals is effectually non-binding apart from universal consensus. However, there was another element in Gregory's subterfuge that neither neatly fits with the patriarchal consensus paradigm nor the direct-jurisdiction paradigm of the later medieval Papacy. For one, Gregory clearly argues that he does not count Constantinople among "all the four Patriarchs."[545] Despite this contradicting what he wrote in his consecration letter,

---

542 Ibid., Book 7, Letter 34.

543 Ibid.

544 Ibid., Book 6, Letter 15; see also Ibid., Letter 24.

545 Ibid., Book 9, Letter 11. Cf Book 2, Letter 52 in a letter critiquing Natalis of Salona, Gregory the Great makes a passing reference to there being "four [P]atriarchs." This is either a subdued insult of John the Faster (Constantinople's Patriarch) or, more likely, a refusal to recognize Gregory of Antioch who was something of a usurper who replaced Saint Anastasius the Sinaite (referred to as "ex-patriarch" while Gregory of Antioch is passed over in silence in Gregory the Great's systatic letter, in Ibid., Book 1, Letter 25). Anastasius was subjected to deposition for his resistance to apthartodocetism, a Christological heresy. By the time that Book 9, Letter 11 was written, Anastasius was Patriarch again (see Ibid., Book 5, Letter 39).

this clearly subjugates Constantinople to any legitimate Patriarch. It also clearly identifies Rome as a Patriarch.

However, this does not mean Gregory understood the Patriarchs to be absolutely equal. Indeed, "the Church of Constantinople… is subject to the Apostolic [S]ee," according to Gregory.[546] If they were not a true patriarchate, why wouldn't they be? However, Gregory likewise perceives an interpatriarchal headship on the basis of Church-wide appeals that is universal:

> he is subject to the [A]postolic [S]ee, if any fault [i.e. appeal] is found in bishops, I know not what bishop is not subject to it. But when no fault requires it to be otherwise, all…are equal.[547]

Gregory makes no reference to whether such appeals apart from consensus are binding. He elsewhere does this with muscular language. For example, Gregory asserts that the Roman Synod's "consent" to councils is necessary as "without the authority and consent of the [A]postolic [S]ee nothing that might be passed would have any force."[548] However, this is a communication of a local right. He refers in the same letter to those who defy Rome as separated from "the peace of the blessed Peter," demonstrating that Gregory maintained the traditional view that Papal excommunications were strictly local. Indeed, localities can nullify councils by chipping away at consensus, but this is not an assertion of a unilateral right to deciding what is binding Church-wide.

Taking his work as a whole, considering that even Papal vicariates and intrapatriarchal synodal elections (and judgments) were exercises in consensus, it is likely he perceived interpatriarchal appeals the same way. Nonetheless, he asserts, as Gelasius did, that Rome's reception of appeals was in some way special. The former explicitly cites the Sardican canons as his basis. While the history of previous centuries demonstrates the existence of appeals against Rome, and just a few decades previous a Pope of Rome was himself

---

546 Ibid., Letter 12.

547 Ibid., Letter 59.

548 Ibid., Letter 68.

judged by an Ecumenical Council, considering Gregory's polemical needs it should hardly be surprising they did not bear mention. In any event, Gregory by no means denies the aforementioned.

What ends the "Ecumenical Patriarch" controversy? In a word, money. Gregory calms down the first time after being given revenue to pay for the local Byzantine garrison.[549] Later, Gregory receives some more money from Byzantium.[550] In his next letter he rails against Constantinople but states "it was not worth my while" to break communion over it,[551] money apparently minimizing his ongoing concerns about the coming (or present) Antichrist in his midst. Gregory never breaks communion again over the issue, despite continually floating the potentiality that John the Faster is the "precursor of [A]ntichrist."[552] Later, Gregory reports receiving more gold to pay for a ransom imposed by the Lombards,[553] and though Gregory makes future complaints he does not act forcefully on the matter.

It appears that Gregory's real concern is not so much over an honorific, but what can be seen in Salona, Prima Justiana, and Ravenna—that Rome's "particular community" would be subsumed by the Ecumenical Patriarch. Gregory is protecting Rome's local jurisdiction and its financial means of existence. It is unlikely Gregory is ignorant of semantics or so legalistic to believe that the self-ascription of an honorific was really part of the coming of the Antichrist. The one consistent thread in the whole controversy was that Gregory affirms the ecclesiology of antiquity, that being of consent and ancient jurisdictional boundaries, vis-à-vis the growing consolidation of power under Constantinople. Indeed, money is a real-world motivator, as the Roman Synod needs to pay its bills. Various similar instances are not unknown in the Church's history.

---

549 Ibid., Book 5, Letter 30.

550 Ibid., Book 7, Letter 26.

551 Ibid., Letter 27.

552 Ibid., Letter 33.

553 Ibid., Book 8, Letter 22.

POPE HONORIUS: ANOTHER HERETICAL POPE?

Honorius is infamous as he is condemned by the Ecumenical Councils of Constantinople III and Nicaea II as a heretic. This evaluation was accepted by Bishops of Rome as well. In some respects, the event is rather unspectacular. Saint Pope Marcellinus lapsed into paganism and Saint Pope Liberius signed an Arianized creed. Vigilius had to be "persuaded" to condemn a set of heretical documents, ardently defending them beforehand. A Pope's heterodoxy was hardly anything new, but what was new was the demand that a Pope be personally anathematized[554]—something that had not occurred with Vigilius. As for the two Popes that are saints, it should go without saying their lapses in faith were forgiven.

It is helpful to understand the historical context surrounding Honorius. The time immediately prior to his Monothelite statements was one of exuberance for the Church. Emperor Heraclius defeated the Sassanid Empire and looked like he was reversing years of ecclesiastical fragmentation. He was what would be called today an ecumenist, expounding Monoenergism (one energy) and then Monothelitism (one will) as doctrinal means of getting both Nestorians and Miaphysites to accept Chalcedon. He successfully established communion with Nestorians in 630, immediately afterwards with the Armenians, and a couple years later with the Severians in Egypt.[555] To be against these subtle Monoenergist/Monothelite formulas was tantamount to breaking apart the greatest Church reunion that had ever occurred (and has never been repeated) in Christian history.

---

554 Patriarchs of Antioch, Alexandria, Constantinople, and Rome have all been historically anathematized by the Orthodox Catholic Church, but never a Patriarch of Jerusalem.

555 The non-Chalcedonian Syriac Orthodox, under Patriarch Athanasius I Gammolo, probably did not go into union, though conversations with the Monoenergist Chalcedonians were friendly. See Phil Booth, *Crisis of Empire: Doctrine and Dissent at the End of Late Antiquity*. Los Angeles: University of California Press, 2013, 202-203.

Indeed, Pope Honorius in favor of such a union writes of there being one will in Christ. He pens the following in the hope of bringing those opposed to Monoenergism (Saints Sophronius of Jerusalem and Maximus the Confessor) on board with the Church union. It inadvertently becomes a new confessional formula in place of the Monoenergist confessions made beforehand:[556]

> *We acknowledge **one will** of the Lord Jesus Christ, since manifestly our nature was assumed by the Godhead but not the sin in it – namely the nature created before sin, not the one corrupted in consequence of the transgression.*[557]

What it seems like Honorius is saying is that Christ had a prelapsarian human will that never contradicted the divine will. This, effectually, is conflated with the divine will and is not (necessarily) mutually exclusive. Honorius was understood to mean that the Christ had a singular hypostatic will. If so, such a view is heretical, because if will proceeds from hypostasis (Person) and not essence/substance/nature, then each hypostasis of the Holy Trinity has an independent will. As Saint Pope Agatho of Rome states in his letter to Constantinople III:

> *For if anybody should mean a personal [hypostatic] will, when in the holy Trinity there are said to be three Persons, it would be necessary that there should be asserted three personal wills, and three personal operations (which is absurd and truly profane). Since, as the truth of the Christian faith holds, the will is natural [i.e. essential/substantial].*[558]

Additionally, a singular hypostatic will would be a denial of independent human willing in the prelapsarian (and glorified) state, because if Christ had one will due to sinlessness, then glorified human will also becomes conflated with divine will by default

556 Price et al., *The Acts of the Lateran Synod of 649*, 3, 11.

557 Ibid., 95.

558 Henry Percival, "The Third Council of Constantinople," in Philip Schaff and Henry Wace (eds.), *From Nicene and Post-Nicene Fathers, Second Series, Vol. 14*. Buffalo, NY: Christian Literature Publishing Co., 1900, 332-333.

and lacks independence. This removes the soteriological aspect of synergy from theosis.

Clearly, these are very fine points of doctrine. Modern scholars surmise that Monothelitism is only nominally different than Dyothelitism, supposing that the former taught that the will is only "one" in its goal or design, but not literally a conflation of two separate wills from two separate essences.[559] This view appears to be the same as the compromise formula of Peter of Constantinople in 658, of "two activities [energies] on account of diversity [of essence, i.e. Christ's human and divine essences], and one [energy] on account of [the hypostatic] union."[560] However, Honorius is condemned along with Peter and others not for attributing will to *object*, but to *hypostasis*. This is due to the Monothelite party in Session 8 of Constantinople III specifically laying claim to this interpretation.[561]

The decree in Constantinople III's condemnation of Honorius for teaching heresy to the whole Church is unambiguous:

> *the author of evil…having found suitable instruments for working out his will (we mean Theodorus, who was Bishop of Pharan, Sergius, Pyrrhus, Paul and Peter, who were Archbishops of this royal city, and moreover, Honorius who was Pope of the elder Rome…), has actively employed them in raising up for the whole Church the stumbling-blocks*

559 Price et al., *The Acts of the Lateran Synod of 649*, 89-90, 92-93, 95.

560 *Saint Maximus' Letter to Anastasius the Monk* in Bronwen Neil, *A critical edition of Anastasius Bibliothecarius' Latin translation of Greek documents pertaining to the life of Maximus the Confessor, with an analysis of Anastasius' translation methodology, and an English translation of the Latin Text: Volume 2.* Ascot Vale, Australia: Australian Catholic University (PhD Dissertation), 1998, 18.

561 During Constantinople III Macarius of Antioch (Monothelite) asserted: "In regard to this issue we have already expounded a confession of faith previously and we are in agreement with the five holy synods as well as with the divinely minded Honorius [of Rome], Sergius [of Constantinople], Paul [of Constantinople], Peter [of Constantinople], and the rest whose memory we invoked in the testimonies we delivered to the master, confessing *one hypostatic will* in our one Lord Jesus Christ and his god-manly activity." Emphasis added to Mark DelCogliano, *The Cambridge Edition of Early Christian Writings: Volume 4.* Cambridge: Cambridge University Press, 2022, 591.

of one will and one operation...disseminating, in novel terms, among the orthodox people, an heresy.[562]

The next Ecumenical Council, Nicaea II, taught the same in what effectively serves as the introduction to its decree, during Session 6 of the council. It condemned:

Honorius of Rome...for having taught there was but one will and operation in the two natures of our Jesus Christ.[563]

Indeed, Honorius begins the Monothelite avalanche with his penning of the term. Evidence suggests there was not so much complicity afterward. Later, he sent a legate to the Council of Cyprus (636) which had Legates/Patriarchs from everywhere other than Antioch (due to Muslim invasion). Alexandria and Jerusalem were the main parties contending with one another, as both Sophronius and Cyrus of Alexandria debated the issue of Monoenergism most stridently. Their constant debating earlier earned the rebuke of Honorius himself.[564] Discussions moved to Constantinople where a council there decreed the *Ekthesis*. It taught Monothelitism as opposed to Monoenergism—obviously taking inspiration from Honorius' coining of the term. Modern scholarship dates the *Ekthesis* to approximately 636.[565] It was seen as a compromise with Sophronius.

There is only one source which describes who accepted the *Ekthesis*—the *Syriac Life of Maximus*—a Monothelite source. It states:

The Emperor at once made a document called an 'Edict' [the Ekthesis], and sent it to the four patriarchal sees...When this order from the

---

Percival, "The Third Council of Constantinople," 344.

563 Mendham, *The Seventh General Council, the Second of Nicaea*, 332-333.

564 Price et al., *The Acts of the Lateran Synod of 649*, 46.

565 Ibid., 3, 23. Traditional dating places the dissemination of the *Ekthesis* to November 638, one month after Honorius' death. Cyrus of Alexandria writes a letter to Sergius of Constantinople in November, confirming receipt of the *Ekthesis*.

emperor arrived and was received by the four sees and all the bishops,
they added the signatures of their agreement.[566]

The Roman and Jerusalem Synods allegedly accepted this
document, which is ascribed to the Emperor Heraclius himself.[567]
At the time, Antioch's Patriarchate was vacant, but they would soon
get a Monothelite *locum tenens*. While it is possible that this source is
not trustworthy, in the end, it is the sole source that directly addresses
the question. Roman legates probably accepted the *Ekthesis* if one
accepts a date for it sometime in 636, though Honorius likely never
officially subscribed.[568] If he ever did, it is curious that such an
acceptance is never cited by any Monothelite source nor ascribed
to them. The next Pope, Severinus, tactfully is silent on the issue—
implying both tacit acceptance but also a lack of explicit approval.

Severinus' posturing implies that the Roman Synod sought less
pliancy with the Byzantine agenda. It did not help matters that the
Byzantines looted the Lateran palace in 640, not out of reprisal
but essentially to help pay for a long list of bills. Expensive internal
rebellions and Lombard aggression against Byzantium arose in
the midst of a rapidly expanding Caliphate, providing the perfect
geopolitical cover to start pushing back against Constantinople's
aggressive proto-ecumenist program. Resistance and a degree of
independence from the Byzantine jackboot became possible. Rome
took the opportunity and ran with it.

On the theological front, Rome's program of opposing
Monothelitism led to the Dyothelite faction (mainly centered in the
same city) concocting varying interpretations of Honorius' words.
They sought to absolve him of responsibility for initiating the very
heresy they were fighting. Honorius' scribe, "John the Councillor

---

566 Sebastian Brock, "An Early Syriac Life of Maximus the Confessor," *Analecta
Bollandiana*, 91, 1973, 317.

567 Price et al., *The Acts of the Lateran Synod of 649*, 232.

568 Though the *Ekthesis* may be dated to 636, Cyrus of Alexandria only seemingly
receives the document officially in November 638. This means Honorius
received the document either near death or it was received by the Roman
Synod somewhat before or slightly after Severinus was made Pope of Rome.
See Price et al., *The Acts of the Lateran Synod of 649*, 48, 235.

claimed that when he composed the letter in Latin....there was no mention of the will of Christ being one in number."[569] The first Pope to vocally break with the *Ekthesis* (John IV) concocted another defense of Honorius, stating that:

> *[Sergius wrote to Honorius] that certain men were speaking of two opposing wills in our redeemer and Lord Jesus Christ. When the aforementioned pope found that out, he wrote back to him that, just as our Savior was one monad, in such a way also he was conceived and born miraculously above the whole human race.*[570]

However, this is a weak defense because it also justifies the Monothelite, Sergius of Constantinople. Sergius presupposed that "it is impossible for two wills that are contrary...to exist at the same time in one...subject."[571] This precise statement elicited Honorius' response, concurring with the sentiment, that created Monothelitism. Honorius inferred from the preceding that the divine will would oppose the postlapsarian human will, apart from Christ's human will being prelapsarian and thereby (hypostatically) singular with the divine will—something that is by definition Monothelitism. Honorius' gloss was perhaps more moderate than Sergius' (the latter perhaps supposing initially that human will, unless one with the divine, would always oppose the divine will by default). However, despite the Lateran Council of 649 ascribing this error to the heretics,[572] definitional Monothelitism is simply

---

569 This is a summary of Maximus' claim in PL 129, 572 C according to Bronwen Neil, *Seventh-Century Popes and Martyrs: The Political Hagiography of Anastasius Bibliothecarius*. Turnhout, Belgium: Brepols Publishers, 2006, 153.

570 In *John IV's Apology for Pope Honorius*. See Neil and Allen, *Conflict and Negotiation in the Early Church*, 179.

571 DelCogliano, *The Cambridge Edition of Early Christian Writings*, 596.

572 Specifically, Themistius claims that human and divine will in Christ would result in them always "fighting with each other," betraying a view that human will by default is defective and not cooperative with the divine will. This is the same presumption that Sergius of Constantinople had in his letter to Honorius in which Honorius responded using the term "one will" to address the same alleged problem. See Price et al., *The Acts of the Lateran Synod of 649*, 352. This problem does not exist if human will, by nature, always follows

the teaching of a singular hypostatic will.[573] It does not necessarily require inferring the specific anthropological aberration at issue, as Honorius, too, is a Monothelite despite not making this error.

The problem with John the Councillor's and John IV's apologies for Honorius is that they contradict. One cannot both disown the very existence of Honorius' statement and then argue it was in fact orthodox all along. Saint Maximus' own apology, that the intention of Honorius' letter must be the same as John IV's apology because John the Councilllor wrote for both of them,[574] is little better. It presumes too much to say the orthodox intentions of the scribe in faithfully presenting John IV's views can be read back into Honorius. The Dyothelites, knowing how problematic his Monothelite statement was, did not know how to "fix it."

Future attempts at repair likewise prove to be equally weak. Two centuries later, Anastasius the Librarian in his *Letter to John the Deacon in Rome*, devises several more excuses.[575] Perhaps, Honorius was not "argumentatively obstinate" in his heresy and therefore not a true heretic. Another possibility was that John the Councillor was the true author and may have entered these statements out of "hatred towards the Pope." It is also possible that John the Councillor may have not made enough "attempts to correct him, or argue back" thereby testing how "devoted to [the] arguments" Honorius was so "that we [should] give the benefit of the doubt" to the latter.

---

the divine will and only a fallen will always "fights" with the divine will. Honorius' explanation, therefore, is more orthodox than Sergius', as at least Honorius recognized that the problem of conflicting wills pertained not to prelapsarian human willing, but to the Fall itself.

573 The same council ascribes the teaching to Nestorians, but being that they confess two hypostases with one will, this somewhat complicates matters. One can more plausibly argue that the Nestorian ascribes will to object and not hypostasis, otherwise they would likewise confess two wills.

574 Joseph P. Farrell, *Disputations with Pyrrhus - St. Maximus the Confessor*. Waymart, PA: St Tikhon's Monastery Press, 2014, 102-103. It should be noted the plural in the title 'disputations' is a typo made by the publisher.

575 Neil, *Seventh-Century Popes and Martyrs*, 153. Generally, they follow the Augustinian criteria of heresy being "maintain[ing] it with passionate obstinacy" from Augustine, *Letter* 43, Par 1.

Anastasius went as far as to cite Luke 6:37 and warned against judging people.

These excuses are as numerous as they are weak. More excuses were to come. Almost a millennium after Honorius, Cardinal Baronius went as far as to accuse the minutes of Constantinople III of being interpolated where Honorius is anathematized.[576]

Not beholden to anachronistic claims to Papal Infallibility and with no need to elicit Honorius onto their side having won on the doctrinal front, Popes subsequent to Constantinople III initially drop the Dyothelite revisionism. For example, Pope Leo II immediately after Constantinople III asserts that Honorius "agreed that the" faith "be contaminated."[577] Adrian II two centuries later writes matter-of-factly:

> For even though Honorius was anathematized after this [sic, "his"] death by the [E]asterners, it should be known that he had been accused of heresy, which is the only offense where inferiors have the right to resist the initiatives of their superiors or are free to reject their false opinions, although **even in this case** no [P]atriarch or other bishop has the right of passing any judgement on him unless the consent of the pontiff of the same first see has authorized it. [578]

The whole thrust of Adrian II's point is that the anathematization for heresy against Honorius only holds water specifically because the Pope of Rome "authorized it." While this ecclesiastical presumption is proven false by controversies covered in earlier chapters, it is a transparent admission of Honorius' heresy. While one may be sympathetic to Honorius in that his attempt at adopting Sergius' doctrine was more nuanced and anthropologically accurate, his passing assertion that Christ had only "one will" misses the mark of orthodoxy.

576 Charles Hefele, *History of the Councils of the Church: Vol. V.* Edinburgh: T & T Clark, 1896, 193-194.

577 *Pope Leo II to Ervigius, King of Spain* in Neil and Allen, *Conflict and Negotiation in the Early Church*, 238.

578 Price and Montinaro, *The Acts of the Council of Constantinople of 869-70*, 314.

THE LATERAN COUNCIL OF 649: NOMINAL ADVANCES IN PAPAL ECCLESIOLOGY

As the last section detailed, almost the whole Christian world devolved into what was later condemned as heresy. Did consensus-based ecclesiology fail? One can point to technicalities to defend the system. For example, the Caliphate overran three patriarchates so several synods did not *fully* accept Monoenergist/Monothelite confessions. Further, Antioch did not presently have a Patriarch amidst the chaos. Technicalities aside, one can forgive the era's contemporaries for thinking the Church was collapsing upon itself and the end of the world was occurring. In fact, Saint Pope Martin in his *Second Letter to Theodore* writes that the "times" are "not to be seen as any other than a clear sign of the beginning of sorrows, just as the Lord foretold (concerning) the coming of the Antichrist."[579]

Such desperate times certainly called for desperate ecclesiastical measures among the Dyophysite faction, strongest in Rome and in the parts of the Near East now under Caliphate rule. This must be kept in mind when interpreting some of the Papal rhetoric during this era.

Additionally complicating matters is the common currency of effusive language during the seventh century. Some fixate on a few of the lofty things said about the Pope of Rome during the Lateran Council of 649. However, only with difficulty can one find loftier language than that penned by Pope Cyrus of Alexandria in writing to his fellow Monothelite, Sergius of Constantinople:

> *To my Master, honored by God, the good chief shepherd, the father of fathers…I was commanded to embark on reading the all-revered report of Your divinely inspired Self…I have learned to take refuge in Your teaching, which speaks from God, even as I beg its precious and clearly instructive message to vouchsafe still brighter clarity…As a result, when our ignorance has been illuminated by Your God-taught Self…*[580]

---

579 Neil, *Seventh-Century Popes and Martyrs*, 173.

580 Pauline Allen, *Sophronius of Jerusalem and Seventh-Century Heresy: The Synodical Letter and Other Documents*. Oxford: Oxford University Press, 2009, 161, 163.

Similar lofty honorifics were ascribed to the Emperor. Sergius of Constantinople and his synod alleges Heraclius to be the "all-wise" author of the *Ekthesis*, supposedly "receiving this grace… from God" to pen the document "accurately and without flaw."[581] Sergius of Alexandria boasts that the same document "proclaims our true and unimpeachable faith correctly and without error" and describes Heraclius in salvific terms such as "The one all-pious and thrice august has saved, has saved us, thrice he saved us."[582]

The Papal chancery likewise was no stranger to such honorifics. A few decades later, Saint Pope Agatho likewise describes the Emperor (Saint Constantine IV) as "taught by the divine" and that in writing "the [I]mperial decrees touching the preaching of our evangelical faith…the Holy Spirit by His grace dictated to the tongue of the [I]mperial [i.e. Emperor's] pen."[583]

In light of the preceding, the titles and such that Lateran (649) ascribes to Pope Martin are less jarring than one may think.[584] Maurus of Ravenna (a bishop who later left Rome's communion in order to declare his own region's autonomy) in a letter calls Martin "the holy and deservedly most blessed lord and apostolic and universal [ecumenical] pontiff throughout the world."[585] Stephen of Dora, the alleged *locum tenens* (i.e. acting Patriarch) "as the first man in the jurisdiction of Jerusalem,"[586] describes Pope Martin as one that "presides over all others (I mean your sovereign and supreme see)…on the basis of its apostolic and canonical authority…with power and priestly authority over them all" in Rome "where are

---

581 Price et al., *The Acts of the Lateran Synod of 649*, 232.

582 Ibid., 235.

583 Percival, "The Third Council of Constantinople," 332.

584 Papal honorifics surrounded Popes other than Martin. Pope Theodore, immediately preceding Martin, was called "father of fathers" and "[E]cumenical [P]atriarch" by Sergius of Cyprus. See Price et al., *The Acts of the Lateran Synod of 649*, 158.

585 Ibid., 126-127.

586 Ibid., 145. Phil Booth identifies this as a claim to authority as *locum tenens* of Jerusalem. See Ibid., 136.

the foundations of the pious doctrines."[587] Benedict of Ajaccio speaks of Martin "having received from God with great and zealous application the inspiration of godlike speech."[588] The *Request of the Devout Hegumens and Monks*, likely written by Maximus himself, calls Martin "the supreme head of the churches."[589]

An overly literal application of the preceding would be a denial of "facts" as Gregory the Great cautions readers to be mindful of when evaluating words. "Godlike" inspiration of speech was not an honorific ascribed solely to the Pope. Nor was the ascription of being "universal" or presiding "over all others." Certainly, there is a consistent, traditional thread pertaining to Rome's prerogatives as the honorary head. This is something the "canons" explicitly delineate (Stephen of Dora surely referring to Canon 3 of Constantinople I and Canon 28 of Chalcedon). Read contextually, none of these statements are extreme. They are fitting for other contemporary figures, such as the Byzantine Emperor and the Ecumenical Patriarch in Constantinople.

Believing facts rather than words, one must evaluate the claim that Lateran 649 and its partisans were expounding Papal direct jurisdiction. If so, then this would be unprecedented in Church history. Martin's *words* imply his direct jurisdiction over foreign patriarchates. Namely, the missions of Stephen of Dora and John of Philadelphia to act as Papal vicars in ordaining Dyothelite bishops, appear to run roughshod over the operations of local synods. One historian observes:

> *A startling feature of these letters [of Martin after Lateran 649] is the extent of the pope's attempted interference in the [E]astern churches... Martin's instructions to John of Philadelphia to consecrate 'catholic' bishops in Syria and Palestine constituted an attempt to replace the patriarchates of Antioch and Jerusalem by direct Roman jurisdiction, and would have been perceived in the East as utterly uncanonical.* **The policy was so startling and so doomed to failure**

587 Ibid., 143-145.

588 Ibid., 252.

589 Ibid., 153.

that one might even begin to doubt the authenticity of these letters…The best Martin could hope to achieve was the creation of what we may call a 'uniate' church in the East, beholden to Rome rather than to Constantinople or the [E]astern patriarchates.[590]

This reveals the problems the historian encounters when imposing an anachronistic view of the Papacy upon seventh century historical events. Any attempt at "direct jurisdiction" is "startling" due to its unprecedented, bordering on unbelievable, nature so that "one might even begin to doubt the authenticity of these letters." If a simpler interpretation more explicitly in line with contemporary ecclesiology is possible so that it does not require one to arrive at "startling" conclusions, this should be preferred.

First, one must dispense with the idea that *Martin* is exercising direct jurisdiction. Stephen of Dora is not a mere *vicar* of Martin—he is the *locum tenens.* Martin explicitly identifies "Stephen," not himself, as the one with the right to ordain new bishops in the Near East: "the [A]postolic [S]ee also ordered this [ordinations] to be done, indeed, through…bishop Stephen."[591] In fact, Martin in dealing with opposition to Stephen by fellow Dyothelites explicitly states that "according to the canons…*power was lacking to us [in Rome] to appoint the [P]atriarch of Jerusalem,* to build up the clerical orders."[592] The preceding demonstrates that Martin in no way conceives of direct jurisdiction, but rather sees himself as giving support to the rightful *locum tenens,* who on his own authority ordains (or reconciles) Dyothelite clergy. As Pope Gregory observed a few decades previously, Papal vicars (here, Stephen of Dora) operate in consensus with their local synods. The whole conception of what is occurring here follows the consensus-based ecclesiological norms of the time.

This does not mean that there were no ecclesiastical irregularities with what the Dyothelite faction was doing, through Martin and

---

590 Ibid., 397.

591 *Pope Martin to John of Philadelphia* in Neil and Allen, *Conflict and Negotiation in the Early Church,* 213.

592 *Pope Martin to Pantaleon, a Cleric in Jerusalem* in Ibid., 223.

others. Clearly, there are other claimants to *locum tenens* and clergy serving the faithful. The problem is that they are Monothelites. Apologizing for their actions, several reasons (or excuses depending on one's perspective) are employed to defend the Dyothelites' irregular program.

Pope Martin repeatedly cites that "the pressure of the [Arab] tribes" created so much chaos that the Jerusalem and Antiochene Synods had no bishops or priests left.[593] This means Martin's official policy was to appoint bishops where *none actually were*—not to explicitly ordain a parallel bishopric due to some *alleged* right to immediate jurisdiction that he never expresses. This justification is questionable, but this is the premise behind the Dyothelite faction's actions. As for the Monothelite clergy in seemingly good standing that opposed the Dyothelites, Martin asserts that these men were "improperly elected" without synodal approval, explaining they "ought to [be] elect[ed] according to the canons."[594] This means that Martin did not assume the authority of deposing actual bishops and replacing them. Rather he supported *Stephen* in ordaining canonical bishops in place of absences and alleged non-bishops—either those who were theoretically imposed by foreign authorities (such as the Arabs or even Constantinople)[595] or self-appointed/ordained.[596]

---

593 *Pope Martin to John of Philadelphia* in Ibid., 213.

594 Ibid., 214.

595 One example is "Sergius of Joppa, usurping the role of caretaker of the see of Jerusalem after the withdrawal of the Persians, in virtue not of ecclesiastical procedure but secular power." See Price et al., *The Acts of the Lateran Synod of 649*, 148. Further, *Pope Martin to the Church of Jerusalem and Antioch* alleges that Constantinople's recognized Patriarchs had "imposed on them the false title of priest...not with any valid election or church succession." See Neil and Allen, *Conflict and Negotiation in the Early Church*, 228.

596 Specifically, "those who elected themselves, apart from their [the synod's] decision and without their knowledge." See *Pope Martin to John of Philadelphia* in Neil and Allen, *Conflict and Negotiation in the Early Church*, 214. One example is Macedonius of Antioch. Pope Martin asserts that "no catholic church acknowledged him as bishop at all, not only because he grabbed this title for himself in a region beyond his own, in contradiction of the canons and without permission, or any decree [by an Emperor?]." See Ibid., 215. If an Emperor's decree is what Martin referenced, this demonstrates that the

Martin circumvents existing *locum tenens*, such as Sergius of Joppa (Jerusalem Patriarchate) and Macedonius of Antioch, on the preceding grounds. He likewise accuses the "tumult" surrounding the election of Peter of Alexandria in making his consecration invalid.[597]

While claims from Martin to operate through Stephen of Dora and John of Philadelphia have some level of legitimacy, without Dyothelite support from the local episcopacy the Antiochene program is more tenuous. (A similar program in Alexandria is completely impossible, given the lack of local support and no contentious jurisdictional claims as had existed and continue to exist between the patriarchates of Antioch and Jerusalem). Yet, desperate times require that *someone* step in to make sure they have bishops. This is similar to Saint Ignatius of Antioch, who said in his absence that Rome presides over his see. This is not an ordinary, but an extraordinary contingency in the "absence" of a (legitimate) Patriarch.

While a direct citation to Ignatius' *Letter to the Romans* is never made (one that would have actually been useful, but perhaps such an interpretation was too unpopular to introduce), Martin does not lack a justification for such an unprecedented measure. The end of the world is at hand, thereby legitimizing such an apparently extreme stance:

> there are now no bishops or priests there who can serve continually at
> the altar and make sacrifices and offerings for the salvation of souls on
> behalf of the people, although they should know that the last hour is at
> hand and the time of scandals draws near.[598]

Martin's program of supporting local Dyothelites in replacing Monothelite clergy thereby extends to local bishops and priests. No one can rightly be called clergy without the "judgment and knowledge of the pope [sic]," or in the Latin *pontifices* (rightly

---

exercise of "secular power" (see n. 595) was perceived as legitimate on some level.

597 *Pope Martin to the Church of Jerusalem and Antioch* in Ibid., 228.

598 *Pope Martin to Pantaleon, a Cleric in Jerusalem* in Ibid., 224.

translated "pontiff" or "bishop"), "who has power over that city [Jerusalem]—either elected or were elected or consented [to elections] or called a council" of *Jerusalem's* Synod due to the "canon [that] was established by the holy [A]postles and our Fathers."[599] What precisely this *canon* is has been wrongly speculated in the past,[600] perhaps due to a misleading inference over *who* the pontiff in question is. The issue is *not* that the Pope of Rome did not specifically recognize local clergy. Rather,

> they [the Monothelite clergy] violate both sees: I mean this [A]postolic [S]ee, which did not give them the right to ordain, as was said before, and the see of holy James, which they sought to hide [from] Sophronius, so **that others could freely control the elections themselves as they wished**, and not as the Holy Spirit commands.[601]

The "*pontifex* who has power over that city" is not the Pope of Rome (as it is wrongly translated), but evidently, Sophronius. Those made clergy without *his* approval and that of his synod, despite Imperial or partial synodal approval, are invalid. It is on this basis that "this [A]postolic [S]ee" (Rome) invalidates the ordinations performed by Sergius of Joppa, as his ascendancy to Patriarch was never approved.

Similar rationales can be applied to Macarius of Antioch and Peter of Alexandria. It was standard practice for all the Patriarchs to write encyclicals which confessed their doctrinal positions, so that other Patriarchs and their synods can affirm their election. As stated in previous chapters, Patriarchs are only legitimate upon

---

599 Ibid., 224-225. Latin is in PL 87, 171. Elsewhere Neil and Allen show an awareness of "pontiff" simply meaning "bishop" when it is used in contrast with the Roman bishop. See *Letter 10* in Neil and Allen, *The Letters of Gelasius I*, 111 and *Letter 27* in Neil and Allen, *The Letters of Gelasius I*, 120-121, 123.

600 Neil and Allen cite Canon 20 from Lateran 649 as the basis for the statement, though based upon what the canon actually states concerning invalid ordinations this is doubtful. See Ibid., 225. PL 87, 171 identifies Canon 2 of Lateran 649, which is even more doubtful as it has nothing to do with ordinations.

601 Ibid.

the acceptance of other Patriarchs—and following the same logic Rome (or any Patriarch for that matter) can rightly oppose *any* such episcopal consecrations (or translations) as illegal and uncanonical.

In light of this, the canon in question is clearly "established by the holy [A]postles and our Fathers" (i.e. an Apostolic Canon). The specific canon is most likely Canon 14, because it denies "a bishop" to "leave his own parish, and pass over into another, although he may be pressed by many to do so…this must be done not of his own accord, but by the judgement of many bishops."[602] Sergius of *Joppa* is such a bishop and his translation, not approved by Sophronius' synod nor Rome's, indicates that his patriarchate is invalid as "the judgement of many bishops" did not approve of it. Thus, there is nothing in Pope Martin's words or actions that defy the consensus-based ecclesiology of the Church which was maintained up to this point in history. Anything allegedly extreme, though "canonical," can be blamed on the need to act fast (and maybe a *little* loose) before the world supposedly would end.

This does not mean the Dyothelite camp lacked extremes. Lateran (649) itself was surely controversial. A Latin council convoked by the Pope of Rome, and not the Byzantine Emperor, conducted in Latin (presuming the authenticity of the minutes)[603] is unlike any Ecumenical Council before or after it *if* it was intended to be an Ecumenical Council. Pope Martin avoids ever calling it such, though he refers to the council itself as being authoritative:

> *We condemned them [the Monothelites] in a synod…everyone recognizes them to be contrary to the Fathers, and* **the synodal definitions**

---

602 Apostolic Canon 14. The spelling of "judgment" is rendered according to the English norm in Schaff and Wace's *Nicene and Post Nicene Fathers*.

603 There have been various speculations over how fanciful the council was, from being a complete fabrication by Maximus to being stage directions where the bishops present simply read their lines provided to them as per the hypothesis of Pietro Conte. In the words of Price et al., "the artificiality of the acts as a record of synodal proceedings is undeniable…The Acts remain a credible record of a council whose proceedings, choreographed in advance, were more akin to liturgy than to a modern parliamentary debate." See Ibid., *The Acts of the Lateran Synod of 649*, 66, 68.

>*of the catholic church from those Acts* have recently been
compiled by us.[604]

Local councils, as the excursus on canon law in a previous
chapter details, were understood in the East to have derived their
authority from the Holy Spirit and thereby shared the pedigree of
Ecumenical Councils. Martin may be thinking in such terms, but
due to such a thought process seemingly absent from the West for
centuries at this point, it is likely that "the synodal definitions of the
catholic church" is a naked assertion of the canons from Lateran in
649 carrying binding authority. The clear implication is that if the
council was not ecumenical, it ought to be treated as functionally
equivalent, such as the Council of Jerusalem in Acts 15 and the
Apostolic Canons traditionally attributed to it.[605]

Maximus was a little less careful in his high estimation of
Lateran (649). Before his exile he wrote in Rome of "six ecumenical
councils" explicitly on the "sole basis and foundation" of the Roman
Church, because "the gates of hell never prevailed over her" as "she
has the keys of the orthodox faith and confession."[606] The consent
of all the synods does not bear mention. The Roman Synod, not
specifically the person of the Pope, is apparently indefectible. This
view is rhetorically without equal in its era, as not even Pope Martin
makes such a claim and neither does the Lateran council itself.[607]

Elsewhere, during the *Disputation at Bizya*, Maximus gives a
different definition of what an Ecumenical Council is. In short,
Maximus demands that Constantinople's Patriarchate receive
"which was made public at Rome," in other words, Lateran

---

604 *Pope Martin to the Church of Jerusalem and Antioch* in Neil and Allen, *Conflict and Negotiation in the Early Church*, 227.

605 The attribution of the Apostolic Canons to the first Council of Jerusalem (see *Apostolic Constitutions*, Book 6, Par 12) is questionable given Canon 85. Additionally, there was another set of allegedly early canons attributed to the Apostles meeting in Antioch circulating from at least the third century. See Alistair Stewart, "The apostolic canons of Antioch. An Origenistic exercise," *Revue d'histoire Ecclésiastique*, 111:3-4, 2016, 439-451.

606 PG 91, 137-40 in Butler and Collorafi, *Keys Over the Christian World*, 352-353.

607 See Price et al., *The Acts of the Lateran Synod of 649*, 144, 158, 186.

(649).[608] His interlocutor, Theodosius of Caesarea, retorts: "The synod which was held at Rome was not ratified, because it was held without the order of the [E]mperor." Obviously, Theodosius puts forward a definition of ecumenicity which implies that what makes an Ecumenical Council is an Imperial convocation. By this definition, Ephesus II and the semi-Arian councils would have been Ecumenical. Maximus rejects this:

> *If it is the orders of emperors which confirm synods which were held, and not [the] orthodox faith, accept the synods which were held against the "homoousios" for they were carried out by order of the rulers...* [609]

Theodosius then concedes to Maximus, "It is as you assert: indeed the correctness of the teaching confirms synods."[610]

The preceding should not be inferred to indicate that Maximus specifically changed his views concerning Lateran (649). Rather, Maximus perhaps understood both claims to be consistent with one another. The Roman Synod is the "sole basis and foundation" of ecumenicity due to their alleged indefectibility. The ecumenical criterion of "correctness" would be consistent with this.

Due to Maximus polemically pushing such a notion, the news of Pope Vitalian's conciliatory policy towards the Monothelites years later must have been a shock to him. According to one historian, "Vitalian...entered into communion with Constantinople without hesitation" and "accepted Peter's [of Constantinople] compromise formula of two natural wills and one hypostatic will in Christ."[611] Vitalian went as far as to personally receive Emperor Constans II into Roman communion during an official visit to Rome in four separate churches and Constans II looted the city's bronze in exchange.[612] Vitalian's flirting with Monothelism ends with

---

608 Neil, *A critical edition of Anastasius Bibliothecarius' Latin translation of Greek documents pertaining to the life of Maximus the Confessor: Volume 2*, 31.

609 Ibid., 31-32.

610 Ibid., 32.

611 Neil, *A critical edition of Anastasius Bibliothecarius' Latin translation of Greek documents pertaining to the life of Maximus the Confessor: Volume 1*, 62.

612 Neil and Allen, *Conflict and Negotiation in the Early Church*, 175. Such looting was

the assassination of Constans II (probably by supporters of the military officer Mizizios). The next Byzantine Emperor, Saint Constantine IV, needing Roman support to deal with Mizizios' rebellion in Sicily proves to be more conciliatory toward the Dyothelite impetus in Italy. He ultimately sides with the Dyothelites in holding Constantinople III.

In fact, Maximus was informed of Vitalian's rapprochement with the Monothelite faction. He is told under interrogation that unless he accepted the compromise formula of Peter of Constantinople (two natural energies/wills and one hypostatic energy/will of Christ) that "through the instruction of the Roman [P]ope [Vitalian], that you [will] be anathematized."[613] In response to this, Maximus simply calls upon "God" to "bring an end to what has been defined" doctrinally "by him," that being Peter of Constantinople. He evidently places all the blame on Peter, never directly confronting that his notions of Roman indefectibility did not pan out.

Perhaps due to Vitalian having resistance within his own synod, Maximus did not see the actions of the individual Pope as an ecclesiastical problem. In other words, his view of indefectibility was broader than the person of the Pope. It is also possible that Maximus in his polemics intentionally exaggerates his actual views of Roman ecclesiology, and so when dealing with the realities surrounding Vitalian, he simply did not have much to say. Maybe the alleged coming of the Antichrist, such as Martin warned about, encouraged devising a new ecclesiological understanding hinging upon something other than consensus. One can only speculate. After Maximus, such peculiar ecclesiastical views wholly lack any mention until documents are penned in the ninth century by the hand of Anastasius the Librarian. Not coincidentally, Anastasius translated the same works of Maximus into Latin.

---

a common occurrence, as it was essentially an Imperial tax.

613 *Saint Maximus' Letter to Anastasius the Monk* in Neil, *A critical edition of Anastasius Bibliothecarius' Latin translation of Greek documents pertaining to the life of Maximus the Confessor: Volume 2*, 19.

Back to Pope Martin, after Lateran (649) he is exiled and experiences Imperial deposition. The Roman Synod consents to this deposition, and ordains a new Pope, Eugene (the Pope preceding Vitalian). While there may have been some initial resistance to Monothleitism, Eugene ultimately sends Monothelite-leaning legates to the capital and enters Peter of Constantinople's communion.[614] Martin was displeased with the Roman Synod. He evidently never stepped down from his Papacy, commanding "in the absence of the pontiff, the archdeacon and the archpriest and the *primeicerius* take the place of the pontiff."[615] The Roman Synod, in defying Pope Martin, evidently did not attempt to provide him any provisions. This is interpreted by Martin as betrayal. He accuses the Roman Synod of a "lack of…sympathy"[616] and laments that they betrayed him despite him having "not shown evils."[617] Surprisingly, Martin at no time acknowledges a theological shift in Rome. His only concern is his own treatment.

Elsewhere, there is a more cryptic statement from Martin where he appears to call Pope Eugene "their [the synod's] member"[618] (Latin: *suo membro*) instead of "our." Further, he refers to him as "the pastor who is now shown to be in charge of them" (Latin: *presses monstratur*) instead of "us."[619] Judging from his overall sense of despair in this and the other letters, the safest interpretation is that Martin is writing dismissively of Eugene and the whole Roman

614 Neil, *A critical edition of Anastasius Bibliothecarius' Latin translation of Greek documents pertaining to the life of Maximus the Confessor: Volume 1*, 61-62.

615 *Second Letter to Theodore* in Neil, *Seventh-Century Popes and Martyrs*, 177, 179.

616 *Fourth Letter of Martin [in Exile]* in Ibid., 227.

617 *Third Letter of Martin [in Exile]* in Ibid., 223.

618 Pope Martin, *Letter 17* in PL 87, 203. The full passage is amidst a complaint that Rome takes care of their own body and their member's needs and not his own. The Latin is: *Miratus quoque multo magis sum in eos qui sunt sanctissimae apostoli Petri Ecclesiae, quoniam tantam dederunt operam de corpore ac membro suo, id est, super dilectione nostra, ad reddendos nos sine sollicitudine. Saltem super corporali usu, quotidianoque sumptu. Nam esti auru Ecclesia sancti Petri non habet, frumento tamen, et vino, et abis necessariis expensa no caret per gratiam Dei, ut modicae saltem exhibitionis curam gessissent.*

619 Ibid, 204. The Latin is: *praecipue pastorem qui eis nunc praeesse monstratur…*

Synod. The same letter complains Rome did not send him food and that he is seemingly judged of bad conscience having "appeared as an enemy to the fullness of the whole Church and an adversary to them."[620] It is unlikely the usage of "them" instead of "us" indicates that he accepts his own deposition. In fact, it implies some sort of (tacit?) universal acceptance to his deposition. By stating that Eugene is "shown to be in charge," instead of simply "in charge," Martin (though praying for this individual and the whole synod) must intend sarcasm or some sort of lack of acceptance. The reason is obvious. The Roman Synod's act in replacing him effectively recognizes his unjust deposition.

In summary, Lateran (649) and its surrounding events on paper are rhetorically a watershed moment in the history of the Papacy. As history will prove, the unprecedented but enhanced view of Papal prerogatives expounded specifically by Maximus are of macro-historical importance, even if they were polemical exaggerations. Nevertheless, the facts at hand demonstrate that Pope Martin explicitly did not assume immediate, direct, and full jurisdiction. Rather, he helped facilitate the ordination of bishops where none allegedly existed. Ultimately, Martin was not heeded by his own synod, who replaced him against his wishes, indivating that the Papal claims made since Popes Gelasius and Symmachus continued to lack serious affirmation and that Rome would wait until a later era (and different historical context) to apply a different meaning and purpose to the advanced Papal rhetoric of the Acacian Schism and Monothelite controversy.

THE LETTER OF SAINT POPE AGATHO TO CONSTANTINOPLE III: THE INERRANCY OF THE ORTHODOX FAITH

As indicated in the previous section, Emperor Constantine IV proved friendlier towards the Dyothelite cause than previous Byzantine autocrats. Constantinople III is a remarkable Ecumenical Council with fantastic elements such as a Constantinopolitan

---

620 Ibid. The Latin is: *inimicus omni plenitudini Ecclesiae apparui, et adversarius illis?*

Patriarch (Saint George of Constantinople) renouncing Monothelitism mid council, the Patriarch of Antioch (Macarius) admitting to being the source behind Monoenergist insertions into earlier Ecumenical conciliar minutes (an admission which unlikely conforms to historical fact unless the truncated version of Constantinople II sources itself from a Latin translation that was modified by Monothelites between the 650s-670s), and even a failed raising of the dead (thereby demonstrating the falseness of Monothelite claims). Constantine IV's intent was that the council was a *fait accompli* from the beginning. Dyothelitism would be vindicated one way or the other. A specific document that played a role in this council is pertinent to this ecclesiological study.

This document is a letter sent to the council by Pope Agatho. In some ways it is unremarkable. Showing continuity with documents in earlier centuries, Agatho warns heretics "not [to] make themselves aliens from *our* communion."[621] This demonstrates that his understanding is that Papal excommunications are local in nature, exhibiting continuity with past Papal claims on the subject.

In the rest of the letter, when read at face value, Agatho extols Rome's Synod, not necessarily the person of the Pope. For example, the letter makes frequent mention to "this spiritual mother of your most tranquil empire" and "this Apostolic Church" with various claims of this church "never" being "turned away from the path of truth in any direction of error" and having "never erred."[622] Though one can infer if not reading or listening too closely that this refers to the whole Church, Agatho himself ascribes the preceding to "the Apostolic pontiffs, the predecessors of my littleness."[623]

Certainly, Agatho did not intend that the Roman Synod "never erred" in a literal, wooden way. In the past, Popes erred in various ways with varying levels of seriousness. Saint Stephen had an incorrect baptismal practice that a subsequent Pope reformed. Marcellinus erred when he apostatized. Saint Liberius erred in ascribing to a semi-Arian creed under torture. Several Popes erred

---

621 Percival, "The Third Council of Constantinople," 337.

622 Ibid., 331.

623 Ibid., 332.

in their schisms with Saints Meletius and Flavian. Anastasius II erred entering into communion with the Church of Thessalonica, who was in communion with non-Chalcedonians. Vigilius erred in defending the Three Chapters. Gregory erred in thinking it was the end of the world. Honorius erred on Monothelitism. Martin erred on also thinking it was the end of the world. Eugene and Vitalian erred by entering communion with Monothelites. While it is possible that Agatho was completely ignorant of history, being that not even Roman Catholic apologists take Agatho completely literally in that they do not infer comprehensive inerrancy from his words, it is wise to presume inerrancy is not actually being expounded.

Agatho, as discussed in the previous section, keeps with the conventions of his time. Honorifics were given out like candy. Agatho himself claimed that the Holy Spirit graced the Emperor's Imperial decrees on religion. The council itself asserted that the Emperor is "appointed by God" and in praising the same exegeted Matt 16:18 by stating "the gates of Hell shall not prevail against your Orthodox empire."[624] With the history of Imperially-imposed Monothelite heresy not even yet in the rear-view mirror, absolute preservation from error at every given moment cannot be what anyone was trying to convey.

Additionally, Agatho's usage of euphemisms such as "mother" appear to be intentionally confusing. His application of this language specifically to Rome is novel.[625] Indeed, "apostolic church" in reference to Rome is not so novel, but it has been historically applied likewise to other churches. Agatho's words are honorifics intended to build Rome up, but were broadly worded enough to permit the interpretation they apply to the Church in a general sense. Agatho demonstrates this near the end of his letter:

> *Therefore the Holy Church of God, the mother of your most Christian power, should be delivered and liberated with all your might (through the*

624 Klaus Schatz, *Papal Primacy: From Is Origins to the Present*. Collegeville, MN: The Liturgical Press, 1996, 50.

625 Earlier Latin sources apply these titles to the whole Church. See Augustine, *Confessions*, Book 7, Par 1; Augustine, *Letter 34*, Par 3; Gregory the Great, *Epistles*, Book 2, Letter 21.

help of God) from the errors of such teachers, and the evangelical and apostolic uprightness of the orthodox faith, which has been established upon the firm rock of this Church of blessed Peter, the Prince of the Apostles, which by his grace and guardianship remains free from all error, the whole number of rulers and priests, of the clergy and of the people, unanimously should confess and preach with us as the true declaration of the Apostolic tradition, in order to please God and to save their own souls.[626]

Here, "the Holy Church" is identified in its entirety as "the mother" of the Roman Empire and it is *this church* that must be "delivered...from the errors" of heretics. Such a statement, of course, is inconsistent with anachronistic conceptions of infallibility or any inference that Agatho intends literal inerrancy for the Roman Synod or the Church at-large. It is specifically "the orthodox faith," not any local church or the entire Church as an institution, that is "free from all error." The literal Latin appears to accord with this.[627] This is further verified by translations from staunchly Roman Catholic sources which make this even more explicit.[628] Additionally, Agatho's last sentence here is arguably receptionist and consensus-based, invoking the input even of the laity.

The interpretation here, that Agatho's letter contained deliberately Roman-centric honorifics only to explain in the end

---

626 Percival, "The Third Council of Constantinople," 337.

627 See Mansi 11, 277. The whole passage is as follows: *Quis exæstuans, piissimi domini, tantæ cæcitatis errores non abominetur & caveat, si utique salvari desiderat, & immaculatem suæ fidei rectitudinem venienti domino cupit offerre? Eximenda proinde, ac summis conatibus cum Dei præsidio liberanda est sancta Dei ecclesia Christianissimi vestri imperii mater de talium doctorum erroribus, & evangelicam atque apostolicam orthodoxæ fidei rectitudinem, quæ fundata est super sirmam petram hujus beati Petri apostolorum principis ecclesiæ, quæ ejus gratia atque praesidio abomni errore illibata permanet, omnis præsulum numerus ac sacerdotum, cleri, ac populorum, unanimitier ad placendum Deo, animamque salvandam, veritatis formulam apostolicæ traditionis nobiscum confiteatur, & prædicet..*

628 "[H]e [Agatho] asked the emperor to rescue the orthodox faith, 'which is founded on the firm rock of this church of Blessed Peter, prince of the [A]postles, which, by his gift and protection remains unblemished from all error.'" See Butler and Collorafi, *Keys Over the Christian World*, 361.

that these applied to the Church at-large being preserved from error, is the only one that reconciles the disparate facts in both the council and history. The council condemned Honorius, something that the legates and subsequent Pope (as Agatho died before Constantinople III ended) accepted without controversy. As cited previously, Pope Leo II told Erbigus, King of Spain, when eliciting support for Constantinople III, that "the Roman Honorius…agreed that the immaculate rule of apostolic tradition which he received from his predecessors be contaminated."[629] This accords with the observation above that it is "the orthodox faith" that was understood by all to be "free from all error." Shochorning that Agatho is expounding Papal Infallibility by inferring a material-formal heresy distinction,[630] something which did not exist for centuries, is without basis given the context surrounding the statements made.

AN EXCURSUS ON THE ACCEPTANCE OF THE CANONS OF THE COUNCIL IN TRULLO

Some discussion of the Council in Trullo (691-692) is necessary in this chapter due to the council occurring during the seventh century. Its delayed and modified acceptance in the West is illustrative of the Byzantine Papacy. As Byzantine power projection in Italy weakened, so did Constantinople's ability to make Rome (and its synod) heel. This affected the reception of Trullo's canons.

Thanks to Emperor Constantine IV, significant rapprochement with the Roman Synod occurred, especially with Constantinople III dogmatizing Dyothelitism. The next Emperor, the aggressive and tactful Justinian II, inherited a politically stable situation which was generally improved by military successes and diplomatic coups against the Arabs and the Slavs. Despite these successes, the reality was that many former Byzantine subjects (and therefore

---

629 *Pope Leo II to Ervigius, King of Spain* in Neil and Allen, *Conflict and Negotiation in the Early Church*, 238.

630 This is a common apologetic in Roman Catholic circles. For example, "White is Wrong," *Catholic Answers*, https://www.catholic.com/magazine/print-edition/white-is-wrong

Orthodox Christians) found themselves outside of his Empire's borders. The Caliphate, thanks to diplomacy, enabled the official synodal recognition of Patriarchs in Alexandria, Antioch, and Jerusalem. Canon 1 of Trullo effectively enabled the full reception of Constantinople III, which occurred 11 years previously.

Trullo had many of the same representatives as Constantinople III and was effectually treated as a continuation of that council. The question then is why would such a council be so controversial in the West? It was not because Justinian II was particularly weak. Rather, Rome did not want (without compulsion) what the canons demanded. The canons were concerned with orthopraxy. In fact, the motivation behind the council appeared to be the standardization of Byzantine orthopraxy—something necessary to address the unity of Byzantines under foreign occupation as well as the declining literacy and religious discipline within the actual empire.[631] However, for those in Rome, they themselves were under occupation. Such canons, instead of being culturally relevant in import, were the opposite. They even contradicted several Latin traditions.

The Roman Patriarchate had some participation in Trullo. Rome had one alleged legate in attendance, Basil of Gortyna. He acted as a legate during Constantinople III, but it does not appear he had explicit permission to act as a legate during Trullo.[632] There were 11 additional bishops in Rome's jurisdiction in attendance, namely Sissius of Dyrrachion and 10 bishops from East Illyricum.[633] All of the aforementioned attendees signed onto the council.

However, Pope Sergius I rejected the council due to portions objectionable to Western practice. Justinian II, experiencing military defeat against the Caliphate in 692, could not push matters. A course of events cascaded where a political rival (Leonitus) had Justinian deposed and mutilated in 695. Leonitus, fighting for the continued

---

631 Warren Treadgold, *A History of the Byzantine State and Society*. Stanford, CA: Stanford University Press, 1997, 396-398.

632 Richard Price, *The Canons of the Qunisext Council (691/2)*. Liverpool: Liverpool University Press, 2020, 35.

633 Ibid., 11.

Byzantine existence of Carthage in Africa, was in no position to stir the pot and pressure Sergius over his predecessor's domestic program with Trullo. Carthage fell and was never recovered by the Byzantines.

Those Byzantines involved with the campaign for Carthage militarily conquered Constantinople and placed Apsimar onto the throne. Renaming himself Tiberius, the Byzantine Emperor concerned himself with stabilizing his eastern flank against the Caliphate. Geopolitically, this allowed the Roman Synod to ignore Trullo with little consequence. However, by 705 Justinian II reclaimed power and not coincidentally the first indications of Roman acceptance of Trullo began to be seen.

In 706-707, Pope John VII (who became Pope shortly before Justinian II returned to the throne) commissioned an icon which deliberately avoided a lamb depiction for Christ in conformance with Canon 82 of Trullo.[634] Due to Roman Christians following this practice in the past,[635] it cannot but be intended to show some level of acceptance Trullo's canons. However, there was no official signing onto the council or agreement made by John VII concerning the canons. The next Pope died after about a month and so one's attention turns to Pope Constantine and his deacon, the future Pope Gregory II.

In 710, Justinian II summoned Constantine (literally arresting him) and transported him to Constantinople. His written command made explicit that "the relentless emperor meant to settle once and for all the issue of Rome's acceptance of the Trullan decrees."[636] What followed was a discussion which included Gregory II. He allegedly remembered something of a debate over Trullo where after receiving "an excellent reply" from Justinian II, his (and

---

634 Ibid., 42.

635 Ibid., 23.

636 Andrew Ekonomou, *Byzantine Rome and the Greek Popes: Eastern Influences on Rome and the Papacy from Gregory the Great to Zacharias, A.D. 590-752.* Landham, MD: Lexington Books, 2007, 270.

Constantine's) earlier opposition to Trullo had vanished as the emperor "resolved every question."[637]

What exactly this reply was cannot be known with certainty, but it must have been an allowance for Rome to disregard some of the anti-Latin canons Trullo included (obviously not Canon 82, which Rome was expected to follow). Likely, Justinian II referred the Pope of Rome and his delegation to Canon 102 which gave permission for the canons in the same council to be applied as a local bishop sees fit.

This, in short, is the canonical principle of *economia*. In effect, Rome would be able to canonically not apply canons they found objectionable or impossible to apply due to circumstance. Trullo's canons, such as Canon 30, had already explicitly applied *economia* in contexts which otherwise forbade Roman practices.[638] So, the basis for the likely compromise can be found in the contents of Trullo itself. Earlier Roman precedent for this canonical thinking already existed, such as when Pope Gelasius wrote that "when there is no compelling necessity, the ordinances of the Fathers should be kept inviolate."[639] During times of necessity, canons ought to be "relax[ed] for a short time."[640]

Further evidence of Roman acceptance of the canons after this point can be gleaned by several sources. A letter between Gregory II and Saint Germanus of Constantinople explicitly quotes Canon 82 of Trullo as from "the assembly of the holy [Fathers]."[641] Pope Adrian I approvingly quotes Saint Tarasius of Constantinople

---

637 Price, *The Canons of the Qunisext Council*, 43.

638 Ibid., 38-39.

639 *Letter* 14 in Neil and Allen, *The Letters of Gelasius I*, 143.

640 Ibid., 145.

641 Price, *The Acts of the Second Council of Nicaea (787)*, 330. There is no doubt that the original letter was in Latin (as evidenced by it having quotations from the Vulgate). See Ibid., 327. Scholars such as Erich Lamberz attribute the quote to the Council of Rome (769). See Ibid., 251. Hence, even if the document is of questionable authenticity, its alleged alternate origins do nothing to actually detract from the evidence that Trullo was accepted in Rome. It would merely shift Papal acceptance from Gregory II (which the explicit recorded evidence actually dictates) to Stephen III.

in accepting "the work of the same holy sixth council with all the canons."[642] Nicaea II, Canon 1 explicitly accepts all:

> *the divine canons...those composed by the holy [A]postles, the celebrated trumpets of the Spirit, those published by the six holy ecumenical councils and by the councils convened locally to issue such injunctions, and those of our holy fathers.*[643]

The reference to "the six holy ecumenical councils" cannot be other than a reference to Trullo, as the fifth and six councils had no canons and Trullo's own introduction explicitly states that it is providing canons on their behalf.[644] Due to disputes over jurisdiction in the Balkans, which will be covered in subsequent chapters, the Latin West's acceptance of Nicaea II is not altogether clear. Whenever the council was actually received (whether immediately after Nicaea II and reneged in part, at Constantinople 869-870, or at Constantinople 879-880), the fact of the matter is Trullo's canons were officially "on the books" in the West.

Yet, *economia* was never explicitly cited in their understanding of Trullo's application (and lack thereof). In the ninth century, Anastasius the Librarian felt it necessary, in his explanation of the approval of Trullo's canons in Pope Adrian I's *Letter to Tarasius*, to modify the statement made with the following opinion: "The principal see [i.e. Rome]...in no way receives those of these [canons of Trullo] which contradict earlier [Roman] canons or the decrees of the holy pontiffs [i.e. Papal decretals]."[645] Pope John VIII echoed this, perhaps due to Anastasius acting as his ghost writer: Rome accepted all canons that "were not contrary to previous canons or decrees of the Holy Pontiff of this see or good morals."[646]

---

642 Ibid., 176.

643 Ibid., 610.

644 Price, *The Canons of the Qunisext Council*, 73.

645 Ibid., 51.

646 Nicolae Dura, "The Ecumenicity of the Council of Trullo, Witness of the Canonical Tradition in East and West," in George Nedungatt and Michael Featherstone (eds.), *The Council of Trullo Revisited*. Rome: Pontificio Instituto Orientale, 1995, 245.

In other words, instead of Rome following the historical principle of *economia* in not applying certain canons (surely the interpretation Justinian II would have intended and his Papal audience understood), Anastasius re-imagined the state of affairs to be that Rome had literally negated canons on the basis of Papal Supremacy. While later Roman Catholic canon lawyers as evidenced by Ivo of Chartres,[647] Gratian,[648] Pope Innocent III,[649] and Bernard Gai[650] all include Trullo in their treatments, their entire sense of canon law is wholly different from the historical Eastern, and earlier Western, view. Gratian literally titled his work "The Concord of Discordant Canons."[651] Canons are seen as contradictory and weighted in authority, Papal Decretals and Roman councils being unquestionable and all others being negotiable on some level. The ethos of this, when compared to the earliest treatments of the canons, is clearly different. However, it is not surprising given the disparate canonical inheritance of the West. Western ecclesiastics gave varying weights to magisterial authority in order to make sense of it all.

SYNOPSIS OF THE PAPACY IN THE SEVENTH CENTURY

The seventh century proves to be in keeping with norms of the Byzantine Papacy from the century previous. Constantinopolitan policy is often aggressive and financially exploitive towards Rome. The Roman Synod, understandably, often operates defensively with an eye towards resistance whenever possible.

Yet, no Pope made a break with previous ecclesiastical precedent. Pope Gregory obviously defended a consensus-based ecclesiology and explicitly affirmed that Petrine prerogatives were not exclusive

---

647 Price, *The Canons of the Qunisext Council*, 52.

648 Ibid., 53.

649 George Nedungatt, "The Council in Trullo Revisited: Ecumenism and the Canon of the Councils," *Theological Studies*, 71:3, 2010, 672.

650 Dura, "The Ecumenicity of the Council of Trullo," 249.

651 Price, *The Canons of the Qunisext Council*, 53.

to Rome. The only prerogative he did uphold was that of canonical appeals, which does not contradict such an ecclesiology.

Pope Honorius taught the heresy of Monothelitism, unintentionally coining the term. His actual views appear akin to what later became the compromise formula of Peter of Constantinople. Both would find themselves condemned by Constantinople III after their deaths.

Certainly, Lateran (649) offers an advance in Papal rhetoric by one of its partisans in particular, Maximus. However, every fact attached to the council reveals that the Papacy was not investing itself with direct jurisdiction or any Vatican I prerogatives. Rather, Pope Martin honors the jurisdiction of Jerusalem and only sought to offer moral support by naming as vicars those who were already part of local synods. The task commended to the vicars was the replacement of vacant bishoprics. Martin would find himself deposed and replaced by a more Monothelite-sympathetic Pope.

Pope Agatho's letter to the Ecumenical Council of Constantinople III, similar to Lateran (649), contains some rhetorical advances in Papal claims. In particular, it appears to expound the inerrancy of the Roman Synod. However, the letter was purposely ambiguous at points allowing for an interpretation which did not contradict the anathematization of Honorius. The simplest explanation is that everyone involved with the council, including Agatho himself, viewed such statements as honorifics or applicable broadly to the Church at-large. Similar honorifics bestowed upon the Byzantine Emperor bear this out. Ultimately, it was the Orthodox faith that was viewed to be preserved from error—not any precise ecclesiastical body.

While the aforementioned gives the impression of "business as usual" for the Papacy during the seventh century, this is not altogether true. Rome was clearly unhappy with their position within the Byzantine sphere. This manifested itself in several outbursts, particularly against Monothelitism during a few Papacies. While Rome proved to be pliant, it was only to the degree that Byzantine muscle could coerce pliancy. The delayed acceptance of the Council in Trullo was a good demonstration of this fact.

Occurring during the twilight of Byzantine authority in Italy, the long-term effects of the council, and its canons never fully permeating the consciousness of the West, provided fertile ground for the re-invention of Latin epistemology and ecclesiology during the ninth century. However, the geopolitical seeds of future disunity were to be sowed in the century before. It is during the eighth century that Rome finally realizes its own independence. It is this political independence, though not immediately leading to theological changes, that is the real impetus behind the Papacy's final fall.

HONORIVS . III . PAPA ROMANVS

Pope Honorius

Emperor Charlemagne

CHAPTER 8

The Eighth Century of the Papacy

The eighth century was the beginning of the end for the orthodox Papacy. At no point during this century in the final analysis does it appear that the Roman Synod solidly breaks, or even anticipates a break, with earlier ecclesiastical precedent. However, for the first time in history, a church synod (Rome) will become an independent political entity in its own right. This requires an ecclesiastical policy which enhances both foreign and domestic policies. Without anyone hugely inventive in the field of ecclesiology, such a change proves not to radically alter the Papacy itself. Ironically, it is the growing domination of the Franks within Italy during this century, and not Rome's own independence, which will prove to be the main factor behind the Papacy's change in the subsequent century.

ROME'S GROWING DISTANCE FROM BYZANTIUM AMIDST ICONOCLASM AND JURISDICTIONAL CHANGES

Since the first century, the Balkans (including the Aegeans) and all of Italy were part of Roman Patriarchal jurisdiction because of the evangelism of Saints Peter and Paul. This was soon to change.

As discussed previously, Byzantine power in the Italian peninsula was slipping away. During the Byzantine Papacy, many of the Popes were ethnic Greeks from locales often far away from Rome. In the beginning of the eighth century, Pope Gregory II (though born in

Byzantine Ravenna), was the first Pope in decades not to be ethnically Greek or from a Greek-speaking family. Though there would still be Greek Popes after Gregory II, some scholarship alleging that Greek was the majority spoken language in the Church of Rome during this time,[652] the fact that Gregory was not Greek suggests a shift in Roman domestic priorities and power structures.

During Gregory II's Papacy, higher taxes were imposed by the Iconoclast Emperor Leo III. In short, iconoclasm is the heresy of destroying and rejecting the religious veneration of icons. During this time, Byzantine protection against the Lombards was mediocre, just as it was more than 100 years previously during Saint Gregory the Great's pontificate. Not getting many services for their taxes, Rome naturally looked for a political exit. At around this time, in 728, the Lombards donated Sutri to the saints "Peter and Paul," a euphemism for the Roman Synod directly.[653] This was *despite* the Lombards having just conquered Sutri from the Byzantines.

Why would the Lombards conquer land and give it away? Traditionally, Lombard King Liutprand's piety is cited as the reason. However, his designs were surely geopolitical. The Lombards had no way to maintain these territories against local rebellion and Byzantine counterattacks, so he "donated" them to Rome as tribute in exchange for rebelling against Byzantium. Like clockwork, the next year Pope Gregory II refused to pay taxes to Byzantium. This emboldened the "troops of the Italian Exarchate," not being paid, to kill their own officers and the Byzantine exarch.[654]

Gregory II did not treat this as an opportunity to declare independence from Byzantium. He refused any calls for the crowning of a new Western Roman Emperor. This reveals Gregory's and his compatriots' "loyalty" to where they were born (the Byzantine Empire), but also the geopolitical independence of Rome from the Byzantines and Lombards. They were able to exploit both sides. To declare complete independence at this juncture would be to forfeit

---

652 Ekonomou, *Byzantine Rome and the Greek Popes*, 245.

653 "Papa Gregorio II," *Liber Pontificalis*, https://fontistoriche.org/papa-gregorio-ii/

654 Treadgold, *A History of the Byzantine State and Society*, 352.

possible Byzantine military protection and naval support, opening Rome up to Lombard domination.

This is the context behind Pope Gregory II's *First Letter to Leo III*.[655] This letter is incredibly important to the present study due to the ecclesiastical presumptions it contains. The Byzantine policy of iconoclasm as supported by Leo III is the theological point of contention.

No stranger to honorifics, Gregory II refers to Leo III as "king and head of Christians." Saint Germanus of Constantinople is referred to as "my Lord" and "Patriarch," a significant honorary advance compared to Gregory the Great's treatment of Saint John the Faster. He describes receiving a letter from the Byzantine emperor who entreated "that we [Rome] should send men" to "an Ecumenical Council." Quoting the Emperor, the following description of an Ecumenical Council is given. It is consistent with the consensus-based ecclesiology of the Church:

> *"I [the emperor] will not preside therein as Sovereign or speak at all authoritatively, but only as one of the Council: and* **as the chief Priests shall agree so will I agree**, *and those who speak aright we will receive…" By God's Grace we sent, and the Sixth Synod was celebrated in peace.*

Gregory II quotes this approvingly against Leo III, because he uses it as the basis of the accusation that the latter is being a hypocrite by his own standards. According to Gregory II, Leo III was imposing iconoclasm by force without the peaceful, free consent of the Church. It is precisely for this reason he rejects Leo III's request for another Ecumenical Council:

> *You should know, O King, that the doctrines of the Holy Church belong not to Kings but to the Priests…thou hast written to us that we should assemble an Ecumenical Synod. To us such an assemblage appears quite*

655 Gregory II's *First* and *Second Letters to Leo III* are quoted from the following translation: "Letters of Pope St. Gregory II (+731) to Emperor Leo Against Heresy of Iconoclasm," *NFTU: True Orthodox and Ecumenical News*, https://web.archive.org/web/20211102193927/http://nftu.net/letters-of-pope-st-gregory-ii-731-to-emperor-leo-against-heresy-of-iconoclasm/

superfluous…Be it so that we should give ear to thee, and Priests from all parts of the world be got together and the Assembly and Council commence its Session—where is the Christ-loving and pious Sovereign who, according to custom, ought to sit in such a Council to honour those who speak well, to expell [sic] those who turn aside from the truth, since thou, O Emperor, art so vacillating and barbarous?

Gregory II views the Emperor's role as executive—he puts into force what the Church freely agrees to. Due to Leo III's inconsistency on the matter of the Church's freedom, an Ecumenical Council is therefore not possible. This would soon turn out to be true as iconoclasm's chief Imperial council, that of Hiera, had no Patriarchs participating, not even Constantinople's. It was headed by the Metropolitan of Ephesus.[656]

Later in the letter, Gregory II asserts episcopal superiority over the Emperor, asserting that both he and Germanus have "received power from God to loose the things that are in heaven or on earth!" While Constantinople's Patriarch can bind and loose sins no differently than Rome, it is the:

High Priests who preside in Rome [who] sit there for the purpose of effecting peace between the East and the West, and are, as it were, a middle and party wall between them.

Rome's special role is seen as a mediating influence between Eastern and Western Christianity. Linguistically and ethnically, this would have been very accurate. However, this is not Gregory II's point. In reality, he is making a geopolitical warning. Rome stands between Byzantium and Western hordes of Lombards and Franks. In response to Leo III's threat to "break down the image of St. Peter" and depose Gregory II "as Constans [II] carried away Martin," Gregory II cautions not only would he hide,

the whole West looks towards our humility…St. Peter, *whose image you threatened to break down and destroy—for him* **all the Princes of the West look upon as an earthly deity…the**

656 Treadgold, *A History of the Byzantine State and Society*, 361.

Princes of the West would avenge the cause of those of the East whom thou hast injured....All the West offer the first-fruits of their Faith to Peter, head and chief of the Apostles, should you send any here for the destruction of St. Peter's image—see—we warn you before hand; we are free from the blood which may be shed on the occasion.

In translation, Gregory is citing foreign protection from the Franks and Lombards, revealing how tentative "Byzantine control" was in Rome. Rome at this juncture was playing all sides against each other so as to avoid paying tribute to foreign powers and establish their own political independence. This is a precursor to the Papal States.

Additionally, it is interesting that Gregory II understands his, and Saint Peter's spiritual importance, as specific to Latin (Western) Christendom specifically. There is not a hint of universal designs in this threat. The conception of Rome's local Patriarchal jurisdiction and geopolitical station is clear.

Pope Gregory II's Second Letter to Leo III is similar in how it treats the same topics. He responds to Leo III claiming, "I am King and Priest" by declaring, "Doctrines belong not to kings, but the Chief Priests, for we have the mind of Christ." His defense is not of the exceptionalness of the Papacy, but of the episcopacy in general. He reiterates that both he and Germanus have "received power from above to loose and to bind things in heaven and things on the earth" and laments that Leo III has "turned a deaf ear to our humility, and to Germanus the President, and all our holy, wonder-working, and glorious teachers and fathers," the latter being the saints.

To modern eyes, a Pope calling an Ecumenical Patriarch "President" can be jarring. It is unlikely by assigning Germanus any sort of Presidency, he implies the superiority of his colleague to himself, simply based upon historical context. The facts of a given time must carry greater interpretive weight than the literal meaning of words.

When Germanus was forced to abdicate his patriarchate, Rome left Constantinopolitan communion, holding the Council of Rome

(731/2) over the issue of iconoclasm.[657] Emperor Leo III responded a few years later during the Papacy of Gregory III. In 733, instead of occupying Rome by force (likely due to lacking the military capacity to do so), he confiscated Rome's "patrimony" (profitable estates). These were in southern Italy, where his grip on power was stronger. Further, Leo III realigned ecclesiastical jurisdiction in the Balkans and southern Italy to be under Constantinople's Synod. Sure, Rome saved on their Byzantine tax bill. However, Leo III compensated for this by seizing their assets and collecting revenue from their former ecclesiastical territories.[658]

Not surprisingly, Ravenna remained under Roman Patriarchal jurisdiction due to the Byzantine geopolitical position there, at the doorstep of the Lombards, being more tenuous. Rome did not explicitly consent to this blatant power and asset grab, but they had no military means to oppose it. Yet, in accepting a new Byzantine exarch, they were clearly not in rebellion. They effectively grieved the issue, but did nothing about it.

The canonical basis for the jurisdictional usurpation was highly questionable. Canon 17 of Chalcedon allows for the redrawing of jurisidictional lines as per Byzantine demands, but only for lands lost to foreign powers that were subsequently reconquered. The Balkans, southern Italy, and the Aegeans, were under constant raids and threats from Slavs and the Arabs; but cities like Thessalonica never outright fell to foreigners.

With the Donation of Sutri, the geopolitical origins of the Papal States are already apparent during the beginning of iconoclasm. However, the ecclesiastical basis for modern Papal claims was then lacking. In diplomatic discourse, consensus-based ecclesiology was presumed upon and Constantinopolitan ecclesiastical usurpations were to a certain degree tolerated.

---

657 Treadgold, *A History of the Byzantine State and Society*, 354.

658 Ibid, 355.

THE END OF THE BYZANTINE PAPACY

Before the complete collapse of Byzantine power in Rome, the Lombards were building up Rome as a counterweight against Ravenna. They did this by granting several cities conquered from the Byzantines to the Roman Synod for reasons delineated in the previous section.

After King Liutprand died, succession crises fragmented Lombardic power creating power vacuums the Franks and Roman Duchy exploited. It was at this time that the first explicit mention of the Papal States is found in the historical record. Pope Gregory III in correspondence with Frankish warlord Charles Martel referred to the citizens of the quasi-independent Duchy of Rome as "the Blessed People of Peter."[659] The Roman Synod was posturing itself as its own regional, secular power broker.

Nonetheless, Byzantine power in Italy was collapsing quicker than Lombard power was disintegrating. When the Lombards conquered Ravenna in 751, this led to a general collapse of Byzantine control in northern and central Italy. Not looking to make domestic enemies so that the Byzantines can turn the tide, the Lombards focused on conquering only Byzantine possessions, not Papal ones. With the Lombards and Byzantines being weak, this invited stronger powers to take advantage of the exhausted military situation in Italy. Just as the Caliphate exploited the weakening Sassanid and Byzantine Empires and incorporated large portions of their empires into their own, the Franks did the same. In 754, the Franks defeated the Lombards decisively in northern Italy. In exchange for Rome's support (and consecrating of their kings as "patricians" of the Romans), they granted Ravenna to the Roman Duchy in 756. This is known as the "Donation of Pepin."

Even still, the Duchy of Rome (the whole Byzantine province) did not declare independence from Byzantium. In so doing, they did not allow themselves to be absorbed into the Lombards or

---

659 In Latin, *"populus peculiaris beati Petri."* See Amedeo Crivellucci, *Studi Storici: Periodico Trimestrale*, Volume 11. Pisa: Coi tipi defli Studi Storici, 1902, 76.

later annexed by the Franks.[660] Being cut off from Byzantium, the Popes appointed new Dukes—being a continuation of the Duchy. In effect, Rome was politically playing all sides so they could be independent. If they outright declared independence, they would lose any Byzantine support which would be necessary to persuade the Franks or Lombards to not annex them. Eventually, the Franks dominated Italy, thereby mostly removing the Lombard threat. At that point, Rome in effect became a quasi-independent client state (the "Papal States") under Frankish "protection."

Sometime during the preceding events, the "Donation of Constantine"[661] was forged to vest Rome with secular power not dependent upon Lombardic and Frankish whims. The donation was allegedly bestowed to "Sylvester, Pope of the city of Rome and to all his successors" *and* "to all the most reverend God-loving Catholic bishops of the same sacrosanct Roman church" (i.e. the whole synod).[662] Sylvester is described as "Universal Pope" and "Universal Pontiff."[663]

The document gives an overtly Chalcedonian Christological confession revealing its obvious inauthenticity and then cites the story of Constantine's baptism where Saints Peter and Paul play a role from beyond grave, a common hagiographic detail. Constantine then cites Matt 16:18 and reflects on Peter's "power" and bestows "our government of great power" and "earthly Imperial power" to the "sacred Roman church."[664]

The document also assigns "principality...over the four principal sees of Antioch, Alexandria, Constantinople, and Jerusalem, and also over all the churches of God in the whole world" to the Pope and that "by his judgment shall be arranged all things which are to be procured for the worship of God or the stability of the Christian

---

660 Treadgold, *A History of the Byzantine State and Society*, 379.

661 All quotes are translations from "Constitutum Constantini," *The Latin Library*, http://www.thelatinlibrary.com/donation.html

662 Ibid., Par 1.

663 Ibid., Par 2.

664 Ibid., Par 10-11.

faith."[665] This appears to be a reference to theological appeals and not direct jurisdiction, which lacks attestation at so early a period.

It bestows superiority to the "Lateran palace" over "all the palaces in the world," seemingly a secular aggrandizement.[666] It also gives commands for Imperial trappings to surround the Pope.[667] This implies that the Pope was styling himself as a king of sorts likely for several decades at this point. It then threatens with eternal damnation anyone who does not concede temporal power to the Pope over the whole Earth.[668]

In summary, the *Donation of Constantine* is a radical document as it says the Duchy of Rome is in fact the inheritor of the entire Roman Ecumene. Terms like "Universal [Ecumenical] Pope" and the brief mention of Rome's superiority in judging appeals are passing statements meant to show that Rome is the center of the Roman Empire. In effect, the forger imagined himself as making a new Roman Empire centered not in Constantinople, but back in Rome itself. The motivation is obviously political. Ecclesiastically there is nothing radical in this document.

Such dreams of grandeur quickly evaporated. Rome would eventually be subjugated by the Carolingians under Charlemagne, who acquired for himself the title "Emperor of the Romans," obviously contradicting the whole intent of the *Donation of Constantine*. Nevertheless, the Roman Synod had officially become a temporal power and client state of the Franks. In the coming century, ecclesiastical concerns would prove to be auxiliary to temporal claims. Church claims were negotiable as long as temporal gain was achievable.

As for the actual end of the Byzantine Duchy of Rome, as this would mark the official beginning of the Papal States, this is not altogether clear. Historical references to a Roman "Duke" are absent for a short period around 778-81, marking the official end of Rome being part of the Byzantine Empire. This makes sense

665 Ibid., Par 12.

666 Ibid., Par 14.

667 Ibid., Par 15.

668 Ibid., Par 19.

given the *Donation of Constantine* styling the Pope as the Roman Emperor himself. The title Duke was later brought back for foreign dignitaries, but at that juncture he officially worked on behalf of the Roman Synod, not Constantinople.[669]

THE COUNCIL OF ROME 769: ATTEMPTS AT PAPAL REFORM AND SUBSEQUENT FRANKISH DOMINATION

Historically, the Bishop of Rome was "popularly elected." This led to controversies during disputed elections, such as that between Saint Cornelius and Novatian. When the Roman Empire became Christian, this popular vote generally became a mere accepting by acclamation whomever the Western Roman Emperor, Roman Senate/nobility, or Ostrogothic king approved of (the latter was removed from consideration by the Council of Palmaris in 502).

During the Byzantine Papacy, "popular" elections continued. In reality, Constantinople effectively chose the Pope until they lost the capacity to assert power in Italy after the reign of Justinian II. At this point, the local nobility generally took over the selection process. This led to a disputed election in the late 760s.

Tuscan nobles installed a layman, Constantine II, by force of arms as Pope. As Desiderius the King of the Lombards was a Tuscan, this demonstrates that Rome, though striving for independence, in fact was subject to foreign influences. Constantine II's Papacy lasted about a year until he had a falling out with the Lombards, who then replaced him by force of arms with a new candidate, Philip. In the chaos, local Roman nobility installed Stephen III as Pope, "deposing" Philip for simony.

Yet, it wasn't really a deposition. It was taken for granted during this controversy that the Pope of Rome was above anyone's judgment. This shows that the Pseudo-Symacchean forgeries and their seeming disappearance from the historical record, had permeated the ecclesiastical consciousness of the Roman Synod by

---

669 Thomas Noble, *The Republic of St. Peter: The Birth of the Papal State, 680–825*. Philadelphia: University of Pennsylvania Press, 1991, 234–235, 249.

this juncture. In all probability, these forgeries were so old (almost 270 years) that they appeared as ancient and authentic as any other document. Any memory of them being questionable in some way would have long deteriorated. Therefore, during the election crisis in question, in order to do away with Constantine and Philip, their elections had to be "uncanonical"—thereby making them not truly Popes to begin with. Instead of devising invented ecclesiastical crimes to licitly depose a Pope, creative ways of invalidating the Papal consecration had to be employed.

The Council of Rome (769) was essentially held to assert the authority of the Duchy of Rome over the Lombards. It forbade the elevation of laymen to the episcopate in quick order (making it impossible for Constantine II to make a comeback).[670] Additionally, the involvement of laity and nobility in "voting"/publicly acclaiming the election of a Pope was officially done away with for the first time. The idea was to prevent foreign powers from strongarming locals politically into choosing who they wanted as Pope. Instead, elections were decided by "cardinals" (then deacons and priests who would elect one of their own number to become Pope). It is ironic that during this council 12 Frankish bishops attended and embraced iconodulia,[671] given in two decades time the Franks would turn against the doctrine when Roman rapprochement with the Byzantines on the question occurred. The council also received the *Letter of the Oriental Patriarchs*, (mostly) the same letter found in Session 3 of the Ecumenical Council of Nicaea II.

The presence of the Franks indicates they were welcomed as military protectors of the Duchy of Rome. The Franks wanted the Duchy propped up as a buffer against Lombardic power in the Italian peninsula. This was accomplished by insulating Roman Papal elections from Lombardic influence. Everyone ordained by Constantine II had to be re-ordained, due to his "invalid" consecration.[672]

---

670 Canon 10 of Sardica already forbade the elevation of laymen, but was vague concerning the timing of such ordinations.

671 Landon, *A Manual of Councils of the Holy Catholic Church, Volume 2*, 98.

672 Price and Montinaro, *The Acts of the Council of Constantinople of 869-70*, 194.

While this council appears to have permanently altered the election of Popes, in 774 it is traditionally believed another Roman Synod (with Charlemagne present) gave the Carolingian autocrat the right of what is called in later eras "investiture" (i.e. choosing Episcopal candidates), including the Pope. Those not invested were anathematized by this council.[673] Even if the 774 council is a later forgery, in coming decades the Franks would dominate the Italian peninsula and manipulate Roman ecclesiastics until the collapse of their power in that region in the 870s. Initially, the Franks had assumed the power of approving Papal elections, manipulating the cardinals who were responsible for them.

This Frankish domination led to the return of Papal elections as soon as local Roman nobility had the capacity to reassert themselves. The motivation was obvious. It was a way to oppose the Franks playing Pope-maker. Pope Valentine was "elected" by local nobility and laity in 827 and this electoral process continued until the Gregorian reforms in the 11th century. The Franks sometimes visibly interfered with the elections of Popes. Pope Sergius II in 844 was one such example. Sometimes there was local Roman pushback, such as when Anastasius the Librarian's Papacy was opposed by the locals who elected Pope Benedict III. Ironically, Anastasius would soon be "welcomed" back after Benedict III's death. He became the ghostwriter (and a significant string puller) behind the next three subsequent Popes, suggesting overt Frankish influence.

In conclusion, the reform program of Rome (769) failed. It was not because the inherent idea behind it was unsound—the Gregorian reforms would return to an election from a College of Cardinals. It was that the motivation behind the program betrayed short-term thinking. The whole design was to up-end a time-honored tradition of (sham) elections and replace it with another system to preempt the Lombards. As soon as Frankish grip over the Italian peninsula

---

673 Landon, *A Manual of Councils of the Holy Catholic Church, Volume 2*, 98. The general practice of investiture is acknowledged to have its beginnings in Charlemagne's reign. See Uta-Renate Blumenthal, *The Investiture Controversy Church and Monarchy from the Ninth to the Twelfth Century*. Philadelphia: University of Pennsylvania Press, 2010, 169.

was strong enough that Lombardic manipulation was a non-issue, the "reform" was dispensed with. Frankish manipulation was more transparently allowed, despite Palmaris (502) and Rome (769), and their canonical precedent, forbidding such a thing. The memory of elections apparently did not fade away quickly and when Frankish domination began to weaken, they reappeared—in contradiction of Rome (769).

So much for the high view of Papal decretals and Roman canons. One is inclined to conclude that the West had a very low view of their own local canons vis-à-vis those received from the East from before the sixth century. In all probability, Western theologians understood that canons derived from consensus carried weightier authority.

THE PAPACY DURING THE COUNCIL OF NICAEA II: CRUCIAL DIFFERENCES IN THE MANUSCRIPT RECORD

Pope Adrian I *perhaps* is the first Pope of Rome who had more in common with the later medieval Popes than the ancient ones. Indeed, he was the first to cite the *Donation of Constantine* in a letter to the Frankish King (later Emperor) Charlemagne. Considering the *Donation*'s contents, Charlemagne evidently did not take the reference to Constantine's donation to heart. It would be Charlemagne, and not a future Pope, who would be crowned the Emperor of Rome (ironically, by the latter). This demonstrates that the Roman chancery at this time used flagrant forgeries as well as made outlandish claims to authority.

Nevertheless, the question remains whether Adrian I made claims consistent with a more advanced Papacy in the mold of Vatican I. This is the context behind the controversy surrounding the allegedly Papal Supremacist statements found in letters received by the Ecumenical Council of Nicaea II (787), those being Adrian I's *Letter to the Emperors* (JE 2448) and his *Letter to Tarasius* (JE 2449). In JE 2448 specifically, the Latin tradition preserves what can be understood to be Papal Supremacist claims. The Greek tradition of the same lacks all of these.

In short, the Latin tradition of Nicaea II is entirely derived from a translation made by Anastasius the Librarian in 873.[674] The historical context surrounding this translation will be fleshed out more in the next chapter. In the 860s, the Roman Synod (led by Pope Nicholas and, in a sense, Anastasius himself as his ghostwriter) refused to consent to the consecration of Saint Photius the Great as Patriarch of Constantinople, nor recognize the deposition of Saint Ignatius of Constantinople. What followed was a diplomatic exchange between Nicholas/Anastasius and Byzantine Emperor Michael III/Photius where interpatriarchal Papal claims and assertions of jurisdiction in the Balkans and Italy were made by Rome which were not recognized by Constantinople. Relations soured so badly that Nicholas deposed his own Papal legates who recognized Photius' consecration. Then, all the Eastern patriarchates deposed Nicholas. The next Pope (Adrian II) and Byzantine Emperor (Basil I) had Photius deposed in 870. A few years after this controversy died down, Anastasius created the Latin tradition that exists today.

It suffices to say that the majority of scholars into the 21st century affirm that *both* the Greek and Latin renderings of JE 2448 and 2449 are authentically from 787, but the Greek was actually read out at the council.[675] Despite being a minority of scholarship,

---

674 Price, *The Acts of the Second Council of Nicaea (787)*, 19.

675 Scholars that believe that both the Greek and Latin renderings of JE 2448 and 2449 are authentic, but the Greek was what was read during the council are as follows, the year of their publication in parentheses: A. Siecienski (2017); A. Louth (2007), M. Maccarrone (1988), F. Dvornik (1966); A. Michel (1956), W. Levison (1948), G. Ostrogorsky (1933), L. Serraz (1926; he implies Anastasius made interpolations into Latin JE 2448), H. Percival (1900), K. Hefele (1877), and J. Mendham (1849). See Ibid., 20; Erich Lamberz, "'Falsata Graecorum more'? Die Griechische Version den Briefe Papst Hadrians I. in der Akten des VII. Ökumenischen Knozils" in Claudia Sode and Sarolta A. Takács (eds.), *Novum Millennium: Studies on Byzantine History and Culture Dedicated to Paul Speck*. London: Routledge, 2016, 222, 223, 226; Siecienski, *The Papacy and the Orthodox*, 213; Andrew Louth, *Greek East and Latin West: The Church AD 681-1071*. Crestwood, NY: St Vladimir's Seminary Press, 2007, 85; Francis Dvornik, *Byzantium and the Roman Primacy*. New York: Fordham University Press, 1966, 97; Luitpold Wallach, "The Greek and Latin Versions of II Nicaea and the 'Synodica' of Hadrian I (JE

a couple recent scholars champion the view that the Greek minutes are falsifications from the 860s-870s due to manipulations made by Photius in response to the aforementioned controversy.[676] Their views will be critiqued in brief here and only within the lens of this study.

Due to the majority view of scholarship being most likely the correct one, this means that Adrian I perhaps advanced Papal claims for domestic or local patriarchal consumption. This may have suited some propaganda purpose in response to the Franks or Lombards. Yet, in any event, he did not yet actually press any interpatriarchal claims on such a level so as to create an ecclesiastical break with past Papal history. If the preceding holds true, this situates the fall of the Papacy from its original consensus-based ecclesiology to a period roughly around the formation of the Papal States. This fall would go unrecognized until future controversies, such as those surrounding the 860s and 11th century, foisted the West's privately held interpatriarchal views onto the world stage.

There is another possibility that deserves serious consideration. That is, the Latin differences are in fact interpolations introduced by their tradition's sole source: Anastasius. Unlike the *Donation*, which is a flagrant forgery, there seems to be nothing in Latin JE 2448 or 2449 that is so blatant. If they contain interpolations, they are much

2448): A Diplomatic Study," *Traditio*, 22, 1966, 115; L. Serraz, "Les lettres du pape Hadrien ler lues au lle concile de Nicee," *Échos d'Orient*, 25:144, 1926, 407-420; Henry Percival, "The Second Council of Nicaea," in Philip Schaff and Henry Wace (eds.), *From Nicene and Post-Nicene Fathers, Second Series, Vol. 14*. Buffalo, NY: Christian Literature Publishing Co., 1900, 537; Hefele, *History of the Councils of the Church: Vol. V*, 349; Mendham, *The Seventh General Council, the Second of Nicaea*, 70. It should be noted that both Mendham and Percival translated Nicaea II, making this view that of most of the council's English translators.

676 Price, *The Acts of the Second Council of Nicaea (787)*, 20 and Lamberz, "'Falsata Graecorum more,'" 213-229. In reality, Price merely reiterates the theory of Lamberz, being indebted to the latter for his critical edition of the council. It should go without saying that Lamberz is the chief living authority on Nicaea II. His theories are an improvement upon those posed by a scholar in the 1960s. See Wallach, "The Greek and Latin Versions of II Nicaea," 103-125.

more subtle akin to the *Pseudo-Isidorian Decretals* that likewise make their appearance in the mid-ninth century. The *Decretals* contain many authentic texts with slight alterations and even their invented texts borrow authentic sounding terminology and quotes from similar letters.[677] Forgeries of this sort escape easy detection.

Leaving aside for now whether the Latin additions to JE 2448 and 2449 are forgeries, it should be stated that the latter does not even really say anything excessively Papal by the day's standards. It critiques Saint Tarasius of Constantinople's elevation from layman to Patriarch (in contradiction of recent Roman forbiddance of such a practice in 769) and complains about Rome's stolen jurisdiction in the Balkans and Italy. Rome surely cared about both of these issues at the time, but they were conspicuously not addressed by Nicaea II itself. This detail is hard to square if the Church of this era had any belief in the Roman Synod having direct and universal jurisdiction. Not surprisingly, the jurisdictional question is entirely excised from Greek JE 2449 and the criticism of Tarasius' ordination is muted. Both such complaints are entirely missing from Greek JE 2448.[678]

Considering Papal honorifics, both Greek and Latin JE 2449 include a quotation of Matt 16:18, applying the promise made in the passage to the whole Church.[679] Nevertheless, the Roman church is identified as "holding the pre-eminence…and exists as the head of all the Churches…and will ever retain the Primacy."[680] Such honorifics, completely consistent with earlier usage such

---

677 The *Pseudo-Isidorian Decretals'* "forgers…did not create them from scratch, but after precise selection from countless authentic works, and, in a way, the composition is reminiscent of a mosaic with of all kinds of tesserae. So they chose passages from the Bible, the Roman and the Frankish legislation, excerpts from authentic letters of the [P]opes, from the acts of councils and synods, from theological treatises and from historiographical works. It is therefore not surprising that the authenticity of these documents was never put in doubt during the Middle Ages." See Evangelos Chrysos, "New perceptions of imperium and sacerdotium in the letters of Pope Nicholas I to Emperor Michael III," *Travaux et Memoires*, 22:1, 2018, 332.

678 Price, *The Acts of the Second Council of Nicaea (787)*, 169, 176, 179.

679 Mendham, *The Seventh General Council, the Second of Nicaea*, 75-76.

680 Ibid., 76.

as during Chalcedon and enshrined in canon law (Canon 3 of Constantinople I and Canon 28 of Chalcedon), though worded assertively, are uncontroversial.

Nevertheless, the Latin differences in JE 2448 command more attention in modern times due to their more advanced Papal claims. Considering the Papacy, Latin JE 2448 cites Matt 16:18. It claims that Saint Peter alone was given "the singular honour" to the "keys of the kingdom of heaven" by Christ Himself, with privileges bestowed to Peter's "successors" in the "Apostolic See."[681] The end of the letter says that this charism gives Rome the greatest "executive role" in the Church, with the Church's "assent," to "confirm each synod" by their own "authority."[682] There are also similar criticisms of Saint Tarasius for being a layman elevated to the episcopacy, but it gets considerably more agitated in tone. For example, it criticizes the title "Ecumenical" being applied to Tarasius on the Papacy's authority, claiming it contradicts that the Pope has been given "primatial authority everywhere on earth."[683] It likewise includes demands over jurisdiction in Italy and the Balkans, worded even more harshly than what is found in JE 2449.

The Latin Papal claims are not radical at first glance. There is some sense that Matt 16:18 can apply to Rome specifically, as covered in the first chapter. Both Chalcedon and JE 2449 invoke Rome's Church-wide role, with Session 6 of Nicaea II itself explicitly delineating that the Roman Patriarchate (among others) has the right to confirm synods.[684] The term "primatial" and similar adjectives have likewise been applied to both Rome and other bishoprics, as covered previously. If the Latin is not anachronistic, the majority thesis that the Latin is authentically what Adrian I had sent to the council, but the Greek was what was actually read out, appears all the more defensible.

There is additional historical evidence of there being modifications made to the Greek at Nicaea II. First, both the

681 Ibid., 49.

682 Price, *The Acts of the Second Council of Nicaea (787)*, 171.

683 Ibid., 172.

684 Ibid., 442.

Latin and Greek minutes specify that Tarasius put an exaggerated emphasis on the Papal legates authenticating that the "letters'" (both JE 2448 and 2449) "interpretation of the Latin"[685] (i.e. Greek translation) was indeed accurate. This virtually guarantees that a diplomatic re-translation of contents had occurred for at least one of the letters, the bizarre detail otherwise being difficult to explain. Second, Anastasius, the sole source for all of the Latin differences, himself explicitly claims that the divergences between the Latin and Greek of JE 2448[686] are the result of "consideration for Tarasios" and the excision "already happened when the letter was read out at the council itself and in the original acts."[687] Anastasius similarly implies that differences in JE 2449 have the same cause.[688] Third, a tenth century Latin gloss of Pope Nicholas' *Letter 86*, a letter which complains emphatically that the Greeks with malintent removed important passages in JE 2449, likewise identifies partisans of Tarasius as responsible for the anomaly between the Latin and

---

685 Mendham, *The Seventh General Council, the Second of Nicaea*, 47, 70-71. Mendham prioritizes the Greek in his translation, which unambiguously delineates letters in the plural are being spoken of: τὰ τοιαῦτα γράμματα. Price wrongly translates the Latin word *litteris* (meaning "letters" in the plural, but it can mean "letter" in the singular if context demands it) as a singular letter in Price, *The Acts of the Second Council of Nicaea (787)*, 174. For the Latin and Greek see Erich Lamberz, *Concilium Universale Nicaenum Secundum: Concilii Actiones I-III*. Berlin: Walter de Gruyter, 2018, 172-173. As for context, immediately before the reading of JE 2448, the "Holy Council" declares that "the letters of the most holy and blessed Adrian" be read. What immediately follows is the reading of both letters.

686 Mansi 12, 1073-1074. This is a marginal note of Anastasius the Librarian included in the midst of the Latin addition to JE 2448.

687 Lamberz, "'Falsata Graecorum more,'" 215. See also Price, *The Acts of the Second Council of Nicaea (787)*, 146.

688 Price, *The Acts of the Second Council of Nicaea (787)*, 179. Therein, Price speculates Anastasius left out the excised section in his translation of Nicaea II simply because of its similarity with jurisdictional requests in JE 2448. If true, this lends credibility to the idea that Anastasius in making his short comment implied the same cause for the difference in the Greek as that he identified in his comments in JE 2448. See n. 686.

Greek.[689] Literally every early source on the question claims the Greek renderings of JE 2448 and 2449 are authentic to Nicaea II, or in the case of Anastasius, reneges on earlier allegations of forgery[690] simply to concede that any differences which existed pertain to controversies surrounding Tarasius himself at the time of the council. As for the Latin versions of JE 2448 and 2449, if it were not for Anastasius (as he explicitly claims) allegedly having recourse to the original letters "in the archives of the Roman Church,"[691] their supposed renderings would have been entirely lost to history.[692] However, due to all this, it is probable the original Latin texts contained some authentic differences, though it is questionable if this would include the Papal claims in Anastasius' version of Latin JE 2448.[693]

It is with the preceding pretext for translation from the Greek and outright textual restoration of the Latin that the differences between the Greek and Latin in JE 2448 are most curious. First,

---

689 Wallach, "The Greek and Latin Versions of II Nicaea," 112.

690 Such allegations of the Greeks altering the minutes of Nicaea II never specifically named Photius, or anyone living, as specifically being responsible for the alleged differences between the "original" Latin and Greek texts of Nicaea II. This implies an awareness in the Papal chancery during the 860s that at least some differences were made during Nicaea II itself, something that Anastasius readily admits to by 873 when translating Nicaea II. Cf Lamberz, "'Falsata Graecorum more,'" 215.

691 Price, *The Acts of the Second Council of Nicaea (787)*, 179.

692 Anastasius asserts there was a Latin version of Nicaea II preceding his own translation in 873. Due to its defects, Anastasius claimed that "nobody reads this translation and no copies of it are made." See Percival, "The Second Council of Nicaea," 581. Percival's above translation of Anastasius is a loose paraphrase, but the Latin (Mansi 12, 1074) conveys essentially the same point: *interpres pene per singula relicto utriusque linguæ idiomate adeo suerit verbum e verbo secutus, ut quid in eadem editione intelligatur, aut vix aut nunquam possit adverti in sastidiumque versa legentium, pene ab omnibus hac pro causa contemnatur. Unde a quibusdam nec ipsa lectione, ut non dicam transcriptione, digna penitus judicatur…*

693 In the opinion of this author, the Latin addition to JE 2449 is so minor that there is no compelling reason to doubt it existed during Nicaea II, but was intentionally excised for political reasons. Theological motivations are difficult to infer. Details considering JE 2448 are subsequently covered.

let's evaluate the differences introduced near the beginning of the letter pertaining to the Papacy.[694] One may legitimately question why, contrary to the Latin, the Greek makes mention of *both* Saints Peter and Paul in reference to the episcopacy, with no mention of Matt 16:18. The invocation of Peter and Paul makes more sense in the Greek *and* Latin, as immediately after the differing passage in question, what follows is a quotation from the *Life of Saint [Pope] Sylvester* where both Peter and Paul appear to Saint Constantine. In the Greek, the details all connect. In the Latin, they do not. In the words of one scholar, "one cannot help but be struck by the fact that the Greek text harmonizes much better than the Latin text…"[695]

Additionally, the peculiar interpretation of Matt 16:18 in the Latin *contradicts* the one given in both JE 2449 *and* later in the council itself (which likewise applies the passage to the entire Church, not Rome specifically).[696] Greek JE 2448 ascribes "the foundation of the Catholic and Orthodox faith" to all who "succeed to their [Peter and Paul's] thrones," a reference to all bishops in common—not as a "singular honour" given to the Pope of Rome. Any claim to Rome being given the keys exclusively is something without earlier attestation,[697] its sudden inclusion during Nicaea II leading one to raise her/his eyebrow. The fact that this detail is found suspiciously

---

694 The differences between the Greek and Latin in JE 2448 are delineated in Mendham, *The Seventh General Council, the Second of Nicaea*, 49.

695 Serraz, "Les lettres du pape Hadrien ler lues au lle concile de Nicee," 412. The quotation is a translation from the French: *on ne peut s'emecher detre frappe du fait que le texte grec s'harmonise beaucoup mieux que le texte latin…*

696 Session 6 of Nicaea II quotes Matt 16:18 and applies it to "the whole Church of God" in its criticism of the iconoclast Council of Hiera. See Mendham, *The Seventh General Council, the Second of Nicaea*, 406. Session 5 likewise attributes infallibility to the whole Church: "Their aim has been to bring to nought the Church of Christ wherefore the Lord shall bring them to nought and shall be set at nought and anathematised by all who are born in her but she hath ever remained undespoiled, unshaken, and immoveable." See Ibid., 327.

697 For example, the Papal legate Philip during the Council of Ephesus did not go as far as to specify Petrine inheritance as a singular honor of Rome's. See Price and Graumann, *The Council of Ephesus of 431*, 377.

only in the Latin text subsequently leads to the raising of the other eyebrow.

Lastly, Greek JE 2448 lacks the end of the letter found only in Anastasius' translation of the Latin. There is good evidence that the Greek does indeed lack portions found in the original, "pre-Anastasian" Latin version of JE 2448. Specifically, Pope Nicholas' *Letter 88* (approximately 865) cites an early part of the ending, noting it is missing in the Greek of his day.[698] This paragraph pertains to asking the Byzantine Empress Irene to issue a *sacra* confessing iconodulia. It is curious that the two sentences preceding what Pope Nicholas cites "are taken verbatim…from the Latin…letter of Constantine IV to Pope Donus," and put into Adrian I's figurative "mouth" without attestation, for *seemingly* no good reason.[699] This indicates an interpolation into this section, matching the style of the *Pseudo-Isidorian Decretals*, was made. However, the overall passage has hallmarks of authenticity. Interestingly, the fact that interpolations were evidently made in the Latin betrays the existence of an authentic Latin JE 2448 whose ending was different than the Greek JE 2448 that exists today.

Later in the ending of Latin JE 2448 (that is missing in the Greek), there is another indication of authenticity. The *Caroline Books* contain a dry reference to Charlemagne, including his royal title that notes that he is a "Roman patrician" (lit. "*patricius Romanorum*") explicitly citing the statement comes from Adrian I's letter.[700] This

---

698 Lamberz, "'Falsata Graecorum more,'" 228. The passage in question cites how the Byzantine state used to persecute iconodules. See Price, *The Acts of the Second Council of Nicaea (787)*, 170.

699 Price, *The Acts of the Second Council of Nicaea (787)*, 170. Price continues to observe that "[t]hey [the verbatim sentences] obscure the point Hadrian [I] is making" in the passage. This implies an interpolation similar to the *Pseudo-Isidorian Decetals*, which employed the practice of adding an insertion from an authentic source into another authentic source intending to change meaning. Though Price does not recognize this, its inclusion was intended to strengthen the criticism given pertaining to Constantinople's bad track record for persecutions.

700 Lamberz, *Concilium Universale Nicaenum Secundum*, 171.

proves that the *original* Latin version of JE 2448 differed from Greek JE 2448, thereby predating Nicaea II itself.

The preceding facts demonstrate that there were indeed differences between the Greek and original Latin version of JE 2448. Yet, one cannot textually verify a reliable parallel text from the preceding that contains any of the Papal Supremacist statements.[701] This permits the possibility of their interpolation into the original Latin by 873. This would mean that the original Latin, Greek, and "Anastasian" versions of JE 2448 all differ.[702]

What lends credence to there being a large, interpolated section introduced by Anastasius between the two preceding verifiably

701 The *Collectio Britannica* contains fragments from JE 2448 that match the Papal interpolations of Anastasius. The Latin matches Anastasius' retroversion of JE 2448 almost *ad verbatim*. Yet, the *Collectio* contains non-Papal fragments which have highly variant Latin when compared with Anastian JE 2448, evidencing the latter's obvious retroversion. The lack of any evidence of retroversion in the Papal fragments indicates that they were not translated from the Greek. Additionally, it indicates Anastasius had made alterations to Adrian I's Papal registry and used those documents to additionally doctor his retroversion of JE 2448. See Folios 100v-101v; 103v-r in British Library, Add MS 8873. <https://www.bl.uk/manuscripts/Viewer.aspx?ref=add_ms_8873_fs001r>, July 21, 2023. Cf Lamberz, *Concilium Universale Nicaenum Secundum*, 123; 143; 157; 163-167; 183.

702 This has been recognized by previous scholarship. See Serraz, "Les lettres du pape Hadrien ler lues au lle concile de Nicee," 420. Even Wallach admits the same, though only about JE 2448's Patristic citations in particular. He asserts that "the *synodica* JE 2448 as inserted in Anastasius Bibliothecarius' Latin version of the Greek Acta of II Nicaea was *verunechtet* [lit. "destroyed," i.e. corrupted] by him in a number of instances." See Wallach, "The Greek and Latin Versions of II Nicaea," 119. He elsewhere admits that "Anastasius… occasionally falsified the genuine text of JE 2448" in Ibid., "The Libri Carolini and Patristics, Latin and Greek: Prolegomena to a Critical Edition," in Luitpold Wallach (ed.), *Diplomatic Studies in Latin and Greek Documents from the Carolingian Age*. Ithaca: Cornell University Press, 1977, 495. In the preceding, Wallach confronts the deliberate methodology of Anastasius in which he corrects a source via insertions from other authentic sources. However, he does not recognize that a similar methodology was expanded upon in the additional Latin portions weighing in on issues relevant to the Papacy akin to how the *Pseudo-Isidorian Decretals* doctored sources from interpolating Patristic statements.

authentic passages in the original Latin JE 2448? There is a marked thematic discontinuity found in the version Anastasius has rendered. Specifically, everything between "[i]n addition" and "against our holy catholic and apostolic church."[703] In Latin JE 2448, what follows the paragraph containing the request for an Imperial *sacra* concerning icons is a long, irate aside. The aside contains suspicious elements, which will be covered in a moment. The paragraph immediately after this suspicious aside invokes Tarasius had already confessed iconodulia in his own encyclical, a detail which is consistent with the request earlier made for the Imperial *sacra*. This implies the authenticity of this subsequent section. The paragraph then gives a criticism of Tarasius' consecration to Patriarch being a layman, a criticism reiterated from the interpolated section only shortly before. This is then significantly expanded with another interpolation, as covered below. The authentic ending to Latin JE 2448 then continues in invoking Charlemagne, thanking him for restoring Roman patrimony from the Lombards. This, though less clearly than the demands made in JE 2449, implied that the Byzantines should do the same. Its absence in the Greek, along with the critique of Tarasius, is not surprising.

Latin JE 2448's ending reads much more naturally with the "in addition" section removed. Even the terminology "in addition" transparently implies the whole section is an addition which does not fit into the original text. In fact, shortly after "in addition" is a long section that in the Latin "is virtually identical" to a section from JE 2449 preserved only in the Collectio Britannica and not Anastasius' translation,[704] implying that he interpolated the section and covered up the evidence. The original Latin text's removal from Greek JE 2448 at the council itself was perhaps motivated by the premise Anastasius himself gives: lessening the offense created by its critique

---

703 Price, *The Acts of the Second Council of Nicaea (787)*, 170-172. "In addition" is *"porro"* in the Latin. See Lamberz, *Concilium Universale Nicaenum Secundum*, 165.

704 Price, *The Acts of the Second Council of Nicaea (787)*, 179. See also Lamberz, *Concilium Universale Nicaenum Secundum*, 165. The Latin in Collectio Britannica Folios 103v-r is practically *ad verbatim*. See British Library, *Add MS 8873*.

of Tarasius, though the original critique likely lacked considerable sections as compared to what Anastasius renders. Subsequent to the "in addition" interpolation, otherwise harmless details to modern eyes, such as calling Charlemagne a Roman patrician and thanking him for his restoration of Roman patrimonies, implies official Byzantine recognition of Charlemagne and his territorial claims—something that was unacceptable in Constantinople. Removing the whole (original) section was an easy solution to the problems the original Latin JE 2448 posed. Its removal does not verify what Anastasius otherwise renders is reliable.

That being said, it is worth reviewing what is found in the interpolated section of the ending of Latin JE 2448. First, there is the sudden textual insertion of Papal correspondence without attestation. JE 2449 and and Gelasius (covered later) are paraphrased and quoted without attestation.[705] As discussed earlier, a letter to Pope Donus is likewise quoted word-for-word, without attestation, right before the addition. Interestingly, shortly after the addition, Gregory the Great is quoted nearly word for word without attestation (not so coincidentally in a section which is a litany of criticisms pointed at Tarasius).[706] These are noticeable indications of a sort of "copy and pasting" typical of high-quality ninth-century Latin forgeries such as the *Pseudo-Isidorian Decretals*. However, this pattern is suspiciously absent in the rest of Latin JE 2448.[707] Furthermore, this is a suspicious textual discontinuity amidst the thematic discontinuity in the section. Considering the controversial

---

705 Ibid., 167.

706 Wallach, "The Greek and Latin Versions of II Nicaea," 122-123. See also Lamberz, *Concilium Universale Nicaenum Secundum*, 169.

707 Lamberz, *Concilium Universale Nicaenum Secundum*, 119-163. Whenever anyone is quoted in JE 2448, he is named. This includes Popes. For example, Pope Gregory is cited by name in Ibid., 127. The one exception to this is a passage from the acts of the Lateran Council of 769 in Ibid., 133. The council was not old enough to have merited explicit citation. The Roman Synod in 785 that penned JE 2448 relied on Lateran (769), especially considering it would have contained relevant source material to draw from. This exception does not betray the pattern of strategically placed unattested quotations of more traditional Papal authorities.

content surrounding these insertions, the motivation for forgery is just as obvious as the textual indications of its existence.

Second, in the large interpolated section there is an oddly anachronistic criticism of Tarasius for using the title "Ecumenical Patriarch."[708] This was something of a dead letter two centuries previous, even in Gregory the Great's time (considering the lack of response he received). The resurrection of such a criticism appears diplomatically foolish in the 780s when the Roman Synod was neither under Byzantine threat of taxation nor imminent military aggression, (as it was in Gregory's time).[709] The entire basis of the complaint is the opposite of Gregory's, as Latin JE 2448 implies the title rightly belongs to Pope Adrian I. Contrarily, Gregory vociferously warned against the pretensions implied by the title and denied its import to the Papacy.

Yet, such a criticism locates nicely to the 860s. The chancery of Pope Nicholas under the helm of Anastasius had a protracted program of asserting interpatriarchal Papal claims in correspondence with Photius and Byzantine Emperor Michael III. Forgeries, such as the *Pseudo-Isidorian Decretals*, were noticeably employed with the intent of expanding unprecedented Papal prerogatives to an apparently surprised Greek audience.[710] At the culmination of this campaign of asserting interpatriarchal prerogatives was the Council of Constantinople (869-870). During this council, Saint Ignatius of Constantinople was not permitted to use the title "Ecumenical Patriarch," because the title "Ecumenical" was explicitly bestowed upon the Pope of that time.[711] In contradistinction, during Nicaea II the title "Ecumenical Patriarch" is used without controversy in the

---

708 Price, *The Acts of the Second Council of Nicaea (787)*, 171.

709 The loss of Rome's southern Italian patrimonies was a serious financial blow, though the sense of imminence caused by this years after it first occurred must have certainly died down.

710 Chrysos, "New perceptions of imperium and sacerdotium," 321-323, 332-333.

711 For the title "Ecumenical Pope" and Ignatius of Constantinople being identified simply as "archbishop" see Price and Montinaro, *The Acts of the Council of Constantinople of 869-70*, 427-429.

Latin and Greek versions.[712] One may perceive that the critique over the title Ecumenical Patriarch is part of a polemical environment expressly concerned with expanding Papal prerogatives during the 860s, rather than the 780s where there was no motive to debate Papal claims.[713]

Third, the addition to Latin JE 2448 also asserts that Rome's "executive role" was given "through an injunction of the Lord…with the church no less assenting" granting Rome "primacy throughout the world" amidst complaints over jurisdiction. This is an uncited paraphrase of an earlier letter by Pope Gelasius which cites in "the rule of each synod" there is an "executive role" for Rome as "approved by the assent of the whole Church" and "enjoined by a saying of the Lord."[714]

The change in emphasis is palpable—Latin JE 2448 implies borderline-direct jurisdiction (in reality, an exaggeration to attain to local jurisdictional rights) as a right given by God Himself. The other invokes Rome's prerogatives in conciliar procedure rooted in the Church's assent, merely citing Matt 16:18 as an additional

---

712 Cosmas the Deacon before the reading of JE 2449 calls Tarasius by his title "Ecumenical Patriarch." The Latin and Greek do not differ on this point. See Lamberz, *Concilium Universale Nicaenum Secundum*, 173-174. Translators make no mention of differences elsewhere between the Latin and Greek concerning the same title. See Mendham, *The Seventh General Council, the Second of Nicaea*, 71 (see also 80, 82-84, 90, 119, 120, 123) and Price, *The Acts of the Second Council of Nicaea (787)*, 175.

713 Price observes that differences between Latin and Greek "are most likely to date to the Photian period, since Constantinople had no motive to play down Roman doctrinal authority in 787, when it needed Roman support against the iconoclasts." See Price, *The Acts of the Second Council of Nicaea (787)*, 143. The preceding acknowledges the 780s lacked a significant reason which would have provided the motive to remove Papal claims in JE 2448, assuming they existed. If one does not assume they existed as Price does, but recognizes that the correspondence between Byzantine Emperor Michael III and Pope Nicholas (by the hand of Anastasius) reveals a specific ecclesiastical controversy at *that* time (as Price recognizes), then this indicates that motive existed among the Latin side to buttress their Papal claims during the 860s-870s. This perhaps motivated forgery, just as it motivated the employment of the *Pseudo-Isidorian Decretals*.

714 Price, *The Acts of the Second Council of Nicaea (787)*, 171.

justification for such prerogatives. In effect, the Anastasian version of Latin JE 2448 puts, what was in Gelasius' personal emphasis, the cart (Rome's position by virtue of the Church's assent) in front of the horse (its institution by Christ). "No less assenting" implies what is of chief importance in Gelasius' actual letter to be of secondary importance in Latin JE 2448. Latin JE 2448's reformulation of Gelasius' words cannot be anything other than an intentional echo of Nicholas' *Letter 86* to Michael III, which boasted:

> *The privileges of the Roman church were founded by Christ upon Saint Peter...These privileges were granted to our church by Christ, not by synods, which merely have celebrated and venerated them.*[715]

The above, uncoincidentally, was also written by Anastasius.

Reviewing the mainstream opinion, the differences between JE 2448 and JE 2449 in the Greek and Latin have an explanation widely attested to in the earliest sources, including Anastasius himself. They refer solely to diplomatic changes to the letter allegedly relevant to disputes over canonical ordinations and jurisdiction. There was no controversy over Papal prerogatives mentioned in any contemporary source surrounding Nicaea II or ninth century observers, such as Anastasius, about the same episode. One can retain this thesis with one slight modification, discussed in detail above. That is, while Latin JE 2448 was excised at Nicaea II, by 873 several suspect passages were interpolated into the original Latin by Anastasius.

Why else does Latin JE 2448 contain a subtle, but decisive emphasis in the (present) Latin pertaining to the Papacy as an institution itself? This is where a review of the scholarly arguments

---

715 Chrysos, "New perceptions of imperium and sacerdotium," 326-327. To be fair to Anastasius, a similar conception of the Roman episcopate was ascribed to the *Gelasian Decretum*, so he may have presumed it was an authentically Patristic idea. However, Anastasius likely acquired the notion from quotations in *the Pseudo-Isidorian Decretals*, a recent source which he must have recognized contained forgeries. See Evangelos Chrysos, "The Principle of Pentarchy at the Council(s) (869-70 and 879-80)," in Maria Youni and Lydia Paparriga-Artemiadi (eds.) *Constantinos G. Pitsakis: In Memoriam*. Athens: Academy of Athens, 2023, 160-161.

in favor of Anastasius' Latin JE 2448 become self-eviscerating for
their cause.

The most convincing argument scholarship asserts in favor
of the priority given to Anastasius' Latin rendering of JE 2448
being authentic (and original to Nicaea II) is that JE 2449 in *both*
the Greek and Latin (the latter more so) includes criticisms of
Tarasius.[716] Therefore, the Latin-priority argument goes, Greek
JE 2448 (presently lacking such criticisms) must have been altered
after Anastasius translated an earlier version of the Greek into
Latin (allegedly) faithfully.[717] Supposedly, Greek JE 2448's Papal
Supremacy claims were excised along with the criticisms. This is
because JE 2449 in both Greek and Latin had (as discussed above)
"claim[s] to primacy" pertaining to "the Roman Church."[718]
According to these scholars, this demonstrates there was a time
where such claims were not objectionable and therefore not excised.
These scholars conclude then that there were at least two rounds of
revision by Photius (or his partisans), once during the 860s (from
which Anastasius faithfully translates this Greek into Latin), and
another round by Photius made after Anastasius left Constantinople
with the earlier (altered) version of the Greek.[719] Otherwise, these
scholars claim, Anastasius would have dutifully reported that
JE 2448 had extensive alterations in the disputed pro-Papal section
when he translated it.[720]

The preceding line of argumentation is peculiar. To make
this theory work, the Greek forger (identified to be Photius or a
partisan) had terrible amnesia and forgot to remove Papal primacy

---

716 This is described in heroic terms by Lamberz, revealing how necessary it is to
his argument: "the letter to Tarasios comes to the rescue." Lamberz, *"Falsata
Graecorum more,"* 215. The German is: *des Briefes an Tarasios zu Hilfe. "Zu Hilfe"*
is a common euphemism in German for being rescued or saved.

717 Ibid., 216.

718 Ibid., 221.

719 Ibid., 226.

720 As noted previously, Anastasius admits the end of JE 2448 was removed just
like a section of JE 2449 due to criticisms aimed at Tarasius in the alleged
Latin originals.

claims from JE 2449, but *surgically* excised them from JE 2448. This
is unlikely.[721] It also uncritically assumes that Anastasius was not
negligent (either intentionally or unintentionally) in mentioning all
the differences in JE 2448. This places a lot of faith in Anastasius,
which will be covered in the next chapter, is not well placed. It
additionally imputes the motive to alter documentation solely upon
Photius when at no point, including during Constantinople IV
(879-880), did Photius manifest a tendency to edit out Roman
ecclesiastical claims.[722]

---

721 In the words of one scholar, "If it was the concern to diminish [Roman]
primacy which motivated the alleged alteration of the *Letter to the Emperors*
[JE 2448] by the Greek translator, we cannot understand the integrity of
[i.e. make sense of] the *Letter to Tarasius* [JE 2449]." See Serraz, "Les lettres
du pape Hadrien ler lues au lle concile de Nicee," 420. The preceding is a
translation of the French: *Si c'etait la preoccupation de diminuer cette primaute qui
avait motive la pretendue alteration de la letter aux empereurs pa le traducteur grec, on ne
s'expliquerait pas l'integrite de la letter a Taraise.*

722 Lamberz in Ibid., 227-228 points out that Pope Nicholas in *Letter 82* does
not mention any alterations in JE 2448 or 2449 and Photius in his response
(*Letter 290*) makes no issue of Nicholas' Papal claims. Lamberz concludes
from the preceding that in 860 (when *Letter 82* was penned) JE 2449 must
have not been altered yet and that the alterations subsequently made left
behind Papal Supremacy language, because Photius did not yet find it
objectionable. Lamberz thereby presupposes that Papal Supremacy was
considered normative in both the East and West at around 860. Therefore,
Photius would have only had the motivation to excise passages pertaining
to jurisdiction, leaving it to years later (and a change of heart) to excise
Papal Supremacy from JE 2448. There are problems with the preceding
theory. First, the presupposition that Papal Supremacy was normative is
incorrect, as this study demonstrates. Second, what plausibly is the occasion
for Photius suddenly finding Papal Supremacy more objectionable after
870 than he did during the 860s so as to provide the motivation to doctor
JE 2448 after Anastasius had received a Greek version of JE 2448 from the
860s without alterations to Papal honorifics alongside JE 2449 with its similarly
unmolested Papal honorifics? Wouldn't Photius have more motivation before
870 to alter these documents than afterwards? And if one were to push the
dating of such presumed alterations into the 880s, what situation provided
the basis for such alterations that was more extreme than the friction of
the 860s? His second deposition cannot be the answer, as he would have
lost control of the levers of power to corrupt the entire Greek manuscript
traditions on the question. The presumption of motive by Lamberz, without

In summary, the ecclesiastical question of Rome's authority was wholly new to the time of Anastasius' tenure. It was exacerbated by Pope Nicholas' deposition, as such a deposition presumed that he was subject to the same disciplinary authority of previous consensus-based Patriarchal depositions. This is what likely motivated Anastasius' interpolations into the present version of JE 2448, as an Ecumenical Council weighing in on the Pope's role in the Church would have been useful *after* 867. Ongoing ecclesiastical disputes among the several Frankish Empires likely also played a role (as will be covered in the next chapter). Additionally, the jurisdictional question in southern Italy and the Balkans was not solved by Constantinople 869-870, which may have poured enough salt in the wound to inspire the creative direct-jurisdictional reasoning latent in Anastasius' Latin JE 2448.

The agreed-to ecclesiology of the Church during Nicaea II was considerably different than that found in Anastasius' Latin JE 2448. The decree of the council itself (Session 7) states that "the divine tradition of the Catholic Church" is "established by our common vote."[723] In the previous session of the council, a definition of an Ecumenical Council is given which delineates that the participation

---

it being applicable to any episode Photius played a role in, inveighs against his thesis. Third, Lamberz poses no rational explanation why Photius was so ham-handed as to excise jurisdictional claims in the 860s from JE 2448 and JE 2449; yet during the 870s excise Papal Supremacy claims in JE 2448, but not from JE 2449. Lamberz's conjecture that there were multiple rounds of Photian forgeries has too many problems to be a compelling thesis. Meanwhile, the inference that Anastasius merely interpolated material in the original Latin JE 2448, with JE 2448 and JE 2449 otherwise already having slight differences between the Latin and Greek since Tarasius' time, requires no ecclesiastical presuppositions or unexplainable motives. A single round of forgery of the Latin manuscript record following a predictable pattern of the era, as gleaned from the methodology of forgery used by the *Pseudo-Isidorian Decretals*, from a known employer of forgeries (Anastasius), works much better. As for *Letter 82* and *Letter 290* discussed above, their tone is explained by mutual relations between Nicholas and Photius having not fully broken down as they have by 862. In fact, it is only after this impasse does controversy over Nicaea II's renderings begin. This implies a change in Roman rhetoric in response to their new tact towards Photius.

723 Mendham, *The Seventh General Council, the Second of Nicaea*, 437.

of all the "[P]atriarchs" and the assent of "the whole earth" are necessary identifying factors. Interestingly, the "Pope of Rome or his priests [i.e. legates]" are assigned the task of "cooperation" (lit.: "*συνέργεια*") and the other Patriarchates age given the task of "assent" (lit.: "*συμφρονοῦντας*").[724]

Concerning the implications of these specific Greek terms, scholarship notes that this is a purposeful "distinction" as "during the sessions of Nicaea II one of the oriental representatives, John the Synkellos, played a more prominent role than either the Roman representatives."[725] In other words, the Eastern patriarchates have an active role in formulating doctrine while the Roman Patriarchate is more passive, either consenting or not. As Saint Celestine cautioned centuries before the Council of Ephesus, Rome was not to insert themselves into the actual doctrinal fray. While Saint Agatho and Rome's legates during Chalcedon did take firm doctrinal stances, they were not the most notable parties in any of the debates or in the formulation of the conciliar decrees. Despite the nuances in exactly how it was understood consensus was achieved by a council, Nicaea II's definition of ecumenicity follows consensus-based ecclesiology and it implies that Roman acceptance in every detail is unnecessary—something that makes sense given ongoing debates over Canon 28 of Chalcedon and Canon 3 of Constantinople I.

Due to disputes over jurisdiction, Nicaea II apparently did not attain to unqualified Roman acceptance. Nevertheless, that did not stop Adrian I from having the council translated and sent to Charlemagne.[726] Further, he defended the same council against newfound Frankish opposition to iconodulia. The Franks hypocritically rejected the council, likely because it effected ecclesiastical rapprochement between the Byzantines and their Roman proxy state. In so doing, they published the *Caroline Books* which in torturous detail accused JE 2448 (Adrian's *Letter to the Emperors* as read out during Nicaea II), in particular, of many theological errors. This disallows for the possibility that the doctrines

---

724 Price, *The Acts of the Second Council of Nicaea (787)*, 442.

725 Ibid.

726 Wallach, "The Greek and Latin Versions of II Nicaea," 113-114.

of Papal Infallibility or Papal Ratification of Ecumenical Councils (being the sole means in which they derive their authority) had any adherents during this period.

With this in mind, a Papal honorific in the *Caroline Books* should bear some mention. It asserts that "the Roman See is eminent over the other [A]postolic [S]ees…from no synodal action of the other Churches, but she holds the primacy (*primatum*) by the authority of the Lord himself."[727] This statement is rhetorically more extreme in some respects than even Anastasius' Latin JE 2448, which at least speaks of Rome's primacy being assented to by the Church.[728]

The statement appears to mirror another forgery, the *Decretum Gelasianum*. The *Decretum Gelasianum* is a document that scholars generally attribute to an anonymous source (likely) without connections to the Papal chancery during the sixth century,[729] though some scholarship allows for it authentically being from Gelasius.[730] One must consider a later origin, at least in part, due to the fact that the original document was continuously altered and amended until it took its final form during the eighth century, within

---

727 Percival, "The Second Council of Nice," 580.

728 Price, *The Acts of the Second Council of Nicaea (787)*, 171.

729 Clare Rothschild, *The Muratorian Fragment: Text, Translation, Commentary.* Tubingen: Mohr Siebeck, 2022, 9-10. See also Chrysos, *The Principle of Pentarchy at the Council(s)*, 160. Contemporary experts on Papal decretals such as Dionysius Exiguus and Cassiodorus are ignorant of its existence. See F.C. Burkitt, "The Decretum Gelasianum," *Journal of Theological Studies*, 14, 1913, 470-471. The actual document itself curiously follows a decree (falsely) ascribed to Pope Hormisdas (or vice versa) as found in PL 62, 537-540. Hormisdas' decree goes in the same order, skipping the first chapter, citing the Biblical canon as found in the *Decretum Gelasianum* verbatim, and then immediately going into a statement essentially identical to *Decretum Gelasianum* 3:1. See PL 62, 537. In J.P. Migne's PL, it is observed that the decretal has suffered corruptions and is likewise ascribed to Gelasius: "*Vides hoc Decretale in quinque titulos apte dividi, ac multis locis depravatum restituti…hoc decretum Gelasio ascriberet.*" See PL 62, 540. The multiple manifestations of this document with ascriptions to different Popes, with nobody "in the know" aware of it, implies it did not originate in any sixth century Papal chancery.

730 Neil and Allen, *The Letters of Gelasius I*, 142.

a Frankish Duchy.[731] The *Decretum Gelasianum* gives a biblical canon, speaks of the Roman church's primacy, gives a list of canonical Patristic works, and then condemns heretical ones (including the apocryphal Scriptures).

Concerning the Roman Synod's primacy, it asserts that "the holy Roman church is given first place by the rest of the churches without a synodal decision, but from the voice of the Lord... obtained primacy."[732] This statement is interpatriarchal in intent, as the *Decretum Gelasianum* explains that the city of Rome is the place of Peter's martyrdom and then lists other Petrine sees (Alexandria and Antioch) as in the second and third place behind Rome.[733]

It is ironic that what appears to be the earliest statement in ecclesiastical history that breaks with the emphasis on Rome's canonical privileges, and instead places emphasis *solely* upon a direct institution from God Himself, is shrouded in so much mystery. This makes evaluating the intent behind its penning difficult. Being that it probably did not originate from a Papal chancery, a sixth century origin may betray forgers writing in opposition to the Three Chapters. For one, its passing comments on Origen increases the probability of this.[734] The anathemas against Origen in 543 were produced almost concurrently with Saint Justinian's demands that the Three Chapters be condemned.[735] The former were assented to without hesitation by Pope Vigilius.[736]

---

731 The first extant copies of the document all originate from a Frankish Duchy in the eighth century. See Rothschild, *The Muratorian Fragment*, 10.

732 *Decretum Gelasianum* 3:1. Cf "Hormisdas'" decree in PL 62, 537: *Post has omnes propheticas, et evangelicas, atque apostolicas, quas superius deprompsimus Scripturas, quibus Ecclesia Catholica per gratiam Dei fundata est, etiam illud intimandum putavimus, quamvis universæ per orbem diffuse catholicæ Ecclessiæ unus thalamus Christi sit, sancta tamen Romana Ecclesia nullis synodicis constitutis, caeteris Ecclesiis prælata est, sed evangelica voce Domini Salvatoris nostri, primatum obtinuit.*

733 *Decretum Gelasianum* 3:3.

734 *Decretum Gelasianum* 4:4.

735 Price, *The Acts of the Council of Constantinople of 553: Volume One*, 17.

736 Ibid., 45.

From this, one may surmise there is a possibility the original document was written during the time immediately before Constantinople II. Then, it was clear the Eastern patriarchates were going to anathematize the Three Chapters, but it appeared Pope Vigilius was not. A concoction explaining Roman exceptionalism within such an environment may have served some sort of immediate propaganda purpose in the West. Perhaps by assigning the document to Gelasius or Hormisdas, the intent was to pressure Vigilius not to acquiesce. However, inveighing against this theory is the sheer emphasis on the apocrypha, a debate which circulated in North Africa in the late fifth century.[737] Perhaps the Papal parts were inserted into an earlier document which emphasized the issue of Scriptural and Patristic canonicity.

Whatever the intentions behind the penning, and the textual history, of the *Decretum Gelasianum*, it is clear that the anti-iconodule *Caroline Books* in quoting it did not infer from it a serious assertion of Papal authority. After all, the very premise behind the *Caroline Books* was to deny the authority of Nicaea II and that of the Synod of Rome (785) which produced JE 2448 (whose purpose was to assert iconodulia).[738] Papal Infallibility and the Pope's capacity to directly impose doctrinal teaching is clearly denied. As the earlier excursus on canon law discussed and the next chapter will further detail, the Franks regularly ascribed honorifics to Rome without meaning much by them. It appears to have been a way to delegitimize the Byzantine churches and buttress the authority of the Roman Patriarchate whose borders largely made up what was soon called the Holy Roman Empire.

Buttressing Roman claims was geopolitical in intent, as both the Byzantines and Franks laid claim to being the true Roman Empire. Rome's "fall" was not perceived to have yet occurred according to either party. An ecclesiastical autarky, reinventing the Church as something which is centered in Rome alone and minimizing the role of the rest of the churches, suited Frankish needs. This

---

737 Vigilius of Thapsus condemned apocryphal works, for example. See PL 62, 540-541.

738 Wallach, "The Greek and Latin Versions of II Nicaea," 115.

was especially the case given both the capacity of the Franks to manipulate the Roman Synod and, when necessary, simply ignore them when it suited their purposes. The *Caroline Books* demonstrate this well.

The events surrounding Nicaea II, being as dense as they are, can be summarized as follows. It is possible that after the institution of the Papal States the first seeds of Papal Supremacist doctrine find themselves in a letter from Pope Adrian I. However, as a careful textual study demonstrates, it is likely that these statements are actually clever interpolations by Anastasius the Librarian about 85 years after the fact. As for Nicaea II itself, the council never endorsed Papal Supremacy as it was an ideology not even posed to them. The council denied Roman demands for local jurisdiction in the Balkans and Italy, revealing the council itself to be the ultimate deciding factor in jurisdictional matters. Further, Nicaea II ascribed Matt 16:18, ecumenicity, and infallibility to the Church at-large— not the person of the Pope of Rome. The council followed the consensus-based ecclesiology of the Church which had prevailed for centuries. Believing "facts rather than words," as the *Caroline Books* demonstrate, the West similarly had no conception of Papal Supremacy. One cannot help but conclude that the doctrines that make up such a view did not yet exist.

SYNOPSIS OF THE PAPACY IN THE EIGHTH CENTURY

As stated previously, the beginning of the end for the Roman Papacy as an orthodox institution is in sight. The century begins with the Byzantine Papacy, though dying, in nominal existence. Ecclesiastical presumptions made by Pope Gregory II, presuming upon the consensus-based ecclesiology of the Church, are unsurprising. Yet, concurrent with the ecclesiastical stasis was an evolving geopolitical situation where Rome's Duchy would become its own independent country. This proved to be short-lived, as their subjugation by the Franks would be complete when Rome forfeited their claims made in the *Donation of Constantine* by crowning

Charlemagne the "Roman Emperor" in 800. Rome effectively was a proxy state of the Franks with only nominal independence.

Depending on one's view of the manuscript tradition, the Papacy was either quickly reinvented sometime after the end of the Byzantine Papacy or ecclesiastically there were no major changes. As detailed here, the latter is more likely, though the former is not impossible and would still betray a disappointing, though inauspicious, beginning of a slow death to orthodox ecclesiology in Rome as a result of changed geopolitical fortunes. However, in the next century particularly, it appears all the seeds of Vatican I's conception of the Papacy are sowed. It seems most proper to locate the fall of the Papacy to this time, but not to a specific pontificate. Rather, a series of Roman pontificates uncoincidentally under the creative thumb of Anastasius the Librarian contain Papal ecclesiology's first radical disjunctures with the consensus-based ecclesiology of the Church.

Anastasius the Librarian

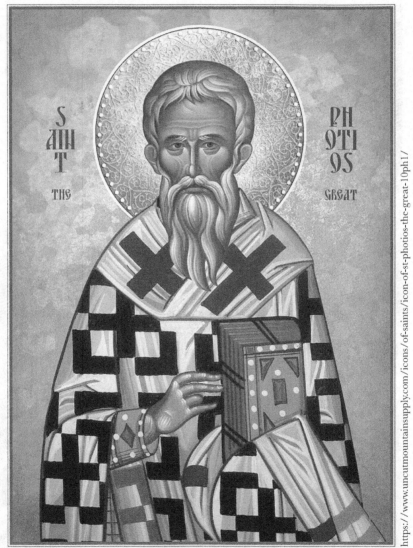

SAINT PHOTIOS THE GREAT

St. Photios the Great

CHAPTER 9

The Ninth to Eleventh Centuries of the Papacy

As detailed previously, the Papacy for centuries had followed a consensus-based view of ecclesiology. Depositions, dogmatizations, and disciplinary canons were all determined by consensus. This was buttressed by a consensus-based epistemology which undergirded the preceding. Consensus revealed the work of the Spirit and informed ecclesiastics of both the authority of their work and its very correctness. The preceding pre-existed the Imperial Church which began under Saint Constantine the Great, subsequent schisms with the Nestorians and non-Chalcedonians, the loss of Rome to the Roman (then "Byzantine") Empire, its reincorporation into the Byzantine Empire, and then its loss and subsequent subjugation to the Franks and their rebooted Holy Roman Empire.

For more than half of the ninth century, the Roman Synod showed no specific signs of having ecclesiastically changed in any interpatriarchal way. In fact, the acceptance of the "Pentarchic Theory" of ecclesiology during this time demonstrates continuity with the past. However, this all began to change with the Papal chanceries that happened to include Anastasius the Librarian. After being a "deposed" Pope himself, he soon returned and became the force behind international Papal correspondence. His literary activity, not coincidentally, is the origin of almost every document which contains an expression, even in seed form, of the Papacy in a Vatican I mold.[739] For those who may cite any other earlier document, such as Latin JE 2448, as the last chapter demonstrated, even this originates from Anastasius' hand.

Ultimately, Anastasius' role in the Papal chancery ended as priorities shifted towards rapprochement with the Byzantines. However, just us the Pseudo-Symmachean forgeries had no real import in Rome until centuries later, Anastasius' writings provided the backbone of the Gregorian reforms almost 200 years afterwards. At that point, the Roman Synod would be ecclesiologically very different than the Byzantines, their epistemology likewise radically altered. With the onset of the Crusades and the creation of a parallel church in the East, the Great Schism would commence. None of this would have been possible if the Papacy had not already fallen, and with it, the original ecclesiastical consciousness of the West.

THE PENTARCHIC THEORY OF ECCLESIOLOGY

As discussed in the previous chapter, Nicaea II not only decreed iconodulia, it also canonized the consensus-based ecclesiology of the Church. It did so explicitly, though not exclusively, along Pentarchic lines.

The Pentarchy refers to there being chief synods in the Church (those having Patriarchs), which decide matters through consensus. Within this Pentarchy there is an order, Rome having the chief rank. The Pentarchy was nothing new and it is implied by previous canons of the Ecumenical Councils.[740] It is certainly a geocentric view of the Church, but with few exceptions, such as Georgia and a short intercommunion with the Nestorians during the seventh century. Even until the ninth century, the Church remained centered along the geographic lines of the same five synods with Patriarchs at their heads.

---

739 The sole (nominal) exception is the *Gelasian Decretum*, though the unknown intent behind its Papal statements makes inferring their intended meaning impossible.

740 Canons 6-7 of Nicaea I, Canon 3 of Constantinople I, and Canon 28 of Chalcedon.

It was perhaps due to this arrangement that during the early-ninth century, when iconoclasm made a comeback and Nicaea II's authority was in question, the Pentarchic theory of ecclesiology was expounded. Its canonical roots were deeper than iconodulia. Saint Theodore the Studite, a Greek iconodule, is useful for this study as he expounded the role of the Papacy within the Pentarchic framework. For example, he writes:

> *What are our opponents to say?* For **they do not have the West, they are deprived of the East;** *they are torn* **from the body of the Church with its five leaders** *(for the sacred Nikephoros [i.e. Saint and deposed bishop of Constantinople] still lives).*[741]

Theodore here asserts that the iconoclasts placed themselves outside of the Pentarchy. He delineates Rome's role not as universal head, but head of "the West." His view of ecumenicity likewise shows a consensus-based understanding. In writing to the Pope, Theodore states:

> *Let [Patriarch Nicephorus] assemble a synod of those with whom he has been at variance,* **if representatives of the other [P]atriarchs cannot be present,** *[although] it certainly is possible* **if the emperor should wish the [Patriarch][742] of the [W]est to be present, to whom belongs authority of the [E]cumenical [S]ynod, but let him make peace and union by sending his synodical letters** *to the protothrone [the pope]…*[743]

Similar to what Pope Gregory II surmised a century previously, the (iconoclast!) Emperor is given the "authority of the [E]cumenical

---

741 Theodore the Studite, *Epistle 497* quoted in Louth, *Greek East and Latin West*, 126.

742 Both the Latin (PG 99, 1419) and Greek (PG 99, 1420) can also be translated "[Emperor] of the West," as a reference to the Emperor Charlemagne. He styled himself the Western Roman Emperor, though there was no official recognition of this in Byzantium. The inference of the translator, that the reference is to the Pope, is more likely.

743 PG 99, 1420 in Butler and Collorafi, *Keys Over the Christian World*, 386.

[S]ynod." This means the authority of convoking it. Nevertheless, the synod requires all the Patriarchs, including Rome (representing the West specifically)—corresponding to Pentarchic theory. If the Pope cannot attend the synod as usual, a synodal letter sent to Rome and consented to by their synod is sufficient. This clearly agrees with Nicaea II's criteria of synodal ratification.

It is with this in mind one must analyze his words to the Pope of Rome:

> For if they, usurping an authority which does not belong to them, have dared to convene a heretical council, whereas **those who follow ancient custom do not even have the right of convening an orthodox one without your knowledge,** it seems absolutely necessary, we dare to say to you, that your divine primacy should call together a lawful council, so that the Catholic dogma may drive out heresy and that your primacy may neither be anathematized.[744]

Similar to what Pope Julius wrote to Antioch's Synod centuries beforehand, nothing may be bound without Rome's consent. In addition to this, Rome is appealed to in order to call a "lawful council." This is not necessarily ecumenical, considering the fact it would not be convoked by the Emperor or explicitly include the rest of the Pentarchy. However, it appears Theodore rightly recognized Rome's traditional interpatriarchal appellate role where the Roman Synod can issue (non-binding) decisions.

Writing to the Byzantine Emperor, Theodore makes the following observation about Rome's (then) schism with Constantinople over iconodulia:

> O Emperor, friend of Christ, now is the day of salvation, the moment to be reconciled with Christ, under the auspices and the mediation of your authority amicable to peace, to **unite ourselves to Rome, the summit of all the Churches of God, and through her to the three [P]atriarchs...**[745]

744 PG 99, 1017-21 in Ibid., 384.
745 PG 99, 1309 in Ibid., 389.

This quote demonstrates that Theodore's ecclesiastical preoccupation was not the Roman Synod in isolation—it was the entire Pentarchy. Apparently, the patriarchates of Alexandria, Antioch, and Jerusalem (under Caliphate domination) were out of communion with Constantinople and in communion with Rome. It would take until the 860s, when the Byzantines started scoring significant victories against the Caliphate, for serious rapprochement with the Patriarchal synods to begin. So strong was the Pentarchic theory, it was being expounded at this time even when all effective communication with the majority of the Pentarchy was impossible due to Arab occupation.[746] Union with the whole Pentarchy was always deemed essential.

The Pentarchy also finds plentiful expression during the Council of Constantinople (869-870). The Byzantine Emperor Basil I, in usurping Michael III, identified Saint Photius the Great as sympathetic to his enemies. Photius needed to be replaced as Patriarch, but this was extremely difficult, considering his popularity. As it will be covered in a later section, while this council barely mustered 12 episcopal attendees for some of its sessions, Photius mustered *1,000* bishops in deposing Pope Nicholas in 867. Even presuming this is a vastly inflated number, the contrast is all too clear. Basil required Roman support for the deposition of Photius as he had few others to draw upon. Saint Ignatius of Constantinople, the former Patriarch, fulfilled Constantinople's function within

---

746 Session 3 of Nicaea II significantly details the difficulties facing the churches there in that time, citing it as the reason behind the secrecy surrounding their participation through the legates ascribed to them. For claims that the legates were pretenders, see Price, *The Acts of the Second Council of Nicaea (787)*, 198-205. One nearly contemporary source with Nicaea II (Theophanes) claims contact was successfully made with at least the Patriarchs of Antioch and Alexandria and they approved the legates. See Mendham, *The Seventh General Council, the Second of Nicaea*, 100. Whatever the truth is, communication was poor due to persecution, which betrays the Caliphate's geopolitical intent to isolate local "Roman" people from the Byzantine Empire. This was surely perceived to be a defensive posture, wanting to prevent a fifth column against their rule in favor of a Byzantine comeback.

the Pentarchic scheme and fake Oriental legates for the rest of the Pentarchy.[747]

Rome's legates were the only individuals with strong (or any) synodal backing. The council was unsurprisingly dominated by them. *Even then*, so strong is Pentarchic ecclesiology, it finds repeated expression in the conciliar minutes. The way it is communicated is inconsistent with Papal Supremacist ecclesiology. The (supposed) Oriental legates stated there needs to be "consensus between all the patriarchal sees."[748] Shortly afterwards the Senators present declare, in response to the Oriental legates: "we all acknowledge that the judgment of the three holy sees was the judgment of God."[749] One of the council's diehard partisans, Metrophanes of Smyrna, notes that *any* of the Patriarchs can receive ecclesiastical appeals.[750] He also lauds the Pentarchy, stating, "[God] placed in the firmament of the church certain great lights (as it were), namely the five patriarchal heads, to illuminate the whole earth."[751]

As referred to previously, the Imperial participants in the council likewise invoke the Pentarchy. Baanes (a patrician) invoked Matt 16:18 in reference to the entire ecclesiastical body:

> *God established his church in five patriarchates and decreed in the gospels that they would never at any time totally fall away, since they are the heads of the church. For the saying "And the gates of the underworld will not prevail against it" has this meaning: if two were*

---

747 "[W]e see no reason to accept the authenticity of the mandate of the legates of Antioch and Jerusalem….[Basil I] investing (that is) two of the Oriental legates with an absolutely invented mandate right on the spot." See Price and Montinaro, *The Acts of the Council of Constantinople of 869-70*, 36. The legates themselves during the council make a bizarre aside without any prompting where they in exaggerated fashion defend their own authenticity. Ibid., 228. Basil I similarly boasts of their validity. Ibid., 273. It is worth noting that Alexandria's legate in the final section may have been legitimate, though this is denied by Alexandria's legate to Constantinople IV (879-880).

748 Ibid., 136.

749 Ibid., 138.

750 Ibid., 258.

751 Ibid., 238.

> *to fall away, people are to have recourse to three, and if three fall away,* *they are to have recourse to two,* **while if it so happened that** **four were to fall away, the single one remaining in the** **head of all, Christ our God, would call back again the** **remnant of the body of the Church.**[752]

In invoking "the single one," there is no implication that the Roman Synod is intended, likely because this would have contradicted the example of Pope Honorius (as discussed in a previous chapter). Without citing Matt 16:18, Basil I made a similar statement:

> *through the protection of our true God the five patriarchates of the* *whole world believe soundly and without any harm to the faith; and* *therefore it is incumbent on you to accept whatever they decide.*[753]

In response to the sham Pentarchic representatives, the Photian partisans brought in for interrogation asserted the superiority of canons to Patriarchs.[754] To this, the Senate responded that no one that defies the Pentarchy can be saved.[755]

The minutes of Constantinople (869-870) are mainly preserved in a Latin tradition translated by Anastasius and a separate Greek abridgment. Not surprisingly, the Latin tradition of the council on the subject of Pentarchy in one point adds a Papal twist. For example, a reading from Pope Nicholas' letter (likely written by Anastasius) in the Greek asserts that appeals must be heard "not from…inferiors… but from greater *persons* of the highest authority."[756] This corresponds with the claim from Metrophanes that the entire Pentarchy can hear appeals, as well as earlier historical precedent throughout the centuries covered in previous chapters. Yet, the Latin rendering of the same states "from a *person* of greater authority."[757] The Latin

---

752 Ibid., 342-343.

753 Ibid., 245.

754 Ibid., 245, 272.

755 Ibid., 272.

756 Ibid., 279.

757 Ibid.

specifies the Pope as the greatest authority, while the Greek speaks to a system more consistent with Constantinople II, which can even judge a Pope.

The preceding must not be pressed too much. The original Latin letter of Nicholas, considering its source (Anastasius), more than likely said what Anastasius translated (or corrected). Later in the council, Nicholas' letter declares that those judged by Rome specifically must be retried in Rome, not elsewhere.[758] This is applied to Gregory of Syracuse, who at that time was judged by Rome on the authority of a blatantly interpolated version of Apostolic Canon 32.[759]

The view of the Roman Synod considering the Pentarchy in Anastasius' time was, in his own words, that "nothing at all is lacking to the universality of the church if all those sees are of one will... the Roman see may deservedly be compared to sight."[760] Essentially, universality exists provided everyone does Rome's will. The idea that Nicholas, through Anastasius' hand, would have contradicted himself in permitting the will of other patriarchates to decide appeals is unlikely. Nevertheless, the difference in the Greek reveals how repulsive the excesses of Anastasius' Papal ecclesiology was even to partisans who *favored* the Council of Constantinople (869-870). In any event, the fact that Anastasius' expression of Papal Supremacy had to find expression within the lens of Pentarchic ecclesiology demonstrates how ingrained consensus-based ecclesiology was. The Pentarchy literally had to be reframed within Anastasius' own preface to the council minutes in order to make sense of how far

---

758 Ibid., 288.

759 Ibid., 293.

760 This is recorded in Anastasius' preface to Constantinople 869-870. See Ibid., 91-92. Before the Council of Constantinople 869-870 Anastasius minimized the importance of the Pentarchy, arguing that only the Petrine sees of Rome, Alexandria, and Antioch are true Patriarchates. This is argued in the *Responsa ad consulta Bulgarorum* (a letter between Pope Nicholas and King Boris-Michael of Bulgaria) and Pope Nicholas' *Letter 88*. Both of the preceding were authored by Anastasius. See Evangelos Chrysos, "The Principle of Pentarchy at the Council(s)," 157-159.

apart the Ignatian and Roman factions were in their understanding of ecclesiology during the pro-Roman council.

THE CONTEXT WHICH CREATED THE *PSEUDO-ISIDORIAN DECRETALS*

The importance attached to the *Pseudo-Isidorian Decretals* by historians pertains to how they have affected the global standing of the Papacy as an institution. Yet, this was not the context behind their creation. Instead, they were concocted to serve the immediate interests of Frankish ecclesiastics who required insulation from local Imperial meddling. It would require another Frankish ecclesiastic, Anastasius, to employ these *Decretals* as a weapon for a whole different enterprise.

During the ninth century, the Frankish position in Italy was collapsing due to Arab invasions, local rebellions, and political fragmentation. Additionally, the Carolingian Empire was split into several areas due to the succession of multiple heirs after Charlemagne. Broadly speaking, the Carolingian Empire had four main parts: western Germany, eastern France, northern Italy to southern Italy (surrounding the Papal States), and western/central France. These sections often were absorbed or lost by an adjacent section after its ruler died.

As for the *Pseudo-Isidorian Decretals*, they originated in Reims (modern-day France). They exaggerated Papal authority and sidelined royal authority, particularly "in the arena of procedural law" so that "the Frankish episcopate" would "have de facto immunity, always and everywhere."[761] They included fake Papal decretals, interpolated conciliar documents, and fake and interpolated Carolingian royal documents. The latest interpolated document quoted is the Council of Paris (829), indicating that this is the earliest possible date of composition for at least part of the

---

761 Eric Knibbs, "Ebo of Reims, Pseudo-Isidore, and the Date of the False Decretals," *Speculum*, 92, 2017, 155.

corpus.[762] The first potential mention of them is in late 830s where a passing statement about a peculiar French liturgical practice was criticized on the basis that it cited "the forged authority of many pontiffs."[763] Research into the marginal notes of three ninth-century manuscripts found that textual notes cited authentic documents from the Corbie scriptorium that were copied and doctored.[764] This interestingly may identify that Paschasius Radbertus (abbot there from the 830s to 865) authored them. He is the same individual who first expounded the later Roman Catholic doctrine of the Immaculate Conception.[765]

Some scholarship concludes that "the forgers wrote to defend the bishops whom Louis the Pious deposed in 835, and none more so than Archbishop Ebo of Reims, Hincmar's controversial predecessor."[766] The *Decretals* are first actually quoted in 852 and Hincmar of Reims notes in passing he knew of them before his nephew's birth, roughly approximated to 840. A reference to Archbishop Otgar of Mainz in the past tense dates the final version of the *Decretals* after April 21, 847, revealing an origin anywhere other than Mainz and western Germany.[767] Hincmar apparently was either imprecise or his comments reveal the evolving nature of the project.

In any event, the obvious intent of the document (as previously stated) was to insulate local French bishops from Imperial deposition by their local Carolingian ruler. A forged decree from Pope Melchiades "required papal approval for the deposition of bishops."[768] This was useful as it impeded the civil authority,

---

762 Ibid., 154.

763 Ibid., 145.

764 Ibid., 151.

765 The Immaculate Conception finds no expression in Byzantine Tradition before or after this point. See Patrick Truglia, "Original Sin in the Byzantine Dormition Narratives," *Revista Teologica*, 4, 2021, 5-30.

766 Knibbs, "Ebo of Reims, Pseudo-Isidore, and the Date of the False Decretals," 145.

767 Ibid., 181.

768 Ibid., 156.

especially when geopolitics isolated the Frankish autocrat from the Pope.

For example, Ebo (bishop of Reims in central/western French part of Carolingian Empire) appealed to Lothair (Carolingian king of then eastern France and northern Italy) *and* Pope Sergius to reinstate him. This was because Charles the Bald, the Carolingian ruler of Ebo's part of France, deposed him. Ironically, Sergius did not help him in this episode, probably because Lothair could not be counted on. Charles the Bald's military position was unassailable. Eventually, Ebo was translated from Reims to Hildensheim, using a forged recommendation letter from Pope Gregory IV.[769] The forgeries gave the Pope (not synods) the final say over translations.[770] This made it easy for forgeries to be used in situations such as this as well as provided justification for ignoring Imperially manipulated synods.

Carolingian ecclesiastics proved adept at using these forgeries selectively as they would defy the Pope when it suited them. For example, anti-Papal partisans asserted their prerogatives so forcefully that at the Synod of Douzy in 871 they taught that in Matt 16:18 "Peter answered for all" bishops and "the same function [of the keys] is given [to] the whole Church in the bishops and the priests."[771] They did this amidst asking the Pope for approval for the translation of Actard so that he would become metropolitan of Tours and the deposition of Hincmar of Reims' nephew, Hincmar of Laon.[772] Pope Adrian II approved the former, but not the latter. Hincmar responded that a Metropolitan sufficed to approve a translation without the need of a Pope,[773] apparently reneging on the council's decision on Actard because the Pope's approval permitted

769 Ibid., 171-172.

770 Ibid.

771 Tavard, "Episcopacy and Apostolic Succession according to Hincmar of Reims," 618.

772 Mary Sommar, "Hincmar of Reims and the Canon Law of Episcopal Translation," *The Catholic Historical Review*, 88:3, 2002, 432-433.

773 Ibid., 433.

him to still lay claim to his former see, Nantes.[774] Hincmar not only wanted to limit Actard's power by denying him Nantes, but this was also revenge for being contradicted concerning the deposition of his nephew.

In *De Iure Metropolitanorum*, Hincmar "defended the rights of Metropolitans" vis-à-vis direct Papal overreach "which provoked opponents to charge him with thinking the [P]ope's powers were no greater than a Metropolitan's."[775] In this book, Hincmar taught that:

> the necessary qualification for a council to be ranked Ecumenical was not merely that it enjoyed magisterial sanction of emperor and pope but also that its decisions were generally received (receptissima) and therefore accepted as manifestly correct guidance for the whole Church...the second council of Nicaea...for Hincmar was a 'pseudo-synod' lacking [W]estern ratification.[776]

When push came to shove, Hincmar held to the consensus-based ecclesiology of the Church.

Not surprisingly, Anastasius responded to Hincmar, quoting several *Pseudo-Isidorian Decretals* and other documents from the Papal archives, including Greek ones.[777] While the *Decretals* were a natural product of the ecclesiastical environment of the Carolingian Empire, they were added to the Papal arsenal by Anastasius. It is perhaps for this reason they were "not widely circulated until the last decades of the ninth century."[778] The usage of otherwise highly questionable documents in official Papal correspondence lent them authenticity (or at least, the need to take them seriously).

---

774 Ibid., 436.

775 Chadwick, *East and West: The Making of a Rift in the Church*, 104.

776 Ibid., 104-105.

777 Sommar, "Hincmar of Reims and the Canon Law of Episcopal Translation," 439-440.

778 Edward Roberts, "Bishops on the Move: Rather of Verona, Pseudo-Isidore, and Episcopal Translation," *The Medieval Low Countries*, 6, 2019, 120.

ANASTASIUS THE LIBRARIAN AND THE PAPAL ECCLESIOLOGY AT THE COUNCIL OF CONSTANTINOPLE (869-870)

Anastasius is perhaps the least known figure of macro-historical importance there is. Little is known of Anastasius' early life. Indeed, he was ethnically Frankish, but apparently a resident of Italy.[779] At that time, Louis II was co-emperor of the Franks and King of Italy. He naturally wanted a Frankish-approved candidate for Pope.

In 855, the local clergy and people elected Adrian and then Benedict III as Pope without Louis II's ratification. Louis II picked Anastasius, apparently an outsider,[780] as Pope with the support of the former's uncle (Arsenius, Bishop of Orta), as well as a few other bishops. A Frankish armed contingent accomplished the task.[781] The local Roman nobility by force of arms expelled Anastasius.[782]

Nevertheless, the next Pope, Nicholas, was appointed by Louis II in 858. Not coincidentally, Anastasius was allowed back into Rome, officially as an abbot of a monastery. At about the same time, Ignatius of Constantinople was deposed and replaced by Photius. During the Council of Constantinople (861), held in the spring, Photius' was confirmed in the patriarchate by 318 clergymen. This included approval by the Roman legates.[783] Evidence suggests that Nicholas had accepted Photius' legates into communion when they subsequently visited Rome, as these legates were interrogated concerning their claim to this during the Council of Constantinople

---

779 Clemens Gatner, "Ad utriusque imperii unitatem? Anastasius Bibliothecarius as a Broker between Two Cultures and Three Courts in the Ninth Century," *Institute for Medieval Research (Medieval Worlds)*, 13, 2021, 37-38.

780 Not only was Anastasius ethnically a foreigner, he was excommunicated in 849, anathematized in 853, and laicized in 854. One does not get to be more of an "outsider" than that. See Reka Forrai, *The Interpreter of the Popes: The Translation Project of Anastasius Bibliothecarius*. Budapest: Central European University (PhD dissertation), 2008, 17.

781 Ibid., 17.

782 Gatner, "Ad utriusque imperii unitatem?," 39.

783 Chrysos, "New perceptions of imperium and sacerdotium," 323.

(869-870).[784] Yet, about a year later, Pope Nicholas had buyer's remorse. Whether or not Louis II had "persuaded" Nicholas to change course is unknown, but it is known that Nicholas wrote to Byzantine Emperor Michael III refusing to consent to the recent council, declaring it "annulled."[785]

"The arrogance of confronting the emperor with such a categorical refusal"[786] cannot have had any other intent other than to pick a fight. Not spoiling for a confrontation, Michael III and Photius refused to dignify Nicholas' letter with a response. Then, Rome in August 863 synodically rejected Photius and officially recognized Ignatius as rightful Patriarch of Constantinople. This "brought an end to…a conciliatory attempt" from Michael III and Photius to resolve their differences with Rome on the question.[787]

At about the same time, Anastasius became an official functionary in the Papal chancery.[788] It is unclear whether Anastasius already had an invisible role or not before this point. By 865, Anastasius' work in the Papal chancery had become so transparent that in Nicholas' *Letter 88* it is "clearly said in the letter" that it was "composed…without any involvement of the [P]ope."[789] According to Anasastius himself, he had written "almost" all of the correspondence in relation to Photius and Michael III, as well as Adrian II's correspondence on the same matters.[790] Anastasius

---

784 Price and Montinaro, *The Acts of the Council of Constantinople of 869-70*, 189-192, 215.

785 Chrysos, "New perceptions of imperium and sacerdotium," 324.

786 Ibid.

787 Evangelos Chrysos, "Greek and Latin in the Confrontation Between Pope Nicholas and Patriarch Photius," in Martina Caroli, Angela Mazzanti, and Raffaele Savigni (eds.), *Per respirare a due polmoni Chiese e culture cristiane tra Oriente e Occidente Studi in onore di Enrico Morini*. Bologna: Bolonia University Press, 2019, 261.

788 Forrai, *The Interpreter of the Popes*, 17.

789 Chrysos, "New perceptions of imperium and sacerdotium," 326.

790 Price and Montinaro, *The Acts of the Council of Constantinople of 869-70*, 59 and Chrysos, "The Principle of Pentarchy at the Council(s)," 157.

apparently had a blank check to act in the Pope's name, at least in foreign correspondence.

It should be noted that Anastasius was also involved in correspondence with Frankish ecclesiastics. A Frankish abbot complained, interpreting such correspondence as from the Pope, that "lord Nicholas, who is called [P]ope and who numbers himself as an [A]postle among the [A]postles, and who is *making himself emperor of the whole world.*"[791] Such impressions about a Pope are previously unknown to history. There was certainly something different coming from Anastasius' pen and Nicholas' chancery. The world took notice.

One would struggle to find any other explanation than Pope Nicholas being a mere figurehead, his policies dictated by Louis II as written by Anastasius. The obvious motivation, at least in the East, was to subvert the Byzantines. Louis II and Michael III were competing for influence in the Balkans. The necessity of Rome's assent to Photius' consecration as Patriarch, as a Patriarch is only legitimate by the assent of the other Patriarchs, was used as leverage against Byzantine designs in the same region.

Khan Boris of Bulgaria in 862 had agreed to an alliance with Louis II and accepted Frankish missionaries.[792] Yet, a neighboring power, Great Moravia, sought help from Michael III in the same year. In so doing, Prince Rastislav of Great Moravia also requested missionaries:

> *Rastislav's request was at least in part politically inspired. West of him was the East Frankish Empire, whose missionaries were pushing eastwards into Moravia, bringing Latin Christianity and with it political suzerainty to the East Frankish emperor, at this time Louis the German, grandson of Charlemagne. East of him were the Carpathian Mountains and beyond them Bulgaria, already on the threshold of accepting Christianity, in its Latin or Byzantine form, and beyond that, the Byzantine Empire itself. Missionaries from Byzantium, preaching the gospel and celebrating the liturgy in Slavonic, would give Rastislav*

791 Louth, *Greek East and Latin West*, 168.

792 Ibid., 180.

alliance with a distant but powerful neighbour, and enable him to retain his independence in relation to the East Franks.[793]

The now infamous saints, Cyril and Methodius, were sent there to complete the work of the former Frankish missionaries.

Bulgaria swiftly soon joined Great Moravia in the Byzantine orbit. Byzantine policy against "Carolingian influence to the very borders of Byzantium" was so forceful they sent "an army to the Bulgarian border and the fleet to the mouth of the Danube."[794] Bulgaria then dropped their alliance with Louis II and requested Constantinopolitan missionaries.

The conversion of the Slavs in the Balkans was a matter of national security. One can see why Louis II pressured the Papacy to take the tact that they did. If Photius was not truly Patriarch, this invalidated any ecclesiastical decisions and ordinations made in the Balkans in league with the Constantinopolitan Synod.[795] In so doing, it opened the door for easier Frankish expansion, or at the very least, reduced the hostility of a neighbor (as they would at least be religiously accountable to a Patriarch under Louis II's thumb if Rome reacquired jurisdiction over the Balkans).

Louis II's use of Anastasius in manipulating Roman foreign policy does not imply that the Popes and local Roman nobility had no power. But, one cannot minimize the power Anastasius wielded. Louis II was officially the protector of the Papal States. In this role, he had enough political capital to insert an excommunicated, laicized, antipope into the role of chief operator behind the Papacy's foreign policy.

In fact, Anastasius' position in Rome would soon become all the more egregiously imposed upon the Pope. When Pope Adrian II was elected without Frankish support, a conspiracy (allegedly headed by

---

793 Ibid., 173.

794 Ibid., 180.

795 Canon 4 of Constantinople 869-870 in Price and Montinaro, *The Acts of the Council of Constantinople of 869-70*, 393. See also Adrian II's *Letter to the Emperors* where he explicitly asserts he will not "depart" from the policy of refusing to recognize Photius' ordinations. Ibid., 460. This implies this policy had been in effect for some time, likely since Rome's synod in 863.

Anastasius), murdered his wife and child. The murderer, Anastasius' cousin Eleutherius, was killed during negotiations for his arrest. Arsenius, Anastasius' uncle, had to "flee Rome."[796] Anastasius was blamed for heading the conspiracy and, being expelled, went to work directly for Louis II.[797] Nevertheless, he "did not suffer any punishment for long, as he was seen again serving in high position within the Papacy in 869,"[798] acting as a "legate" to help negotiate a marriage alliance between Louis II and Byzantine Emperor Basil I.[799] As stated previously, Anastasius took credit for writing almost all of Adrian II's correspondence with Constantinople, indicating that even in exile his pen was still speaking for the Pope. The Council of Constantinople (869-870) started soon after and Anastasius himself would attend during its last session in 870. Even if Anastasius was not officially back in the Roman chancery's employ until 871, the fact he ever was during Adrian II's lifetime reveals that the Pope had little input over such appointments—or at least *less* than Louis II did.

Yet, the Frankish position in Italy was collapsing. Louis II died in 875, leading to quick successions from Charles the Bald, Charles III the Fat, and Carloman of Bavaria. The Byzantines were establishing new footholds in Italy. The present Pope (John VIII), realizing where the winds were blowing, saw:

> the Frankish empire weakening and dissolving, unable to assist him in overcoming dangers such as the Arab threat…[H]e was compelled to conduct a more conciliary [sic] policy towards Byzantium, hoping to gain military assistance from there. The foreign policies of Rome in this period were governed predominantly by these military interests, since it

---

796 Gatner, "Ad utriusque imperii unitatem?," 40.

797 Ibid.

798 "Hincmar and Anastasius: Lying, Treacherous Villains—Paper by Shane Bobrycki," 2011 Haskins Society Conference, Boston College, https://www.medievalists.net/2011/11/hincmar-and-anastasius-lying-treacherous-villains/

799 Forrai, *The Interpreter of the Popes*, 18.

was under constant Arabic threat, thus it continuously needed help from both empires.[800]

John VIII, perhaps not requiring the services of an overt Frankish manipulator, officially retired and replaced him with Zaccharias of Anagni. Interestingly, recent scholarship infers that Anastasius "further penned John VIII's correspondence," dying sometime after 882 (as the hallmarks of his work disappear).[801] Anastasius always proved competent so it makes sense he would have been retained in some capacity.

With this in mind, it is now possible to evaluate how Anastasius' literary production in the Papal chancery pertains to this study. During Nicholas' Papacy, Anastasius quoted the *Pseudo-Isidorian Decretals* 40 times in correspondence against Photius and Michael III.[802] Bizarre, interpatriarchal claims "beyond any precedent known from the past"[803] were made such as asserting that only a Pope can convoke a synod (and not the Byzantine emperor),[804] citing an altered canon of Chalcedon[805] (something that surely telegraphed a certain brashness as the correct rendering would have been well known), and claiming that Roman prerogatives cannot be modified by conciliar action, being granted by Christ and irrespective of synodal assent.[806] The last of these claims at least had some basis in the *Gelasian Decretum*, not that this held any weight in the East this time. It would have been brand new to a Byzantine audience.

Initially, Byzantine correspondence was relatively measured in response. Soon Michael III became too irritated by their tone or (more likely) emboldened by Louis II's weakening position in the Balkans and his attention being diverted to southern Italy in his war

---

800 Ibid., 27.

801 Price and Montinaro, *The Acts of the Council of Constantinople of 869-70*, 59.

802 Chrysos, "New perceptions of imperium and sacerdotium," 333.

803 Ibid., 323.

804 Ibid., 321-322.

805 Ibid., 334. Photius politely replied that this alleged canon was "never received" in Constantinople. Ibid., p. 336

806 Ibid., 326-327.

against the Emirate of Bari. Michael III went as far as to threaten to invade Rome, though the success of such an endeavor would have not been very likely. Nevertheless, he convoked a council in 867 which supposedly enlisted the consent of the Patriarchs and 1,000 signatories (by Anastasius' admission) that deposed Pope Nicholas.[807] Nicholas died before ever receiving word, but presuming the authenticity of the Patriarchal legates' participation, he certainly was canonically deposed.

The Roman Synod responded in 869 and excommunicated Photius again. The new Byzantine Emperor, Basil I, wanted Photius deposed for political reasons. Due to the popularity of Photius, this was not going to be easy. Louis II was able to exact an ecclesiastical price. The forging of an alliance between Basil I and Louis II, the latter looking for Byzantine naval support to fight the Emirate of Bari, had been ongoing. Later, during autumn, a new "Ecumenical Council" was held in Constantinople.

At this council, Photius was treated like an antipope—he was never really bishop, so he was not really deposed. He was anathematized without a trial.[808]

The council itself was conducted with an air of Papal superiority. Pope Nicholas' letter (likely penned by Anastasius), read out during Constantinople (869-870) clearly asserted Papal Supremacy:

> These are the enactments of the [A]postolic [S]ee...[whatever] it decrees has always been held by the universal church—and this in such a way, when particular heresies have arisen...according to the authority of its primacy, settles the matter with a decree, and then the universal church...approves at some time or other.[809]

This, ironically, is the inverse of Nicaea II, where the East settles doctrinal issues and Rome later approves. Due to the council's *Letter to Adrian II* ascribing to both the Pope and Emperor the capacity of

---

807 Price and Montinaro, *The Acts of the Council of Constantinople of 869-70*, 87. Anastasius unsurprisingly alleges the subscriptions are fake.

808 Ibid., 325.

809 Ibid., 289.

acting as "judges,"[810] claims that Rome definitively settles matters must have been understood as empty honorifics. It is telling that when the council had about 12 bishops in attendance, the Roman honorifics were far more flagrant than when the council closed with 102-103 bishops. Roman partisans were not going to press matters too strongly considering the difficulty Basil I had getting episcopal approvals for his endeavor. In contrast, Photius' comeback synod in 879-880 during Basil's reign had 383 bishops in attendance.[811]

Constantinople (869-870) also contained the seeds of Papal Infallibility. For example, Canon 2 alleged that, "The most blessed pope Nicholas" was "an instrument of the Holy Spirit."[812] This appears to echo a statement from a letter written by Adrian II, where an odd emphasis on the Pope "opening his mouth" is made, implying prophetic power.[813] In fact, the Papal legates were called "prophets."[814] Considering that Anastasius took credit for nearly everything the Papal chancery was writing at this time on the question of Photius, he may have even suggested these words to their speakers. At the very least, he translated them.

The preceding is not entirely unprecedented in conciliar documents. In the past, Saint Cyril of Alexandria had his *Second Letter to Nestorius* received by the Council of Ephesus and attributed Spiritual authority.[815] Yet, he was not described as prophetic or having such authority by virtue of being Pope of Alexandria. In the past *the council's work* was imbued with such words, not specific bishoprics.

In any event, it does not appear that Adrian II (or perhaps Anastasius, if he was unofficially writing on his behalf in 869) truly ascribed to Papal Infallibility. Adrian II, as already discussed, candidly admitted in his conciliar letter that Pope Honorius was

---

810 Ibid., 451.

811 Ibid., 43.

812 Ibid., 391.

813 Ibid., 318.

814 Ibid., 187.

815 Price and Graumann, *The Council of Ephesus of 431*, 235.

rightly deposed as a heretic—with Roman consent.[816] Additionally, Honorius was deposed in Constantinople's (869-870) decree "for following the doctrine and false opinions of the impious heresiarch Apollinaris."[817]

All this reveals that the proper interpretation of these "seeds" was that they were hollow honorifics. Even Photius had allegedly acquired titles such as "supreme priest"[818] and "[P]atriarch of [P]atriarchs and the high priest of high priests."[819] The pseudo-Oriental legates even spoke of "Ignatius" who "presides in this see" of Constantinople of "enjoying such primacy."[820] Perhaps such Byzantine flatteries had created an honorifics arms race that demanded the response of the Papal chanceries of Nicholas and Adrian II—or vice versa.

Yet, in 874, Anastasius appears to assert the honorifics as literal fact. He went as far as to argue (torturously, as covered previously) that even Honorius did not teach heresy, implying that the Papacy at no time "had any trace of the serpent."[821] In short, Papal Infallibility finally finds expression in Anastasius' personal writings. As speculated earlier, it appears that translating Saint Maximus inspired him to water the seeds found in Constantinople (869-870), that perhaps he himself planted, into a literal idea.

Anastasius first expounds this idea in his *Letter to John the Deacon in Rome*. He not only defends Honorius through various means, he ascribes to the words of Pope Anastasius II "the heavy weight of the authority of Holy Scripture."[822] What follows is a radical discussion positing an entirely new Christian epistemology. While consensus-based epistemology was so ingrained in Church history that it led to phenomena such as "conciliar fundamentalism"/

---

816 Price and Montinaro, *The Acts of the Council of Constantinople of 869-70*, 314.

817 Ibid., 414.

818 Ibid., 271.

819 Ibid., 149.

820 Ibid., 228.

821 Neil, *Seventh-Century Popes and Martyrs*, 157.

822 Ibid., 155.

conciliar contextualism (as covered previously), Anastasius posits an epistemology where the declarations of a Pope are above even Ecumenical Councils.

He proves this out by first delineating there are limits to what is infallible and binding in an Ecumenical Council:

> *lest we seem to be making an accusation against a council so holy and venerable, or to criticise it carelessly, we think it fitting for us to consider them in the way we know our holy fathers considered the great council of Chalcedon. One of them, namely holy Pope Gregory, indicated that this was to be accepted only "up to the issuing of the canons."*[823]

It cannot be emphasized enough that such thought had found no previous expression in Christian history. As one can see, Anastasius gives a restricted view of "authority" as it corresponds to Ecumenical Councils, (mis)citing Saint Gregory the Great as his precedent. In fact, Anastasius surprisingly does not explicitly endorse the *decrees* of Ecumenical Councils, given that he only speaks of them being accepted "up to the issuing of the canons." This was intentional as Pope Honorius was condemned in both the decrees of Constantinople III and Nicaea II. However, canons discussing disciplinary matters tend to be issued with conciliar decrees, so Anastasius' tact here seems peculiar at first glance.

Anastasius makes sense of the preceding by arguing that Ecumenical Councils were only accepted up to the point that Rome accepted them in matters of faith and morals. This appears to defend the conciliar decrees of the councils which anathematized Honorius by in effect negating any disciplinary measures, such as anathemas, they contain. He (mis)quotes Pope Gelasius' *Tractate 4* on this point:

> *Pope Gelasius decided the Chalcedonian council should be accepted, that is, "for the communion of the faith and the Catholic and apostolic truth, on behalf of which the [A]postolic [S]ee commanded that this be done, and confirmed that it had been done."*[824]

---

823 Ibid.

824 Ibid., 157.

Anastasius effectively created an epistemology where only selective parts of Ecumenical Councils were specified as infallible. This was predicated upon the authority of Papal pronouncements and to the extent that "the [A]postolic [S]ee commanded." Was either Pope Gregory's or Gelasius' view of authority in contradiction to conciliar contextualism and in the mold that Anastasius claims? In short, no.

Pope Gregory was responding to accusations made by those who opposed Constantinople II on the basis it contradicted Chalcedon.[825] In the passage that Anastasius is quoting from, Gregory asserts that "the Holy Synod of Chalcedon spoke of general causes [i.e. the ecclesiastical sessions] up to the definition of the faith [i.e. the decree] and the promulgation of the canons."[826] As one can see, he is simply stating that Chalcedon conducted ecclesiastical business in addition to issuing a decree and canons. It appears that Anastasius excised the part of the quotation about the decree to attain to his polemical purpose. Gregory then goes on to defend Ibas against any allegation that he had taken credit for the (heretical) letter ascribed to himself, in effect defending the integrity of Chalcedon's work on the question. This in effect denies that anything "contrary to the definition of the Holy Synod" occurred within the acts of the same council.[827] Any sort of restricted acceptance of Chalcedon is not explicitly communicated by Gregory in this letter.

Tractate 4 from Pope Gelasius,[828] contrary to the claims of Anastasius, defends the entirety of Chalcedon in a different way. Gelasius argues that:

> *for either it **[Chalcedon] must be admitted in its entirety, or if it is partially redeemable, it is no longer possible to stand firm in its entirety:** let them therefore know it*

---

825 PL 77, 986-987. This is Book 9, *Letter 52* in the PL. Neil identifies this as Gregory the Great, *Registrum IX*, 148, 702.95-97.

826 PL 77, 986. The Latin is as follows: *sancta Chalcedonensis synodus usque ad definitionem fidei, et prolationem canonum, de generalibus causis locuta est.*

827 Ibid. The Latin is as follows: *definitioni sanctæ synodi probatur adversa.*

828 Andreas Thiel, *Epistolae Romanorum Pontificum Genuinae*, 558.

> *[Chalcedon] according to the Holy Scriptures and the tradition of the*
> *elders, as well as the canons and rules of the Church, for the faith,*
> *communion, and Catholic and apostolic truth, for which this is delegated*
> *by the [A]postolic [S]ee and confirmed that it be done, admitted without*
> *doubt by the whole Church.*[829]

Clearly, all of Chalcedon's acts have integrity. This is Gelasius' point vis-à-vis Anastasius' framing of him. Gelasius then goes on to complain about Canon 28:

> *But another [Canon 28], which through incompetent presumption there*
> *was brought forward, or rather aired, which the Apostolic See has in*
> *no way delegated to carry out, which was afterward contradicted by the*
> *vicars of the Apostolic See, it is manifest...*[830]

Gelasius' point is that all of Chalcedon "must be admitted in its entirety" like the Scriptures and the saints, otherwise it would not be an Ecumenical Council at all. In defense of Chalcedon against a critique that disagreement over Canon 28 would compromise the integrity of the whole council, Gelasius argues that this canon lacked consensus–particularly Rome's approval. This was recorded in the minutes of Chalcedon itself in Session 16 (which he alludes to), so this would not be at all inconsistent with the acceptance of the "entirety" of the said council.

Like Gregory, Gelasius actually defends conciliar contextualism. Therefore, they are damaging to Anastasius' whole point. In fact, Gelasius is merely expounding that consensus determines what precisely is authoritative within the "entirety" of an Ecumenical Council. The fact Anastasius distorts the meanings of his own

---

829 The Latin is as follows: *aut enim ex toto eam admitti oportere, aut si ex parte repudiabilis est, firmam ex toto constare non posse: cognoscant igitur illud secundum Scripturas Sanctas traditionemque majorum, secundum canones regulasque Ecclesiae, pro fide, communione et veritate catholica et apostolica, pro qua hanc fieri sedes apostolica delegavit factamque firmavit, a tota Ecclesia indubitanter admitti.*

830 The Latin is as follows: *Alia autem, quae per incompetentem praesumptionem illic prolata sunt vel potius ventilata, quae sedes apostolica gerenda nullatenus delegavit, quae mox a vicariis sedis apostolicae contradicta manifestum est...*

prooftexts reveals that the epistemology of ecumenicity he is posing is wholly novel for its time.

Leaving aside whether Constantinople's (869-870) acts contained the latent presumption of Papal Infallibility, the council represented the zenith of Anastasius' (in reality, Louis II's) agenda. For the first time a form of Papal Primacy not matching canonical norms was expounded in the East. However, the council had nearly no attendance and it did not concede Roman jurisdictional claims, as evidenced by Adrian II's *Letter to the Emperors*. Therein he complains that "Ignatius," whom Rome helped have reinstated, "presumed to consecrate the bishop for the region of the Bulgars...he will not escape canonical punishment, nor will those who usurp the title of episcopacy..."[831] This betrays that direct jurisdiction was not consented to and, probably, not even conceived of. Not surprisingly, Anastasius' subsequent translation of Nicaea II sowed the seeds of undoing the indignity in the Balkans by creating a new rationale for Rome's claims in the region, as covered in the previous chapter.

In light of the preceding section and chapters, one can summarize the several changes to the Papacy that were introduced *specifically* by Anastasius the Librarian. The way canon law was treated in the West became fundamentally different. Difficult canons were previously treated with *economia*, but now Papal nullification in effect acted as a line-item veto. Rome's Petrine succession was recast as a singular honor, instead of a Church-wide inheritance. Rome's jurisdiction in the Balkans was justified with reasoning akin to direct jurisdiction. Pentarchic ratification, and thereby consensus-based ecclesiology, was merely submission to Rome's whims. The *Pseudo-Isidorian Decretals* were employed to effectively undo Apostolic Canon 34 in response to Frankish ecclesiastics who regularly ignored Papal policies they did not agree with. One example of this was the Papacy's refusal to recognize the Frankish deposition of Hincmar of Laon. The same *Decretals* were popularized by their usage in international correspondence, fundamentally changing Rome's posture in interpatriarchal disputes. Thanks to these forgeries, no longer were Sardica's canons the epitome of Roman prerogatives (as

---

831 Price and Montinaro, *The Acts of the Council of Constantinople of 869-70*, 459.

they were in Gelasius' time). Rather, Rome had complete authority, even above Ecumenical Councils. Roman ecclesiastical prerogatives could not be modified or dictated by conciliar action. Lastly, Papal Infallibility found its first explicit defense and consensus-based epistemology its first explicit opposition.

Certainly, Anastasius could not get everyone to concede, agree, or even acknowledge part, let alone the whole, of his program. Yet, if one is looking for a specific origin for the underlying basis of Papal Supremacy and the Papacy of Vatican I, the Papal chanceries during the career of Anastasius the Librarian certainly are it. As for Anastasius, he had a grand view of his own activity, describing himself as "possessed" (his word) "by the challenge" of his work, "implying a boundless authority for himself" through the skill of writing.[832] He had the ingenuity, creativity, and Imperial support to accomplish the task. The fact that one struggles to find a manifestation of Papal Supremacy in any historical circumstance before this point, or even nominal textual claims to it, is telling. It is a set of coincidences which cannot be arbitrary. One scholar's evaluation of Anastasius as "*the* architect and promoter of the papal claims" is justified.[833]

THE FORGED *FORMULA OF ADRIAN II*

As discussed previously, Constantinople (869-870) was an unpopular council. It was foisted upon the Church due to Louis II of the Franks and Basil I of the Byzantines seeking an alliance in southern Italy against the Saracens. Despite all the Papal pronouncements throughout the council, only about 12 bishops were subjected to the indignity of the exaggerated claims that were made. When approximately 102 bishops were cobbled together to

---

832 Anastasius had a grand view of his work, comparing himself to Rufinus, Jerome, Dinoysius Exiguus, and Cassiodorus. See Forrai, *The Interpreter of the Popes*, 22-23.

833 Chrysos, "The Principle of Pentarchy at the Council(s)," 168. Emphasis added.

sign the council's decree, it is clear that they had only subscribed to its final session.[834]

Along with the signed conciliar decree were individual *libelli*, containing subscriptions to the *Formula of Adrian II*. Presuming the *Formula* shared the same language ascribed to it during Session 1, the subscriber effectively swore fealty to the Pope. Through a set of suspicious circumstances documented by Anastasius, these *libelli* and the minutes of the council itself were stolen by Basil I[835] and "pirates."[836] As luck would have it, though Anastasius was officially acting as a legate to the Frankish Imperial delegation and in no supposed capacity for the Pope, he *personally* acquired all of the *libelli* and had luckily preserved his own copy of the council's minutes.[837]

The preceding textual history of these *libelli* increases the chance of their manipulation. In addition to this, Anastasius when translating the council's minutes into Latin "consult[ed] a second Greek manuscript" of the *libellus* "supposedly brought to Rome" allowing Anastasius to correct "the *faulty Greek version* of the Roman *libellus* included at Session I" presumably found in his primary Greek manuscript.[838] This implies additional revisions in the supposed content of the *Formula*, at least in the only extant Latin version preserved in the conciliar minutes.

A comparison of the Greek and Latin versions of Adrian II's *Formula* virtually guarantees that a forgery took place. In the extant Greek minutes of Constantinople 869-870, the *Formula* asserts that:

> *The chief means of salvation is that we…in no way deviate from the decrees of God and the Fathers. We anathematize all the heresies… We embrace with all our heart whatever the authority of the Apostolic throne decreed, concerning Ignatius…I, N[ame], bishop of such a church, have made this profession of argument, and by my hand I*

834 See Donatus' subscription in Price and Montinaro, *The Acts of the Council of Constantinople of 869-70*, 428.

835 Ibid., 45.

836 Chadwick, *East and West: The Making of a Rift in the Church*, 166-167.

837 Price and Montinaro, *The Acts of the Council of Constantinople of 869-70*, 45, 59.

838 Ibid., 62. Emphasis added.

deliver it to you, a most holy despot and great pontiff, and an ecumenical father Hadrian through the legates.[839]

The preceding has all the hallmarks of authenticity, quoting a short portion of the *Formula of Hormisdas* without embellishment and matching the details concerning the *Formula*'s contents discussed in passing during the council.[840]

The Latin[841] includes a longer section of the *Formula of Hormisdas*. It quotes Matt 16:18 and adds that "the catholic religion has always been preserved without stain…in the [A]postolic [S]ee." It then includes that in addition to following "the decrees of God and the fathers" (as found in the Greek) one must also follow "in particular…the holy bishops of the [A]postolic [S]ee." It adds that Ignatius is to be "revere[d]" as "the [A]postolic [S]ee has decreed" and those opposing the Pope not be commemorated. It then adds a redundant statement about the non-negotiability of communion with Rome:

---

839 Mansi 16, 316. The Greek is difficult to re-render without typos, but a Latin translation of the entire Greek formula is provided by Mansi 16, 315, which is as follows: *Prima salus est, rectæ fidei regulam custodire, deinde a consitutis Dei & partum nallerenus deviare; quæ nos secuti anathematizamus omnes hæreses simul cum Iconomachis. Anathematizamus etiam Photium, qui adveresus sacros canones repente de curiali administratione, & fæculari militia, superstite sancissimo patriarcha Ignatio, Constantinopolitanam ecclesiam latronum more per quosdam schismaticos invasit. Amplectimur & sanctam synodum, quam beatæ papa Nicolaus celebravit; cui tu quoque domine coangelice summe pontifex Hadriane subscripsisti; recipimusque omnes quos recipit illa; damamus omnes quos damnavit illa, praesertim Photium & Gregorium Syracusanum, parricidas videlicet, qui contra spiritualem patrem suum linguas exerere minime sormidarunt; sectatores item eorum in schismate perseverantes, quiequie cum illis in communionis societate permanent. Ecclesias vero malignantium, & perverforum dogmatum adinventiones sub Michaele imperatore bis contra beatissimum patriarcham Ignatium, & semel adversus fedis apodtolicæ principatum coactas, insolubilibus anathematis nexibus innodamus, unaque omnes qui eas (synodos) desendunt, aut impia carum acta occultant. De Ignatio porro reverendissimo patriarcha, & iis qui cum illo sentient, quidquid apostolici throni decrevit auctoritas, tota mente complectimur. Hanc ergo prosessionem ego N sanctae ecclesiæ N episcopus feci, & manu mea subscripsi, ac tibi sanctissimo domino & magno pontifici, oecumenicoque papae Hadriano per apocrisiarios tradidi.*

840 Price and Montinaro, *The Acts of the Council of Constantinople of 869-70*, 271.

841 Ibid., 128-132.

as we have already said, *we follow the [A]postolic [S]ee in all things and observe all its decrees, we hope for the favour of enjoying the single communion that the [A]postolic [S]ee proclaims, in which is the complete and true totality of the Christian religion.*

Lastly, it embellishes the Pope's honorific so that it reads, "most holy, thrice blessed and coangelic lord the supreme pontiff and universal Pope Hadrian."

These differences are suspicious. All the high-Papal parts are missing in the Greek. Though the Greek minutes of the same council is an abridgement of sorts, it is curious that in this precise section of the council the supposed abridgements would occur primarily where there are Papal claims.

The Latin and Greek *Formulas* begin identically: "keeping the rule of the orthodox faith and then in departing in no way from the decrees of God and the fathers." However, the Latin veers into a long explanation about Rome (quoting the *Formula of Hormisdas*). It modifies the original point as found in the Greek that one does not deviate from the fathers by redundantly reiterating the same idea a second time and then adding "and in particular the holy bishops of the [A]postolic [S]ee." This is typical of the *Pseudo-Isidorian Decretals*, which inserted into real documents sections from other real documents to produce an authentic sounding document with a new meaning. An interpolation can be inferred by the sloppy redundancy that is found in the Latin. This redundancy serves no other purpose than to further exaggerate Roman ecclesiastical claims on the heels of the older Roman claims quoted from the original *Formula of Hormisdas*. In so doing, it effectively reframes the meaning behind Hormisdas' words and passes them off as Adrian II's.

Additionally, the Latin *Formula of Adrian II* requires not commemorating those who oppose the Pope. This requirement was largely dropped from the *Formula of Hormisdas*' subscriptions centuries earlier due to it being so unpopular. Why would such an unpopular element be reincorporated if it were not for the fact of slavishly following the details in the original *Formula of Hormisdas* in an Isidorian-styled forgery? A forger can be forgiven for lacking the nuance to permit the sort of modifications allowed by Hormisdas himself, who ultimately permitted such commemorations.

Another hallmark of inauthenticity is that *both* the Greek and the Latin preserve that the one signing the document authenticate his own signature. Additionally, a witness is required to sign for the same reason. This exaggerated emphasis upon authentication indicates that forgery was expected and that these "safeguards" were intended to give the impression that nothing unseemly occurred. Perhaps, a subscriber was told to sign a blank piece of paper[842] and the language of the *libellus* that was attached to his individual subscription was reconstituted in Rome itself. The textual history previously described implies this.

It is no wonder the council had such low attendance. It was only a matter of time that the record was corrected.

THE LAST CANONICAL ECUMENICAL COUNCIL: CONSTANTINOPLE IV (879-880)

The mid to late 870s experienced geopolitical changes in quick succession. As referred to previously, Louis II died and subsequent Frankish emperors were weak. Pope John VIII (the Pope who succeeded Adrian II) backed Charles the Bald, Louis II's successor. However, this marginalized John with future successors to the Frankish kingdoms. They retaliated by cutting off tribute and military support to Rome.[843]

In the meantime, Byzantine control in southern Italy greatly increased under Basil I. This was especially the case when they captured Otranto from the Saracens in 873 and Bari (the former Emirate) from the Franks in 876. In Constantinople, Basil allowed Photius to make a comeback before Ignatius ended his life. He was soon Patriarch of Constantinople again.

---

842 Signing a blank subscription was not unknown in Church history. The repentant attendees to Ephesus II claimed this. See Price and Gaddis, *The Acts of the Council of Chalcedon: Volume One*, 134.

843 Barbara Kreutz, *Before the Normans: Southern Italy in the Ninth & Tenth Centuries*. Philadelphia: University of Pennsylvania Press, 2011, 58.

While the Byzantines were experiencing a resurgence in Italy, the Papal States were in dangerous straits. John VIII was no longer able to secure Frankish protection amidst regional uprisings. No longer receiving tribute from the Franks and those in active resistance within his domain, the Papal treasury was not being replenished at the rate it was emptied paying tribute to placate the Saracens and local Dukes. This ruinous financial situation led to his murder in 882.[844]

With the preceding context in mind, John VIII's openness to rapprochement with Byzantium in exchange for military protection makes all the more sense.[845] Pope Nicholas in the 860s needed nothing from the Byzantines, but was reliant upon the Franks. His anti-Byzantine posturing in light of this should be expected. John VIII's only real motive to continue the policies of the 860s would have been simply to save face. However, under urgent necessity, he was expected to make compromises with the Byzantines to secure their naval support. This required accepting Photius' restoration and conceding jurisdictional claims in southern Italy specifically. Concessions in Italy made sense as Rome was in no position to press territorial claims where the Byzantines had civil control, considering they were looking for Byzantine support to secure the integrity of their own borders. Nevertheless, claims in the Balkans were not dropped, likely because Canon 17 of Chalcedon could not be argued to apply there.

This is the background to the Council of Constantinople IV (879-880). Its chief purpose was to gain the support of the Patriarchs, including Rome's, to Photius' restoration. Secondarily, the undoing of Constantinople (869-870) was necessary as it called into question the holy orders of many clergymen. Not surprisingly, there was legitimate enthusiasm to restore Photius and this is further evidenced by its large episcopal attendance, as detailed previously.

Despite a lot of controversy surrounding the council in modern times, it was in some respects doctrinally lackluster in its own day. Indeed, it accepted Photius and officially condemned Constantinople

---

844 Ibid., 59.

845 Ibid., 59-60.

(869-870). However, contrary to popular imagination, it was not very assertive in addressing the controversy surrounding the *filioque*. The council simply disallowed changes to the Constantinopolitan Creed. This implied a stance against the *filioque*, but no actual theological rationale contrary to the doctrine was put forward. Additionally, it failed to resolve specific points of differences with Rome (such as jurisdiction in the Balkans and the role of the Papacy).[846] The latter would prove to be of paramount theological importance and it was essentially neglected, even though it was posed by the Roman legates during the council.

Session 1 of the council contains an exchange between the Papal legates and Photius which is illustrative for the purposes of this study. The legates assert Papal prerogatives and appear to resume the "honorifics arms race" which may have been in full swing since the 860s. Photius appears to treat these as vain flatteries and only subtly pushes back. For example, "Peter, the Cardinal and Vicar of Pope John [VIII]" declared, "Saint Peter is visiting us" in reference to his own attendance. Photius responded, "May Christ our God, through the chief of the disciples Peter...have mercy on us all." As one can see, Cardinal Peter is making hay out of Saint Peter so as to imply Rome's authority. Photius concedes this authority, with the intent of looking for "mercy." This is simply code for Rome going along with the Byzantine program.

Cardinal Peter responded, "The most-holy and [E]cumenical Pope John venerates your holiness [Photius]." Photius, seemingly unphased by the honorific "[E]cumenical Pope" accepts the title with a subtle qualification. He speaks of their "common Master" and later says of the Pope "we record him and being our brother, co-liturgist and spiritual father....all having as our common head Christ." In short, this "[E]cumenical Pope" is a fellow Bishop, the Head of the Church being Christ and not the Pope. Clearly, Photius understood the latent Papal Supremacist claim being made. He

---

846 What follows are quotations from "'Photios the Great and the Eighth Ecumenical Synod' by Metropolitan Hierotheos Vlachos," *Orthodox Christianity Then and Now*, https://www.johnsanidopoulos.com/2016/02/photios-great-and-eighth-ecumenical.html

felt his response was sufficient to address any implicit assertions of Papal prerogatives. Due to Photius failing to be more forceful, this implies a lack of appreciation for the seriousness of such a claim and what it would mean in the future.

Cardinal Peter then speaks of John VIII's letter sent to the council, stating that it demonstrates "the care and attention he procures for your holy Church." These patronizing words imply Rome's headship over Constantinople, but it was nothing new in and of itself. Nearly identical language was employed by the Papal legates in the Council of Ephesus in reference to Saint Pope Celestine's letter.[847] Photius, understanding the intent behind what was stated, responded that "the letters 'are not lessons, but an addition and verification of what had already been known.'" In other words, the Constantinopolitan Synod had conducted its own business and Rome is merely approving, instead of enforcing, what had occurred. Photius even continues to approve of John VIII for not being "schismatic," an obvious swipe at his predecessor Nicholas. It appears that Photius took more offense at this specific statement. This implies that he understood that John VIII's letter was being presented as an ultimatum and this was unacceptable according to consensus-based ecclesiology.

What follows are comments about the Pope's health and the state of the Roman Synod which one scholar[848] infers carry the connotation that Photius was asserting that Rome had local, instead of universal, jurisdiction. Certainly, it is a measured response pertaining to which churches are actually under John VIII's care. For example, Photius asks, "How is his [John VIII's] holy Church of God and all the pontiffs and priests he has?" Cardinal Peter responded, "All is healthy through your holy prayers, but what do you have to say about the love and faith the most holy Pope has towards your holiness?" This retort effectively reasserts that the Pope's care is not just local in nature, but also for Constantinople.

---

847 Price and Graumann, *The Council of Ephesus of 431*, 369.

848 "'Photios the Great and the Eighth Ecumenical Synod' by Metropolitan Hierotheos Vlachos," *Orthodox Christianity Then and Now*. What immediately precedes and follows are quotations from this work.

Photius, probably in amusement, responds, "Words have authority when visible actions make them apparent, and with the most holy Pope, our spiritual father, his actions overthrow his words…" In other words, the legates and John VIII are talking a big game, but the facts at hand indicate otherwise. They are there to make rapprochement, not issue ultimatums. At this point, Cardinal Peter breaks his exchange with Photius, giving him the last word.

After that exchange, Cardinal Peter addresses the council at-large with similar patronizing language to which John of Heraclea responds that, "we have one true Shepherd…Photios our most holy Master and Ecumenical Patriarch." In effect, the council rejects all overtures of Papal Supremacy and reasserts the legitimacy of the title "Ecumenical Patriarch," something that as discussed previously the Papal chancery under Anastasius had taken issue with. However, they fail to censure the Papal legates on this point, and similar ones, throughout the council. From an Orthodox perspective, this would be the council's chief failure. Historically speaking, the point of the council was to keep the status quo, receive pan-Patriarchal acceptance for Photius, and concede no concrete claims to Rome. In this, the council was successful.

During a later session, a letter from John VIII is read. Upon hearing what the letter demands, the council rejected his call for restoring jurisdiction in the Balkans to Rome. In fact, the council referred the issue to "the [E]mperor to solve it, especially when the Empire was to be restored to its 'ancient boundaries.'" Effectively, the council's attendees cited Canon 17 of Chalcedon as justification for reconfiguring the jurisdiction in the Balkans according to the civil model. The preceding demonstrates two things. First, that John VIII, as discussed previously, had conceded claims in Italy as he laid no claims to it at this juncture. Second, that "direct jurisdiction" was a notion not seriously asserted by the Roman legates and by virtue of no such local jurisdiction being conceded, implicitly rejected by default. In reviewing the same letter, they also rejected John VIII's call for banning the promotion of laymen to the episcopate.

Interestingly, John's letter asserted Constantinople (869-870) was not "subscribe[d]" by Pope Adrian II (ironically over the Bulgarian question) and "annulled" by Rome.[849] There is no reason to doubt the authenticity of this given what Rome's demands were at the time. Further, the Latin and Greek versions of this letter match.[850]

Session 5 decreed Canon 1 of the council. The canon is worth unpacking:

> *This holy and ecumenical Council has decreed that so far as concerns any clerics, or laymen, or bishops from Italy that are staying in Asia, or Europe, or Africa, under bond, or deposition, or anathema imposed by the most holy Pope John, all such persons are to be held in the same condition of penalization also by the most holy Patriarch of Constantinople Photius…All those persons, on the other hand, whom Photius our most holy Patriarch has condemned or may condemn to excommunication, or deposition, or anathematization, in any diocese whatsoever, whether clerics or laymen or any of the persons who are of prelatical or priestly rank, are to be treated likewise by most holy Pope John….Nothing, however, shall affect the priorities due to the most holy throne of the Church of the Romans, nor shall anything redound to the detriment of her president, as touching the sum-total of innovations, either now or at any time hereafter.[851]*

In short, Rome and Constantinople were not to take appeals from one another, but were to treat each synod's ruling as final. It is a surprising abrogation of any interpatriarchal interpretation of Sardica and a timely one at that. In a passive aggressive sense, its banning of "innovations" affecting "the priorities due to" the Roman Synod is in fact banning Papal Supremacy. In effect, the canon decrees that Rome's prerogatives are only those that the canons (Canon 6 of Nicaea I, Canon 3 of Constantinople I, and Canon 28 of Chalcedon) have already specified. The Sardican

---

849 "The 8th Ecumenical Council: Constantinople IV (879/880) and the Condemnation of the Filioque Addition and Doctrine by: Fr. George Dion. Dragas," *The Orthodox Dogmatic Research Group*, https://www.oodegr.com/english/dogma/synodoi/8th_Synod_Dragas.htm. This article appeared in *The Greek Orthodox Theological Review*, 44:1-4, 1999, 357-369.

850 Ibid.

851 Canon 1 of Constantinople IV (879-880).

canons, which were on the books Church-wide, appear to be given their specifically local interpretation by this canon. This is despite the fact that it contradicts (or at least minimizes) the interpretation given by Saint Pope Leo that these canons pertained to Rome's role in an Ecumenical Council (as covered previously).

One can see why this arrangement was a concession for the Roman Synod (who did indeed accept the canons of this council), as it truncates Sardica. Nevertheless, if one simply presumes upon Papal Supremacy (which obviously had become the party line in the Papal chancery since Anastasius), then preserving supposedly ancient "priorities" would in fact only strengthen Rome's claims. Additionally, the naming of the Patriarchs in the "reciprocity deal" laid out in the canon can, in effect, abrogate the canon from having future application. (It should be noted that Sardica similarly contained the name of Pope Julius, so such canonical thinking would also invalidate Sardica.) Judging from John VIII's qualified acceptance of the council, as covered later, this canon was not accepted according to its full meaning from the very beginning.

Session 6 of the council forbade any additions to the Creed "with illegitimate words, or additions, or subtractions," threatening defrocking to those who defied it.[852] However, they failed to condemn anyone by name or even mention what was added (to prevent stirring the pot). Again, Photius appears to have won the day, but similar to Saint Hezekiah the Righteous,[853] did not sufficiently appreciate that the door being left open for future problems on both the ecclesiastical and Pneumatological fronts.

Lastly, Photius invited the attendees to sign "*all* the synodical acts and ordinances."[854] This was a rhetorical slap at the limited documentation made available for review during the final session of Constantinople (869-870). As discussed previously, only the decree

---

852 "'Photios the Great and the Eighth Ecumenical Synod' by Metropolitan Hierotheos Vlachos," *Orthodox Christianity Then and Now.*

853 2 Kings 20:19 MT.

854 What follows is from: "'Photios the Great and the Eighth Ecumenical Synod' by Metropolitan Hierotheos Vlachos," *Orthodox Christianity Then and Now.* Emphasis added.

was made available at the time and the *libelli* attached to the council were hidden and then manipulated.

Interestingly, the Papal legates endorsed consensus-based ecclesiology at the close of the council, the following statement being ascribed to all of them:

> *Blessed is God for by His judgement*[855] *and will all the most-holy [P]atriarchs came together as one, and through common harmony and peace all things came to a good end from what was ruled and passed at this holy and ecumenical synod.*

The preceding interestingly implies a certain cowing of the legates at this juncture, as the statement implies the Pope is a fellow Patriarch and "common harmony" had decided matters. The invocation of God's judgment is a concession that the Holy Spirit superintended the work of the council. The aforementioned evaluation of the legates does not appear to be disingenuous. Pope John VIII's letters to the emperor, council, and even in written instructions to his legates "refers to the Patriarchs of the East as integral parts of the common pentarchic leadership of the Church."[856] The legates entered the council with some notion of consensus-based ecclesiology.

Scholarship concurs that John VIII accepted the synod, even though he was displeased that his letter was not accepted on all points.[857] John VIII's letter of (partial) acceptance survives, stating:

> *true to apostolic custom and taking pity on the Church of Constantinople, we have decided that the advantage of one should not be the detriment of another…After summoning our Church, urged by the necessity of the times, we have turned our attention to the Church of Constantinople in the exercise of our apostolic authority and power and instructed our legates to proceed cautiously. We rejoice at her unity of peace and*

---

855 Spelling of "judgment" as "judgement" is original to the translation in Ibid.

856 Chrysos, "The Principle of Pentarchy at the Council(s)," 164-165.

857 Ibid. See also "The 8th Ecumenical Council: Constantinople IV (879/880) and the Condemnation of the Filioque Addition and Doctrine by: Fr. George Dion. Dragas," *The Orthodox Dogmatic Research Group.*

concord…it is a wonder to us why so many things that we had decided [in reference to his letter to the council] should have been obviously altered, transformed and, we do not know through whose mistake or design, distorted…if you try to increase in devotion and loyalty to the Holy Roman Church and to our insignificant person, we also embrace you as a brother…We also approve what has been done in Constantinople by the synodal decree of your reinstatement and if perchance at the same synod our legates have acted against apostolic instructions, neither do we approve their action nor do we attribute any value to it.[858]

In short, this is a synodal approval of Constantinople IV with the proviso that Rome's Synod still pressed all the claims made in John VIII's letter. Any assurance from the legates that they were "perchance" negotiated according to the demands of the council, where demands of both parties did not align, are abrogated. In other words, John VIII continued to demand jurisdiction in the Balkans, future bans on promoting laymen, and the restoration of Ignatian bishops. Despite the Roman Synod accepting the council's canons,[859] the latter demand is at least a partial abrogation of Canon 1— something that post-Anastasian Latin canon law allowed, as covered in an earlier excursus.

The tone of the letter is intentionally patronizing, matching that of the Papal legates found during the beginning of the council as compared to its end. Additionally, the mention of "many things" that "have been obviously altered" likely is not a reference to the actual forging of documents, such as John VIII's letter. Not only is his letter as read out during the council essentially the same in Greek and Latin,[860] what is preserved in the Greek has all the hallmarks of authenticity, including its honorifics and outrageous demands which the council deliberately contradicted.

---

858 Francis Dvornik, *The Photian Schism*. Cambridge: Cambridge University Press, 1970, 205-206.

859 For example, Constantinople IV's canons (879-880) are found in Gratian's collection of canon law.

860 "The 8th Ecumenical Council: Constantinople IV (879/880) and the Condemnation of the Filioque Addition and Doctrine by: Fr. George Dion. Dragas," *The Orthodox Dogmatic Research Group*, n. 7, 8.

If the letter was forged and then the Latin manuscript record deliberately corrupted (somehow), it would have had a much different character. The comment therefore must be referring to unwritten assurances made by legates in reference to the conciliar letter or to something more along the lines of the sort of face-saving edits that previous conciliar documents, such as JE 2449 in Nicaea II, had. Even then, they had to be minor as jurisdictional claims found themselves in the former, but not the latter. John VIII's words appear to be intentionally making much out of very little, as Anastasius had done during the 860s. One can perhaps detect Anastasius' hand in its writing, or someone having acquired his style and temperament.

FAST-FORWARDING TO THE GREGORIAN REFORMS

With Anastasius, the Papacy had already fallen from its original design—at least in the realm of ecclesiastical theory. The actions of the Papal legates and John VIII's subsequent acceptance of the Constantinople IV (879-880) were not evidence of a victory for consensus-based ecclesiology and the total undoing of the Anastasian Papal program. Rather, they are indicative of a Roman Patriarchate that is increasingly distancing itself from its ecclesiastical roots. Some make much out of the fact that the Roman Synod did not confess the *filioque* at this juncture. However, the Roman church never confessed it anyway and it would not be officially confessed in Rome until the 11th century. This was not really where the battle was being fought.

Rather, the battle during Photius' and Anastasius' tenures was over Papal Supremacy. Photius certainly won the battle and outlived his opponent. However, the war (at least for the heart of believers in the Roman Patriarchate) was lost. The Papal legates not only implied Papal Supremacy without censure in front of the largest ecclesiastical audience of its day, John VIII (by defending Ignatian bishops' claims to legitimacy) though accepting the council essentially abrogated Canon 1. This, in effect, undid the feeble work the council had undertook on the question of Papal ecclesiology. It makes sense that as long as the patriarchates "lived and let live," the honorary expression of Papal Supremacy was tolerated. However, it appears that Photius and his contemporaries failed to appreciate the earnestness of what was being asserted by the Papal chancery and what the ramifications of this would be if geopolitically the Roman Patriarchate had the means to enforce their claims.

For the purposes of this study, detailing the ebbs and flows of the Papacy after John VIII into the 10th century are not entirely relevant. The question is when did the literary program of Anastasius find manifestation throughout Christendom? After all, Karl Benz (the inventor of the automobile) is eclipsed by Henry Ford, because the latter made the same invention ubiquitous. In applying the previous example, if Anastasius is Karl Benz, then Pope Gregory VII (Hildebrand of Sovana) is the Vatican I Papacy's Henry Ford.

As covered previously, Frankish power was in a state of decline throughout the ninth century. Nevertheless, the Eastern Franks under Otto the Great had a resurgence of sorts and claimed the mantle to the Holy Roman Empire in 962. In so doing, "[P]apal incumbents would have to take an oath of allegiance" to the Holy Roman Emperor and Papal elections were annulled "without German imperial authorization."[861] Frankish control over the Papacy laid the foundation for the ecclesiastical reforms necessary to break free from their grip—just as the Papacy had done in 769 with the Lombards.

In the 1050s, Pope Leo IX was Pope. He also happens to be the same Pope whose legates notoriously began the Great Schism. Interestingly, he was not an Italian—the first such Pope in 50 years. He appointed to the College of Cardinals other Franks like himself. His design appeared to be to buttress a faction not under the thumb of local Italian nobility, but more becoming to himself. This policy would be continued and, due to reforms to the Papal election process, this put the Papacy into the hands of ethnic Franks.[862] As this ethnic replacement to the College of Cardinals was occurring, ecclesiastical reforms involving the same College were initiated.

861 Papadakis and Meyendorff, *The Christian East and the Rise of the Papacy*, 28.
862 Ibid., 35.

Pope Nicholas II in 1059 invested the right to vote for the Pope to the College of Cardinals, but the "royal clause" retained the Holy Roman Emperor's prerogatives to investiture.[863] Nevertheless, this reform insulated the Papacy from the control of local Italian nobility—something the Holy Roman Empire would accept.

However, the clique of Frankish Cardinals proved to be incrementalists. A mere 16 years later, one of their own (Gregory VII) officially banned investiture, insulating the clique from any outside influences whatsoever.[864] History is not so neat and tidy. Overt conflict with Holy Roman Emperor Henry IV ensued, Gregory VII dying in exile under Norman protection.[865] The Normans themselves had earlier invaded Byzantine Italy and created for themselves their own kingdom there. The Holy Roman Empire only renounced claims over the Papacy in 1122, generally due to domestic weakness. One must consider that the Capetian dynasty was consolidating their control over what was modern-day France, offering a growing threat to the Holy Roman Empire which the Papacy did not fail to exploit.

Despite Gregory VII's inauspicious end in exile, what he had kicked off were the ecclesiastical reforms that created the same College of Cardinals that exists today. Additionally, he had given voice to Papal Supremacy in unequivocal terms in the *Dictatus Papae*.[866] In this document:

> *The [P]ope is throughout represented as an absolute monarch, as the supreme authority over bishops, councils, clergy, and all temporal rulers. Simultaneously, [P]apal authority is everywhere deemed preeminent, especially in administration and legislation, as Rome's arbitrary right to review petitions, authorize canon law, convene ecumenical councils, and deliver judgments (from which there is no appeal) illustrate… transforming obedience to the [P]ope into virtual dogma, or in declaring*

863 Ibid., 40-41.

864 Ibid., 41.

865 Ibid., 43.

866 The document, though not ascribed to him, is entered into the registry of his letters. See Ibid., 47, 54.

conciliar legislation invalid, just because it contradicted [P]apal decrees.[867]

Twelfth century canonists followed suit, themselves members of holy orders "known for their reliability and loyalty to the Roman see" vis-à-vis the Benedictines.[868] Gratian, the most important canonist of medieval Roman Catholicism, is alleged by most scholars to be a Camaldolese monk.[869] Ivo of Chartres, himself important in opposing investiture, was an Augustinian.[870] The *Dictatus Papae*, apparently written to replace previous understandings of canon law,[871] and the subsequent canonists (Papal partisans as they were) had re-envisioned the canons along such Papal lines. For example, "the *Decretum Gratiani*" had become "an instrument of [P]apal absolutism" as Gratian and the other canonists had rediscovered "supposedly forgotten privileges of the Roman pontiff."[872] These were buttressed by the numerous *Pseudo-Isidorian Decretals* that were preserved as canonically authentic.[873] Scholarship has asserted that this "new juridical understanding of primacy as supremacy was, arguably; the most decisive chapter in the entire history of the Roman patriarchate."[874] However, considering its contents, the *Dictatus Papae* was not new.

Quoting the *Dictatus Papae*, "[t]he Roman Church was founded solely by God"[875] is found in the *Gelasian Decretum* and Anastasius'

---

867 Ibid., 49.

868 Ibid., 59.

869 John Noonan Jr, "Gratian Slept Here: The Changing Identity of the Father of the Systematic Study of Canon Law," *Traditio*, 35, 1979, 145. At the very least, Gratian was explicitly connected with the Camaldolese. See Ibid., 149.

870 Christof Rolker, *Canon Law and the Letters of Ivo of Chartres*. Cambridge: Cambridge University Press, 2009, 23.

871 Papadakis and Meyendorff, *The Christian East and the Rise of the Papacy*, 55.

872 Ibid., 174.

873 Out of 324 canons gleaned from Papal decretals, only 11(!) are not derived from forgeries. See Froom, *The Prophetic Faith of our Fathers*, 788-789.

874 Papadakis and Meyendorff, *The Christian East and the Rise of the Papacy*, 54.

875 *Dictatus Papae*, 1.

version of JE 2448. "Only the Pope can with right be called 'Universal'"[876] was the operating assumption of the Papal chancery during Constantinople (869-870), a concern flagrantly inserted in JE 2448 by Anasastasius. Then there is, "[h]e alone can depose or reinstate bishops," "[a] sentence passed by him may be retracted by no one. He alone may retract it," and "[h]e himself may be judged by no one."[877] This finds expression in Rome's response to Pope Nicholas' deposition by a Pan-Orthodox Synod. Pope Adrian II commented on the preceding by explicitly stating concerning Pope Honorius's condemnation by an *Ecumenical Council* that "no [P]atriarch or other bishop has the right of passing any judgement on him [the Pope] unless the consent of the pontiff of the same first see has authorized it."[878] In other words, the Pope cannot be deposed nor is his judgment appealable, unless he agrees to it. "No synod shall be called a 'General Synod' without his order"[879] harkens back to the same claims by Anastasius through Pope Nicholas. "The Roman Church has never erred. Nor will it err, to all eternity,"[880] likewise finds explicit precedent in Anastasius in his defense of Honorius. "He who is not at peace with the Roman Church shall not be considered 'catholic,'"[881] though not original to Anastasius or the Papal chancery of his time, is found in the *Pseudo-Isidorian Decretals*[882]—something popularized by Anastasius. Likewise, "It

---

876 Ibid., 2.

877 Ibid., 3 , 18, 19.

878 Price and Montinaro, *The Acts of the Council of Constantinople of 869-70*, 314.

879 *Dictatus Papae*, 16.

880 Ibid., 22.

881 Ibid., 26.

882 "Although the dignity of his [Peter's] authority is passed on to all Catholic bishops, yet by a certain singular privilege it remains in the bishop of Rome as in the head, forever remaining higher than in the other members. Whoever therefore does not reverently show him due obedience, being separated from the head, makes himself guilty of the schism of the Acephalous [headless]." PL 83, 908 quoted in in Butler and Collorafi, *Keys Over the Christian World*, 435-436. For its attribution to Pseudo-Isidore see R.W. Dyson, *James of Viterbo: De Regimine Christiano—A Critical Edition and Translation*. Leiden, The Netherlands: Brill, 2009, 323.

may be permitted to him to transfer bishops, if need be"[883] is found in the same *Decretals*.

The document does have some originality. "He may depose and reinstate bishops without assembling a Synod"[884] is an interesting evolution in its own right, as it claims Papal exceptionalism over and beyond Roman synodal exceptionalism. "It may be permitted to him to depose emperors"[885] betrays a political concern situated nicely to Gregory VII's spat with the Holy Roman Empire.

SYNOPSIS OF THE PAPACY BETWEEN THE NINTH AND ELEVENTH CENTURIES

The ninth century would prove to be the Orthodox Papacy's last. It began with the Roman Synod expressing some independence from the Franks, as they reasserted themselves with local elections. When the Franks imposed candidates, such as Anastasius himself, Rome was independent enough that they were able to forcefully remove him and choose their own Pope. However, with the consecration of Nicholas to the Papacy, a certain rapprochement with Rome's imperial protector, Louis II, occurred. It required restoring a laicized cleric, Anastasius, and ultimately directly employing him.

What followed was one of the most important literary programs in human history. Anastasius is not only important in intellectual history, as he translated many pivotal documents from Greek into Latin. He was also the creative mind behind the Papal chancery and its correspondence with foreign powers—something directly relevant to Rome's role in an international ecclesiastical body which historically valued consensus. There are signs that he was in effect his own actor over and above the day's Popes in this capacity, as evidenced by him transparently taking credit for writing Papal correspondence and being implicated in murdering Pope Adrian II's own family, yet ultimately maintaining his employment.

---

883 *Dictatus Papae*, 13.

884 Ibid., 25.

885 Ibid., 12.

Anastasius appreciated that "the pen is mightier than the sword." By cunning, the citing of forgeries such as the *Pseudo-Isidorian Decretals*, and (from all appearances) the creation of his own forgeries, Anastasius through the Papal chanceries of Nicholas, Adrian II, and John VIII had effectively reimagined what the Papacy was. However, he not only made a new Papacy but through the pen he gave it a basis in the historical record it never before had. Even after his (forced?) retirement, the Papal posturing that was manifested in Anastasius' earlier writing appeared to be maintained, unrepudiated. In fact, Photius (Anastasius' chief nemesis throughout his career) proved to be too much of a pragmatist to fully appreciate what was occurring. In his defense, he certainly had no awareness of the extent of Anastasius' literary program.

By the time the Gregorian reforms occurred in the 11th century, one could not blame a contemporary for believing that the movement was conservative. The Frankish Popes of this era were demanding a return to Rome 769, Nicaea II, and the slew of *Decretals* which appeared to be authentic as long as anyone can remember. As far as anyone in the West knew, the reinvented Papacy of the ninth century having found expression in the pen of Anastasius alone, was patently historical. A person living in the Latin West at the time would be hard-pressed to not conclude that the Gregorian reforms had an authentic historical basis.

However, outside of the Latin-speaking world, Anastasius' literary activity (and the *Decretals*) had literally no import. His name probably was scarcely even remembered. The ecclesiology remained unchanged; the Church continued operating according to the consensus-based ecclesiology that it had always operated under since the first century. Its epistemic presumptions, also pertaining to consensus, remained unchanged. Everything did not hinge upon a single synod, let alone a singular man within a single synod. Gregory VII during the Council of Rome (1080) declared that, "We desire to show the world that we can give or take away at our will kingdoms, duchies, earldoms, in a word, the possessions of all men; for we can bind and loose."[886] Such a declaration would be unthinkable in the East.

When the Crusades occurred, for the first time the East had to directly confront Papal Supremacist ecclesiology. Unlike Constantinople IV (879-880) where such a theory was able to be ignored as mere posturing, now it was reality. Parallel episcopates were set up wherever the Westerners invaded. Every single Patriarch was replaced with a Western pretender without synodal approval, let alone Pan-Patriarchal consent. For the West, this was *now* ecclesiologically justifiable. Merely being out of communion with the Pope was schism. The Pope's decrees, infallible as they were, carried more weight than what was earlier derived by consensus. In effect, if the Papacy approved of an ecclesiastical realignment, this carried indisputable authority.

With this, the history of the Papacy's rise and fall comes to a close. The Lord said, "Whoever exalts himself will be humbled, and he who humbles himself will be exalted."[887] It cannot even be said that it is ironic that the Papacy fell just as it began its radical ascent to the greatest secular heights. The Lord's warning is clear. Such secular aggrandizement demands a spiritual fall. One may hope that by returning to the Gospel principle, the Papacy's story within the Church may begin a new chapter.

---

886 Froom, *The Prophetic Faith of our Fathers*, 539.

887 Matt 23:12.

Sts. Peter and Paul

BIBLIOGRAPHY

A

Allen, Pauline. 2009. *Sophronius of Jerusalem and Seventh-Century Heresy: The Synodical Letter and Other Documents.* Oxford: Oxford University Press.

Avery, Lowe Elias. 1954. *Codices Latini Antiquiores. A Palaeographical Guide to Latin Manuscripts Prior to the Ninth Century. Part VII: Switzerland.* Oxford: Clanderon Press.

B

Babylonian Talmud: Tractate Sanhedrin. 2023. *Sanhedrin.* https://www.sefaria.org/ Sanhedrin.2a.1?lang=bi&with=all&lang2=en

Blumenthal, Uta-Renate. 2010. *The Investiture Controversy Church and Monarchy from the Ninth to the Twelfth Century.* Philadelphia: University of Pennsylvania Press.

Bobrycki, Shane. 2011. *Hincmar and Anastasius: Lying, Treacherous Villains—Paper by Shane Bobrycki.* https://www.medievalists.net/2011/11/ hincmar-and-anastasius-lying-treacherous-villains/

Bogatyrev, Sergei. 2007. "Reinventing the Russian Monarchy in the 1550s: Ivan the Terrible, the Dynasty, and the Church." *The Slavonic and East European Review* 85 (2): 271-293.

Booth, Phil. 2013. *Crisis of Empire: Doctrine and Dissent at the End of Late Antiquity.* Los Angeles: University of California Press.

Brock, Sebastian. 1973. "An Early Syriac Life of Maximus the Confessor." *Analecta Bollandiana* 91: 302-313.

Bunsen, Christian Charles Josias. 1852. *Hippolytus and His Age: Volume 1.* London: Longman, Brown, Green, and Longmans.

Burkitt, F.C. 1913. "The Decretum Gelasianum." *Journal of Theological Studies* 14: 469-471.

Butler, Scott, and John Collorafi. 2003. *Keys Over the Christian World.* Scott Butler and John Collorafi (self-published).

C

Catholic Encyclopedia. 1907. *Pope Saint Marcellinus.* https://www.newadvent.org/cathen/09637d.htm

Chadwick, Henry. 2005. *East and West: The Making of a Rift in the Church.* Oxford: Oxford University Press.

Chrysos, Evangelos. 2018. "New perceptions of imperium and sacerdotium in the letters of Pope Nicholas I to Emperor Michael III." *Travaux et Memoires* 22 (1): 313-339.

Chrysos, Evangelos. 2019. "Greek and Latin in the Confrontation Between Pope Nicholas and Patriarch Photius." In *Per respirare a due polmoni Chiese e culture cristiane tra Oriente e Occidente Studi in onore di Enrico Morini,* by Martina Caroli, Angela Mazzanti and Raffaele Savigni, 261-278. Bologna: Bolonia University Press.

Chrysos, Evangelos. 2017. "Minors as Patriarchs and Popes." In Prosopon *Rhomaikon: Ergänzende Studien zur Prosopographie der mittelbyzantinischen Zeit,* by Alexander Beihammer, Bettina Krönung and Claudia Ludwig, 221-239. Berlin, Boston: De Gruyter.

Chrysos, Evangelos. 2023. "The Principle of Pentarchy at the Council(s) (869-70 and 879-80)." In *Constantinos G. Pitsakis: In Memoriam,* by Maria Youni and Lydia Paparriga-Artemiadi, 155-169. Athens: Academy of Athens.

Collectio Britannica. 2023. *Add MS 8873.* https://www.bl.uk/manuscripts/Viewer. aspx?ref=add_ms_8873_fs001r

Collorafi, John. 2023. *Pope Hormisdas Letters 77 and 80: A Translation.*
    https://orthodoxchristiantheology.com/2021/08/26/
    pope-hormisdas-letters-77-and-80-a-translation/

Constantinou, Maria. 2020. "Synodal Decision-Making Based on
    Archived Material." In *Konzilien und kanonisches Recht in Spätantike
    und frühem Mittelalter: Aspekte konziliarer Entscheidungsfindung*, by
    Wolfram Brandes, Alexandra Hasse-Ungeheuer and Hartmut
    Leppin, 81-105. Berlin: De Gruyter.

Constas, Nicholas. 2014. *On the Difficulties of the Church Fathers:
    Volume I.* Cambridge, MA: Harvard University Press.

Council of Constantinople (1351). 2023. *The Synod of Constantinople
    (1351).*
    https://maximologia.org/2020/05/17/
    the-synod-of-constantinople-1351/

Crivellucci, Amedeo. 1902. *Studi Storici: Periodico Trimestrale, Volume
    11.* Pisa: Coi tipi defli Studi Storici.

D

Daley, Brian. 1998. *On the Dormition of Mary.* Crestwood, NY: St.
    Vladimir's Seminary Press.

DelCogliano, Mark. 2022. *The Cambridge Edition of Early Christian
    Writings: Volume 4.* Cambridge: Cambridge University Press.

Denny, Edward. 2013. *Papalism.* Christian Resources.

Diacastery for Promoting Christian Unity. 2016. *Synodality
    and Primacy During the First Millennium: Towards a Common
    Understanding in Service to the Unity of The Church.*
    http://www.christianunity.va/content/unitacristiani/en/
    dialoghi/sezione-orientale/chiese-ortodosse-di-tradizione-
    bizantina/commissione-mista-internazionale-per-il-dialogo-
    teologico-tra-la/documenti-di-dialogo/testo-in-inglese1.html

Dragas, George. 1999. "The 8th Ecumenical Council: Constantinople IV (879/880) and the Condemnation of the Filioque Addition and Doctrine." *The Greek Orthodox Theological Review* 44 (1-4): 357-369.

Duffy, Eamon. 2014. *Saints and Sinners: A History of the Popes.* London: Yale University Press.

Duffy, Eamon. 1999. "Was there a Bishop of Rome in the First Century?" *New Blackfriars* 80 (940): 301-308.

Dunn, Geoffrey. 2012. "The Appeal of Apiarius to the Transmarine Church of Rome." *Journal of the Australian Early Medieval Association* 8: 9-29.

Dura, Nicolae. 1995. "The Ecumenicity of the Council of Trullo, Witness of the Canonical Tradition in East and West." In *The Council of Trullo Revisited*, by George Nedungatt and Michael Featherstone, 229-262. Rome: Pontificio Instituto Orientale.

Dvornik, Francis. 1966. *Byzantium and the Roman Primacy.* New York: Fordham University Press.

Dyson, R.W. 2009. *James of Viterbo: De Regimine Christiano–A Critical Edition and Translation*. Leiden, The Netherlands: Brill.

E

Edgecomb, Kevin. 2023. *The Apostolic Tradition of Saint Hippolytus of Rome.* https://www.stjohnsarlingtonva.org/Customer-Content/ saintjohnsarlington/CMS/files/EFM/Apostolic_Tradition_ by_Hippolytus.pdf

Edmundson, George. 1913. *The Church in Rome in the First Century*. New York: Longmans, Green and Co.

Ekonomou, Andrew. 2007. *Byzantine Rome and the Greek Popes: Eastern Influences on Rome and the Papacy from Gregory the Great to Zacharias*, A.D. 590-752. Landham, MD: Lexington Books.

Elliot, Michael. 2013. *Canon Law Collections in England ca 600–1066: The Manuscript Evidence*. Toronto: Centre for Medieval Studies University of Toronto (PhD dissertation).

F

Farrell, Joseph P. 2014. *Disputations with Pyrrhus - St. Maximus the Confessor*. Waymart, PA: St Tikhon's Monastery Press.

Feltoe, Charles. 1918. *St. Dionysius of Alexandria: Letters and Treatises*. New York: The Macmillan Company.

Field, Lester Jr. 2004. *On the Communion of Damasus and Meletius: Fourth-century Synodal Formulae in the Codex Veronensis LX*. Toronto: Pontifical Institute of Mediaeval Studies.

Forrai, Reka. 2008. *The Interpreter of the Popes: The Translation Project of Anastasius Bibliothecarius*. Budapest: Central European University (PhD dissertation).

Fortescue, Adrian. 1955. *The Reunion Formula of Hormisdas*. Garrison, NY: Chair of Unity Apostolate.

Francis Dvornik. 1970. *The Photian Schism*. Cambridge: Cambridge University Press.

Frend, W.H.M. 1952. *The Donatist Church: A Movement of Protest in Roman North Africa*. Oxford: Oxford University Press.

Frend, W.H.M. 1972. *The Rise of the Monophysite Movement: Chapters in the History of the Church in the Fifth and Sixth Centuries*. Cambridge: Cambridge University Press.

Froom, Leroy. 1950. *The Prophetic Faith of our Fathers: The Historical Development of Prophetic Interpretation: Volume I*. Washington D.C.: Review and Herald.

G

Gatner, Clemens. 2021. "Ad utriusque imperii unitatem? Anastasius Bibliothecarius as a Broker between Two Cultures and Three Courts in the Ninth Century." *Institute for Medieval Research (Medieval Worlds)* 13: 36-53.

Giles, E. 1952. *Documents Illustrating Papal Authority AD 96-454.* London: S P C K.

Green, Bernard. 2008. *The Soteriology of Leo the Great.* Oxford: Oxford University Press.

Gwynn, David. 2009. "The Council of Chalcedon and the Definition of Christian Tradition." In *Chalcedon in Context: Church Councils 400-700,* by Richard Price and Mary Whitby, 7-26. Liverpool: Liverpool University Press.

H

Hefele, Charles. 1997. *History of the Councils of the Church: Vol. 2.* Albany, OR: Books For the Ages.

Hefele, Charles. 1896. *History of the Councils of the Church: Vol. V.* Edinburgh: T & T Clark.

Hieromonk Encoh. 2023. *Letters of Pope St. Gregory II (+731) to Emperor Leo Against Heresy of Iconoclasm.* https://web.archive.org/web/20211102193927/http://nftu.net/letters-of-pope-st-gregory-ii-731-to-emperor-leo-against-heresy-of-iconoclasm/

Horn, Cornelia. 2023. *The Correspondence Between the Monks of Syria Secunda and Pope Hormisdas in 517/518 A.D.* http://www.maronite-institute.org/MARI/JMS/october97/The_Correspondence_Between.htm

J

Javakhishvili, Manana. 2008. "Canon Law in Georgia in the Middle Ages." *In Sacri Canones Servandi Sunt, Ius canonicum et status ecclesiae XII-XIV*, by Pavel Kraft, 305-309. Prague: Historický ústav AV ČR.

K

Knibbs, Eric. 2017. "Ebo of Reims, Pseudo-Isidore, and the Date of the False Decretals." *Speculum 92*: 144-183.

Kosinski, Rafal. 2015. "The Exiled Bishops of Constantinople from the Fourth to the Late Sixth Century." *Studia Ceranea* 5: 231-247.

Kreutz, Barbara. 2011. *Before the Normans: Southern Italy in the Ninth & Tenth Centuries*. Philadelphia: University of Pennsylvania Press.

L

Lamberz, Erich. 2018. *Concilium Universale Nicaenum Secundum: Concilii Actiones I-III*. Berlin: Walter de Gruyter.

Lamberz, Erich. 2016. "'Falsata Graecorum more'? Die Griechische Version der Briefe Papst Hadrians I. in den Akten des VII. Ökumenischen Knozils." In *Novum Millennium: Studies on Byzantine History and Culture Dedicated to Paul Speck*, by Claudia Sode and Sarolta A. Takács, 213-229. London: Routledge.

Landon, Edward. 1909. *A Manual of Councils of the Holy Catholic Church*. Edinburgh: John Grant.

Liber Pontificalis. 2023. *Papa Gregorio II*. https://fontistoriche.org/papa-gregorio-ii/

Liber Pontificalis. 2023. *Papa Pelagio I*. https://fontistoriche.org/papa-pelagio-i/

Louth, Andrew. 2007. *Greek East and Latin West: The Church AD 681-1071*. Crestwood, NY: St Vladimir's Seminary Press.

M

Mantel, Hugo. 1967. "The Nature of the Great Synagogue." *The Harvard Theological Review* 60 (1): 69-91.

Mendham, John. 1850. *The Seventh General Council, the Second of Nicaea, Held A.D. 787, in which the Worship of Images was Established*. London: William Edward Painter.

Menze, Volker-Lorenz. 2008. *Justinian and the Making of the Syrian Orthodox Church*. Oxford: Oxford University Press.

Metropolis of Corinth. 2023. *ΟΙ ΜΗΤΡΟΠΟΛΙΤΕΣ.* https://www.imkorinthou.org/index. php?option=com_content&view=article&id=55&Itemid=52

Metzger, Bruce. 1987. *The Canon of the New Testament*. Oxford: Clarendon Press.

Meyendorf, John. 1992. *The Primacy of Peter*. Crestwood, NY: St. Vladimir's Seminary Press.

Moorhead, John. 1978. "The Laurentian Schism: East and West in the Roman Church." *Church History* 47 (2): 125-136.

Moscow Patriarchate. 2013. *Statute of the Russian Orthodox Church: Adopted by the Council of Bishops in 2000, Amended by the Council of Bishops in 2008 and 2011 and Adopted As Amended by the Council of Bishops in 2013.* https://mospatusa.com/files/STATUTE-OF-THE-RUSSIAN-ORTHODOX-CHURCH.pdf

Moss, Yonatan. 2016. *Incorruptible Bodies: Christology, Society, and Authority in Late Antiquity*. Oakland: University of California Press.

Muir, Edward. 1981. *Civic Ritual in Renaissance Venice*. Princeton, NJ: Princeton University Press.

N

NASSCAL. 2023. *Acts of Timothy Acta Apostoli Timothei*. https://www.nasscal.com/e-clavis-christian-apocrypha/acts-of-timothy/

Nedungatt, George. 2010. "The Council in Trullo Revisited: Ecumenism and the Canon of the Councils." *Theological Studies* 71 (3): 651-676.

Neil, Bronwen. 1998. *A critical edition of Anastasius Bibliothecarius' Latin translation of Greek documents pertaining to the life of Maximus the Confessor, with an analysis of Anastasius' translation methodology, and an English translation of the Latin Text*. Ascot Vale, Australia: Australian Catholic University (PhD Dissertation).

Neil, Bronwen. 2006. *Seventh-Century Popes and Martyrs: The Political Hagiography of Anastasius Bibliothecarius*. Turnhout, Belgium: Brepols Publishers.

Neil, Bronwen, and Pauline Allen. 2020. *Conflict and Negotiation in the Early Church: Letters from Late Antiquity, Translated from the Greek, Latin, and Syriac*. Washington DC: Catholic University of America Press.

Neil, Bronwen. 2014. *The Letters of Gelasius I (492-496): Pastor and Micro-Manager of the Church of Rome*. Turnhout, Belgium: Brepols Publishers.

Newman, John Henry. 1920. *Historical Sketches, Vol. 1*. London: Longmans, Green and Co.

Noble, Thomas. 1991. *The Republic of St. Peter: The Birth of the Papal State, 680–825*. Philadelphia: University of Pennsylvania Press.

Noonan, John Jr. 1979. "Gratian Slept Here: The Changing Identity of the Father of the Systematic Study of Canon Law." *Traditio* 35: 145-172.

P

Papadakis, Aristeides, and John Meyendorff. 1994. *The Christian East and the Rise of the Papacy: The Church 1071-1453 A.D.* Crestwood, NY: St Vladimir's Seminary Press.

Perry, S.G.F. 1881. *The Second Synod of Ephesus: Together with Certain Extracts Relating to It.* Dartford: Orient Press.

Price, Richard. 2009. *The Acts of the Council of Constantinople of 553 with related texts on the Three Chapters Controversy.* Liverpool: Liverpool University Press.

Price, Richard. 2020. *The Acts of the Second Council of Nicaea (787).* Liverpool: Liverpool University Press.

Price, Richard. 2020. *The Canons of the Qunisext Council (691/2).* Liverpool: Liverpool University Press.

Price, Richard, and Federico Montinaro. 2022. *The Acts of the Council of Constantinople of 869-70.* Liverpool: Liverpool University Press.

Price, Richard, and Michael Gaddis. 2005. *The Acts of the Council of Chalcedon.* Liverpool: Liverpool University Press.

Price, Richard, and Thomas Graumann. 2020. *The Council of Ephesus of 431.* Liverpool: Liverpool University Press.

Price, Richard, Phil Booth, and Catherine Cubitt. 2014. *The Acts of the Lateran Synod of 649.* Liverpool: Liverpool University Press.

Puller, Frederick. 1900. *The Primitive Saints and the See of Rome.* London: Longmans, Green, and Co.

R

Richards, Jeffrey. 1979. *The Popes and the Papacy in the Early Middle Ages*. London: Routledge and Kegan Paul.

Roberts, Alexander, and James Donaldson. 1882. *Ante-Nicene Christian Library: Translations of the Writings of the Fathers Down to A.D. 326* Vol. XXI. Edinburgh: T. & T . Clark.

Roberts, Edward. 2019. "Bishops on the Move: Rather of Verona, Pseudo-Isidore, and Episcopal Translation." *Medieval Low Countries* 6: 117-138.

Rolker, Christof. 2009. *Canon Law and the Letters of Ivo of Chartres*. Cambridge: Cambridge University Press.

Romanian Patriarchate. 2016. *MISIUNE ORTODOXĂ ÎN SINODALITATE ASTĂZI*. https://patriarhia.ro/misiune-ortodoxA-n-sinodalitate-astAzi-8703.html

Rothschild, Clare. 2022. *The Muratorian Fragment: Text, Translation, Commentary*. Tubingen: Mohr Siebeck.

Runciman, Steven. 1986. *The Great Church in Captivity: A Study of the Patriarchate of Constantinople from the Eve of the Turkish Conquest to the Greek War of Independence*. Cambridge: Cambridge University Press.

S

Salmond, S.D.F. 1882. *The Works of Gregory Thaumaturgus, Dionysius of Alexandria, and Archelaus*. Edinburgh: T&T Clark.

Schatz, Klaus. 1996. *Papal Primacy: From Is Origins to the Present*. Collegeville, MN: The Liturgical Press.

Serraz, L. 1926. "Les lettres du pape Hadrien Ier lues au IIe concile de Nicee." *Échos d'Orient* 25 (144): 407-420.

Shoemaker, Stephen. 2002. *Ancient Traditions of the Virgin Mary's Dormition and Assumption*. Oxford University Press: Oxford.

Siecienski, A. Edward. 2017. *The Papacy and the Orthodox: Sources and History of a Debate*. New York: Oxford University Press.

Sommar, Mary. 2002. "Hincmar of Reims and the Canon Law of Episcopal Translation." *The Catholic Historical Review* 88 (3): 432-433.

Stewart, Alistair. 2016. "The apostolic canons of Antioch. An Origenistic exercise." *Revue d'histoire Ecclésiastique* 111 (3-4): 439-451.

Surius, Laurentius. 1567. *Concilia omnia, tum generalia, tum provincialia atque particularia*. Calenius & Quentel.

T

Talbert, Richard. Princeton. *The Senate of Imperial Rome.* 1984: Princeton University Press.

Tavard, George. 1973. "Episcopacy and Apostolic Succession according to Hincmar of Reims." *Theological Studies* 34 (4): 594-623.

Terian, Abraham. 2008. *Macarius of Jerusalem: Letter to the Armenians, A.D. 335*. Crestwood, NY: St Vladimir's Seminary Press.

The Hebrew University of Jerusalem. 2023. *Qumran Community Leaders*. http://virtualqumran.huji.ac.il/moreInfo/ CommunityLeaders.htm

The Latin Library. 2023. *Constitutum Constantini*. http://www.thelatinlibrary.com/donation.html

Theodosius the Great. 2023. *TITULI EX CORPORE CODICI THEODOSIANI*.

https://web.archive.org/web/20120127105031/http://
ancientrome.ru/ius/library/codex/theod/liber16.htm#1

Thiel, Andreas. 1868. *Epistolae Romanorum Pontificum Genuinae: et quae
ad eos scriptae sunt A.S. Hilaro usque ad Pelagium II.* Braunsberg: In
aedibus Eduardi Peter.

Townsend, W.T. 1937. "Councils Held Under Pope Symmachus."
Church History 5 (3): 233-259.

Treadgold, Warren. 1997. *A History of the Byzantine State and Society.*
Stanford: Stanford University Press.

Truglia, Patrick. 2021. "Original Sin in the Byzantine Dormition
Narratives." *Revista Teologica* (4): 5-30.

V

Vlachos, Hierotheos. 2016. *'Photios the Great and the Eighth Ecumenical
Synod' by Metropolitan Hierotheos Vlachos.*
https://www.johnsanidopoulos.com/2016/02/photios-great-
and-eighth-ecumenical.html

W

Walker, G.S.M. 2008. *Letters of Columbanus.* Cork: Corpus of
Electronic Texts, University College.

Wallach, Luitpold. 1966. "Luitpold Wallach." *Traditio* 22: 103-125.

Wallach, Luitpold. 1977. "The Libri Carolini and Patristics, Latin
and Greek: Prolegomena to a Critical Edition." In *Diplomatic
Studies in Latin and Greek Documents from the Carolingian Age,* by
Luitpold Wallach, 451-498. Ithaca: Cornell University Press.

Weickhardt, George G. 2001. "The Canon Law of Rus', 1100-
1551." *Russian History* 28 (1): 411-446.

Weinrich, William C. 2005. *Ancient Christian Commentary on Scripture,
NT Volume 12.* Downers Grove IL: IVP Academic.

Whiting, Colin. 2015. *Christian Communities in Late Antiquity: Luciferians and the Construction of Heresy.* Riverside, CA: University of California, Riverside (PhD dissertation).

Wirbelauer, Eckhard. 1993. *Zwei Papste in Rom: Der Konflikt Zwischen Laurentius und Symmachus (498-514).* Munchen (Munich): Tuduv-Verlagsgesellscaft, mbH.

ΙΓΝΑΤΙΟΣ. 2023. *ΡΩΜΑΙΟΙΣ ΙΓΝΑΤΙΟΣ.* https://www.ccel.org/l/lake/fathers/ignatius-romans.htm

Note: *Additional works that are part of Schaff and Wace's volumes of the Ante- and Post-Nicene Church Fathers, PL and PG, Mansi, as well as conciliar canons and decrees which are open source are not included as part of this bibliography.*

UNCUT MOUNTAIN PRESS TITLES

Books by Archpriest Peter Heers

Fr. Peter Heers, *The Ecclesiological Renovation of Vatican II: An Orthodox Examination of Rome's Ecumenical Theology Regarding Baptism and the Church*, 2015

Fr. Peter Heers, *The Missionary Origins of Modern Ecumenism: Milestones Leading up to 1920*, 2007

The Works of our Father Among the Saints, Nikodemos the Hagiorite

Vol. 1: *Exomologetarion: A Manual of Confession*

Vol. 2: *Concerning Frequent Communion of the Immaculate Mysteries of Christ*

Vol. 3: *Confession of Faith*

Other Available Titles

Elder Cleopa of Romania, *The Truth of our Faith*

Elder Cleopa of Romania, *The Truth of our Faith, Vol. II*

Fr. John Romanides, *Patristic Theology: The University Lectures of Fr. John Romanides*

Demetrios Aslanidis and Monk Damascene Grigoriatis, *Apostle to Zaire: The Life and Legacy of Blessed Father Cosmas of Grigoriou*

Protopresbyter Anastasios Gotsopoulos, *On Common Prayer with the Heterodox According to the Canons of the Church*

Robert Spencer, *The Church and the Pope*

G. M. Davis, *Antichrist: The Fulfillment of Globalization*

Athonite Fathers of the 20th Century, Vol. I

St. Gregory Palamas, *Apodictic Treatises on the Procession of the Holy Spirit*

St. Hilarion Troitsky, *On the Dogma of the Church: An Historical Overview of the Sources of Ecclesiology*

Fr. Alexander Webster and Fr. Peter Heers, Editors, *Let No One Fear Death*

Subdeacon Nektarios Harrison, *Metropolitan Philaret of New York*

Elder George of Grigoriou, *Catholicism in the Light of Orthodoxy*

Archimandrite Ephraim Triandaphillopoulos, *Noetic Prayer as the Basis of Mission and the Struggle Against Heresy*

Dr. Nicholas Baldimtsis, *Life and Witness of St. Iakovos of Evia*

On the Reception of the Heterodox into the Orthodox Church

Select Forthcoming Titles

Orthodox Patristic Witness Concerning Catholicism

Homilies of Metropolitan Neophytos of Morphou

George, *Errors of the Latins*

Fr. Peter Heers, *Going Deeper in the Spiritual Life*

Abbe Guette, *The Papacy*

Athonite Fathers of the 20th Century, Vol. II

Collected Works of St. Hilarion (Troitsky), vol. 2

This 1st Edition of

THE RISE AND FALL OF THE PAPACY:
An Orthodox Perspective

written by Patrick (Craig) Trugila typeset in Baskerville in this two thousand twenty third year of our Lord's Holy Incarnation is one of the many fine titles available from Uncut Mountain Press, translators and publishers of Orthodox Christian theological and spiritual literature. Find the book you are looking for at

uncutmountainpress.com

GLORY BE TO GOD
FOR ALL THINGS

AMEN.